Nebraska
Symposium on
Motivation
1989

Volume 37

University of Nebraska Press

Lincoln and London 1990

Nebraska Symposium on Motivation 1989

Cross-Cultural Perspectives

Richard A. Dienstbier   *Series Editor*

John J. Berman   *Volume Editor*

Presenters

Gustav Jahoda
*Professor of Psychology
University of Strathclyde,
Glasgow*

Harry C. Triandis
*Professor of Psychology,
University of Illinois
at Urbana-Champaign*

Çiğdem Kağıtçıbaşı
*Professor of Psychology,
Boğaziçi University,
Bebek-Istanbul*

J. W. Berry

Juris G. Draguns

Michael Cole

Professor of Psychology,
Queen's University
Kingston, Canada

Professor of Psychology,
Pennsylvania State University

Professor of Psychology,
University of California,
San Diego

Nebraska Symposium on Motivation, 1989, is Volume 37 in the series on CURRENT THEORY AND RESEARCH IN MOTIVATION

Copyright © 1990 by
the University of Nebraska Press
All rights reserved
Manufactured in the United States of America
International Standard Book Number
0-8032-1193-7 (Clothbound)
International Standard Book Number
0-8032-6078-4 (Paperbound)

The paper in this book meets the minimum requirements of American National Standard for Information Sciences—Permanence of Paper for Printed Library Materials, ANSI Z39.48–1984.

"The Library of Congress has cataloged
this serial publication as follows:"   *BF*
Nebraska Symposium on Motivation.
Nebraska Symposium on Motivation.
[Papers] v. [1]–1953–
Lincoln, University of Nebraska Press.
v. illus., diagrs. 22cm. annual.
Vol. 1 issued by the symposium under
its earlier name: Current Theory and
Research in Motivation.
Symposia sponsored by the Dept. of
Psychology of the University of Nebraska.
1. Motivation (Psychology)
BF683.N4   159.4082   53-11655
Library of Congress
74 753

Preface

The volume editor for this 37th edition of the Nebraska Symposium on Motivation is John J. Berman. He assumed major responsibility for drawing together the contributors and coordinating all aspects of the editing. My thanks to our contributors for excellent chapters delivered in timely fashion, and to John for his editorial care in seeing the volume through to its conclusion.

The symposium series is supported largely by funds donated to the University of Nebraska Foundation by the late Cora L. Friedline in memory of Harry K. Wolfe. This symposium volume, like those of the recent past, is dedicated to Professor Wolfe, who brought psychology to the University of Nebraska. After studying with Wilhelm Wundt, Professor Wolfe returned to his native state to establish the first undergraduate laboratory of psychology in the nation. As a student at Nebraska, Professor Friedline studied psychology under him.

We are grateful to the late Professor Friedline for her bequest and to Edward J. Hirsch of the University of Nebraska Foundation for his assurance of continuing financial support for the series. Our thanks also to Vice-Chancellor for Research John K. Yost and Chancellor Martin A. Massengale for their continued support of and interest in the symposium. RICHARD A. DIENSTBIER
Series Editor

Contents

Introduction

John J. Berman

University of Nebraska–Lincoln

Almost all of what we know as scientific psychology has been developed in Western cultures. In fact, in the first two or three decades after World War II—probably because of the devastation in Europe caused by the war—the overwhelming majority of psychological research and theorizing was conducted in an even smaller part of the world—the United States. Furthermore, almost all of this work was performed by and focused on white, middle-class Caucasians.

Although this narrow focus has been changing somewhat in the past decade or two, psychology is still very much an American discipline. For example, in a typical psychology library in a major university in countries as diverse as India and West Germany, at least 80% of the material will be in English, and over 90% of that will be from America. Furthermore, the courses in these countries will use the same United States–authored and United States–published textbooks used in America. Many students in these countries prefer to have their psychology examinations conducted in English rather than their native language, because English is the language in which they learned the material. This is so despite the fact that many of the subjects treated in the textbooks are totally inappropriate for these cultures. For example, most texts in social psychology used in India today have a chapter on interpersonal attraction that includes large sections on dating and marital choice behavior, which rarely occur in India, where over 90% of marriages still are arranged.

Such domination by one cultural and linguistic group may not be a problem for some other disciplines, but it is crippling to one that purports to explain human behavior in a generalized way. It is obvious that the mainstream of psychology must become more aware of the cultural limitations of its theories and data. Thus the subarea of cross-cultural psychology has an important role because, if nothing else, it serves as a reminder to the discipline—almost a conscience—of the narrow focus of much of its theory and research.

Whether or not mainstream American psychology begins paying more attention to what cross-cultural researchers are saying, it is clear that the rest of the society is doing so. Driven by advances in transportation, communication, and antidiscrimination movements, more and more people from differing cultures are finding themselves interacting with each other. This is especially apparent in business, where strong pressures for cross-cultural interaction come both from the evolution of the world economy and from the need for nations to emphasize exports. Thus, in business colleges across the country cross-cultural work has come into vogue; and given the causes just mentioned, there is no reason for the interest to abate.

The purpose of this book is twofold. One goal is to communicate some of the substantive developments in the area of cross-cultural psychology. The second is to sensitize social science researchers pursuing a wide variety of topics to the potential cultural influences and limitations on their work. In selecting the contributors I wanted to sample some of the major areas of psychology and to find the very best representatives I could. It is worth noting that each of these participants was my first choice to represent that particular area.

This volume contains chapters of interest to social and personality psychologists (the chapters by Triandis, Berry, and Kağıtçıbaşı), clinical psychologists (Draguns), developmental psychologists (Kağıtçıbaşı and Cole), cognitive psychologists (Cole), and to those interested in the history and systems of psychology (Jahoda and Cole). Besides being useful to researchers, several chapters will interest all who have been, or soon will be, involved in a cross-cultural experience. This is especially true of the chapters by Berry, Triandis, and Kağıtçıbaşı. Anyone who has interacted, or will interact, regularly with someone from another culture will profit from reading them, for they offer a set of ideas and conceptual frameworks with which to interpret cross-cultural experiences and behavioral differences.

The first chapter in the book is by Gustav Jahoda, who gives a historical analysis of the conceptual roots of cross-cultural psychology, tracing the development of the field from the 18th century through the beginning of the 20th. By presenting the ideas of outstanding figures of those times, he makes a strong case for his organizing theme—that there is nothing new under the sun.

Harry Triandis then presents a comprehensive review of the theory and research surrounding the dimension of individualism/collectivism. Because this dimension seems to capture well many of the differences observed between cultures that are typically called "developed" versus "developing" (or "West" versus "East," or "North" versus "South"), it has received a great deal of attention from cross-cultural researchers, including Triandis himself. All of this is summarized and interpreted in a thorough treatment of the topic. He concludes by suggesting that neither extreme individualism nor extreme collectivism is desirable, but that a combination of some versions of the two might well be ideal.

Çiğdem Kağıtçıbaşı then presents an extensive summary and integration of the cross-cultural work on families and child-rearing practices. After an extensive critique of psychological and sociological approaches to studying the family, she reviews several important dimensions on which the cultures of the world have been found to differ with regard to family life and socialization practices (e.g., parental beliefs and values, parent-child interaction patterns, and dependence/independence). She then presents various models of family life and proposes that the two found most frequently in the world today might be evolving into a common third model.

John Berry defines acculturation as the psychological processes that occur when two distinct cultures come into continuous contact. He then proceeds to provide a detailed framework for thinking about the acculturation process. He identifies the important variables, discusses various research designs and strategies that can be used to study acculturation, emphasizes the importance of the attitudes toward acculturation held by the members of the acculturating group, reviews the research on cognitive and behavioral changes that have been documented to have occurred as a result of acculturation, and discusses acculturation stress, including what can be done to alleviate it.

Juris Draguns addresses the topic of abnormal behavior from a cross-cultural perspective. He reviews the evidence about the universality of various psychopathological manifestations, especially schizophrenia and depression, and concludes that as far as we now know they are universal, although with, as he terms it, "a variety of cultural characteristic accretions and transformations." He then explores the possibility of relationships between some major variables of interest in the cross-cultural psychology of normal behavior (e.g., individualism/collectivism) and psychopathology in various cultures. Although the results of this effort are not as successful as one might hope, the attempt does prove thought provoking and generates stimulating ideas for future research.

Michael Cole has for some time been proposing what he calls a "cultural psychology," as opposed to "cross-cultural" psychology or, for that matter, to mainstream psychology. That is, he believes all psychology should be cultural psychology. Stimulated by the Soviet sociohistorical school, he argues that human psychological functions are different from those of other animals because they are culturally mediated. Culture here is defined as the collection of artifacts, both material (e.g., an ax) and symbolic (e.g., a spoken word) accumulated over the history of the human race. That is, all behavior is cultural in the sense that human beings live in an environment transformed by the artifacts of prior generations. Other aspects of his argument are that the starting point for the study of a psychological process should be practical, everyday activity rather than artificially contrived laboratory tasks. After detailing his position, Cole gives an example of how one does psychological research within this framework. The psychological process used for the example is learning to read, and his extensive analysis of reading, from the several perspectives implied by cultural psychology, is informative.

One of the goals of the Nebraska Symposium on Motivation each year is to provide a resource for graduate courses in the particular topic covered. This year I believe the contributors have more than adequately met that goal. They have provided a comprehensive, up-to-date synthesis of their areas of expertise in cross-cultural psychology. For that we at Nebraska, and the people who will use this volume, owe them a debt of gratitude.

Our Forgotten Ancestors

Gustav Jahoda
University of Strathclyde, Glasgow

The thing that hath been, it is that which shall be;
and that which is done, is that which shall be done;
and there is no new thing under the sun.
Ecclesiastes 1:9

Commonly rendered these days as "there is nothing new under the sun," the phrase has become trite. I wonder how many of the people using it realize that it goes back to one of the major sources of Western civilization. As far as the human predicament is concerned, the thought is a useful reminder of historical continuity. I have always found it difficult to persuade my students that anything other than the most recent of books and journals is worth reading. Moreover, many of those in the field of culture and psychology, with which we are concerned here, seem to imagine they are breaking entirely new ground. This is no doubt true as regards sophistication of research tools, but the questions asked and the answers put forward centuries ago are sometimes remarkably similar to present ones.

Since there are no sharp discontinuities, the choice of how far back one should go is bound to be somewhat arbitrary. Klineberg (1980), writing a chapter on historical perspectives on cross-cultural psychology, decided the crucial date was 1860, the year of the founding of the *Zeitschrift für Völkerpsychologie und Sprachwissenschaft*. Although this was undoubtedly an important landmark, in my view it is desirable to go further back, for two main reasons: first, the journal represents only one particular strand in a complex web of traditions; second, this starting point omits what for me are perhaps the most exciting beginnings in the *siècle des lumières*. Hence I propose to begin with the 18th century.

Before making this start, I must explain that this is not the place, nor is there the space, for a coherent and chronological history. My aim is merely to provide some indication of the roots of major contemporary ideas. These roots are complex and tangled, but by greatly simplifying, three main strands can be discerned, to which I shall attach modern labels: empiricism, the sociohistorical tradition, and racism. Although the last of these was important, especially during the 19th century, it is now scientifically (though unfortunately not politically) dead and will thus be treated only peripherally. Among the other two empiricism has been, and remains, dominant, though its rival has been gaining in strength.

My plan is to begin with a sketch of the mainstream philosophical models of man during roughly the first half of the 18th century, then switch to the contrasting beginnings of the sociohistorical tradition and pursue this to the present. I shall then jump back to the second half of the 18th century and trace the course of positivism and empiricism. In my probably foolhardly attempt to paint such a broad canvas in so short a time, my chief method will be to present the ideas of some outstanding figures. In concluding this lengthy preamble I ought to make it clear that what I am offering is my particular perspective, which at least in some respects is certainly open to debate.

Models of Man in the Age of Reason

During the 18th century the horizons of the known world were rapidly expanding, most coastlines (though not interiors) having been explored. Travel literature was very popular, being rapidly translated and widely circulated, and between 1700 and 1740 a whole series of synthetic collections appeared in several European countries. With few exceptions, reports by travelers and explorers about the inhabitants of the places they had visited were superficial and stressed the exotic. A notable exception was the writings of the Jesuits, who lived for years among their peoples and learned their languages. Mention should be made of the well-known work of Joseph François Lafitau (1724) on Canadian Indians; although he had an ax to grind, his observations read almost like those of a modern ethnographer. But apart from such exceptions, the usual accounts of "savages" were commonly unreliable and sometimes grotesque.

This presented a problem for the great naturalists of the period, whose taxonomy for the first time included humans as part of the animal kingdom. In view of the weaknesses of their sources, it is not surprising that they had trouble dealing with the human species and were somewhat uncertain about its boundaries. The great Linnaeus, whose general system of classification has stood the test of time, included in the genus *Homo* some mythical "wild men" with tails as well as the orangutan. Georges Buffon, though somewhat more skeptical, also referred to reports of such marginal creatures.

Such aberrations were only minor flaws in a burgeoning scientific quest to understand both nature and human nature. René Descartes, following Plato, had taught that the pure activities of the mind consist of ideas that are independent of the world of objects. These "innate ideas," of which God and self are prime examples, were said not to originate from any external causes. John Locke refuted this doctrine in this famous *Essay Concerning Human Understanding* (1690) by pointing out that if there were such ideas they ought to be found in children and savages but were not. The first book of his *Essay* is largely devoted to surveying contemporary accounts of the beliefs of uncivilized peoples to demonstrate this. Locke based his psychology on the analysis of experience, not merely of the physical but also the social world, dispensing with the metaphysical assumptions of Descartes. Although Locke's refutation of innateness was generally accepted in the 18th century, Etienne de Condillac considered that it did not go far enough in shedding hypothetical entities, a shortcoming he sought to remedy. In his *Traité des sensations* (1754) the ambitious aim was to discover a law as simple and universal as Newton's that governs the working of the human mind. Condillac wanted to get rid of the unexplained "faculties" Locke retained, though he had to reluctantly concede the existence of some innate principle. Without going into the details of his system, one can summarize by saying that sense impressions are the basic building blocks not only of all knowledge, but also of the development of the various faculties of the mind. He conducted what we would call a "thought experiment" in which a statue, originally given only a sense of smell and a modicum of motivational "unease," would develop all the faculties Locke had taken as given.

A critical issue was accounting for the emergence of reflective thought, and here Condillac's theory of language was crucial. It began, according to him, with cries and gestures elicited by felt needs. Such natural signs evoked analogous feelings in others, and thus began through the law of association the formations of words and deliberate communication. It follows that reflective thought is a consequence of language and cannot be separated from it. Condillac saw in the "law of association of ideas" the equivalent of Newton's law of attraction.

Condillac's "sensationalism" is important, since it implies that humans are almost infinitely malleable by external influences, a view then widespread and one that can still be found in, say, Margaret Mead's earlier writings. At the same time, the passivity suggested by his image of the statue worried some of his disciples, who sought to account for the *progress* of humanity. This was one of the major aims of the *philosophes*, as indicated by the title of the main work of the last of them, the marquis de Condorcet: *Sketch of a Historical Picture of the Progress of the Human Mind* (1795/1966). Returning to Condillac, we shall find his "sensationalism" adopted by the *idéologues* and *observateurs* who may be regarded as the precursors of social science; and it might be added that his ideal of a psychology modeled on physics still lingers on.

Condillac's ideas on language pervaded 18th-century discussions and beyond—echoes can be found in Edward B. Tylor and Wilhelm Wundt. The notion of a close link between language and thought is much older; the Greek term "barbarian" is supposed to derive from the unintelligible noises made by uncouth peoples. Languages of savages were regarded as poverty stricken, reflecting their undeveloped minds. Here is what Montesquieu wrote in an essay entitled *On the Causes That Can Affect the Spirits and Characters*, probably published in the early 1740s: "A proof that they lack ideas is that their languages are all very sterile; not only have they few words, because they have little to say, but they have few modes of conceiving and sensing. The fibres of their brains, little used to being flexed, have become rigid."

The notion that primitive languages are simple and poor survived until quite recently, in spite of the fact that Lafitau (1724) had already sought to combat this stereotype, stressing the richness and beauty of Indian languages. Typically, however, philosophers of the Enlightenment relied more on travelers' tales, and in any case they were concerned with the abstract image of the "savage" rather than with particular peoples. They perceived the "savage" not as a race apart, but as representing a stage in the development of humanity. They were often ethnocentric, as when the Abbé de Saint-Pierre praised the forethought of Providence in arranging that dark fleas would be highly visible on white skin; they were apt to be condescending toward savages without history, morals, or government. But on the whole they were tolerant in their attitudes, commonly deploring the cruelties of Europeans in their relations to native peoples.

On the other hand, one must also remember that most of them were ardent reformers, and when it suited them they held up the savages as examples to be emulated—free, without masters, priests, oppressive laws, or any vices. Not that they were so foolish as to fail to realize that all humans have a mixture of virtues and vices; rather, they wanted to project an image for certain purposes, and their accounts must therefore be looked at from this perspective.

One has to distinguish this from real attempts to explain the causes of human differences. Montesquieu, for instances, put forward a physiological interpretation in terms of the effects of climate on nerve and muscle "fibers." In a significant passage he stated that "it is this different constitution of the *machine* [my italics] that produces the differing strengths of the passions." Thus the predominant temper of the 18th-century approach to humanity has been well captured by Frankel (1969) in the phrase "the experimental physics of the soul."

The Sociohistorical Approach

Whereas the ferment of ideas generated by Descartes and Locke captured the imagination of Europe, a seemingly minor figure working in isolated obscurity in Italy remained long unnoticed. Yet Giambattista Vico (1688–1744) was a revolutionary thinker whose *New Science* (1725/1948) is at the opposite pole to the quasi-mechanical interpretation of human nature typified by Condillac. It is a book written in a baroque style with heavy theological overtones; this, together with the fact that its golden nuggets are often buried in dross, makes it hard to read. It is perhaps presumptuous for someone who is not a Vico scholar to suggest that there is some tendency to attribute to him more coherence and similarity to some modern notions than his writings warrant. Whether or not such a judgment is correct, there is no doubt that his contribution was remarkable.

Whereas the dominant theme of the Enlightenment was that of bringing man wholly into the realm of nature, the *New Science* is based on the premise that there is a fundamental distinction between our knowledge of external nature and that of man. In the latter case we possess a unique insight lacking in the former:

> But in the night of thick darkness enveloping the earliest antiquity, so remote from ourselves, there shines the eternal and never failing light of a truth beyond all question: that the world of civil society has certainly been made by men, and that its principles are therefore to be found *within the modifications of our own human mind* [my italics]. Whoever reflects on this cannot but marvel that the philosophers should have bent all their energies to the study of the world of nature, which, since God made it, He alone knows; and that they should have neglected the study of the world of nations, or civil world, which, since man has made it, men could come to know. (1725/1968, p. 96)

Vico was against giving undue attention to "bodily things" instead of looking inside ourselves. For him there is no fixed universal and permanent core of human nature; mind constantly changes and develops in parallel with the stages of transformation undergone by different societies. Moreover, such changes are not the outcome of any mechanical causation but represent the play of purpose and intention within certain broad limits laid down by Providence. In this manner humans come to change both themselves and their world.

The *New Science* is, in one of its aspects, a history of human ideas in their progressive development. The first men were "stupid, insensate and horrible beasts" (p. 116), and their initial groping effort to come to some understanding of the world was through "poetic wisdom"; this seems to refer to a kind of metaphorical imagery, said to have first elevated man beyond the animals confined to their senses. By a slow and gradual process, associated with the stage of society reached, through other forms of symbolism and eventually language, men acquired the use of reason and became capable of abstract thought.

Language also plays a crucial part in Vico's scheme. Man, he says, is essentially mind, body, and speech. At the beginning there was only the mute body language of gesture; then articulate languages were invented, initially with a very limited vocabulary that expanded only when reason was fully developed. His description of the corresponding three "stages"—the "divine," "heroic," and "human" periods—is highly fanciful, as are the linguistic examples supposed to characterize the three periods. However, the underlying notion that the development of symbolic systems is closely linked to particular cultural contexts is important.

Vico did not regard the rich varieties of languages and customs as limitless; rather, there is kernel of common elements determined by the requirements of the social life of the species:

There must in the nature of human institutions be a mental language common to all nations, which uniformly grasps the substance of things feasible in human social life and expresses it with as many diverse modifications as these same things may have diverse aspects. A proof of this is afforded by proverbs or maxims of vulgar wisdom, in which substantially the same meanings find as many diverse expressions as there are nations ancient and modern. (p. 67)

In sketching his ambitious panorama of the development of the human spirit, Vico confined himself mainly to the classical and later civilizations. His account of the mentality of "primitive" man remained rather nebulous and fantastic, admittedly an armchair effort at reconstruction that did not even take account of such evidence as was available.

In spite of its weaknesses it was a monumental opus, whose central message is that human nature is not constant but a function of specific sociohistorical conditions; hence a genetic and historical approach is necessary for its study.

Although Vico tends to be contrasted with the thinkers of the Enlightenment, by no means all of them followed the pattern of Condillac and his disciples. Rousseau, in his *Discourse on Inequality*

(1754), also seems to make the point that human nature is shaped by various stages of culture rather than being unchangeable; but his views on the virtues of "savages" lost by civilization were not always well received. When Rousseau sent Voltaire a copy of *Discourse,* the latter replied in characteristically caustic fashion:

> I have received your new book against the human race, and thank you for it. Never was such a cleverness used in the design of making us all stupid. One longs, in reading your book, to walk on all fours. But as I have lost that habit for more than sixty years, I feel unhappily the impossibility of resuming it. Nor can I embark in search of the savages of Canada, because the maladies to which I am condemned render a European surgeon necessary to me; because war is going on in these regions; and because the example of our actions has made the savages as bad as ourselves. (Cited in Russell, 1946, p. 715)

This passage illustrates how the "savages" were usually little more than lay figures used by the philosophers to display their arguments. Claude-Adrien Helvétius (1715–1771) criticized Rousseau for presenting an oversimplified picture of the "savages"; he himself, while accepting the prevailing stereotypes about lazy Hottentots or cruel Indians, argued that they differed as much among themselves as do people in civilized societies. Helvétius (1773) also explicitly rejected any racial explanations, stating that differences in physiognomy have nothing to do with minds. Especially in his later writings, Helvétius also maintained that there is no innate core of human nature that remains constant—that it changes as a result of changes in society.

It is therefore possible to find ideas similar to those of Vico among some Enlightenment thinkers. However, none of them came as close as Vico to our modern conception of "culture" when he characterized "nations" in terms of patterns of language, customs, and institutions. From a completely different starting point as an ardent disciple of the Enlightenment, Johann Gottfried Herder (1744–1803) arrived at a very similar position. He came to reject the view that regards man as a kind of rational animal. This comes out clearly in his essay on *The Origin of Language* (1772/1969), in which he opposes Condillac's theory (with which Rousseau agreed) that language began with animal sounds. According to him language and thought, indissolubly linked, are what differentiates man from animals equipped only with instincts. Moreover, language serves not merely as a mode of communication between living individuals, but also as a way of transmitting the ideas and feelings of past generations. Thus what Herder called "tradition" is not just a static bundle of beliefs and customs, but a *process* in which past and present are fused and which gives people their sense of identity.

The key term Herder applied to such an organic community is *Volk*. A *Volk* is characterized by a shared language and historical tradition that shape the mentality of its members, not into any permanent mold but in a constant movement of growth and development—or decay. A *Volk* may or may not coincide with a nation-state and refers essentially to what we nowadays mean by "culture"; and Herder's somewhat flowery descriptions of the way from infancy onward not just collective ideas but also feelings and images are conveyed is tantamount to an account of socialization into a particular culture.

The diversity of human cultures constituted for Herder a positive value, something good and "natural." In contrast to most Enlightenment thinkers, who established scales of progress by which to evaluate various societies as "high" or "low," "savage" or "polished," he was a relativist who considered that each culture must be approached, and valued, on its own terms: "Thus nations change according to place, time and their inner character; each carries within itself the measure of its perfection, incommensurable with others" (1785/1969, Vol. 4, p. 362).

Herder also rejoiced in the richness and variety of human languages. He believed that those of primitive peoples contain more emotional than abstract terms, but he rejected the notion, fairly common until well into the 20th century, that "primitives" are incapable of abstraction: "Since human reason cannot remain devoid of abstractions, and since no abstractions can be made without language, it follows that the language of every people must contain abstractions" (cited in Barnard, 1969, p. 152).

Nor did Herder share the complacency about European superiority; he envisaged a future when the tables might be turned and other parts of the world "cheated and plundered" by Europeans might get their own back. Moreover, he criticized the assumption of any *general* European superiority even in his own time, arguing that not everybody who makes use of an invention thereby shares the genius of the inventor. Thus he anticipated this very point made in the well-known discussion of African thought by Horton (1970).

It should be apparent even from this brief sketch that Herder's ideas about the relationship between cultural development and change, with the resulting diversity of human nature, foreshadow some of the central themes of Lev S. Vygotsky's theory concerning the sociohistorical determinants of the varieties of the human psyche. Some of Herder's followers, not excluding the founders of *Völkerpsychologie*, distorted his message by giving a somewhat mystical flavor to the notion of a *Volk*. His name has even been evoked in support of racialism, but Herder himself emphatically rejected such an ideology.

Herder was a major source of inspiration for Moritz Lazarus and Heymann Steinthal, the founders of *Völkerpsychologie*, which marked the first explicit statement of the need for a cultural psychology. I should mention in passing that the common translation of this term as "folk psychology" is misleading, since it lacks the connotation of a shared identity that was the heritage from Herder.

Another important influence was that of Johann Friedrich Herbart (1776–1841), who for the modern reader was a strange mixture: on the one hand he sought to establish a mathematical foundation for psychology, while on the other he discussed the probable structure of concepts in the soul after death! On a more mundane plane, Herbart pointed out the one-sidedness of a psychology confined to isolated individuals, predicted a "science of politics," by which he understood what we would call social psychology or sociology; and said that "after it would follow an empirical summary of that which may be found in the history of nations as permanent contrasted with the transient" (1816/1891, p. 191). Mention should also be made of Wilhelm von Humboldt, to whom the term *Völkerpsychologie* is attributed. Humboldt (cf. Leitzman, 1903) also put forward the view that language has a powerful effect on thought, so that people speaking different languages will have different worldviews—essentially the Sapir-Whorf hypothesis!

It is from the confluence of these and some other (e.g. Hegel's) streams of ideas that Lazarsfeld and Steinthal's *Völkerpsychologie* took shape. In the first issue of the *Zeitschrift für Völkerpsychologie und Sprachwissenschaft* (the last word meaning "philology") in 1860, their vastly ambitious and not altogether coherent program for an as yet nonexisting discipline was put forward. Both men were philologists, a field still being defined in dictionaries as "the science of language"; in fact, it had been transformed early in the 19th century from a rather arid concentration on the formal aspects of classical languages to a wider focus on what we would call the culture of the speakers of various languages. Hence it is not surprising that Lazarus and Steinthal believed in an intimate connection between language and the spirit of a *Volk*; but they went further in their view that language is a "psychic organ" requiring psychology for its study.

Here it is possible to offer only a scanty and crude outline of their complicated ideas. Their main focus is on the *Volk*, viewed as a community of individuals sharing a language and tradition giving them a common fate and identity; with the exception of some quasi-mystical overtones, this is much the same as what we now understand by "culture." Humanity at large, viewed in a broad time perspective, is made up of a gradually changing collection of such units. The task of *Völkerpsychologie* is twofold: one approach, abstract and general, deals with humankind as a whole and seeks to establish the laws of its development; in this context such aspects as language or religion are treated as general categories with a view to discovering universal laws. The second approach is concrete and specific, dealing with the psychologies of existing *Völker* and their particular modes of development, considered as manifestations of the working of the universal laws. For the purpose of achieving this objective, *Völkerpsychologie* (which is taken to include philology) has to join with anthropology and history so as to encompass all the salient aspects of a culture as it changes over time. As will be apparent, the task Lazarsfeld and Steinthal set out for the new discipline was a formidable one, and so it is no wonder the contributions to the journal over the three decades of its existence have practically nothing to say about general laws and made only modest advances as regards the more specific issues.

When one scans the contents, philological and often highly specialized linguistic topics predominate. There is much folklore, a little ethnographic material from outside Europe, and a good deal of indigestible philosophizing. An example of one of the articles probably closest to the intentions of the founders will help us understand the approaches. It is by Fluegel (1880), entitled *The Self [das Ich] in the Life of Peoples.* The author begins by noting that the concept of self is central in humans, from childhood onward. For the bulk of the article he draws on ethnographic and historical material, which he categorizes in terms of various ways of conceptualizing the self: beginning with the bodily self, he goes on via personal names and particular material objects to more abstract notions such as that of the self as an active principle. He then postulates a developmental principle according to which the concrete, predominating among "primitives," gradually gives way to more sophisticated ideas among civilized peoples. In the concluding sentence the author states that he wanted to show "how the development of the self in the life of peoples goes through the very same stages as the self of the individual" (p. 160). This postulated analogy between individual and collective development was one of the guiding ideas of Lazarus and Steinthal's *Völkerpsychologie.*

Wilhelm Wundt (1888) subjected the whole of their theoretical edifice to what can only be called devastating criticism. His own interest in *Völkerpsychologie* dated back to the 1860s and was reflected in his early writings. In his article entitled "On the Aims and Ways of *Völkerpsychologie*" he contrasted his own position with that of Lazarus and Steinthal. He objected to the excessive scope of their scheme, involving the "psychologizing" of history and anthropology; he also rejected the distinction between individual and cultural "laws," contending that there could be only one set of such laws.

From the present standpoint two issues are of major importance. First is Wundt's critique of the Herbartian psychology underpinning the writings of Lazarus and Steinthal, relating especially to their conception of general "laws." Herbart sought to establish mechanical connections modeled on the natural sciences, expressed in mathematical form. Wundt maintained that psychological laws are not of this kind; rather, they are *developmental* principles, whereby changes occur in psychological processes through interaction with physical and social contexts. Usually he was more concerned with phylogeny than ontogeny.

Second, just as Wundt was not greatly interested in individual differences, so he dissociated himself from that part of the Lazarus and Steinthal program that concerned the differential psychological study of particular cultures. Although it is true that he later (Wundt, 1917) acknowledged its legitimacy as a kind of subordinate field, it was entirely omitted from his own work. At the beginning of his monumental 10-volume study this was explicitly stated: "[For *Völkerpsychologie*, in contrast to history,] local and national differences . . . are a matter of indifference, unless they in some way help to throw light on the [general] lawfulness" (Wundt, 1911, Vol. 1, p. 3). His purpose was to trace the lawful development, through collective experience, of the higher mental processes; and he based this primarily on inferences from changes in languages, myths, and customs, traced in minute detail from the mass of ethnographic material then available. It should be noted that the later book translated into English as *Elements of Folk Psychology* (1916), far from being a summary of the extensive 10-volume work, represents a much more speculative "psychological history."

In the period that followed, *Völkerpsychologie* went into a decline, and such discussions as appeared tended to be critical, with Lazarus and Steinthal being largely forgotten. Alfred Vierkandt (1914) accused Wundt of not having carried through his program, suggesting that the study of psychological types in different cultures should be a major task. Erich Stern (1920), in an article entitled "Problems of Cultural Psychology," in essence went back to Lazarus and Steinthal (but without mentioning them) in proposing a dual aim of establishing both general "culture-psychological" laws and a special cultural psychology in which these laws would be applied to particular cultures. Richard Thurnwald (1924, 1929), who himself had been an anthropological fieldworker, reproached Wundt with never having been in contact with any of the "primitives" about whom he had written so extensively. Thurnwald, this time referring to Steinthal, also wanted to distinguish a general from a specific *Völkerpsychologie*, taking the view that the general aspect is the business of sociology.

Summing up, the proponents of *Völkerpsychologie* has some important new ideas about cultural influences on psychological processes. However, they remained locked in abstract discussion, lacking the means to carry out relevant empirical studies. How some of these began will be mentioned later.

Empiricism

This term does not refer here to the opposition common in psychology of nativism/empiricism but is treated as more or less synonymous with positivism. This means it is intended to cover all those approaches that assume a lawful determinism of the natural science type to be applicable to human affairs.

Unlike the sociohistorical approach that is characterized by a certain unity and coherence, empiricism in the broad sense used here takes a great many different forms in relation to a variety of specific issues. Hence it is not feasible in the present context to tell a story in chronological sequence. Instead I will employ a mixed strategy, surveying a number of relevant themes in roughly the temporal order of their prominence.

IDEOLOGUES AND OBSERVATEURS DE L'HOMME

Toward the end of the 18th century and early in the 19th an outstandingly talented group of men were active in France promoting the observational (i.e., scientific rather than speculative) study of man. Constantin-François Volney (1757–1820) spent three years in the Middle East for the specific purpose of studying the habits and characters of its peoples. As what we would call a "participant observer" (apart from the world of women, from which he was excluded), he not only provided a detailed ethnographic account, but also raised some important questions. He maintained that it was the business of the philosopher to discover the reasons for the diversity of customs and characters in human populations. Volney refuted Montesquieu's simplistic climatic determinism, putting forward instead a much more sophisticated hypothesis:

> In order to arouse activity, objects of desire are needed first of all; in order to sustain it, one needs hope in order to be able to enjoy them. If these two circumstances are absent, there is no activity, neither in the individual nor in the nation; and such is the case of the Orientals in general. . . . Who could get them to move, if no movement offers them the hope of a benefit arising from the effort they have had to make? (Volney, 1787/1959, p. 405)

This is enough to indicate his theory of social motivation, relating to the sociopolitical institutions. Volney also graphically described the culture shock he experienced on returning to France, where everything at first appeared rather strange.

In the course of his subsequent visit to America, Volney worked through an interpreter with an informant, a Miami Indian war chief. With him he not only discussed tribal customs and traditions, but was also interested in social change, seeking to discover why the Indians were reluctant to adopt the ways of the dominant Americans. Of particular interest are Volney's reflections on the Indians' ability to endure extreme pain without complaint, then usually attributed to innate insensitivity. Volney suggested that it was probably a function of a particular physiological state, a violent "exaltation of the passions." He drew parallels with the stoicism of religious and political martyrs and said that the phenomenon was worthy of study in medical schools.

Although Volney was on good terms with Jefferson, his book, which contained some critical comments on the United States, was not well received there. In the introduction to his translation Brockden Brown sarcastically asked why it was necessary to ask if savages could be improved by civilization when they were doomed to extinction. On Volney's proposal that an institute for the study of Indian languages be set up, Brown commented that it would be a waste of good money (Gaulmier, 1980).

Volney has justly been described as a precursor of psychological anthropology; his contemporary, François Péron (1775–1810), may be credited with having carried out the first empirical test of a cross-cultural hypothesis. The ideologists held the view that the range of sensations people are capable of experiencing determines their capacity to produce and combine ideas, and therefore to create and develop values. Péron, with a medical background, extended this idea by postulating a correlation between susceptibility to illness and moral sensitivity. This means that savage peoples will be physically strong and healthy but lacking in moral sentiment. Needless to say, the argument is much more subtle than my crude summary.

At any rate, when Péron became one of the scientific members of an expedition to Australasia, he decided to put the matter to the test. Using the dynamometer then newly invented by Edme Régnier, he compared the physical strength of the savages with that of

European sailors. The outcome was the opposite of what he anticipated, the Europeans proving stronger. Moreover, in the course of
the voyage another incident occurred that made a great impression
on Péron: a group of natives, encountering white men for the first
time, were allowed to inspect one of the young sailors and evidently
wanted to ascertain that he was white all over. The sailor had an
erection, which the savages are said to have greeted with exclama-
tions of surprise and delight. On this slender basis Péron jumped to
the conclusion that it was for them an unusual occurrence and that
savages were in fact also sexually weak. The image of the paradise of
"natural man" was shattered for him; instead, the physically as well
as morally weak savage needed to be rescued by making him civilized. It might be noted, incidentally, that Péron's dynamometer
study continued to be cited until the late 19th century.

Both Volney and Péron had firsthand experience of other peoples, but two others lacking this nevertheless made notable contributions entirely on the basis of the by then very extensive travel literature. Joseph-Marie de Gérando (1772–1842) wrote a kind of manual
on the methods of observing savage peoples (de Gérando, 1800/1978)
that was so far ahead of its time that it can still be read with profit today.
For the sake of brevity, I shall express examples of his ideas in modern
jargon, thereby laying myself open to the risk of being accused of
anachronism, but in my view the distortions are minimal.

De Gérando refers to sample size and representativeness and
to the importance of avoiding ethnocentrism and taking account of
the role and impact of the European observer. He stresses the need
for acquiring the language, including gestures; one should also take
care to avoid ambiguities in questioning, repeating inquiries in different forms to assess reliability. The topics listed for study include
many psychological ones: acuity of the different senses, modes of
thought (e.g., Do they make use of analogy?), and the incidence of
mental handicap; the sense of identity, and opinions; attention and
memory, and the extent to which they are future oriented.

This should be sufficient indication of de Gérando's incisive insights, but here, as a last example, is a direct quotation concerning
child training:

> It is certain that one can expect with the savages highly inter-
> esting details about the moral education of their children. Nev-

ertheless there are several circumstances worthy of a few remarks. What is the extent of attachment of parents to their children, and how much interest do they display towards them? How far do they supervise them, and with what degree of severity? Is it the father or the mother who is particularly concerned with their care? Until what age does that care continue? Is it equal for all children, or do they indicate some preference? How do children learn their language? How are they initiated into the moral ideas of their parents? Lastly, how rapid is the development of the emotions and of intelligence? (de Gérando, 1800/1978)

Finally mention should be made of Jean-Nicholas Démeunier (1751–1814), who undertook the enormous labor of collating the information then available about peoples and their customs (Démeunier, 1776). His work consisted of three volumes containing well over 2,000 references to nearly 500 authors; it was published when Démeunier was just twenty-five years old. The work is systematically structured according to what were regarded as the major stages of savage, barbarous, and civilized. Within these the organization is remarkably similar to our familiar concept of the life cycle: birth, the family and education, sexual behavior, everyday life, illness and death. The whole opus is strongly reminiscent of the Human Relations Area Files, and Démeunier ought to be credited with being their pioneer.

These sketches dealing with a few outstanding figures should make it clear that the ferment of the French Revolution produced some remarkable thinkers, who raised a number of issues concerning psychology and culture that remain salient today.

THE ISSUE OF "PSYCHIC UNITY"

In the 18th century, as I have already noted, the basic potential of the human mind was generally taken to be the same everywhere. The gap that divided savagery from civilization was viewed as a difference not in capacity, but in stage of historical development. The psychological model was that of the developing human individual from infancy to maturity, explicitly stated by Adam Ferguson (1723–1816) when he likened the advance from "rudeness" to "civilization" to that from infancy to manhood (Ferguson, 1767). Marie-Jean Condorcet (1743–1794) believed that all humans had an innate need for new sensations and ideas leading to steady progress, which in turn generated new and more complex needs. Perfectibility was taken for granted, and such debate as there was focused on the external obstacles to progress and the hypothetical presocial or "natural" state of man (Condorcet, 1795/1966). The central notion that fundamental psychological characteristics are shared by all humans subsequently came to be labeled "the psychic unity of mankind."

The broad consensus of the Age of Reason began to break down early in the 19th century, as a result of several intellectual and political currents. These included the rise of physical anthropology and the persisting debate about the status of the great apes, which led to renewed and increasingly vociferous questioning about whether humanity really constituted a single species. This trend is typified by the great naturalist Georges Cuvier (1769–1832), who in 1790 had ridiculed the idea that Negroes and orangutans may be interfertile, or that differences in "intellectual faculties" could be explained by cranial features. A decade later he discussed the strong possibility of a relationship between body structure and the moral and intellectual characteristics of different races; and by 1817 he had become convinced of the inferiority of the dark races (see Stocking, 1964).

Such a line of thinking also provided welcome "scientific" ammunition for those who opposed the abolition of the slave trade. Moreover, in France the restoration of a rather weak monarchy was threatened by the claims of the social revolutionaries that the distribution of status within human societies was capable of rapid change. The view that class as well as race differences are "natural" was highly convenient for buttressing social privilege. Thus, well before Darwin a biologically oriented explanation of the chasm between "savage" and "civilized" first became intellectually respectable and later gained wide ascendancy.

This meant that the proponents of "psychic unity" were to some extent thrown on the defensive. Thus James Cowles Prichard (1786–1848) in his *Natural History of Man* begins his chapter on the "mental endowments of human races" as follows:

Psychology is, with respect to mankind, the history of the mental faculties; it comprehends, likewise, an account of those properties in the different races of animals which most nearly resemble the mental endowments of man. . . . If now it should appear, on inquiry, that one common mind, or psychical nature, belongs to the whole human family, a very strong argument would thence arise, on the ground of analogy, for their community of species and origin.

But can it be maintained that such is really the fact? On first adverting to this inquiry, most persons would be likely to adopt the negative side of the question; for what greater contrasts can be imagined than those which present themselves when we compare in their actual state the different races of mankind? (1848, pp. 486–487)

We see from this passage that Prichard took the prevalence of skepticism for granted and made allowance for it before surveying the evidence in detail. His conclusion was that "the same inward and mental nature is to be recognized in all races of men" (1848, p. 564).

A similar strategy of presentation was employed by Theodor Waitz (1821–1864)—to review the arguments of the opponents of "psychic unity" (a term Waitz used) in order to counter them. He had more material at his disposal, and his discussion is rather more subtle than that of Prichard, who had in the main been content to list the common psychic elements found everywhere. Waitz sought to grapple with the problem of the interrelation between disposition, environmental influences, and individual differences. He refused to accept such abstractions as "the spirit of the people," nor was he willing to allow absolute judgments of the mental capacity of a people or a race, pointing to the prevalence of important intragroup differences everywhere. The mental capacity of a people is not constant and does not "alter merely in the course of time, but according to its historical fate" (Waitz, 1863, p. 324). The allegedly "natural" superiority of whites is not one of race but one of civilization, and he cites examples of "uncultivated white races." The conclusion he reaches is essentially the same as Prichard's: "On casting a retrospective glance at the numerous facts . . . we are irresistibly led to the conclusion that there are no specific differences among mankind with respect to their psychic life" (1863, p. 327).

Note that the supporters of psychic unity and those who believed in biologically determined differences in mental capacity based their cases on much the same material. What varied were the inferences drawn, with one party stressing similarities and the potential indicated thereby, while the other emphasized contrasts in actual achievements. The problem for the advocates of biological determinism was how to account for the similarities, which they tried to do by invoking what later came to be known as "diffusion"—the borrowing of beliefs, customs, and artifacts from other societies. However, it was frequently pushed to absurd lengths such as postulating a link via Atlantis or searching for some of the lost tribes of Israel in America.

This was the issue tackled by Adolf Bastian (1826–1905), a prolific but very obscure writer. In the words of Eisenstaedter (1912, p. 11) who produced a dissertation on Bastian's work, "With great effort one can peruse at most two or three of the shorter pieces in succession; then one's strength fails." In my experience this is an understatement, but it applies only to his theoretical work. Bastian traveled all over the world as a ship's doctor, and the accounts of his adventures are often lively and entertaining. Unlike his more bookish predecessors, it was probably his experiences that prompted his conviction of the basic similarity of human minds everywhere.

In seeking to formulate his views in a scientific manner, Bastian's background predisposed him toward a biological analogy, though in his case the intention was, in our terminology, antiracist. He envisaged an original uniform state of humanity where the similarity of modes of existence generated everywhere a restricted set of basic ideas (*Elementargedanken*). These gradually came to be modified and elaborated as different communities changed their ways of life, and also (but secondarily) as a consequence of contacts with other peoples; to these he applied the term "folk thoughts" (*Völkergedanken*). They contained within them the essence of the former basic ideas, and by careful analyses of folktales, myths, and so on these can be retrieved. One can discern here some remote similarity with the notions of Claude Lévi-Strauss (1962), who also saw the ultimate source in the characteristics of the human brain. The main difference lies in the fact that Bastian postulated simple, if not naive, parallels between biological laws and the laws of thought: "The same necessity of organic growth which, in indissoluble interaction with the environment, forms cells in plants, elicits ideas in men and predisposes them towards further unfolding" (Bastian, 1868, p. xii). Thus he regarded *Elementargedanken* as the fundamental units for psychological study, in explicit analogy with the cell for the botanist or the atom for the physicist. He advocated what he called "thought statistics" whereby each thought should be recorded as one records a variety within a species. Here is an example of the tortuous ways his own thoughts are encoded in pompous and dense prose:

> The damaging weed demands to be studied just as much as the useful plant that yields fruit, but soon interest will lead to the elimination of the former if it cannot be ennobled through culture. It is only when the human spirit has succeeded in growing its roots throughout the universe and to draw nourishment from the combined harmonies of the separate parts that the unity of self-consciousness will emerge organically out of the manifold appearances. (Bastian, 1860, Vol. 1, p. 429)

Given such a baroque style, it is hardly surprising that there were numerous disputes about the interpretation of Bastian's writings. In particular, he was unjustly criticized by the diffusionist Friedrich Ratzel (1882), who complained that what he called Bastian's "psychological theory" ignored culture contact; in fact Bastian did not ignore it, but he treated it as less important. His general message, too often buried in pretentious verbiage, was sometimes made quite clear: "Comparative psychology can be established only on the basis of ethnology, which traces in various populations the genetic development of thought creations and explains their local coloring in terms of the geographical conditions or historical context" (Bastian, 1868, p. xi).

Notice that this is a fair approximation to what is now regarded as the objective of culturally oriented psychology. Bastian's attempt to put his program into practice cannot be said to have been very effective. It consisted of assembling a rather heterogeneous mass of ethnographic material and seeking to draw out similarities at various levels. There is a certain resemblance between his efforts and those of some followers of Lazarus and Steinthal, in spite of the fact that their theoretical aims were quite disparate.

The idea of the psychic unity of all humankind, which was to be proclaimed anew by Franz Boas (1911) in the early 20th century, went against the *Zeitgeist* of the latter part of the 19th century, which was dominated by biological determinism. Thus the message of Edward B. Tylor's earlier writings was similar to that of Bastian's. In his *Researches into the Early History of Mankind* (1865), he commented on the similar irrationality of the beliefs of "kafirs" and European spiritualists; and in his famous definition of culture that opened his book *Primitive Culture* (1871) he noted that its study was relevant for understanding the "laws of human thought and action." A few years later, however, he had shifted his position toward biological determinism, as I will show next.

PRIMITIVE CHILDREN AND CHILDLIKE PRIMITIVES

There seems to be in mankind inbred temperament and inbred capacity of mind. History points the great lesson that some races have marched on in civilization while others have stood still or fallen back, and we should partly look for an explanation of this in differences of intellectual and moral powers between such tribes as the native Americans and Africans, and the Old World nations who overmatch and subdue them. In measuring the minds of the lower races, a good test is how far their children are able to take a civilized education. The account generally given by teachers who have had the children of lower races in their schools is that, though these often learn as well as the white children up to about twelve years old, they then fall off, and are left behind by the children of the ruling race. (Tylor, 1881/1937, Vol. 1, p. 58)

This idea of what later came to be known as "arrested development" was by no means new at the time Tylor came to adopt it. In 1860 Theodor Waitz had cited numerous reports of arrested development, together with others giving the opposite testimony. Waitz himself dismissed the idea, attributing the instances to climatic and social environmental factors. Nonetheless, it became increasingly widespread. In 1863 the notorious James Hunt said in an address to the British Association that Negro children are precocious but cease to grow mentally after puberty. The first edition of *Notes and Queries on Anthropology,* published in 1874, contains the following passage in the section titled "Psychology":

> Care should be taken to ascertain whether the slight progress made by savages in acquiring habits of civilized life arises from incapacity or the influence of acquired habits, customs and modes of thought which are antagonistic to progress. Particular notice should therefore be taken . . . of the influence of culture upon natives of the same race who have been removed at an early age from native surroundings and brought up in European schools.

There follow a series of questions concerning among other things their precocity and whether intelligence is being maintained or stops at a certain age. Evidently based on a questionnaire devised by Francis Galton (cf. Pearson, 1924), it was at least phrased in the form of a hypothesis to be tested. I have not been able to find any relevant published evidence arising therefrom, though the questions appeared in essentially the same form in two subsequent editions until 1899.

Although the official organ of anthropologists at least adopted an open-minded stance, arrested development was widely taken for granted as an established fact for which sometimes biological causes were sought. A. E. Chamberlain (1900), in an article on "arrested development," cites anatomists who believed premature closure of the sutures of the skull to be the main cause.

The persistence of these ideas is noteworthy. *The Child in Primitive Society* by N. Miller, published in 1928, refers to the "extreme precocity" of primitive children as well as the supposed "fact" that they become dull and sluggish between about 12 and 15 years of age, the reason being that the primitive adolescent "falls into a slough of sensuality." What is even more remarkable is a post–World War II statement in a monograph that appeared under the auspices of the World Health Organization (Carothers, 1953) to the effect that "the psychology of the African is essentially the psychology of the African child. The pattern of his mental development is defined by the time he reaches adolescence, and little new remains to be said" (p. 106).

The cause was said to be just the old saw about excessive preoccupation with sex, and that in itself was regarded as merely one of the symptoms of a lack of personal integration characterizing African mentality.

If one accepts the doctrine of arrested development, it follows logically that primitive adults must be mentally like children in their early teens. This was indeed, and has in fact long remained, a prevalent view reflected in the burgeoning literature on ethnic psychology from the latter part of the 19th century onward. There were exceptions such as Richard Andree (1878), an anthropologist who was an admirer and follower of Bastian; he insisted that mental functions are essentially the same everywhere. The bulk of the often semipopular writings, many of them published in France, perpetuated the stereotype. A few examples will illustrate this.

Elie Reclus (1885) began his book by telling his readers not to despise the primitives, who are well adapted to their environment. As he proceeds, it becomes evident that he viewed them basically as children—though of course we like children. Similarly, F. S. Schultze (1900) suggested that the brains of primitives failed to develop owing to lack of proper stimulation; he not only compared them to children but claimed that they were similar to dogs insofar as they lived in a world of smells! Charles Letourneau (1901) wrote about black Africans that their character and intelligence was of a level characteristic of European children, though he did add that this did not mean that they could never advance beyond such a level. There is little point in multiplying examples, but I should like to pause briefly at Gustave Le Bon (1894), usually considered one of the founders of social psychology. In a little-known work on the psychological laws governing the evolution of peoples he displayed a quite different biologically grounded set of ideas. According to him, "One must have lived with people of a different mental constitution . . . in order to appreciate the chasm separating the thought of different peoples. Without going on distant voyages [as he never did] one can get some idea when one observes the great mental divergence between a civilized man and a woman, even if she is well educated. They may have common interests and sentiments, but never similar chains of thoughts" (1894, pp. 34–35).

In an earlier work (1881) he had sought to demonstrate this by elaborate charts of relative brain volumes, concluding that women are at a lower evolutionary level and closer to children and savages than to civilized men. Le Bon also seems to have originated the notion of the "veneer of civilization": you can easily make a Negro or a Japanese into a university graduate or a lawyer, but any number of diplomas will be only superficial varnish, and his mentality is bound to remain below that of an ordinary European.

This is a view that has filtered down to be conventional wisdom, lingering until quite recently. In the introduction to what purports to be the autobiography of an African, LoBagola (1930), it is said that he became highly educated, wrote books, and lectured. Nevertheless, "Ibn LoBagola is interesting because he is just what he is, a savage civilized merely on the surface" (p. xiii).

DRAWINGS AND PERCEPTION

The notion of the childlike mentality of savages was based on two sets of beliefs held either separately or together: that they constitute an early stage of the development of humanity, and that they are subject to innate limitations on mental growth. The later Tylor combined both views, as is apparent from the continuation of the passage previously quoted: "It [the arrested development of savage children] agrees also with what the history of civilization teaches, that up to a certain point savages and barbarians are like what our ancestors were and our peasants still are, but from this common level the superior intellect of the progressive races has raised their nations to heights of culture" (1881/1937, p. 58).

The phrase "what our peasants still are," of course, begs the question, unless the peasants are regarded as an "inferior race." Tylor was not unusual in trying to have it both ways, and the issue was frequently fudged. Another line of thought that must be mentioned originated in 1866, shortly after the first impact of Darwinism. In that year Ernst Haeckel (1834–1919) put forward his "biogenetic law" best known under the slogan "ontogeny repeats phylogeny" (Haeckel, 1874). Although first conceived in relation to the embryo, it later came to be extended to postnatal child development, as in Stanley Hall's "recapitulation theory"; this held that the child in its development to maturity "recapitulates" the evolution of humanity from anthropoid to *Homo sapiens*. In fact, as the names of Baldwin, Binet, Preyer, and Sully indicate, child psychology as a special field took off in the 1880s and 1890s.

The second half of the 19th century also saw the beginnings of serious interest in African, American, and Oceanic art (though some refused to regard it as "art"), and the first discovery of the Stone Age paintings in Europe was made at Altamira in 1878. In 1887 Corrado Ricci published his book on children's art, which attracted much attention and subsequently led to the collection of literally hundreds of thousands of children's drawings. Ricci also made reference to the similarity between children's art and primitive art.

Although I have been unable to disentangle the connections between these various strands, there is little doubt that they all came together to generate an enthusiasm for studying the drawings of savages. Ethnographers went into the field and pressed pencils into hands that had never wielded one, asking people to draw. This was probably the first time since Péron's use of a dynamometer that empirical data other than pure observations were obtained.

Most of this work was done in South America and Africa by German ethnographers, who also treated the material most thoroughly. Members of the Cambridge expedition to Torres Straits also collected drawings, but they had little to say about them. Alfred C. Haddon (1904) began an article in which such drawings were reproduced by stating that "drawings by uncultured people possess considerable interest." However, he failed to explain further what the interest was, most of the article being devoted to descriptions and some comparisons of the skills of different peoples. The only general conclusion was as follows: "All these drawings exhibit a very rudimentary power of delineation, and they correspond very closely with the drawings by members of the Bororo and of other central Brazilian tribes. . . . Indeed, they are similar to many other drawings of nature-folk, and those of our own children" (p. 33).

The Brazilian study he referred to was one of the earliest ones by Karl von den Steinen (1894). Referring to Corrado Ricci, he attempted a comparison of the Bororo and (European) children—both sought to characterize the object rather than rendering it in faithful detail. For instance, in drawing a picture of Steinen, they showed the head with beard and the sexual organs, though these were not visible. Indians, unlike children, never used a profile representation for persons but always did so with animals. Again, Steinen carefully noted the number of fingers drawn and advanced an interesting explanation for why they usually showed only three. He also commented on their handling of space, which in spite of some oddities was superior to that of children. It will be noted that "children" were treated as a homogeneous category, no account being taken of developmental differences.

This and similar ethnographic reports gave rise to a great deal of theoretical speculation, which can only be briefly sketched. Georg Buschan (1906), citing the biogenetic law, claimed that drawing fulfilled the same functions for small as well as "large" children (i.e., savages) and pursued the parallels in considerable detail.

Max Verworn (1907, 1917) introduced a distinction between what he called *physioplastic* and *ideoplastic* art. Physioplastic art is the faithful reproduction in drawing of an object present to the senses; ideoplastic art refers to drawing from memory images, but it must be stressed that this includes what the person thinks and knows about the object. The typical drawing of children and most primitives is ideoplastic, because of their lack of coherent logical thinking and their unbridled fantasy. The awkward problem is that Bushmen, one of the most primitive peoples, have physioplastic art. Verworn's answer was that they are a people who do not speculate or fantasize about life and death but are totally preoccupied with hunting, and this also makes them good observers. The same applies to prehistoric peoples and their cave art.

Although much of Verworn's argument was, in hindsight, weak, he did make an effort to analyze drawing behavior, distinguishing between conceptual aspects and motor skills. He also pioneered some experiments in serial reproduction of drawings. In the ensuing debate, whose details need not detain us, opinions were sharply divided over Verworn's thesis about prehistoric peoples. On the other hand there was general agreement with Wundt's view that in spite of some differences drawings of children and primitives have much in common. Johannes Kretzschmar (1910), in an article comparing children's art with prehistoric art, seems to have expressed a wide consensus when he wrote: "There is a need for numerous scientific studies on the relation between individual and collective development; if the researchers are constantly aware that it has to do with psychological problems, they will enhance the value of child psychology for all phylogenetic *Geisteswissenschaften*, prehistory, universal history and ethnology/folklore [*Völkerkunde*]" (p. 366).

With the demise of the "recapitulation theory" postulating a close parallel between individual and collective development, anthropological interest in drawing waned. Margaret Mead (1954) still recommended it as a method of research with primitive children. There were some who used it this way during the 1930s (e.g., Fortes, 1981), but it has become rare. In cross-cultural psychology a few have continued the tradition, though the aims have become rather modest—perhaps too modest. For instance, it has been shown that when children in different cultures are asked to draw fruit trees, they tend to draw trees that are familiar to them (Adler & Adler, 1977). On the other hand, Goodnow, Wilkins, and Dawes (1986) have used drawings in a novel and imaginative way.

There is, however, another aspect on which attention has increasingly focused, that is, pictorial perception, or the *understanding* of drawings. There were a number of reports during the 19th century suggesting that certain peoples cannot make sense of pictures. Here is what was written about an aboriginal tribe: "They are totally incapable of understanding the most lively pictorial representation. Shown a large coloured illustration of a native New Hollander, one declared it to be a ship, another a kangaroo, and so on. Not one out of a dozen recognized that the portrait had some connection with themselves. They are able to comprehend a rough drawing in which all the essential parts are greatly exaggerated" (Oldfield, cited in Andree, 1887).

Reactions to such reports varied. Lubbock attributed the lack of understanding to an innate racial deficiency. Others, like the distinguished French anthropologist Paul Topinard (1878), were skeptical, because other evidence indicated that these people "possess a certain amount of intellectual capacity" (p. 150). Recent research (Deregowski, Muldrow & Muldrow, 1972) has confirmed Oldfield's observations.

A related issue is that of visuospatial skills, and here I want to jump right back to Christoph Meiners, whose *Researches into the Differences in Human Nature* (1815) contains some relevant comments. It is worth mentioning in passing that Meiners put forward an exceedingly simple classification of human races into the beautiful and the ugly. As one might guess, the beautiful are the Europeans, but with the exception of the Slavs; the ugly covers everybody else.

Meiners noted that the senses of Negroes, American Indians, and certain Asiatic peoples are extraordinarily acute. This assertion, repeated throughout the 19th century, gave rise to much debate and was later tested and disproved by William H. R. Rivers (1864–1922). Yet in spite of this, Meiners maintained, they have certain deficiencies that neither practice nor training can correct: "Owing to the complete lack of adequate visual judgement [*richtigem Blick*] or of a sure eye [*Augenmaas*], these people never learn to draw properly. . . . The Negroes are totally incapable of drawing a straight line, or to orient a dining table in a straight line" (1815, Vol. 3, p. 222).

The latter complaint must have been echoed innumerable times over more than a century by colonials and especially their wives—I have heard it myself as late as the 1950s. On the other hand, there have also been reports of outstanding spatial-perceptual abilities. Thus Francis Galton (1883) commented on the exceptional "visualising faculty" as it was then known of the Eskimos; although unschooled, many are able to draw amazingly accurate maps of vast territories over which they had traveled. The basic correctness of such observations has since been confirmed (Pick, 1980), but though we now know more about the issue, the causes of such differences remain far from clear.

Some of the problems mentioned were investigated by W. H. R. Rivers (1901) in the course of the Cambridge expedition to the Torres Straits. He concentrated on vision, partly because he seems to have agreed with Wundt that higher mental processes cannot be studied empirically, and partly because he held the view that the excessive concentration of primitive people on sensory objects was inimical to the development of higher mental processes. In this he seems to have been influenced by the evolutionist Herbert Spencer, who had advanced precisely that argument. Spencer believed there is only a fixed amount of mental energy, which savages all expend on perception, so that none is left for abstract thought: "For in virtue of a general antagonism between the activities of the simpler faculties and the activities of the more complex faculties, it results that this dominance of low intellectual life hinders the higher intellectual life. In proportion as the mental energies go out in restless and multitudinous perception, they cannot go out in calm deliberate thought" (Spencer, 1876, Vol. 1, p. 89).

I should add that later, after more personal contact with "primitives," Rivers came to abandon this view. Since Rivers's work is deservedly famous, it hardly needs to be described. Instead I propose to give some account of German studies whose contribution, though less weighty than that of Rivers, deserves to be rescued from oblivion.

The most notable empirical researcher was Richard Thurnwald (1869–1954), an anthropologist brought up in the broad 19th-century tradition before specialization had become the rule. His writings throughout his career testify to his conviction that a psychological approach must be part of any attempt to understand primitive cultures.

Since he himself had not been trained in psychology, he asked a prominent psychologist for advice before leaving for a research trip in Melanesia, where he worked during the years 1906 to 1909. There he undertook a series of what he called ethnopsychological studies (Thurnwald, 1913). In his introduction to the report he made it clear that his primary goal was ethnographic and the psychological work was done merely "on the side." Hence that work was essentially exploratory, raising questions rather than providing definitive answers. The topics he investigated will be briefly outlined.

1. Relative strength of the left and right hands, measured with a dynamometer;

2. color vision, assessed with Holmgren's wools, and color nomenclature;

3. attention and memory, requiring subjects to reproduce the order of sets of briefly exposed colored threads and picture postcards;

4. suggestion, using the same materials but trying to shake the subjects' confidence in their answers;

5. counting, the subjects being required to give the number of a group of matches displayed; here Thurnwald sought to determine how many matches could be counted at a mere glance, and for larger aggregates he tried to analyze the counting strategies employed;

6. associations; this involved naming or describing such stimuli as geometric figures or stereometric objects;

7. word associations, employing the translation of a standard German list;

8. transmission of reports, whereby a story was passed on from one subject to another;

9. experimental drawing, regarded more or less as an intelligence test; this included copying stereometric objects and making free drawings of the human figure, animals, everyday objects, and so on.

Thurnwald's approach was in most respects entirely different from that of Rivers. Apart from a concern with color, their topics had little in common, and Thurnwald lacked Rivers's experimental sophistication; in fact it is unlikely that he had come across Rivers's work before he went into the field. The number of people studied was small, usually amounting to no more than half a dozen for each experiment. On the other hand, he did have some novel ideas, in particular his approach to counting, where he departed from the then-customary concentration on purely linguistic aspects (e.g., Schmidl, 1915), and he could be regarded as having anticipated current cognitive psychology. Moreover, his "transmission of reports" is essentially the same as Frederic C. Bartlett's (1932) later "method of serial reproduction," and it is possible that Bartlett may have indirectly obtained the method from Thurnwald (cf. Jahoda, 1989).

The consultation mentioned above led to a discussion among various psychologists at a congress in Würzburg regarding the kinds of issues that might fruitfully be studied in primitive cultures. The eventual outcome was a collection of proposals for ethnopsychological research (Institut für Angewandte Psychologie, 1912), intended as a kind of guide not only for professional researchers but for anyone in close contact with primitive people, such as missionaries, teachers, officials, and medical personnel.

The content of the publication is heterogeneous and very uneven in quality. Some of the contributors merely suggested replications of laboratory experiments that were totally unrealistic, while others evidently made a real effort to take account of the constraints of the field even if they themselves had no personal experience.

It had been hoped that any material collected would be sent to the Institute, thereby accumulating an ethnopsychological data bank. However, the Great War intervened, and with the loss of the German colonies the project came to naught. In any case some of the proposals, in particular that for the study of modes of thought, were incredibly naive. Thus the question whether people had any purely theoretical interests was treated as follows: "How far is it a matter of curiosity or a desire for knowledge, of mere astonishment or a serious need for explanations? Example: Perhaps the question could be tested in connection with the moon, which plays a great role in many myths; one gives the natives the opportunity of closely viewing its character through the telescope, and one can then see how receptive they are to this" (Institut für Angewandte Psychologie, 1912, p. 91).

In complete contrast to such absurdity, one finds an article published at the same time on the thinking of primitive peoples by Max Wertheimer (1912). He begins by saying that the reports then available are inadequate for assessing the thinking of primitives. Researchers tend to impose their own categories, and their prejudice leads them to regard the thinking of primitives as representing an earlier stage and thus as rudimentary and inadequate. Wertheimer, with his Gestalt orientation, considers modes of thinking as biologically based though modified through environmental factors, especially formal education. Thus primitives have not acquired our habit of hypothetical thinking in a closed system, their thinking being rooted in reality. He cited the example of the Red Indian who has been told to translate the sentence "The white man has shot six bears today" but absolutely refuses on the grounds that it would be impossible to do that. A good deal of Wertheimer's argument is closely similar to that of Alexander Luria's (1976) report on research in Uzbekistan. He also concluded with a series of concrete research proposals, in which he stressed the need to adapt the questions investigated to the particular cultural system. In sum, it is probably no great exaggeration to say that much of the article could have been written in the 1980s.

Another writer worthy of mention was Johannes Lindworsky (1917/1918, 1926), who tackled the same issue from a different starting point. Lindworsky complained that ethnologists in his time were still taking their cue from Wundt, who had declared that the higher mental processes are not amenable to empirical study. Consequently ethnologists still relied on fallible impressions and perpetuated notions such as the supposed lack of "mental energy" of primitives, or the *Ohnmacht*—a favorite term at the time meaning "weakness" or "impotence"—of their intellect.

In opposition to this Lindworsky maintained that not only had experimental studies of reasoning been shown to be feasible, but their results were highly relevant to the issue. His own studies showed that the thinking of even highly educated Europeans was itself primitive when applied to unfamiliar fields. On the other hand, if we look at the everyday life of primitive peoples and the ways they gain their livelihood, we find everywhere the same capacity for causal thinking as our own. Such a view, which anticipated some of the basic arguments of Shweder (1977), was in sharp opposition to the conventional wisdom of the period, supposedly buttressed by the results of intelligence tests. It was a view also shared by Frederic Bartlett (1923), though he failed to support it with adequate evidence. It was not until almost the middle of the 20th century that the doctrine of the mental inferiority of people in nonliterate culture ceased to be scientifically respectable.

In retrospect, the continuity of some ideas over the centuries is remarkable. In the 13th century Albertus Magnus, discussing whether pygmies belonged to the human species, made some shrewd observations on the comparative psychology of animals and humans. He concluded that the pgymies are not human, since they are capable only of a low level of thinking tied to particulars and sensory impressions, as shown by their language, which he compared to that of mental defectives (Koch, 1931). During the 18th century savages were seen as humans at an earlier stage of development, but one finds again the notion that their supposedly crude languages reflected undeveloped minds largely tied to sense impressions. George J. Romanes (1888), a post-Darwinian scientist, stated in his book *Mental Evolution in Man* that intellectual progress is very slow and that the thinking of most uncivilized races remains at the level of what he calls "recepts," that is, between percepts and true concepts; in support of this he referred to the languages of such "low races" as Bushmen and Hottentots, whose "clicks" were said to constitute a remnant of an inarticulate system of sign making. Last, one might mention Christopher Hallpike (1979), admittedly an odd man out in the second half of the 20th century. While no longer arguing on the basis of language and employing Piagetian terminology, he did maintain that primitive societies remain largely at the preoperatory stage, and this means that their reasoning is supposed to be perception bound—essentially the same case made by Albertus Magnus.

A broader thread that runs throughout history consists of two closely related questions that still occupy us today: What are the shared characteristics of all humans? And how does one account for their differences? Although in the 18th century the outer boundaries of humanity remained somewhat uncertain, the unity of the human species was generally taken for granted. Differences in degree of civilization were viewed as consequences of varying rates of progressive development. However, differences between peoples at a given level were also noted, and the empiricists from Locke onward proposed certain causal factors that were either physical, such as climate, ecology, and nutrition, or what was then called "moral" and we would call "social," namely, education, social and political institutions, religion, and contact with other peoples.

Such general categories are still prevalent and are treated by present-day empiricists as "independent variables." The same applies to the model put forward by the philosophers of the Scottish Enlightenment, who referred to the four stages of society as "hunting, pasturing, farming, and commerce." The "culture-and-personality" school that flourished during the 1940s and 1950s bears some resemblance to the grand theories of the 18th century, eventually collapsing under the weight of its excessive ambition.

The period that followed saw the emergence of a more hard-nosed cross-cultural psychology along the lines pioneered by Rivers. It tackles what appear to be more manageable problems such as perception, memory, values, and attitudes. Undeniably a great deal has been achieved, but there remains a lingering doubt regarding the fundamental nature of the enterprise. This is reflected in a divergence between the reasons put forward for doing cross-cultural psychology and actual practice. Most declarations of aims are couched in the spirit of de Gérando, who wrote in 1800 that "the science of man is also a natural science" (Copans & Jamin, 1978). The aim is often said to be the development of universal theories (e.g., Brislin, 1983; Segall, 1983), and the method usually advocated is the closest possible approximation to the experimental approach of mainline psychology. Many formulations contain the hidden assumption of "psychic unity," as when Sechrest (1987, pp. 55–56) proposed that "in essence every cross-cultural study is a quasi-experiment directed at discovering the effects of culture as a virtual (in the sense of computer jargon) independent variable."

However, when one scans the findings of a wide range of cross-cultural research it becomes evident that the bulk of it, with all its quasi-experimental or psychometric sophistication, remains essentially descriptive in character. This is not to deny that much of it is interesting and valuable, but in general one searches in vain for universal laws or the establishment of "causes." The single most common outcomes tend to be accounts of differences related to certain (often classical) "independent variables."

The reason for this state of affairs was clearly understood by John Stuart Mill. In his *System of Logic* he discussed problems of generalization and inference, taking as an example a comparison of

Frenchmen with Englishmen resulting in a finding that more French than English have a particular characteristic. After pointing out the limitations in terms of sampling and so on of such a generalization, he went on: "If we could even obtain . . . a much more satisfactory assurance of these generalizations than is really possible, they would still be only empirical laws. They would show, indeed, that there was some connexion between the type of character formed, and the circumstances existing in the case; but not what the precise connexion was, nor to which of the peculiarities of those circumstances the effect was really owing" (1879, Vol. 2, p. 455).

Mill also pointed out the local and time-bound nature of such empirical generalizations, and I cannot forbear citing his prescient illustration: "A long list of mental and moral differences are observed, or supposed to exist between man and women: but at some future, and, it may be hoped, not distant period, equal freedom and an equally independent social position come to be possessed by both, and their differences of character are either removed or totally altered" (p. 456).

Now most of the findings of cross-cultural psychology consist of such empirical generalizations. They are often of great interest, but their limitations should be recognized and more freely acknowledged. It seems likely that failure to do so is a consequence of an implicit belief in "psychic unity," the notion that psychological processes are exactly the same in all humankind. In extreme cases this can lead to the justification for conducting all one's research with college students (Gerard & Conolley, 1972).

Although Bastian's notion enshrined an important truth in opposition to the racial ideas of his time, "psychic unity" today is merely the expression of a sentiment, admirable as such but in my view no longer useful as a concept. It would be difficult to maintain nowadays that one can readily characterize "human nature" in vacuo and partition psychological functioning neatly into the human essence versus environmental accretions. Psychological functioning develops within particular sociocultural settings and thereby takes on a local color. This had been a basic insight of Lazarsfeld and Steinthal, but they sought to understand it in terms of collective development, viewed as parallel to individual development, and were therefore unable to translate that insight into empirical research.

It was members of the Soviet sociohistorical school, inheritors of the Hegelian tradition that also nurtured *Völkerpsychologie*, who pioneered the study of individual development from this perspective. Although they concentrated on cognition, I am convinced that affect, the organization of emotional dispositions (an old-fashioned term I prefer to "personality") is open to the same approach. Luria was the first to apply these new ideas in the cultural field, but more recently most of exciting work has been done by American adherents of that school, most notably Michael Cole and his colleagues and lately, more eclectically, Shweder. What they have in common is a turning away from inferences about central processing mechanisms and would-be universal laws that constitute the elusive targets of mainstream cross-cultural psychologists. Their banner reads simply "cultural psychology," and an increasing number of theorists and researchers flock to it. There is apparently only a short step, which some seem inclined to take, from this to claiming that all psychology is really "cultural psychology."

This, I submit, would imply a rejection of the view, taken by the *observateurs de l'homme* and powerfully confirmed by Darwin, that humans are part of nature as well as being creatures of culture. Although the emphasis many cross-cultural psychologists place on universals is sometimes naive and usually unjustified, it does not follow that the aim of establishing some universals is necessarily futile. For as even Vico had already noted, there are limits to human variability. One could surely expect nontrivial specieswide uniformities based either on common modes of central processing or on shared aspects of the human condition. Psychology's dilemma is that it spans both nature and culture and is unable to escape, since no clear boundary divides them. This quandary was well recognized in its essence by Wilhelm von Humboldt in 1795 (Leitzmann, 1903) when he sketched his *Plan for a Comparative Anthropology*, though our current concept of "culture" was not available to him. He argued that on one hand man as a species is a link in the chain of nature, and as such can be studied by experiment. On the other, he is capable of seemingly arbitrary actions governed by his reason, impulse, or striving, which will have common characteristics in the same sex or nation; and from that perspective man can be interpreted only historically. Hence anyone who wishes to advance our knowledge "has so to speak to combine within himself the differing approaches of the observer of nature, the historian and the philosopher" (Leitzmann, 1903, p. 397).

For the greater part of the 20th century the one-sided emphasis in psychology has been on nature, tacitly equated with the characteristics of humans in Western cultures. There is a certain parallel here with the Enlightenment thinkers, who regarded 18th-century Europeans as the most perfect embodiment of the human species. It is likely that a time will come when both these positions are viewed as equally untenable.

In concluding, I should say once again that my survey has had to be highly condensed and unavoidably selective. Nonetheless, I hope it will have become apparent that there is a distinct family resemblance between our ancestors and ourselves.

REFERENCES

Adler, L. L. & Adler, B. S. (1977). The "fruit tree experiment" as a cross-cultural measure of the variations in children's drawings due to regional differences. In L. L. Adler (Ed.), *Issues in cross-cultural research*. New York: New York Academy of Sciences.

Andree, R. (1878). *Ethnographische Parallele und Vergleiche*. Stuttgart: Maier.

Andree, R. (1887). Das Zeichnen bei den Naturvölkern. *Mitteilungen der Anthropologischen Gesellschaft in Wien*, n.s., *7*, 98–114.

Barnard, F. M. (1969). *J. G. Herder on social and political culture*. Cambridge: Cambridge University Press.

Bartlett, F. C. (1923). *Psychology and primitive culture*. Cambridge: Cambridge University Press.

Bartlett, F. C. (1932). *Remembering*. Cambridge: Cambridge University Press.

Bastian, A. (1860). *Der Mensch in der Geschichte* (3 vols.). Leipzig: Wigand.

Bastian, A. (1868). *Beiträge zur vergleichenden Psychologie*. Berlin: Dümmler.

Boas, F. (1911). *The mind of primitive man*. New York: Macmillan.

Brislin, R. W. (1983). Cross-cultural research in psychology. In M. R. Rosenzweig & L. W. Porter (Eds.), *Annual review of psychology* (Vol. 34). Palo Alto, CA: Annual Reviews.

Buschan, G. (1906). Primitive Zeichnungen von Kindern und Primitiven. *Die Umschau, 10*, 461–467.

Carothers, J. C. (1953). *The African mind in health and disease*. Geneva: World Health Organization.

Chamberlain, A. E. (1900). Die Entwicklungshemme des Kindes bei den Naturvölkern und bei den Völkern von Halbkultur. *Zeitschrift für Pädagogische Psychologie und Pathologie, 2*, 303–309.

38

Condorcet, M. J. (1966). *Esquisse d'un tableau historique des progrès de l'esprit humain*. Paris: Editions Sociales. (Original work published 1795)

Copans, Jean, & Jamin, Jean. (1978). *Aux origines de l'anthropologie française*. Paris: Sycomore.

Démeunier, J.-N. (1776). *L'esprit des sages et des coutumes des differens peuples*. Paris: Pichot.

de Gérando, J.-M. de. (1978). Considérations sur les diverses methodes à suivre dans l'observation des peuples sauvages. In J. Copans & J. Jamin. *Aux origines de l'anthropologie française*. Paris: Sycomore. (Original work published 1800)

Deregowski, J. B., Muldrow, E. S. & Muldrow, W. F. (1972). Pictorial recognition in a remote Ethiopian population. *Perception, 1*, 417–425.

Eisenstaedter, J. (1912). *Elementargedanke und Übertragungstheorie in der Völkerkunde*. Stuttgart: Strecker und Schroeder.

Ferguson, A. (1767). *An essay on the history of civil society*. Edinburgh.

Fluegel, O. (1880). Das Ich im Leben der Voelker. *Zeitschrift für Völkerpsychologie und Sprachwissenschaft, 11*, 43–80, 141–160.

Fortes, M. (1981). Tallensi children's drawings. In B. Lloyd & J. Gay (Eds.), *Universals of human thought*. Cambridge: Cambridge University Press.

Frankel, C. (1969). *The faith of reason*. New York: Octagon.

Galton, F. (1883). *Inquiries into human faculty and its development*. London: Macmillan.

Gaulmier, J. (1980). *L'idéologue Volney*. Paris: Slatkine.

Gerard, H. B., & Conolley, E. S. (1972). Conformity. In C. G. McClintock (Ed.), *Experimental social psychology*. New York: Holt, Rinehart and Winston.

Goodnow, J. J., Wilkins, P., & Dawes, L. (1986). Acquiring cultural forms. *International Journal of Behavioral Development, 9*, 485–505.

Haddon, A. C. (1904). Drawings by natives of British New Guinea. *Man, 4*, 33–36.

Haeckel, E. (1874). *Anthropogenie*. Leipzig.

Hallpike, C. R. (1979). *The foundations of primitive thought*. Oxford: Clarendon Press.

Helvétius, C. A. (1773). *De l'homme, de ses facultés intellectuelles et de son éducation*. London.

Herbart, J. F. (1891). *A textbook in psychology*. New York: Appleton. (Original work published 1816)

Herder, J. G. (1969). *Herders Werke* (5 vols.). Berlin: Aufbau. (Original work published 1772)

Horton, R. (1970). African traditional thought and Western science. In B. R. Wilson (Ed.), *Rationality*. Oxford: Blackwell.

Institut für Angewandte Psychologie. (1912) Vorschläge zur psychologischen Untersuchung primitiver Menschen. *Zeitschrift für Andewandte Psychologie und Psychologische Sammelforschung*, No. 5.

Jahoda, G. (1989). Zum Ursprung der Serial-Reproduction-Methode. *Psychologie und Geschichte 1*:46–48.

Klineberg, Otto. (1980). Historical perspectives: Cross-cultural psychology before 1960. In H. C. Triandis & W. W. Lambert (Eds.), *Handbook of cross-cultural psychology,* Vol. 1. Boston: Allyn and Bacon.

Koch, J. (1931). Sind die Pygmäen Menschen? *Archiv für Geschichte der Philosophie, 40,* 194–213.

Kretzschmar, J. (1910). Kinderkunst und Urzeitkunst. *Zeitschrift für Pädagogische Psychologie, 11,* 354–366.

Lafitau, P. (1724). *Moeurs des sauvages Ameriquains.* Paris: Saugrain.

Le Bon, G. (1881). *L'homme et les sociétés.* Paris: Rothchild.

Le Bon, G. (1894). *Les lois psychologiques de l'évolution des peuples.* Paris: Alcan.

Leitzman, A. (Ed.). (1903). *Wilhelm von Humboldts Werke* (Vol.1). Berlin: Behrs.

Letourneau, C. (1901). *La psychologie ethnique.* Paris: Schleicher.

Lévi-Strauss, C. (1962). *La pensée sauvage.* Paris: Plon.

Lindworsky, P. J. (1917/1918). Vom Denken des Urmenschen *Anthropos, 12–13,* 419–423.

Lindworsky, P. J. (1926). Die Primitiven und das kausale Denken. *Internationale Woche für Religionsethnologie, 5,* 60–75.

LoBagola. (1930). *An African savage's own story.* New York: Knopf.

Locke, J. (1690). *An essay concerning human understanding.* London.

Luria, A. R. (1976). *Cognitive development: Its cultural and social foundations* (M. Cole, Ed.). Cambridge: Harvard University Press.

Mead, Margaret. (1954). Research on primitive children. In L. Carmichael (Ed.), *Manual of child psychology* (pp. 667–706). New York: Wiley.

Meiners, C. (1815). *Untersuchungen über die Verschiedenheiten der Menschennaturen* (Vol. 3). Tübingen: Cotta.

Mill, J. S. (1879). *System of logic* (10th ed., Vol. 2). London: Longmans, Green.

Miller, N. (1928). *The child in primitive society.* London: Kegan Paul.

Notes and Queries on Anthropology. (1874). London: British Association for the Advancement of Science.

Pearson, K. (1924). *The life, letters and labour of Francis Galton* (Vol. 2). Cambridge: Cambridge University Press.

Pick, A. D. (1980). Cognition: Psychological perspectives. In H. C. Triandis & W. Lonner (Eds.), *Handbook of cross-cultural psychology: Vol. 3. Basic processes.* Boston: Allyn and Bacon.

Prichard, J. C. (1848). *The natural history of man* (3rd ed.). London: Baillière.

Ratzel, F. (1882). *Anthropogeographie.* Stuttgart: Engelhorn.

Reclus, E. (1885). *Les primitifs: Etudes d'ethnologie comparée.* Paris: Chamerot.

Rivers, W. H. R. (1901). Part 1: Introduction and vision. In A. C. Haddon (Ed.), *Reports of the Cambridge anthropological expedition to Torres Straits.* Cambridge: Cambridge University Press.

Romanes, G. J. (1888). *Mental evolution in man.* London: Kegan Paul.

Russell, B. (1946). *A history of Western philosophy.* London: Allen and Unwin.

Schmidl, M. (1915). Zahl und Zählen in Afrika. *Mitteilungen der Anthropologischen Gesellschaft in Wien, 45,* 165–209.

Schultze, F. (1900). *Psychologie der Naturvölker.* Leipzig: Veit.

40

Sechrest, L. (1987). Critical issues in the development of cross-cultural research methodology. In K. F. Mauer & A. I. Retief, *Psychology in context.* Pretoria: Human Sciences Research Council.

Segall, M. H. (1983). On the search for the independent variable in cross-cultural psychology. In S. H. Irvine & J. W. Berry (Eds.), *Human assessment and cultural factors.* New York: Plenum.

Shweder, R. A. (1977). Likeness and likelihood in everyday thought. *Current Anthropology, 18,* 637–658.

Spencer, H. (1876). *Principles of sociology.* London: Williams and Norgate.

Steinen, K. von den. (1894). *Unter den Naturvölkern Zentral-Brasiliens.* Berlin: Reimer.

Stern, E. (1920). Probleme der Kulturpsychologie. *Zeitschrift für Gesamte Staatswissenschaft, 75,* 267–301.

Stocking, G. W., Jr. (1964). French anthropology in 1800. *Isis, 55,* 134–150.

Thurnwald, R. (1913). Ethno-psychologische Studien an Südseevölkern. *Zeitschrift für Angewandte Psychologie und psychologische Sammelforschung,* No. 6.

Thurnwald, R. (1924). Zum gegenwärtigen Stande der Völkerpsychologie. *Kölner Vierteljahrschrift für Soziologie, 4,* 32–43.

Thurnwald, R. (1929). Grundprobleme der vergleichenden Völkerpsychologie. *Zeitschrift für Gesamte Staatswissenschaft, 87,* 240–296.

Topinard, P. (1878). *Anthropology.* London: Chapman and Hall.

Tylor, E. B. (1865). *Researches into the early history of mankind and the development of civilization.* London: John Murray.

Tylor, E. B. (1871). *Primitive culture* (2 Vols.). London.

Tylor, E. B. (1937). *Anthropology* (2 Vols.). London: Watts. (Original work published 1881)

Verworn, M. (1907). Kinderkunst und Urgeschichte. *Korrespondenzblatt der Deutschen Gesellschaft für Anthropologie, Ethnologie und Urgeschichte, 38,* 42–46.

Verworn, M. (1917). *Zur Psychologie der primitiven Kunst.* Jean: Fischer.

Vico, G. (1948). *The new science.* T. G. Bergin and M. H. Fish (Trans.). Ithaca: Cornell University Press. (Original work published 1725)

Vierkandt, Alfred. (1914). Der gegenwaertige Stand der Völkerpsychologie. *Neue Jahrbücher für des Klassische Altertum, Geschichte und Deutsche Literatur, und für Pädagogik* 17:625–641.

Volney, C.-F. (1959). *Voyages en Égypte et en Syrie.* Paris: Mouton. (Original work published 1787)

Waitz, T. (1863). *Introduction to anthropology.* London: Anthropological Society of London.

Wertheimer, M. (1912). Über das Denken der Naturvölker. *Zeitschrift für Psychologie, 60,* 321–378.

Wundt, W. (1888). Über Ziele und Wege der Völkerpsychologie. *Philosophische Studien, 4,* 1–27.

Wundt, W. (1911). *Völkerpsychologie: Vol. 1. Die Sprache.* Leipzig: Engelmann.

Wundt, W. (1917). Völkerpsychologie und Entwicklungspsychologie. *Philosophische Studien, 10,* 189–238.

Cross-Cultural Studies of Individualism and Collectivism

Harry C. Triandis
Professor of Psychology
University of Illinois, Urbana-
Champaign

In introducing the *Handbook of Cross Cultural Psychology*, I remarked (Triandis, 1980a) that the major contributions of the field were methodological, not theoretical. Now, however, the time is ripe for the field to begin making theoretical contributions as well. One strategy is to identify dimensions of cultural variation (e.g., Triandis, 1984) and study them intensively. Multimethod procedures should be used in such studies (Fiske, 1986), ideally including ethnographies, systematic observations, measures of beliefs, attitudes, norms, roles, values, and other elements of subjective culture (Triandis, 1972), content analyses, experiments, and the Human Relations Area Files. The multimethod strategy is needed because cultural variables are impregnated with meaning and interact with measurement methods, which also depend on meaning. Different subjects understand the measurements differently, and depending on whether we analyze the data within or between cultures, we often discover different meanings. Thus it is essential to triangulate across

John Berman, Michael Bond, C. Harry Hui, William Gudykunst, and Shalom Schwartz provided useful comments that improved this chapter. Correspondence can be sent to H. C. Triandis, 603 East Daniel Street, Champaign, IL 61820, telephone (217) 333–1894.

methods and discover common elements in several cultural settings in order to establish a cultural dimension.

The meaning of a construct needs to be established by moving back and forth between theory and measurement. For example, what individualism is was determined by examining how the term was used in the literature—what researchers thought the concept meant (Hui & Triandis, 1986). Then the measurements of the various aspects suggested by such reviews were factor analyzed and treated in a number of analytic ways. The meaning is still evolving as more measurements are made in different cultures.

Once the meaning of the dimension is clear, we need to examine separately variables that reflect the common ecology, history, and social/economic structures of those who are high and of those who are low on that dimension. From such studies we can develop causal links between the determinants of culture and cultural variables and thus understand why these cultural variations appear. In addition, we need to examine the consequences of these cultural variables. What social behaviors are associated with a high or low position on the variable?

As an example of the first steps toward theory in cross-cultural psychology, the work on individualism and collectivism is a rudimentary theory of cultural/social behavior. Much more needs to be done, but a journey of a thousand miles starts with one step. Here it is.

Perhaps the most important dimension of cultural difference in social behavior, across the diverse cultures of the world, is the relative emphasis on individualism versus collectivism. In individualist cultures most people's social behavior is largely determined by personal goals that overlap only slightly with the goals of collectives, such as the family, the work group, the tribe, political allies, coreligionists, fellow countrymen, and the state. When a conflict arises between personal and group goals, it is considered acceptable for the individual to place personal goals ahead of collective goals. By contrast, in collectivist cultures social behavior is determined largely by goals shared with some collective, and if there is a conflict between personal and group goals, it is considered socially desirable to place collective goals ahead of personal goals.[1]

The individualism/collectivism construct can be found in discussions of the West versus the East or the West versus Africa (Centre Nationale de la Recherche Scientifique, 1973). For example, Hsu

(1983) provides interesting literary analyses, arguing that most of ancient Greek literature (e.g., the *Iliad* and the *Odyssey*) celebrates the exploits of *individuals*, most Western novels emphasize individual action, and love conquers all; individuals do what is enjoyable rather than what they must do as it is dictated by groups, authorities, parents. Conversely, the Eastern novel is commonly a celebration of doing one's duty as determined by parents and kin, emperor, or other authorities, in spite of the tremendous temptations that the hero faces from all sorts of enjoyable activities. Thus Hsu suggests that the roots of individualism in the West and collectivism in the East are very deep.

MacFarlane's (1978) historical analysis finds individualism in England as early as the 12th century. Hazard (1953) sees the critical years of shift to individualism in the period 1680–1715 in England. Tocqueville (1840/1946) identified individualism as an important attribute of America. Toennies (1957) contrasted *Gemeinschaft*, with its intimate exchanges more commonly found in collectivism, with *Gesellschaft*, which is more characteristic of individualism. He identified as essential attributes of the former that people have many common goals and engage in interpersonal relationships with a long time perspective (such as mother-son, while the child is growing), whereas he considered the latter's essential attributes to be a short time perspective and equal exchange (reciprocity of equal value).

The tendencies toward collectivism and individualism can coexist, so it is incorrect to think of them as opposites. In fact, empirically, our attempts to measure the construct (e.g., Triandis et al., 1986) have identified two orthogonal factors related to individualism and two orthogonal factors related to collectivism, so that the constructs under discussion can best be indexed by four orthogonal factors.[2]

An analogy might help. Just as water and ice can coexist, so can collectivism and individualism. Being primates, humans are intensively dependent on the protection of family during their early years. As they become independent of the family and emotionally detached from it, they become self-reliant and more individualistic. But some of the bonds of family integrity and interdependence remain. So collectivism is like water and individualism is like ice. Each molecule of water may be transformed into ice, but ice can melt back into water. The molecules of ice correspond to particular relationships of the individual with friends, co-workers, neighbors, those with similar demographic attributes, those with whom the individual experiences common fate and who are similar in attitudes—that is, those with whom the individual shares time, place, language, and experience. In each culture a different pattern of those self-other links becomes ice. So there are different kinds of individualism and different kinds of collectivism, depending on whether the predominance of the molecules are water or have been transformed into ice.

What are some of the major determinants of this transformation? In my opinion two factors are most important: cultural complexity and affluence. The effect of cultural complexity is to create separation, distinction, and different life-styles. Then the individual is confronted with conflicting norms and worldviews. This conflict requires that the individual decide how to act on the basis of internal factors rather than the norms of a collective, and thus individualism is born. Cultural complexity can be found whenever there are economies based on functional specialization, where different individuals do different jobs and that is beneficial for the whole. It also occurs where there is separation, such as when the geography involves mountains and islands, or when people have migrated to distant lands. Individualism developed first in ancient Greece. Note that Greece was, and still is, cut up by mountains and the sea. Different cities developed distinct life-styles.[3]

The next major thrust occurred in England and was accelerated by the Renaissance, Protestantism (humans related to God directly, no longer through the church hierarchy), and the industrial revolution. Migration was also a major factor. England established colonies and an empire on which the sun never set. Australia, Canada, New Zealand, and the United States are among the most individualistic cultures of the world (Hofstede, 1980).

Affluence is also an important factor. One can be independent when rich, and financial independence is correlated with independence from ingroups. One does not have to do what others want.

China, as the prototypical collectivist culture, was unified rather early, about 2,500 years ago. It called itself the Central Kingdom and could ignore the barbarians outside who did not share its life-style. It could emphasize solidarity between lord and citizen, father and son, older brother and younger brother, husband and wife, friend and friend, as the cardinal Confucian virtue. The rest of the social relationships were conducted "appropriately" (*li*), based on the models provided by the five cardinal relationships. A unity of perspective was developed and maintained within an immense land mass where millions of people lived while Europe still had a small population. Although some families were wealthy, the wealth was used to maintain the social structure rather than to change it. The idea of the individual's leaving the ancestors to establish colonies abroad had limited appeal. The Chinese did not establish colonies as independent states until the very recent period (Brunei, Singapore). There was nothing comparable to the Greek colonies or the British Empire.

The cardinal values of collectivists were reciprocity (*pao*), obligation, duty, security, tradition, dependence, harmony, obedience to authority, equilibrium, and proper action (*li*). The cardinal values of the individualists were bravery, creativity, self-reliance (Emerson), solitude (Thoreau), and frugality (Franklin). The eight extolled virtues of China were social and included shame (*ch'ih*) and filial piety (*hsiao*), so they were designed to cement interpersonal relationships. In the West emotions are linked to enjoyment of sexual activity, and so Freud overemphasized libidinal processes. In the East emotions are linked to doing one's duty, reciprocity, and proper action. So to Confucius proper action (*li*) is as central as libidinal processes are to Freud (Hsu, 1983).

Individualists must conquer frontiers (see Alexander the Great; missionaries; the insistence on making the whole world adopt one's own religion and political system) in order to feel that they are "good people," whereas collectivists are satisfied to cultivate their own habitat. When the individualist cannot dominate others, he turns to dominating things (owning objects) or animals (pets). The collectivist is much more interested in maintaining harmony with humans. But of course, as Eastern societies become affluent they also become individualistic, and they too begin to emphasize ownership and pets (Hsu, 1983).

With the emphasis on proper relationships, collectivists have, other things being equal, less crime, particularly fewer sex crimes, fewer hospital admissions, and less drug abuse than individualists. Collectivists are not religious missionaries, and they pay little attention to supernatural issues. Individualists exclude those who are too different (e.g., South Africa; British colonies), whereas collectivists try to include them, and if that does not work they fight them openly. Giving gifts is one of the ways collectivists increase their circle of influence.[4]

Individualism is linked to additional ideas and processes. Hsu (1983) sees self-reliance,[5] competitiveness, aggressive creativity, conformity, insecurity, large military expenditures, prejudice toward racial and religious groups that are too different, and unrealistic interpersonal relationships—and by extension international relationships (trying to play policeman of the world)—as characteristics of individualism. Collectivists, according to Hsu, are low in emotionality, seek the protection of the group, and are not interested in competition. But they pay a price in low creativity.

Although Hsu's ideas are well developed in his book, there is a need for empirical work to test them. It is not clear that all the theoretical statements he makes are valid. Their validity is based on anthropological observations, content analyses of literary products, and the like. Multimethod measurement of the constructs is needed to check exactly what relationships occur in individualist and collectivist cultures.

Much of the work reported below tests some of these ideas. We will find, in the course of this empirical work, that individualism is a complex construct that does not necessarily include all the links postulated by Hsu. Yet much of his theoretical structure has been confirmed. For example, individualism has been found to be linked to competitiveness.

Hsu also makes many value statements and is clearly in favor of traditional Chinese culture. Although the empirical work is too incomplete to challenge all his value statements, one must admit that on a number of occasions his analysis is correct. For example, whereas early individualism was linked to the idea of the public good (Tocqueville, 1840/1946), more recent versions of individualism have emphasized hedonism, and little remains of the emphasis on ethics and the common good (Bell, 1976).

Although there is anthropological evidence concerning the construct (e.g., Mead, 1967) the major focus of this review will be on psychological data. Nevertheless, Margaret Mead's work must be mentioned. She analyzed the ethnographies of 13 primitive societies to extract themes emphasizing cooperation, competition, or individualism. I used the ideas that psychologists have generated concerning collectivism/individualism (collectivism=subordination of individual goals to group goals, achievement aimed at improving the position of the ingroup; individualism=primacy of individual goals; achievement benefits primarily the individual) to classify Mead's societies into individualistic (Manus, Ifagao, Dakota, Kwakiutl, Ojima, Eskimo, in that order, with the Eskimo most typical) and collectivist (Maori, Arapesh, Bathonga, Iroquois, Samoan, and Zuni, with Zuni most typical). I then did Fisher exact tests and found a number of statistically significant relationships: individualist societies tend to be hunting, gathering, fishing, or foraging, whereas collectivist tend to be agricultural; individualists do much trading, collectivists do not; individualists prod children to become adults, collectivists allow them to become adults when they are ready; individualists use property for self-glorification, collectivists for the good of the group; in individualist cultures power of the individual over others is desired and often achieved.

However, one of the distinct findings from a review of these ethnographies is that both individualism and collectivism are *setting specific*. For example, the Kwakiutl are individualists in competition with other chiefs and collectivists in their households. Collectivists are very nice to those who are members of their ingroups but can be very nasty, competitive, and uncooperative toward those who are members of outgroups. This complexity must always be kept in mind in the discussion that follows, which tends to oversimplify and assumes that other factors are the same (i.e., the setting is the same).

Figure 1 presents the general framework for the analysis of cultural-social behavior links that will be used in this chapter. I will begin by defining individualism and collectivism, and in the process I will describe cultures that differ on those attributes. Next I will examine the antecedents of individualism and collectivism—that is, the ecological variables that determine them. Then I will examine the links between cultures and socialization, and finally the links between socialization and social behavior. Thus the chapter provides a

ECOLOGY → CULTURE → SOCIALIZATION → PERSONALITY → SOCIAL BEHAVIOR

Figure 1. Simplified framework for the study of culture-social behavior links.

theory of the linking of culture and social behavior—the consequences of individualism and collectivism.

The Importance of the Study of Individualism and Collectivism

The importance of the cross-cultural study of individualism/collectivism cannot be overstated. Almost all the data of psychology come from individualistic cultures (Triandis, 1980a), yet about 70% of the population of the world lives in collectivist cultures (Bell, 1987). The behavior of people from the collectivist part of the world shows common elements (Gaenslen, 1986). Thus, by studying how our social-psychological theories operate in the collectivist part of the world we can extend social psychology in a major way.

Many social science findings can be integrated around the dimensions of individualism and collectivism. For example, understanding of economic development (Adelman & Morris, 1967), moral views (Shweder, 1982), religious behavior (Bakan, 1966), the concept of limited good (Foster, 1965), the relationship of food accumulation (Barry, Child, and Bacon, 1959) to child rearing (Berry, 1979), and the structure of state constitutions (Massimini & Calegari, 1979) have benefited from the distinction of individualism and collectivism or from equivalent constructs such as group versus individual orientations.

Individualism has been criticized (e.g., Bellah, Madsen, Sullivan, Swindler, & Tipton 1985; Hogan, 1973, 1975; Lasch, 1978; Rakoff, 1978; Sampson, 1977, Smith, 1978) and defended (Perloff, 1987; Riesman, 1954, 1966; Waterman, 1981). Some (e.g., Kanfer, 1979; Rotenberg, 1977) have attempted to define patterns of desirable behavior that combine elements of high and low individualism.

The importance of the topic is reflected in the fact that two recent presidents of the American Psychological Association chose to discuss it. Spence (1985) recognizes that at least since the time of Alexis de Tocqueville individualism has been considered central to the American character. Emerson and Thoreau emphasized self-reliance and independence. But recently, critics such as Bellah et al. (1985), have decried it as selfishness. Spence argues that the critics have lost sight of the positive contributions of individualism to social and political institutions. She stresses the roots of individualism in Protestantism. She notes the role of individualism in the framing of the Declaration of Independence and the Constitution, in the way psychology defines parent-child relationships, and in the definition of an autonomous self and then examines in some detail its role in theories of achievement. Related to McClelland's conception are theories emphasizing that the achievement motives must be understood in terms of the sociocultural context. She agrees that our theories may be more appropriate for individualist cultures than for collectivist cultures. She seems to approve of the arguments of some of the critics of extreme individualism—the extreme competition associated with it leads to dishonesty in science (too many people make up their data); she points out, from her own research, that scientists who are too competitive are less effective than others, and at the end she praises the political stability, material prosperity, and freedom of opportunity associated with individualism but argues that "freedom and autonomy, however, leave people vulnerable to feelings of alienation and narcissistic self-absorption and tempt them to pursue narrow self-interests" (Spence 1985, p. 1293). She ends with a plea to psychologists to contribute to a better understanding of how individualism is linked to social and psychological problems.

Perloff (1987, p. 3), by contrast, is a "proud advocate of self-interest." He admits to a nonobjective analysis, based on reading of the literature in psychology, evolutionary biology, and economics and on his own observations of everyday affairs. He argues that self-interest is an effective force underlying behavior.

A key point about the importance of cross-cultural studies emerges from the discussion of definitions. It is clear from a review of the literature, and also from the discussion of Spence (1985) and Perloff (1987), that self-reliance is a key concept of American individualism. In support of this, Triandis, Bontempo, Villareal, Asai, and Lucca (1988) found, in a factor analysis of items measuring individualism and collectivism obtained from a sample in Illinois, that the most important factor was Self-Reliance with Competition (accounted for 35.2 of total variance) and included items such as "To be superior a man must stand alone," "Winning is everything," "What happens to me is my own doing." A collectivist second factor accounted for 14% of the variance (e.g., "I like to live close to my friends," "I would help within my means if a relative told me s(he) was in financial difficulties"), but the third factor, accounting for 12% of the variance, was also individualist. It was given the name Distance from Ingroups and included items like "I am not to blame if one of my family members fails," and "My happiness is unrelated to the well-being of my co-workers."

Although the American definition of individualism is self-reliance, competition, and distance from ingroups, the interesting point is that these dimensions are of little importance in contrasting the cultures of the world. Cross-culturally, Triandis et al. (1986) found that the most important contrast was obtained on a factor called Family Integrity, which included the items "Aging parents should live at home with their children" and "Children should live at home with their parents until they get married." The latter factor accounted for 57% of the common variance in a discriminant function analysis, while the Separation from Ingroups factor accounted for only 11% and the Self-Reliance factor for only 7% of the variance. In short, what is most important in the United States is least important worldwide. This is an interesting example of how concepts are defined locally but have limited importance in understanding worldwide phenomena. The self-reliance factor has a lot of variance in the United States. One can find people who agree as well as people who disagree with extreme self-reliance and competition. But the Family Integrity factor does not have much variance. Almost all Americans indicate they do not want to live with their parents until they get married or after their parents are old. The small variance results in the small importance of this factor. But worldwide the Family Integrity factor is the *really* important one. It is the only factor that correlates (-.73) with Hofstede's (1980) index of individualism. It contrasts cultures like those of East Asia with the cultures of Europe and North America.

The individualism/collectivism constructs reflect, in part, values. There is evidence that values are linked with attitudes and with behavior (Triandis, 1980b). Thus, understanding how individualism/collectivism operates in different parts of the world will allow us to understand, at least in part, why social behavior is different in different places.

At an even more fundamental level, the analysis of individualism/collectivism will inform a major debate in contemporary social science, reflected in Schwartz's (1986) devastating critique of the social sciences. Schwartz makes a very convincing case that economics, evolutionary biology, and the behavioral sciences are based on individualistic assumptions that reflect not "human nature" but the scientists' culture. It is not the case that human nature is individualist, but scientists assume it is. So these sciences are not describing or accounting for "human nature" but reflect the scientists' cultural values. Schwartz does a masterly job of challenging basic assumptions. He argues that these sciences assume people are governed by greedy self-interest, but that the assumption is false—it is not "an eternal law of human nature" (p. 317). His critique shows that people often violate the assumptions of these sciences and that the data are distorted (e.g., preferences are not always transitive, people do not always prefer the lowest price, preferences are not stable, people rarely maximize preferences; sociobiology is a post hoc science; rats behave as behavior theorists say they do only if placed in environments where other behaviors are not possible).

He points out that self-interest has entered most Western institutions as a basic principle in family, church, school, and state. But people must see the importance of cooperation and self-sacrifice as "moral imperatives" or democracy will collapse. In a democracy one has to do what is good for the majority of voters, even if that is not good for oneself. In collectivist cultures people internalize the norm of helping others and only infrequently ask "What's in this for me?" He argues that we cannot build a society merely on economic exchanges and reinforcements. We have to use moral forces; otherwise sexual behavior becomes prostitution, people will lie and steal whenever they are unlikely to be caught, and social life will break down. Schwartz accepts an economic basis of exchanges when the goods are produced, the producers and consumers are strangers, goods are enjoyed only by their owners, and commodities are interchangeable and produced for a profit. But economics does not provide a sound basis of exchange when goods are enjoyed in the family, when they are used by more people than their owners, when they are not exchangeable, and when they are not produced for a profit. In short, only *some* aspects of social behavior can be governed by individualist principles. In many situations, such as behavior in the family, other principles are needed.

To go back to the analogy of water and ice, just as water (collectivism) turns into ice (individualism) and can turn back into water under specifiable conditions, so one can think of the myriad social relationships between an individual and others. Each relationship can be defined in an individualist or a collectivist manner. That is, one can place personal goals over the goals of the group or the other person, or one can place the goals of the other person ahead of personal goals. When common fate (e.g., an external threat) is clear, individuals turn collectivist in many relationships. The point Schwartz makes is that in certain settings, such as the family, it is important that most relationships *be* collectivist, while in the marketplace individualist principles are fine.

Finally, the importance of the topic is made greater by noting the parallel between individualism/collectivism and male/female social behavior. Eagly (1987) has presented an excellent review of gender differences in social behavior. The parallel with collectivism/individualism is striking. One point will suffice. Just as collectivists place ingroup goals ahead of personal goals, so females in most societies are expected to place the interests of their children and their families ahead of their personal goals.

Definitions

Gould and Kolb (1964) defined *individualism* as "a belief that the individual is an end in himself, and as such ought to realize his 'self' and cultivate his own judgment, notwithstanding the weight of pervasive social pressures in the direction of conformity."

Collectivism means greater emphasis on (a) the views, needs, and goals of the ingroup rather than oneself; (b) social norms and duty defined by the ingroup rather than behavior to get pleasure; (c) beliefs shared with the ingroup rather than beliefs that distinguish self from ingroup; and (d) great readiness to cooperate with ingroup members. In the case of extreme collectivism individuals do not have personal goals, attitudes, beliefs, or values but only reflect those of the ingroup. One's behavior is totally predictable from social roles, and performance of duties associated with roles is the path to salvation (Shweder & Bourne, 1982). In extreme collectivism the person *enjoys* doing what the ingroup expects.

It is useful at this point to provide formal definitions of group and ingroup. A *group* is a set of individuals who are perceived as a "group" by themselves or by others. This is most likely to happen when (a) these individuals are similar to each other (e.g., same family, tribe, age, gender, nationality, religion, social club, scientific organization, activity, preferences, subjective cultures, political party, economic institution); (b) there is a common fate of the members (owing to same location, economic activity, threat from other groups, common boundaries, past grouping as one group, minority status); and (c) there is stability and impermeability of the boundaries of the group.[6]

An *ingroup* is a group whose norms, goals, and values shape the behavior of its members. Thus both actual groups (e.g., family) and reference groups (e.g., a social club one aspires to belong to) can be ingroups for the particular individual. The size of ingroups is of the order of a hundred or less (Campbell, 1983).

An *outgroup* is a group with attributes dissimilar from those of the ingroup, whose goals are unrelated or inconsistent with those of the ingroup, or a group that opposes the realization of ingroup goals (competing). Note that we are dealing with perceptions. It is not necessary that the outgroup actually threaten the ingroup. All that is needed is the perception that it is threatening. Also, outgroups must be moderately stable and impermeable. Another person is perceived as part of the outgroup if there is a dissimilarity (e.g., in status or attitude), if the goals appear contrary to the individual's goals, or after a failure has been experienced that can be attributed to the other.

The definition of the ingroup is different in different cultures. In traditional Greece, for instance, collectivists define the ingroup as "family and friends and people who are concerned with my welfare" (Triandis, 1972), and other Greeks are outgroup. But in the United States Rokeach's (1960) research on the importance of belief similarity suggests that ingroup is frequently defined as "people who are in agreement with me on important issues and values." Of course "people" has to be qualified, because in some cases (e.g., when whites think of blacks in intimate situations) "people" includes whites only, and for some people similar social class, religion, or other attributes (e.g., life-style) may be required before they are considered ingroup.

A person can see another person as ingroup in one context and as outgroup in another. For example, an employee of Toyota may see another employee as outgroup along a labor/management axis but as ingroup along a Toyota/Nissan axis. Also, people belong to multiple ingroups. Depending on the situation or the issue that becomes salient at a particular moment, one or more of these ingroups become salient. For example, a black woman may see "black" as the relevant attribute in a group that includes three white women but see "woman" as the relevant attribute in a group that consist of her and three black men. The same person may see "black" as the relevant attribute in a discussion about the fairness of the nonpromotion of a black man and "woman" as the relevant attribute in a discussion about the fairness of the nonpromotion of a white woman. Some people develop habits of focusing on particular ingroups. For example, members of many extremists group tend to see most interpersonal relationships along a dimension that is of special importance to their group (e.g., the Ku Klux Klan: black/white).

Conceptualization of Individualism and Collectivism

Lukes (1973) used content analyses of Western texts to arrive at a definition of individualism that includes several themes: dignity of humans, individual self-development, autonomy, privacy, the individual as the basis of society; individuals as used to analyze social phenomena, as the bases of political, economic, religious, or ethical analyses; individuals as the sole locus of knowledge. Kashima (1988) used the Lukes categories to analyze the conceptions of persons found in different cultures.

Hui and Triandis (1986) asked a sample of social scientists, residing on all populated continents, to give their views of the meaning of the individualism/collectivism constructs. They found considerable agreement across the world. Collectivists are concerned about the results of their actions on others, share material and nonmaterial resources with group members, are concerned about their presentation to others, believe in the correspondence of outcomes of self and ingroup, and feel involved in the contributions and share in the lives of ingroup members.

Collectivism often is internalized to such an extent that members of ingroups respond as ingroup norms specify without doing any sort of utilitarian calculation. It is not a case of "What's in this for me?" The response is automatic. We can call this "unquestioned attachment" to the ingroup. It includes the perception that ingroup norms are universally valid (a form of ethnocentrism), automatic obedience to ingroup authorities, and willingness to fight and die for the ingroup. These characteristics are usually associated with distrust of and unwillingness to cooperate with outgroups.

Based on these findings Hui (1984, 1988) and Triandis, Leung, Villareal, and Clack (1985) devised methods for measuring the constructs. The latter also made the distinction between individualism/collectivism at the cultural level and *idiocentrism/allocentrism* at the individual level. This allows for a discussion of the behavior of allocentrics in individualist cultures and of idiocentrics in collectivist cultures.[7]

If we summarize the many factor analyses we have done (see notes 7 and 10 for details), we can conclude that, in discriminant function analyses where we contrast cultures, collectivism differs from individualism primarily in the dimensions of Family Integrity and Detachment from Ingroups, with the collectivists wanting to stay with their parents and extended family more than do the individualists, who feel emotionally detached from these groups. However, within culture the allocentrics are primarily high on Interdependence and Sociability and the idiocentrics are high on Self-Reliance and Competition. Interestingly, much of the United States literature on collectivism/individualism refers to the within-culture dimensions, whereas the cross-cultural literature refers mostly to the Family Integrity dimension, which is the only one that correlates with Hofstede's (1980) index.

As we will see later, individualism is higher among the affluent, socially and geographically mobile, more modern segments of every society. Thus, within each society there will be people high or low on this attribute. The idiocentrism/allocentrism terminology allows us to distinguish them within a culture. Basically, idiocentrics in individualistic cultures tend to be narcissistic and self-sufficient; allocentrics in individualist cultures tend to be socially integrated, to receive much social support when they need it; idiocentrics in collectivist cultures tend to be rebels, ready to migrate from the oppression of the culture; allocentrics in collectivist cultures tend to be well-adjusted, enthusiastic supporters of whatever ingroups are salient.

Marin and Triandis (1985) reviewed several studies[8] that indicate that United States Hispanics tend to be more collectivist than non-Hispanics in the United States, and that they become more and more individualist as they become acculturated. Several studies indicate that Hispanics in the United States pay more attention to the needs of ingroup members, avoid interpersonal competition, stress family obligations, and so on (e.g., Triandis, Marin, Hui, Lisansky, & Ottati, 1984; Triandis, Marin, Lisansky, & Betancourt, 1984).

Traditional Greeks (Triandis, 1972) have been found to depend on ingroups (family, friends, and those concerned with my welfare) for protection, social insurance, and security. They readily submit to ingroup authorities and accept their control; they are willing to sacrifice themselves for the ingroup. They relate to ingroup members with great intimacy; they achieve to glorify the ingroup. They perceive the self as weak but the ingroup as strong. They view themselves largely (74% in surveys) as having *philotimo* (as being polite, virtuous, reliable, truthful, self-sacrificing, tactful, and diligent). They believe that social control (e.g., severe punishment) is desirable (Triandis, 1972, pp. 324–325). They value ingroup success, honor, kindness, and dependability. They define *freedom* and *progress* as societal (e.g., national) constructs rather than as individual constructs. Their supreme values are good social relations and social control within the ingroup. By contrast, Americans value achievement and efficiency. Among Greeks behavior toward the ingroup is consistent with what the ingroup expects; behavior toward everyone else (e.g., strangers) is characterized by defiance of authority, competition, resentment of control, formality, rejection, arrogance, dogmatism, and rejection of influence attempts that have the outgroup as a source.

Collectivism is also high among Asian Americans. An excellent comparison of Americans and Chinese can be found in Hsu (1981) and one of Americans and Filipinos in Church (1987).

An important aspect of Filipino culture is that Tagalog, the local language, recognizes eight levels of interpersonal relationships, thus making explicit the differences in interaction with ingroup and outgroup members. A sharp distinction between ingroup and outgroup is an important element of collectivism (Triandis, 1972, 1984).

Collectivist patterns can be seen in many other studies such as of the Chinese (Yang, 1986), Japanese (Lebra, 1976), and so on. Patterns of collectivism can be seen in a wide literature, such as Guthrie (1961) and Church (1987) on the Philippines; Kaiser (1984) on the USSR; Doumanis (1983), Katakis (1984), Georgas (1986, 1989), and Triandis and Vassiliou (1972) on Greece; Northrop (1949) on the Navaho; Strodtbeck (1958) on Italians and Jews; Tallman, Marotz-Baden, and Pindas (1983), Holtzman, Diaz-Guerrero, and Swartz (1975), and Diaz-Guerrero (1979) on Latin Americans; Sinha (1982) on Indians; Holzberg (1981) on Africans; and Geertz (1963) on Bali, while individualism has been discussed by Bellah et al. (1985), Kerlinger (1984), and Triandis et al. (1985) for the United States. Although one can recognize common collectivist elements all over the world, at the same time it must be emphasized that there are many kinds of collectivism, characterized by different emphases on the family, tribe, country, and so on, more or less breadth of automatic, unquestioned response to a wide range or a narrow set of ingroups, and different mixtures of self-reliance and family integrity.

Similarly, there are different kinds of individualism, such as the individualism that is strongly associated with competition (as in the United States), the individualism that is associated with strong attachment to the family but complete freedom to be exploitative outside the family, as in southern Italy, the individualism that has elements of narcissism, and so on. Waterman (1984) provided a conceptual analysis that identified individualism as involving a sense of personal identity, the actualization of the "true self," internal locus of control, and postconventional moral reasoning (ethical universality). However, his literature review supports only the claim for the case of internal locus of control.[9]

Collectivism is a broader construct and includes power distance; that is, collectivists tend to see a large difference between those with power and those without, so it is difficult to know whether the emphasis on harmony within the ingroup is due to collectivism or to power distance. Certainly people in authority in most cultures do not like to have their views challenged. This may be functional when there is time pressure—when prompt carrying out of the boss's orders may help the collective. Socialization toward obedience seems associated with both collectivism and power distance. Thus individualists tend to value equality in social relationships. Hofstede and Bond (1984) found rank-order correlations of the order of -.7 between individualism and power distance, using very different methods for the measurement of values.

Hsu (1981) provides numerous contrasts between China and the United States that reflect the collectivism/individualism constructs. Thus collectivism includes a very positive attitude toward ancestors, whereas individualism emphasizes the importance of youth and the future. Success and prestige are defined in terms of ingroup goals versus personal goals. According to Hsu, competition is an important element of American individualism that is driving the arms race and bankrupting the country; it permeates every aspect of American life. The struggle of children for the attention and affection of parents, the struggle of parents to win their children's approval, the concern of American women for beauty and style, the anxiety of the husband to prove he is successful and thus deserves his wife's affection, the competition for success in all organizations, the readiness of the churches to vie with each other for membership are traced to aspects of United States individualism. Keeping up with the Joneses, the readiness to switch organizations, the notion that everyone has the right to happiness, the acceptance of the notion that happiness consists of the fulfillment of individual wishes are all linked to individualism.

Naroll's (1983) review of the empirical evidence suggests that very positive social indicators characterize societies in which the primary group is a normative reference group that provides strong social ties, emotional warmth, and prompt punishment for deviance; is culturally homogeneous; and includes active gossip, frequent rites, memorable myths, a plausible ideology, and badges of membership. Specifically, such societies have low rates of homicide, suicide, crime, juvenile delinquency, divorce, child abuse, wife beating, and drug and alcohol abuse and are characterized by good mental health. On the other hand, such societies are also characterized by dissatisfaction with the excessive demands of family life and by low gross national product per capita.[10]

As we studied collectivism and individualism over the years we realized that there are many varieties of these constructs. Although there are some basic similarities among the various kinds of individualism and of collectivism (see below), there are also many differences. First there is the question of how many groups (collectives) are important. In familism only the family is important (e.g., southern Italy as described by Banfield, 1958). Second, there is the question of how widespread is the influence of the collective. For example, in China the "work unit" was the important collective (e.g., see Henderson & Cohen, 1984) and decided a wide range of questions such as how many children one could have, how to raise them, where they would study, and what medical attention they would receive. During the Mao period the state had something to say about all domains of life represented by the six Spangler values—aesthetics, economics, politics, religion, science, and society. In other collectivist cultures the influence of the collective is more limited. For instance, in many Arab countries it is very strong on the religious axis, somewhat strong on the political and social axes, relatively mild on the aesthetic axis, and nonexistent on the economic and scientific axes.

Turning to individualism, here too we have many kinds. With so many ingroups to relate to and consult before a major action is taken, the United States government is characterized by consultative individualism. But there are also narcissistic individualists and anarchic individualists. The individualism of a hunting and gathering society is characterized by attachment to the band but includes freedom to roam about and do one's own thing while hunting.

Thus our theory links attributes of the culture, including the relative tendency toward individualism/collectivism observed on each of the six Spangler values and the number of ingroups that dominate social behavior in specific areas of social life and in particular settings, to predict social behavior.

In summary, the major contrasts between individualism and collectivism can be found in the following areas.

EMPHASIS ON THE PRIVATE SELF VERSUS EMPHASIS ON THE INGROUP

Among individualists the self is defined almost entirely in individual terms. Personal goals are more important than ingroup goals; the person is emotionally detached from ingroups; social control depends more on guilt than on shame and reflects contractual arrangements; personal fate is emphasized; internal control is high; values are personal (e.g., creative, brave, happy); and there is congruence between private self and public self.

Among collectivists the emphasis on the ingroup is reflected in the definition of self in ingroup terms and in its influence on much of social behavior. For example, how one behaves depends on whether the other is an ingroup or outgroup member. Among Filipinos different words are used to describe grades of relationships of self to others. The emphasis within the ingroup is on sharing, concern for ingroup members, correspondence of outcomes with ingroup members, common fate, acceptance of control by the ingroup, and importance of proper action. Key terms are defined in collective rather than personal terms; there is no necessary consistency between private and public self (what one does reflects what the ingroup expects); social control depends more on shame than on guilt and reflects moral considerations; ingroup goals are more important than personal goals; harmony within the ingroup is most important; values are social (e.g., duty, politeness, conformity to ingroup authorities); and even small deviations from normative action may be punished.

The emphasis on individuation versus relationships corresponds also to the emphasis found among men and women. Men have difficulty with relationships, while women have difficulty with individuation (Gilligan, 1982), and that may explain why many of the findings for individualism/collectivism correspond to male/female findings (Eagly, 1987).

EMPHASIS ON SHORT- VERSUS LONG-TERM TIME PERSPECTIVES

Interaction is conceived in a longer time perspective by collectivists than it is by individualists. Specifically, goals are closer in time among individualists; one expects tit-for-tat rewards from social interaction. Distant goals are more common among collectivists. One does not expect immediate reciprocity, but long-term reciprocity is most important. Furthermore, the time frame of individualists is bound by their birth (hence the great importance of one's birthday) and thoughts about the possible influence on one or two generations of descendants. The time frame of collectivists is likely to include a chain of dozens of generations of ancestors and descendents. For Buddhist collectivists one's acts have consequences for many generations to come and can determine whether one may enter nirvana.

EMPHASIS ON HIERARCHY AND HARMONY IN COLLECTIVISM

The genesis of collectivism involved the realization that collaborative action leads to survival. Such collaboration had to be coordinated by authorities. To maximize their effectiveness, the authorities required obedience and harmony within the group. Thus an important attribute of collectivism is the emphasis on hierarchy. Hofstede (1980) found collectivism to be highly correlated with "power distance" (the perception that those at the top of the hierarchy are very different from those at the bottom and that it is appropriate for them to be distant). The emphasis on harmony within the group means that the authorities do not have to be concerned with dissent or internal conflict and can devote their energies to guiding the group toward its goals.

EMOTIONAL ATTACHMENT TO FEW INGROUPS OR DETACHMENT FROM MANY INGROUPS

Collectivists are emotionally attached to a few ingroups and are very concerned about preserving them and doing what will promote them. Individualists have many ingroups and would be emotionally drained if they were quite as concerned about all of them. So they invest primarily in their first-degree relatives and feel rather detached from the remaining ingroups, which they can pick and choose so as to maximize their "profit" and minimize the "cost" of membership. Individualists have excellent skills in interacting superficially with many ingroup members but have fewer skills in interacting intimately with others than do collectivists.

THE CONSTRUCTS ARE POLYTHETIC, NOT MONOTHETIC

We must conceive of these constructs in polythetic rather than monothetic ways (Jensen, 1970). That is, no single attribute is sufficient to classify an individual as an individualist or a collectivist. Rather, scores of attributes must be used. At this time we do not know all the defining attributes that should be used. The discussion above presents some of these, and future research is likely to identify more. Then we will be able to use classification methods such as multidimensional clustering, to classify individuals as more or less collectivist. For the time being the list of attributes presented above can be used as a guide to thinking about the constructs.

RELATED CONSTRUCTS

Two social-psychological works seem to have direct relevance to the discussion of individualism and collectivism. The first is by Mills and Clark (1982), who discuss communal and exchange relationships. The second is by Ziller (1965), who discusses open and closed groups.

Mills and Clark (1982) contrast communal relations, such as those found in families among first-degree relatives, and exchange relationships, such as one finds in commercial exchanges. Communal relationships are characterized by greater concern for the welfare of the other; equality of affect (if one is sad, the other is sad); high rates of responding to the other's needs; benefits exchanged without attention to their size or temporal contiguity; relationships that vary in strength (e.g., father has a favorite daughter); and an expectation of long-term interactions.

According to Mills and Clark, people have communal relationships with everyone, but their strength may be very weak. For example, if a stranger asks for help one may give it, but only if the costs of this help are minimal. People also have exchange relationships with everyone; for example, one may employ the neighbor's child. Mills and Clark made a number of deductions from this theoretical framework that they tested experimentally. For example, they hypothesized that benefit from another after the other has benefited (an attribute of exchange relationships) should reduce attraction if the relationship is defined as a communal relationship. The data supported the hypothesis.

Clark, Ouellette, Powell, and Milberg (1987) developed a communal orientation scale (typical item: I often go out of my way to help another person; reversed item: People should keep their troubles to themselves) and found that it predicted helping behavior.

The items have much in common with the Interdependence and Sociality factor of Triandis et al. (1986).

Ziller (1965) discussed open and closed groups. Open groups keep changing their members; closed groups have relatively stable memberships. The attributes of closed groups resemble those of collectivists, and the attributes of open groups have much in common with individualist cultures. Ziller argues that in open groups (in constant flux) there are short time perspectives, reciprocation norms apply between individual and group, there is an expanded frame of reference (e.g., more creativity), and little power can be exerted on the members (since they can leave the group). Thus there are some advantages (e.g., creativity) and some disadvantages (e.g., more internal conflict, instability, and short time perspective). In closed groups (stable), on the other hand, there are long time perspectives, people have a more stable self that derives largely from group membership, reciprocity norms apply among individuals, and the group is in equilibrium (if an outside force is applied the group will change only temporarily and will return to its previous condition). On the other hand, members have a narrow frame of reference (fixed ideas, inflexible beliefs), and more power can be exerted on them by high-status members. Thus, again there are both advantages and disadvantages.

Ziller's theorizing is surprisingly parallel to the arguments I have been advancing about individualism and collectivism. Moreland and Levine (1982) took it a bit further. They noted that the greater the rewards received from group membership, the greater is the commitment to the group, indexed by consensus, cohesion, control, and continuance (p. 148). That pattern is common in collectivist cultures, where there usually are consensus and cohesion, control is high, and the social environment does not change quickly.

Measurement of the Construct

As outlined earlier, it is essential to measure dimensions of cultural variations with multimethod strategies. Many arguments favor such strategies (e.g., Campbell, 1986; Fiske, 1986), but the main one is the possibility of interaction between the meaning of cultural variables and the meanings of the measurements. Even when using the same method but analyzing the data from within- versus between-cultures perspectives, one can obtain different meanings. For example, *achievement* is usually associated with individual achievement in individualist cultures and with group achievement in collectivist cultures. *Self-reliance* means independence from the ingroup in individualist cultures and not being a burden on the ingroup in collectivist cultures (Triandis et al., 1988). The antecedent-consequent meaning method (Triandis, 1972) is very useful in discovering differences in the meanings of key constructs in different cultures.

If a multimethod strategy is to be used, one might ask: How can I study the cultural variables by different methods? For example, one might identify two cultures high and two cultures low on the cultural variable (two is desirable because cultures vary in myriad ways, and examining what is common across the two high ones and across the two low ones is just as informative as examining the differences between the two lows and the two highs), then do ethnographies of the four cultures, make systematic observations of behavior, conduct surveys to measure beliefs, attitudes, norms, values, and other elements of subjective culture, use projective instruments (e.g., Holtzman, 1980), do experiments (e.g., Bochner, 1980; Brown and Sechrest, 1980; Ciborowski, 1980), examine the spontaneously generated products of the cultures through content analyses, and even examine the variable through analyses based on the Human Relations Area Files (e.g., Barry, 1980).

In this section I will review studies that utilize observations, laboratory behaviors, analyses of the self, attitude items, value items, content analyses of autobiographies, reactions to scenarios, and studies of goals.

OBSERVATIONS

My first thought was observing the frequencies of people seen in public (streets, squares, restaurants, movies, etc.) alone (A) or together (T). I did some observations in two cities of equivalent size, one in northern Greece (Kozane) and the other in the United States (Urbana, IL). These cities of 35,000 people were suitable because Urbana, though not a major United States city, is relatively cosmopolitan and hence likely to be more individualist, and Kozane is in the heart of Greece, in a relatively traditional area, not close to any other country's border. One needs a city large enough that people will not notice they are being observed, but small enough to be easy to study.

I made a map of each town. Urbana already had a satisfactory map, but Kozane did not. In Urbana I took five streets to the north, south, east, and west of center (Broadway and Main), thus forming a 10 × 10 street grid. This grid defines 100 corners. I selected 10 corners by consulting a table of *random* numbers. Similarly, I divided the daylight period (excluding the time when people obviously go to work, such as 8:00 A.M. or come back from work, such as 5:00 P.M.) into 30-minute segments. Then I *randomly* picked 10 segments and observed for 10 minutes at the 10 randomly picked locations. It so happened that the observations were made at 10:00, 10:30, 12:00 noon, 12:30, 1:30, 2:00, 3:30, 4:30, 6:00, and 6:30. In each case the first 10 minutes of the interval constituted the period of observation. Having selected those times in Urbana, I tried to do the same in Kozane, but I had to take into account that people there go home for lunch at 2:00 P.M. and *start* work again at 5:00 P.M. So the density of observations is lower between 2:00 and 5:00 P.M. In the case of Kozane, rather than sampling I observed at 9:00, 9:30, 10:00, 10:30, 11:00, 11:30, 12:00 noon, 12:30, 1:00, and 1:30. That gave me 10 periods "during the main work hours."

Sampling locations in Kozane was not as easy as in Urbana. For one thing, the town is not built on a grid. There is a central street with two squares at its ends, and the streets fan out from those squares. So I constructed my own map (it took almost a day) and located all corners of the main street and all corners away from the two squares until I had 100 corners. Then I sampled randomly 10 of these corners.

In each corner I tallied the number of cases where people were alone or together in cars and as pedestrians. This kept me very busy, and in some cases I had to estimate because people were walking by faster than I could record. It would be good to have two observers to get interrater reliability data, so this is very exploratory.

In Kozane I also sampled in the evening after work. Here the situation is quite different. The alone/together ratio shifts from being quite a bit larger than 1.00 to being less than 1.00, showing that "sociability" increases in the evening.

RESULTS

In Urbana the alone/together ratios varied from 3.05 to 8.67, for cars, with a mean of 3.94, and from 1.50 to 7.00 for pedestrians, with a mean of 3.42. In Kozane, the A/T ratio ranged from 0.8 to 2.7 for cars, with a mean of 1.49, and from 1.69 to 7.71 for pedestrians, with a mean of 3.50. There is *no* overlap in the distributions for the car indexes. In short, there is no doubt that Greeks ride together more often than alone relative to Americans. But that may just reflect affluence and the number of cars per family . The pedestrian data are uncannily similar.[11]

Informal observations carried out in the People's Republic of China (PRC) confirm that in collectivist cultures a larger percentage of social interactions occur in groups of three or more, and in individualist cultures more people are alone or in pairs. The causes of these differences may be in the full employment policies of the PRC (which result in featherbedding), in the fact that collectives or organizations control funds (e.g., the bill in restaurants is paid by the organization, not by individuals), it is more convenient to deal with large groups when the population density is large, and so on. But whatever the forces that result in larger groups, the fact remains that social life is significantly different, and that is observable.

These exploratory studies suggest that further research on observational indexes of collectivism/individualism is justified.

LABORATORY BEHAVIORS

Knight (1981) used chips to represent different outcomes. One outcome included five chips for self and five for a friend; another five for self and three for the friend; and a third outcome five for the self and one for the friend. Many such studies suggest that the more individualist the culture the more likely children are to select outcomes that favor the self, but not too strongly (the second rather than the third of the three outcomes mentioned above).

PAPER-AND-PENCIL MEASURES

Self. Self-definition is likely to be different in collectivist cultures, where the self is like an appendage of the ingroup, and in individualist cultures, where the self is an entity separate from the ingroup. Nevertheless, even in individualist cultures people use ingroup-related concepts to define the self. One way to study the self is to use the Kuhn and McPartland (1954) method of eliciting completions to 20 sentences that begin with "I am . . . ." Content analysis of the response focuses on whether the answers refer to an ingroup. Any demographic entity or reference or membership group is scored as a "social category." The percentages of social categories ranged from 0 to 100% for particular individuals. The means of collectivist samples ranged between 29% and 52%; the means for individualist samples ranged from 15% to 19%. In addition, one can examine which categories are mentioned frequently and how early in the rank order a particular social category is mentioned. Typical findings are that *family, nation,* and *gender* are mentioned more frequently and earlier in the rank order by collectivist samples, while *occupation* is more mentioned often and earlier by individualist samples. Results differ from sample to sample, but these trends reveal differences in the way the self is defined in the two kinds of cultures (Triandis, McCusker & Hui, submitted).

Self-Report Measures. Hui (1984, 1988) has provided measurements using attitude items validated in the United States and Hong Kong. Triandis et al. (1985) used both attitude items and reactions to a variety of scenarios within the United Sates to determine the convergent and discriminant validity of various measures. Triandis et al. (1986) used attitude items in 15 locations around the globe; Triandis et al. (1988) used attitude items in four cultures.

Hui's (1984) attitude items suggest low but significant correlations between collectivism and Crandall's (1980) "social interest" and Swap and Rubin's (1983) reaction to social rather than economic relationships scales. Triandis et al. (1985) found low positive relationships between allocentrism and cooperative tendencies (Johnson & Norem-Hebeisen, 1979) and low negative relationships between allocentrism and loneliness (Schmidt & Sermat, 1983).

Values. Hofstede (1980), Hofstede and Bond (1984), the Chinese Cultural Connection (1987), and Triandis, McCusker, and Hui (submitted) investigated values. For example, in the last study subjects rated values, such as *freedom*, on a scale from −1 ("I reject this") to 7 ("of the utmost importance in my life"). Such value surveys (e.g., Rokeach, 1973) are useful, for one can see what patterns of values emerge in individualist and collectivist cultures and how different values are intercorrelated. American samples generally emphasize individualism (ambitious, courageous, capable) and goals such as freedom and accomplishment that have individualist meanings. Consistent with our previous discussion, in the United States Rokeach found more individualist values in the upper social class and more collectivist values in the lower and more individualist values among Republicans than Democrats.

The method Schwartz and Bilsky (1987) used to measure values can be used to tap specific aspects of collectivism and individualism. They presented a list of values to Israeli and German subjects and asked them to rate their importance. Smallest space analysis revealed a structure of these values that was reasonably similar in those two cultures. Clusters corresponding to individualism were identified: self-direction (sense of accomplishment, imaginative, intellectual), achievement (ambitious, social recognition, capable), and enjoying life (comfortable life, pleasure, happiness). Clusters corresponding to collectivism were also identified. They were prosocial (equality, helpful, forgiving), restricted conformity (obedient, polite, clean), and security (national security, world of peace, inner harmony). Schwartz (1988) argues that these clusters are subfactors of individualism and collectivism and will give a more refined measurement of the constructs than will more global measures.

Triandis, McCusker, and Hui (submitted) argued that the most typical collectivist values are those that show similarities between the People's Republic of China and American allocentrics, or contrasts between the PRC and the United States. In their study they identified them: for collectivists *social order, self-discipline, social recognition, humble, honoring parents and elders, accepting my position in life,* and *preserving my public image.* For individualists, *equality, freedom, an exciting life, a varied life,* and *enjoyment.* Clearly the first set of values are in the service of the collectivity and the second in the service of the individual.

Bond (1988) studied values in 21 cultures. His most important factor contrasted *intellectual* and *independent* with *family security*, suggesting considerable resemblance to individualism/collectivism.

Content Analyses. Morsbach (1980) content analyzed autobiographies obtained from Japanese and Western samples and found more individualist themes in the Western autobiographies.

Scenarios. Jones and Bock (1960) used abbreviated versions of Morris's 13 ways of life as stimuli in a cross-cultural study and identified one way of life (sympathy, concern for others, restraint of one's self-assertiveness) that seems related to collectivism/individualism. United States whites were very low, whereas Asians were quite high on this factor. Bond, Wan, Leung, and Giacalone (1985) found that responses to a verbal insult, presented in scenarios, were related to collectivism. Leung (1987) found that conflict-resolution scenarios were responded to differently by collectivists and individualists. An insult by a high-status ingroup member is tolerated more in collectivist than in individualist cultures; collectivists are more concerned with maintaining harmony over long periods than are individualists.

Finally, Shannon (1986) content analyzed 30 United States young children's favorite books and found a clear tendency for the self to be the focus of most activities, with very little emphasis on harmony with others.

Goals. Tanaka (1978) surveyed samples from the Pacific rim and found the individualist Australians and New Zealanders agreeing with the goal "to do whatever I think worth doing" 50% and 64% of the time, respectively, while the Japanese agreed only 32% of the time, the Indians (12%), and Pakistanis (8%) even less often. But the samples from the Indian subcontinent agreed with the goal "to acquire high status" 36% of the time, while the Australians did so only 1% of the time. Triandis (1972) found that the definitions of *success* were more individualist in the United States than in India (e.g., antecedent in the United States *ability*; in India *huge army*; consequence in the United States *achievement*, in India *fame*).

Collectivists tend to pay more attention to the views of others in deciding what to do, whereas individualists tend to pay most attention to their personal enjoyment and the consequences their actions have for themselves (see Davidson, Jaccard, Triandis, Morales, & Diaz-Guerrero, 1976).

Antecedents: Probable Causes of Collectivism and Individualism

ECOLOGY

Life in groups has definite advantages for primates (Chency, Seyforth, & Smuts, 1986) in that it raises the probability of finding food, and food of higher quality, lessens the probability that the animal will become a victim of other animals, contributes to reproductive success, and increases the enjoyment of mutual care. In short, it results in a higher probability of receiving rewards.

However, among humans, as the society gets to be more heterogeneous (an attribute of a complex culture) and affluent, the advantages of group living are less clear. For example, a very affluent individual can ensure reproductive success by buying it (mistresses) and protection by employing bodyguards.

The advantages of groups, such as the greater probability of survival when both successful and unsuccessful hunters or food gatherers belong to the same food ingroup, need to be examined against the advantages of individualism in the form of freedom to do one's own thing and to maximize pleasure, self-actualization, and creativity without having to pay the penalties of doing one's duty to the collective, doing what the group expects, meeting one's obligations, and the like.

In different ecologies the advantages of group versus individual life will be different. Although in low food accumulation societies the advantages of group life are significant and common fate creates goals shared by groups and individuals (e.g., getting enough food, adequate shelter), in high food accumulation societies (e.g., modern industrial societies with large food surpluses) the advantages of the group fade. We find empirically, in simple cultures, that as food accumulation increases there is more emphasis on conformity, obedience, and interdependence in child rearing (Barry, Child, & Bacon, 1959). But as societies move from the agricultural to the industrial phase and become information cultures, the advantages of individual action increase. We note a similar pattern among the social classes in modern societies. The lower social classes emphasize obedience and socialize severely; their "ideal child" is one who is a good follower (Kohn, 1987). The professional classes, by contrast, socialize for independence, creativity, and self-reliance; their ideal child is a professional.

Thus if we examine societies moving from hunting/gathering to agricultural to industrial to information societies, we see a move from protoindividualism to collectivism and then to neoindividualism. Hunters can do their own thing to some extent because their success does not depend too much on the actions of others. Agriculturists, however, have to work together (e.g., building canals, distributing surplus food to cities). Common fate is more obvious to those who depend on the weather than to those who depend on the presence or absence of hunting targets. Thus ecology, in the form of what the environment provides (availability of resources), is directly linked to individualism or collectivism.[12]

Many similarities between the simple hunting/gathering cultures and the modern industrial cultures can be identified: both emphasize the nuclear family, whereas collectivists emphasize the extended family. Both value the new more than old (e.g., the new hunting grounds); both are high in food availability, whereas collectivists often do not have enough food; both are characterized by geographical mobility, whereas collectivists usually stay in one place; both use linear dance forms, whereas collectivists use curvilinear forms; both are high in cognitive differentiation (Witkin & Berry, 1975); both emphasize self-reliance and independence in their child rearing, whereas collectivists emphasize dependence and obedience; both show a high self/other differentiation, whereas collectivists often identify so much with their ingroups that are simply a personalization of their group; both emphasize rights, whereas collectivists emphasize duties; and both allow the individual to have privacy, whereas collectivists do not.

As societies evolved (Boyd & Richardson, 1985) from food gathering and hunting to agricultural to industrial, there was a shift in the functional utility of the individual's submitting to the ingroup. As cultures moved from collectivism to individualism, numerous changes in social behavior were observed. For example, behavior moved from intimate to formal (Adamopoulos & Bontempo, 1986). As wealth increased, trading became a key activity. Trading is a behavior found in individualist cultures (Pearson, 1977). Contracts became important. Behavior was determined by short-term considerations, whereas in collectivist cultures it was determined by long-term considerations. In collectivist cultures one does not expect immediate reciprocity.

In sum, changes in ecology, affluence, mobility (both social and geographic), and movement from rural to urban (complex) societal settings contribute to the changes of cultures from collectivism to individualism. Finally, those societies that are exposed to the mass media also shift in the individualist direction, because the origin of television and other programs is predominantly Western. But where state policy precludes such influences (e.g., Iran), collectivism remains strong.

Consequences of Individualism and Collectivism

SOCIALIZATION

As I mentioned earlier, ecology results in shifts from proto-individualism to collectivism and then to neoindividualism. We can see this in the way people socialize their children. In simple hunting societies children are urged to be independent and self-reliant and to explore their hunting grounds; in complex agricultural societies they are required to be obedient; in modern industrial and information societies, again, they are supposed to be independent and self-reliant. Among preliterate societies only, Zern (1982, 1983) showed that the more complex the culture, the more child rearing favored collectivism. The more complex the culture, the more children are required to pay attention to the instructions of elders, up to a point, after which there is a reduction in this requirement. Thus the individualists (proto or neo) are socialized largely by peers and the collectivists largely by elders. The vertical relationships are more important than the horizontal for the collectivists, and the reverse is true for the individualists. The corresponding skills also differ: the collectivists know how to get along with the boss and with subordinates; the individualists know best how to relate to peers.

Traces of such differences continue in modern industrial environments. Leung and Sedlacek (1986) found among international students (mostly from collectivist cultures) studying in the United States that the students were more comfortable with faculty members and counselors (vertical relationships) than with friends (horizontal relationships). Specifically, the students were asked to imagine that they faced a particular problem, that they had tried unsuccessfully to solve it and had to get help. They were presented with a list of 12 sources of help. The collectivist student selections clearly were more vertical than horizontal.

Excellent discussions of the shift from collectivism to individualism have been provided by Doumanis (1983), Katakis (1984), and Sinha (1988). The last describes changes in the Indian family, with the transition from extended kin to the nuclear family, the segregation of children from adults, which increases individuation, the absence of clear-cut role models, changes in the status of women, and the impact of migration. The convergence in the presentations of these three authors, dealing with data from Greece and India, suggests that some of the phenomena they describe have cross-cultural generality.

The importance of cultural complexity is suggested by a famous six-culture study of child rearing (Whiting & Whiting, 1975). The greater the cultural complexity, the greater the family complexity (extended family) up to a point, and then the family became less complex (Blumberg & Winch, 1972). That is, the simple cultures had nuclear families; the complex had extended families; and the very complex, such as the United States, had nuclear families again. Interpersonal relationships within the family were more formal in the collectivist cultures than in the individualist ones. Mothers in the simple cultures demanded and obtained obedience, but their demands were simple (get some firewood, fetch some water, prepare this food, do some gardening or herding). In the more complex cultures the same activities were more complex, and children did not undertake them until they were older (age 5–10 instead of 3–4). In the complex cultures children were trained to be competitive and to achieve, and the greater the cultural complexity, the more the training was concerned with tasks and achievement. The same pattern was noted in Greece (Doumanis, 1983), where collectivism was linked to social relations and individualism to task achievement.

Child rearing is very intrusive in collectivist cultures; privacy for children is unknown. Dependence of the child on the parents is encouraged, and breaking the will of the child, so as to obtain complete obedience, is considered desirable (Guthrie, 1961). Thus the ideal is the "well-socialized child" (obedient, reliable, a good worker).

The value of children is also different (Hoffman, 1987). Children have an instrumental value, as good workers, in the collectivist cultures and an expressive value (ways to have fun) in the individualist cultures. In that study also, independence and self-reliance were not stressed as much in collectivist cultures as in individualist cultures.

Collectivists control their children by means of high ratios of interaction, consultation, guidance, and socialization. One thing they cannot be accused of is neglecting them. The strong mother-child bond is assumed to result in a well-adjusted adult. Children live with their parents until they get married and even after that. Parents live with their children until they die. Thus filial piety (taking good care of parents) is a cardinal virtue. But also, children are told that they are the center of the world. They are constantly rewarded with love and status. Cooperation with ingroup members is rewarded, and aggression toward them is severely punished. The interdependence of the ingroup members is stressed. If a child has a fight, this may affect the whole ingroup, and it cannot be allowed. Data from a range of societies (e.g., Guthrie, 1961, for the Philippines; Triandis, 1972, for traditional Greece; Shweder & Bourne, 1982, for East India; Wu, 1985, for China; Rugh, 1985, for Egypt; Kaiser, 1984, for the USSR) are striking in the extent to which they suggest similarities in child rearing that contrast with child rearing in the United States, Scandinavia, England, or Germany (Hoffman, 1987).

Hui (personal communication, 1989) points out that familistic collectivism can result in rugged individualism when there is only one child in the family (as is the case in urban China at this time). At least the Chinese press seems to suggest that the excessive pampering of that one child by two parents and four grandparents can lead to the creation of "little devils" who are selfish and highly individualistic. Research that is currently under way by Jing and his collaborators (personal communication, 1988) will determine if these fears are justified.

Whereas collectivists rarely neglect their children, this is not always the case with individualists. In fact, cases of child neglect and abuse have reached epidemic levels in the United States. Such levels were not known even one generation ago and may be linked to the change of individualism from the perspective that emphasized the public good (Tocqueville) to narcissistic individualism. Pilisuk and Parks (1985) document the perpetuation of cultural patterns of child abuse and neglect, where parents who were neglected by their parents neglect their children. Abused children had parents who were abused as children. The high mobility of individualist societies implies low interdependence with others, so the burden on the mothers is extreme and they sometime escape from their responsibilities. Mobility also means loneliness, which children cannot always remedy, so the mother may go to a bar to find companionship or receive social support and thus may neglect the child.

Children learn the most important skills for being good members of their society rather early. That is, children in collectivist cultures first learn those behaviors that allow the ingroup to function smoothly, and learn about independence later. Conversely, children in individualist cultures first learn to be independent and may or may not acquire skills relevant to the smooth functioning of the ingroup (Rosenthal & Bornholt, 1988).

The child-parent bond is generally the strongest human bond in collectivist cultures, though the strongest bond differs from one culture to another (e.g., in China it is father-son; in India it is mother-son; in Africa south of the Sahara, it is older brother–younger brother; see Hsu, 1971). The key difference is that the spouse-spouse bond is not as strong in the collectivist as in the individualist cultures. Data reported by Triandis, Vassiliou, and Nassiakou (1968) are illustrative. Consider the intimacy levels that are perceived to be appropriate, on 9-point scales, for mother-son and wife-husband in traditional collectivist Greece and individualist America. The Greek means of 6.7 and 4.9 contrast with the American means of 6.3 and 6.9. Clearly these means suggest an interaction.

Given these patterns of importance, the most difficult marriage is that of a collectivist male to an individualist female. The collectivist will see the relationship with his mother as more important than that with his wife, whereas his wife will expect his relationship with her to be more important. Only if wife and mother-in-law are separated in a major way (e.g., mother's death, large geographic distance) can such a marriage survive.

In terms of predictions about divorce, the most favorable prediction is for collectivist-collectivist marriages; next for individualist-individualist, and least favorable for collectivist-individualist marriages. However, the gender of the spouses also plays a role. The marriage of a collectivist wife and an individualist husband is not quite as problematic as that of a collectivist husband and an individualist wife. For example, to go back to the traditional Greek data, the intimacy in the daughter-father role was 5.4 and 5.5 in Greece and the United States, respectively, while that of the wife-husband was 4.9 and 6.9. So, while the parent-child bond is still more intimate in the collectivist culture than the spouse-spouse role, the difference is not as large as in the case of the son-mother role.

Collectivist child rearing is characterized by the great control that parents exert over their children. As a result, the more collectivist the culture, the more likely children are to do what the adults expect them to do. Thus Shouval, Kav, Bronfenbrenner, Devereux, and Kiely (1975) found more adult-approved behavior in the USSR than in the United States, and more in an Israeli kibbutz than in the USSR.

Given that patterns of child rearing persist over several generations, even when samples from collectivist cultures raise their children in an individualist culture (Lambert, Hammers, & Frasure-Smith, 1979), it seems important to consider, as a minimum, the following antecedents of collectivism and individualism in both kinds of cultures: cultural background of parents, migration, social mobility, urban environment, exposure to the mass media, education, and rapid social change, all of which tend to contribute to individualism.

Quite revealing of the emphasis in child rearing in collectivist and individualist cultures is a study of the role perceptions of children (Setiadi, 1984). Setiadi tested children in Indonesia and the United States with the "role differential" (Triandis et al., 1968), which requires the respondent to rate the probability of a particular behavior (e.g., obey) in a particular role relationship (e.g., child-mother). The data were factor analyzed to determine what patterns of behavior would emerged in the various roles. In such analyses the first factor is the most important (the one that accounts for most of the variance in the judgments of role behaviors). Setiadi found that the most important factor in Indonesia was Obedience (subordination to ingroup authorities), whereas the most important factor in the United States was Enjoyment (having fun together).

This reflects the more "authoritarian" character of child rearing in collectivist cultures, where physical punishment is used frequently, though the correlation of collectivism and physical punishment is not necessarily strong, since there are collectivist cultures (e.g., Japan) where other means of securing obedience are used. Japanese mothers employ the technique of announcing that they feel hurt when the child misbehaves and feel happy when the child behaves appropriately. Since the mother-child bond is extremely strong (mothers rarely work and are totally devoted to upbringing), rejection by the mother (e.g., putting the child out of the house and closing the door) is totally devastating. Physical punishment is quite unnecessary under these conditions. Note the interesting contrast: in the United States children sometimes run away; in Japan they are punished by exclusion from the house!

In collectivist cultures socialization includes a major emphasis on learning a good deal about who one is (one's ancestors, one's history); in individualist cultures it involves learning what one is able to do. In the former, socialization is primarily the formation of a social identity as the member of an ingroup and secondarily a set of skills. The reverse is true in individualist cultures.

PERSONALITY

Definition of the Self in Individualist and Collectivist Cultures. The self is here defined as all the statements a person makes that include the words "I," "me," "mine," and "myself." This definition means that all aspects of social motivation are included in the self. Attitudes (e.g., *I* like . . .), beliefs (e.g., X has attribute Y in *my* view), intentions (e.g., *I* plan to do . . .), norms (*my* ingroup expects *me* to do . . .), roles (*my* ingroup expects people who hold this position to do . . .), and values (e.g., *I* feel that . . . is very important), are aspects of the self.

The self is coterminous with the body in individualist cultures and in some of the collectivist cultures. However, it can be related to a group the way a hand is related to the person whose hand it is. The latter conception is found in collectivist cultures, where the self often overlaps with a group, such as family or tribe (Centre National de la Recherche Scientifique, 1973; Shweder & Bourne, 1982).

Obviously, with such a broad construct, if we are going to describe different kinds of selves in individualistic and collectivist cultures it is necessary to limit the meaning of the term in some way. One way is to consider the contrast between the private, public, and collective selves (Greenwald & Pratkanis, 1984). The private self consists of statements that refer to traits, states, or behaviors, such as "I am honest"; the public self refers to statements that refer to the generalized other's view of the person, such as, "People think I am honest"; the collective self refers to statements that an ingroup has made about the self, such as, "My family thinks I am honest."

There is evidence that people in collectivist cultures sample the collective self more than people in individualist cultures. This can be seen from studies in which subjects were asked to write 20 statements that begin with "I am. . . ." Working in Hawaii, I (Triandis, McCusker, & Hui, submitted) asked students from the University of Hawaii to respond to this task, as suggested by Kuhn and McPartland (1954). Each response was examined by a coder to determine if it was a "social category." For example, "I am an uncle" was coded *family*; I live in Honolulu" was coded *location*, "I am a woman" was coded *gender*, and so on. A total of 12 social categories were mentioned with substantial frequency. Note that a response of "I play tennis" was not scored as a social category, but "I am a member of the tennis club" was. Interrater reliabilities were .97 across three raters. The percentage of the 20 responses that was coded as a social category provided the %S score. In addition, we noted the "availability" (number of responses referring to a particular social category, such as the *family*) and "accessibility" (e.g., How early in the sequence of the 20 responses was the *family* mentioned?) of each response.

The subjects were also asked to specify their cultural background. Since many had Japanese or Chinese backgrounds, the "collectivism" of the background of the Hawaii sample was relatively high. A sample of students from Illinois went through the same routine, but their collectivism score, based on their background, was low.

Using the %S score as a measure of sampling of the collective self we found that the mean of the Hawaii sample was 29% and that of the Illinois sample 19%. A sample from the People's Republic of China averaged 52%. The ratings of collectivism/individualism based on the ethnic background of the parents of these students ranged (on a 7-point scale) from 1=foreign students from Japan or China to 7=native-born Americans of northwest European background. This scale correlated with the %S score -.24 (N=183, $p <$ .001). Thus the more individualist the background of the subjects, the less they used social categories in the response to the "I am" instructions.

A different student sample, again from Illinois, responded to the 21-item instrument measuring different aspects of individualism and collectivism mentioned earlier (Triandis et al., 1986). The factor structure of that instrument was replicated with this new sample. That is, as in the study that used data from Illinois, California, Chile, Hong Kong, Indonesia, India, Greece, France, the Netherlands, and Costa Rica, the factors were called Distance from Ingroups, Self-Reliance, Interdependence, and Family Integrity. The same factors were obtained with this sample. Since the Illinois students showed very little variance in the Family Integrity factor, we disregarded that factor and defined subjects as "idiocentrics" (high on Distance and Self-Reliance) or "allocentrics" (low on Distance and Self-Reliance). We found that the mean %S of the allocentrics was 35% and that of the idiocentrics 29% ($p < .04$). The allocentrics referred to their families twice on the average, while the idiocentrics did so 1.5 times, a difference in availability that was significant. The allocentrics also referred to an athletic group more frequently in defining themselves (1.2 vs. 0.5 times; $p < .002$). The accessibility of the athletic group was also higher for the allocentrics than for the idiocentrics (6.4 vs. 3.8, where 20 means that the category was mentioned first; $p < .007$). The allocentrics also mentioned their social class (0.6) more often than the idiocentrics (0.2; $p < .03$).

Tesser and Moore (1986) argued that the public and private selves will tend to converge, because people fear that being dishonest will lead to difficulties, because having two inconsistent selves causes information overload, and because both selves are influenced by the same outside factors. However, it is likely that these arguments hold only in individualist cultures. In collectivist cultures inconsistency between private self and public self is much more likely. In fact, Doi (1986) considers this the major difference between Japan and the United States. In the United States people pride themselves on being honest and frank—"telling it like it is." In Japan, a sophisticated person will not behave as the private self requires. Rather, though that person may have a poor opinion of the other, he will show the best face and will be most polite.

Evidence supplied by Iwao (1988) supports Doi's view. Iwao presented Japanese and Americans with three scenarios in which there was some conflict between an actor and another person. Subjects were asked to indicate how the actor would behave, giving their preferred position, second most preferred position, and so on, and also indicating how the average Japanese and average American would behave. These data clearly supported Doi's view about the inconsistency of private self and public self in a collectivist culture. For example, one scenario was about a racially prejudiced father whose daughter brought home a person of the "wrong race" as a future husband. One of the ways for the father to respond was to "think that he would never allow them to marry, but tell them he was in favor of their marriage." In the United States only 2% of the 169 subjects chose this response, out of the total of five responses available to them. In Japan, 44% of the 150 subjects chose that response. This is so dramatic a difference that it requires no statistics to show its significance.

Of course, in the United States also, people do not always speak up. Certainly, even when they disagree with the boss they might show a favorable face. The point is that in a society where harmony is the ideal and "doing the right thing" is essential for good relations, one often does what one believes to be socially desirable even if one's attitudes are inconsistent with the action. The private and public selves are different in collectivist cultures.

Thus Doi (1986) makes a distinction between *tatemae* (self-presentation) and *honne* (behind the mask). He argues that the two selves are not linked in the United States, although they are interrelated, but that they are independent of each other in Japan. His analysis leads him to argue that United States individualism is linked to the United States emphasis on equality. If all are equal, all must make their way without the help of others. He further argues that individualism and conformity are two sides of the same coin, because if all are equal all must behave the same way. In Japan hierarchy is the essence of social order. People depend on their relative status to determine their social behavior.

Doi indicates that the Japanese dislike stating personal opinions and prefer to express opinions that emerge from social consensus. Self-definition is based on the groups one belongs to. This reminds me of the famous incident during the Second World War when Japanese prisoners of war offered to spy for the United States. Anthropologists were asked if the offer should be accepted, and they indicated that indeed it should. The prisoners became excellent spies. Once they had changed ingroup, having been taken prisoner against the explicit instructions of their superiors, they no longer defined the self as Japanese.

Especially interesting is Doi's argument that "real" individuals exist only in Japan because, although Japanese people do what is socially appropriate, their "real" self is their private self, which is very different from what they do. By contrast, in individualist societies, with the emphasis on equality that leads to conformity and the strong convergence of public and private selves, there are no individuals. He suggests that the Japanese emphasis on poetry is an escape from the duality of the two selves. He further argues that modernity results in consistency between the private and public selves and weakens the public self, which is one of the weaknesses of modernity.

Doi also distinguishes individualism, collectivism, and totalitarianism: individualism is putting private goals ahead of ingroup goals; collectivism is the situation where private goals *are* the ingroup goals; totalitarianism is the situation where private and ingroup goals are not the same and the ingroup goals are imposed on the individual. Clearly, he sees Japan as a collectivist culture, but one in which there is no conflict between ingroup and private goals.

As a Japanese psychiatrist, Doi argues in favor of people's having secrets and not revealing their private life in public. However, the coordination of two selves, he admits, is taxing and tiring, so the Japanese escape into nature, where they do not have to coordinate them.

Geertz (1983) examined the self in Java, Bali, and Morocco and provided a description that suggests Bali is the most collectivist and Morocco the most individualist of the three. Bali is an exaggerated version of Java. Nothing suggestive of individuality is allowed. One plays a role, as prescribed by Balinese life. People come and go, but "the masks they wear, the stage they occupy, the parts they play, and most important, the spectacle they mount remain, and comprise not the facade but the substance of things, not least the self" (p. 62).

In Java there is also the assumption that a private and a public self are different. The "inside" is pure, polished, exquisite, ethereal, civilized, and smooth, while the outside is action, movement, posture, and speech, and in many cases is impolite, rough, uncivilized, coarse, and insensitive. The inside is cultivated through religious discipline, while the outside responds to etiquette. Etiquette rules have the force of law. The outside is predictable, undisturbing, elegant—a "rather vacant set of choreographed motions and settled forms of speech" (p. 61). The parallel with Doi is striking.

Morocco is quite different. Although the self is intimately linked to the *nisba* (relationship, affinity, connection, kinship), and one knows the person by knowing his or her *nisba*, there is a choice of *nisbas* that allows the person to behave differently depending on the situation. In Egypt he is a North African; in Sefrou he is called by his tribe's name; within the tribe by the name of the tribal fraction; within the fraction by some other fraction; and finally marriage, worship, diet, law, and education provide additional social contexts. But these social categories are only the skeleton. The interaction provides the flesh. This is individualism because in public individuals determine what to do to maximize their returns. One can be a fox among foxes without losing one's sense of who one is.

Identity is defined by what one has in individualist cultures— what I own, what experiences I have had, what I have accomplished (e.g., my list of publications!). Identity in collectivist cultures is defined by relationships to groups of others—I am a member of this family; I am the mother of X; I live in Y. Furthermore, individualists tend to give importance to attributes like being logical, balanced, rational, or fair, whereas in other cultures, such as in Africa, the important attributes are the person's unique movements, the spontaneous self, sincere self-expression, unpredictability, and emotional expression. The contrast between classical music (e.g., Bach and Mozart) and jazz reveals this difference musically.

Weldon (1984) reasoned that in an individualist culture, such as the United States, a person who is characterized as not unique—as "similar to an average person"—would be offended. She predicted that offended subjects would be less cooperative toward the person who offended them. She showed subjects who were performing a laboratory task a bogus rating supposedly made by their task leader. The rating indicated in half the cases that the student was not unique (was similar to the average student). She found, as predicted, that after seeing this rating the subjects were less likely to volunteer to help this leader, and were less productive when they thought such production would benefit the leader, than a control group who had not seen such a rating.

Morality. There is empirical evidence that morality is viewed differently in collectivist and individualist cultures. In collectivist cultures it is more absolute, more contextual, and depends more on the actor's position in the social system. That is, the norms of the ingroup are seen as correct no matter what the norm of other ingroups (absolute), and a person's transgression is judged depending on the social situation (e.g., Was he drunk?) and social position (e.g., Was he a high-status person?) to a greater extent than is the case in individualist cultures (e.g., see Hamilton & Sanders, 1983; Shweder, 1982).

Ma (1988) has a very interesting discussion of the Chinese perspective on moral judgment. He follows Kohlberg (1976, 1981), yet provides Chinese versions of Stages 4, 5, and 6. The main differences he postulates between the Chinese and Western perspectives at Stage 4 are a collectivistic and affective perspective versus an individualist and rational perspective, a soft attitude toward conflict resolution versus less tolerance for compromise, a person-oriented government and loose legal system versus constitutional government and public institutionalized law. At Stage 5 the collectivist perspective is more rigid, with more rules and clear values than the individualist. The Chinese emphasize a natural, autonomous, affective, and self-sacrificing altruistic disposition, whereas in the West the emphasis is on "the greatest good for the greatest number." The conflict between the majority and the individual is resolved in China by the individual's sacrificing to the majority, whereas in the West it is decided on the principle of the "greatest good to the greatest number." At Stage 6 the Chinese view emphasizes that one must comply with nature harmoniously; to achieve autonomy and freedom, one must have few desires and nonvaluative judgment—that is, everyone is treated as ethically neutral. Every opinion is equally good and right. The Western view emphasizes the free choice of principles by the individual, that people are ends, and that all persons have an equal right for consideration of their claims.

Ma (1988) sees three possible types of development: purely Chinese, for example, Stage 1-2-3-4C (where C stands for Chinese)-5C-6C, purely Western 1-2-3-4W-5W-6W, or a mixture, such as 1-2-3-4W-5W-6C. Thus, although the society may be collectivist, particular individuals may adopt individualist perspectives at certain points of their development, and vice versa.

SOCIAL BEHAVIOR

Mate Selection. An important study by Buss and his associates (1990) carried out in 37 cultures examined the attributes that men and women considered most important in selecting a mate. The largest effect of culture was on *chastity*, to which collectivist cultures such as China, India, Indonesia, Iran, Taiwan, and the Palestinians of Israel gave great importance, but which subjects from individualist cultures such as Sweden, Finland, Norway, the Netherlands, and West Germany accorded little importance. A second contrast between collectivists, such as Zulus and Colombians, and individualists, such as the people of the United States, Canada, and Western Europe, was on the importance of being a *good housekeeper*. The next contrast between the individualists or moderate collectivists from France, Japan, Brazil, the United States, Spain, and Ireland and the collectivists from Zulu areas, China, India, and Iran was on the importance of an *exciting personality*, which was important for the individualists and unimportant for the collectivists.

In general Buss et al. (1990) found that the effects of culture were much larger than the effects of gender.

If family integrity is a high value for collectivists, as the Triandis et al. (1986) study has suggested, it seems reasonable that *chastity* and *good housekeeper* will be major considerations for them in mate selection. Lack of chastity may suggest "cheating," and those who cheat on their partners are likely to do things that will disintegrate the family. Also, those who are poor housekeepers certainly will not provide the optimal family environment. By contrast, an *exciting personality* interests individualists because they consider "pleasure" an important value. Also, in winning the battle of competition, a mate with an exciting personality may be most valuable.

Dion and Dion (1988) use the individualism/collectivism constructs to discuss patterns of romantic love. Individualists ask, "How does my heart feel?" Collectivists ask, "What will other people say?" Individualists emphasize physical attractiveness and intensity of feeling (*eros*), and collectivists stress practical and friendship-based styles of love. The individualist's love relationships have some narcissistic qualities (p. 284), whereas collectivists were found to be fonder of their partners. They speculate "that individualism makes it difficult for individuals to become intimate and loving with one another. It is likely, for example, that the high divorce rate that characterizes American society is due in good part to the culture's exaggerated sense of individualism" (p. 286).

Support for Dion and Dion's speculation can be found in a study by Brodbar and Jay (1986). They examined the relationship of allocentrism (measured by synagogue attendance, having many Jewish friends, belonging to Jewish organizations, contributing to Jewish charities) to divorce rates among 4,505 Jewish households in New York City. They found that the more collectivist the sample, the lower was the divorce rate.

Social Behavior in Different Contexts. *Collectivists pay more attention to ingroup/outgroup distinctions than individualists.* This point becomes clear when we review the following quote from Evans-Pritchard (1940, p. 183): "If you wish to live among the Nuer you must do so on their terms, which means that you must treat them as a kind of kinsman and they will then treat you as a kind of kinsman. Rights, privileges, and obligations are determined by kinship. Either a man is a kinsman, actually or by fiction, or he is a person to whom you have no reciprocal obligations and whom you treat as a potential enemy." This description is one step more extreme than my discussion (Triandis, 1972) of the ingroup in traditional Greece. The ingroup is "family and friends and other people who are concerned with my welfare." Triandis et al. (1968) studied the role perceptions of traditional Greeks and Americans concerning a wide range of roles, such as nuclear family (e.g., wife-husband), extended family (e.g., uncle-niece), host-guest roles (e.g., native-tourist), exchange roles (e.g., lawyer-client), co-worker roles (e.g., boss-secretary), competition roles (e.g., administrator-university student) and competition/exchange roles (e.g., client-prostitute). The two cultures perceived roles very similarly in the family and in competitive situations. As might be expected, there was more association (help, support, cooperate with) in family roles than in competitive roles; more superordination (order, criticize) in competitive than in family roles; more intimacy in family than in competitive roles. However, a major cultural difference could be seen at a point between the exchange roles and the co-worker roles. There is a discontinuity in the Greek perceptions of role relationships at the point between exchange roles (which include people who might be interested in the individual's welfare, such as teachers, psychologists, etc.) and work roles, which are seen in competitive (outgroup), distrustful, and distant ways.

The sharper difference between collectivists' ingroup and outgroup behavior than between individualists' is also well illustrated by a study of Gudykunst, Yoon, and Nishida (1987). They examined the ratings of behavior toward an ingroup member (friend) or an outgroup member (stranger) by students from Korea (very collectivist), Japan (slightly collectivist), and the United States (very individualist). The subjects rated the interaction with the ingroup or the outgroup member on a set of scales. Factor analysis of the scales indicated that three dimensions accounted for most of the variance of the ratings: *Personalization* (e.g., we share secrets with each other), *Synchronicity* (e.g., our conversation is spontaneous, informal, and relaxed) and *Difficulty* (e.g., we find it hard to talk to each other). They hypothesized that Koreans would see more Personalization and Synchronicity and less difficulty in ingroup than in outgroup interactions and that this difference would also be true for Japanese and for Americans, but decreasingly so. One can examine the size of the t-tests, when comparing the factor scores for these three qualities, for ingroups versus outgroups. Table 1 presents these t-tests. It is clear that the more collectivist the culture, the larger the t-test, so the sizes of the t-test correspond to the hypothesis.

Gudykunst, et al. (cited in Gudykunst, Nishida, & Schmidt, 1989) examined the influence of collectivism/individualism on communication behavior. They predicted major differences in such behaviors in collectivist cultures (Hong Kong, Japan) when the other

Table 1

Size of Significant t-Tests
for Differences between Ingroup and Outgroup Social Interactions

Factor	Culture		
	Korea	*Japan*	*United States*
Personalization	12.2	9.9	5.9
Synchronization	9.2	8.9	7.1
Difficulty	10.9	7.7	4.9

Source: Gudykunst, Yoon, and Nishida (1987).

Note: Largest differences between ingroup and outgroup ratings occur in the most collectivist cultures, smallest differences in the most individualist cultures. All *t*-tests are $p < .001$.

person is an ingroup versus an outgroup member, but no such differences in individualist cultures (the United States and Australia in this study). The data supported this prediction. Gudykunst, Nishida, and Schmidt (1989) reviewed several studies, including the one just mentioned, which examined communication with ingroup and with outgroup members in the United States and Japan. They conclude that, consistent with Triandis et al. (1986), there is more self-disclosure, attraction, perceived similarity, display of nonverbal affiliative expressiveness, shared networks, and "attributional confidence," that is, confidence in making attributions (assigning causes to behaviors) in ingroup relationships than in outgroup relationships in collectivist than in individualist cultures. "Attributional confidence" here refers to the extent to which a person feels confidence when making attributions about the attitudes and behavior of another person. "Shared networks" refers to the number of common friends and acquaintances.

When interacting with ingroup members, collectivists tend to be very cooperative and helpful, whereas when interacting with strangers they tend to be competitive and not helpful. The ingroup/stranger contrast is much less important for individualists, who behave more or less equally well toward both ingroup and strangers. The result is that when groups are formed for a first time members from individualist societies behave more cooperatively than members of collectivist societies (Gabrenya & Barba, 1987). Furthermore, collectivists are more competitive when they are a minority, whereas individualists are less competitive than usual when they are in a minority position (Espinoza & Garza, 1985). Thus it is not true that collectivists are cooperative across the board. It depends on the situation.

Neglecting to pay attention to the difference between ingroups and outgroups leads social scientists to be surprised by the results of experiments. For example, the typical Asch-type conformity study uses strangers, and thus outgroup members. In a collectivist culture (Japan) subjects not only did not show more conformity but actually showed anticonformity; that is, when the majority made the correct response, they made an incorrect response (Frager, 1970). Here we have to enter the subject's phenomenology: "If these strangers are saying silly things, it's a good idea for me to respond the opposite way." Presumably, had Frager used an ingroup that made the incorrect responses, the subject would have tried to correct the erring majority, but since he used an outgroup there was no such obligation for the collectivist subjects.

The ingroup/outgroup distinction, though useful, is often too coarse (inaccurate). Atsumi (1980), while discussing Japanese social behavior, suggests that the categories benefactors, true friends, co-workers, acquaintances, and outsiders are needed to understand this behavior. With benefactors the sense of obligation (*giri*) is of great importance as a determinant of social behavior; with friends the enjoyment of the relationship as well as the sense of obligation is important; with kin the norms of kin behavior are primary determinants of social behavior; with outsiders the advantages and disadvantages that can be derived from the relationship are of the greatest importance. In business/professional relationships, norms and perceived advantages are of equal importance. In other words, Atsumi suggests that exchange theory (e.g., Thibaut & Kelley, 1959) is applicable in Japan, but only for relationships with strangers. In the other relationships it may have minor importance or even not be important.

One can obtain empirically the categories of "others" that are used by collectivists and individualists. This was done by Triandis, McCusker and Hui (submitted) by asking subjects in the People's Republic of China and in Illinois to "consider the person with whom you feel closest. It might be one of your parents, a friend, a spouse, or a brother. Assume that the distance between yourself and that person corresponds to *one* point. Now we want you to indicate how many points correspond to the distance between yourself and several social stimuli, using the same meaning for the points."

Using the psychophysical method of direct magnitude estimation, each subject developed a idiographic scale of social distance. By dividing the values of each social category with the geometric mean of the social stimuli that constituted that scale, it was possible to develop comparable scales across subjects.

The subjects were 34 students in a course given in Beijing, 200 introductory social psychology students in Illinois, 45 students in a cross-cultural psychology course, and 45 other University of Illinois students tested with the same procedure. In the last case those students who came from Europe and North America were asked to test a student from Asia, Africa, or Latin America; conversely, those from the latter countries were asked to test students from the former countries.

The method of direct estimation was also used to determine idiographic scales for six attributes of social behavior: *association* (e.g., marry, consult, admire), *dissociation* (e.g., insult, murder, criticize), *superordination* (e.g., scold, order to do something, fire from a desirable job), *subordination* (e.g., obey, serve, accept point of view of), *intimacy* (e.g., kiss, pet), and *formality* (e.g., say "hello" when meeting for first time; say "nice to have met you" after meeting).

Since each subject had a social distance scale (*x*-axis) and six scales concerning attributes of social behavior (association, formality, etc.), it was possible for each of them to plot the relationships between each attribute of social behavior (*y*-axis) and social distance. The $Y = f(x)$ functions were plotted separately for collectivists and individualists. By averaging across subjects, one could see differences in the way subjects from the two kinds of cultural backgrounds conceived of social behavior.

Details of this study can be found in Triandis, McCusker, and Hui (submitted). First, the curves from the PRC and Illinois were overall very similar. This is desirable, since it is only in the context of similarities that one can interpret cultural differences (Campbell, 1964). Second, the PRC subjects were closer to their parents than the Illinois subjects, but the Illinois subjects were closer to their closest friends and their roommates than were the PRC subjects. Third, although the functions were generally similar, there were statistically significant differences at certain points. These differences indicated that the PRC sample considered it more appropriate to show subordination within their very close ingroup, intimacy toward their extended family, co-workers, and people of the same religion, nationality, and neighborhood as themselves, and more formality and superordination toward strangers and disliked groups than was the case for the Illinois subjects. In other words, the PRC made more of a distinction between ingroups and outgroups, showing more intimacy and subordination to ingroups and more formality and superordination to outgroups than was the case for the Illinois samples.

The large difference in the area of intimacy was also found by Argyle, Henderson, Bond, Iizuka, and Contarello (1986). It was the most distinct difference in the rules of social interaction, contrasting England and Italy on the one hand with Hong Kong and Japan on the other.

Conflict Resolution. The importance of ingroup harmony in collectivist cultures is well reflected in the studies of Leung (Leung 1987, 1988; Leung & Lind, 1986). Leung shows that collectivists prefer bargaining and mediation to a greater extent than individualists do, because they perceive these methods of dispute resolution as leading to less animosity than adversarial methods. Leung (1988) asked college students in Hong Kong and the United States to read a conflict scenario and indicate how likely they were to pursue the conflict. A conflict was more likely to be pursued when the stakes were large and when the would-be disputant was an outgroup member. Chinese subjects were less likely than Americans to pursue a conflict with an ingroup member and more likely than Americans to pursue one with an outgroup member.

However, among collectivists manipulative behavior to the disadvantage of outgroups is generally approved of (Pandey, 1986). When negotiating with outgroups it is acceptable to act in immoral ways, because morality applies only to the ingroup. When competing with outgroups collectivists are often more competitive than individualists (Espinoza & Garza, 1985), even in situations where extreme competitiveness is counterproductive.

Ting-Toomey (1988) proposed a theory concerning differences

in the strategies that individualists and collectivists are likely to use in conflict situations. She hypothesizes that individualists will be more concerned with saving their own face, autonomy, domination, control, and solutions to the problem; they will use direct negotiation strategies. By contrast, collectivists will be more concerned with saving face for the other or for both, approval, being obliging and smooth, and avoiding conflict. They will use indirect negotiation strategies—for example, they will welcome mediators.

Communication. Individuals in collectivist cultures tend to use more of the social context when communicating. Gudykunst (1983) noted that in high-context cultures people are more cautious in initial interactions, and base more of their social perceptions on the other person's group memberships, than do people in individualist cultures. In one experiment in which he contrasted students from the United States, Germany, and Switzerland with students from Japan, China, and Korea, he found that the former smile, shake hands, and look directly in the other's eyes, whereas the latter greet formally and ask if the other is married and about father's occupation and religious background.

The rated intimacy levels of various social stimuli also revealed differences in interaction. Gudykunst and Nishida (1986) found that the Japanese saw more intimacy with acquaintances, co-workers, colleagues, and classmates than did Americans, whereas the latter saw more intimacy with a lover, sister, roommate, fiancé, son, and neighbor.

SOCIAL PERCEPTION

Bond and Forgas (1984) had subjects in Hong Kong (collectivists) and Australia (individualists) read descriptions of target persons who varied on the dimensions of extroversion, agreeableness, conscientiousness, and emotional stability. After reading a description, the subjects indicated their intention on a behavioral differential (Triandis, 1964). Although conscientiousness and agreeableness were found to be desirable by both samples, the Hong Kong sample (collectivists) were more favorably impressed by these attributes than were the individualists. Similarly, Bond, Chu, and Wan (1984) found that collectivists were especially impressed by group-serving partners (people who attribute success to the whole group rather than to individuals) and liked them more than other partners.

SOCIAL VERSUS TASK FACTORS

An interesting study along these lines is Forgas and Bond's (1985) examination of the multidimensional scaling of 27 social episodes (e.g., arrive very late for a tutorial) done by collectivist (Hong Kong Chinese) and individualist (Australian) subjects. The most important dimension in Hong Kong was a combination of *power distance and collectivism*. Semantic differential scales such as unequal-equal, communal-isolated, and commonplace-rare related to that dimension. The most important dimension in Australia was *competitiveness*, with scales such as cooperation-competition, pleasant-unpleasant, and relaxed-anxious related to it. Second in importance, in both cultures, was a *task* versus *social interaction* dimension. Fourth in Hong Kong and third in importance in Australia was an *involvement* dimension. Finally, Hong Kong had an *evaluation* (pleasant-unpleasant) and Australia a *self-confidence* (I'm in control) dimension. So two of the dimensions were culture common and two were culture specific. The culture specific in the collectivist culture reflected collectivism and pleasantness; that in the individualist culture reflected competition and control. Thus social episodes have somewhat different meanings in the two kinds of cultures. In collectivist cultures they may be viewed according to the extent to which they permit communal feelings and social usefulness, as well as acceptance of authority, while in individualist cultures they may be viewed according to the extent to which they are competitive and allow one to be in control and free.

The greater importance of social factors than of task factors, characteristic of collectivism, is reflected in the expectations people have about what others will remember. For example, in a study of beliefs that Sumatrans and Australians had about the memory of the aged, it was found that the Sumatrans expected the aged to remember social information (e.g., names of family ancestors, how to go about buying a house, the stages in a traditional wedding, who came to the wedding) much more than did Australians (Noesjirwan, Gault, & Crawford, 1983).

Differences in social behavior reported by subjects from the United States and Hong Kong keeping a diary over a two-week period are consistent with the Triandis (1988) conceptualization about the importance of few ingroups for the collectivists and the emotional detachment of the individualists from the many ingroups they belong to. The United States sample, with more ingroups, engaged in a greater frequency of interaction, but the Americans disclosed to their partners less information than did the Chinese. Furthermore, the Chinese had a higher percentage of interaction in groups than in a one-on-one setting (see the observations in Kozane and Urbana reported above, for convergence); they had longer interactions, fewer interaction partners, and more task and fewer recreational interactions than did the American subjects (Wheeler, Reis, & Bond, 1989).

DISTRIBUTIVE BEHAVIOR OF COLLECTIVISTS AND INDIVIDUALISTS

There is considerable evidence, reviewed by Marin (1985), that collectivists tend to use equality and need when distributing resources in a number of situations in which individualists use equity. In other words, collectivists do not follow the norm "to each according to his contributions" with the same level of probability as individualists do (Bond, Leung, & Wan, 1982; Leung & Bond, 1984; Murphy-Berman, Berman, Singh, Pachauri, and Kumar, 1984). Some complexities have been identified, however, that make the statement above too simple. For example, Hui and Triandis (submitted) found that when resources are limited Chinese subjects had a tendency to use an allocation rule that favored their partner in a job setting to a greater extent than American subjects did. When resources were unlimited, the Chinese used an equality norm more often than an equity norm in distributing resources. The tendency toward equality was eliminated when the subjects' level of collectivism was statistically controlled. However, the tendency toward generosity was not eliminated with this statistical control.

More recently, Leung and Iwawaki (1988) also found that collectivism was related to tendency to use the equality norm.

SOCIAL SUPPORT AND HEALTH

There is evidence that within cultures individuals who are allo-centric (Triandis et al., 1985) receive more social support than individuals who are idiocentric (Triandis et al., 1988). In one study, 26% of Americans reported they felt lonely, which is consistent with findings by Triandis (1972), who found that loneliness was a problem in individualist but not in collectivist cultures. Pilisuk and Parks (1985) review studies indicating that in a 1981 survey 80% of Americans supported the view that "the search for self-fulfillment is a primary concern" (p. 21), but this orientation is not likely to result in receiving much social support when one needs it.

Lack of social support is associated with poor physical and mental health when major negative life events occur (e.g., a person gets fired, there is illness in the family). The wealthy can buy support (they hire companions), which the poor cannot afford. This may explain in part the differential incidence of mental illness across social classes in the United States. Among the poor, even when much social support is available there is poor health.

Many other factors complicate the relationship between collectivism/individualism and social support. First, individualists are more affluent, have more ingroups (Verma, 1985), and often have an orientation that leads to the solution of their problems (e.g., internal locus of control). On the other hand, collectivists set up their societies so that negative life events associated with high competitiveness do not occur, spend more time interacting with their kin, and expect less from life.

The impact of a negative life event also depends on expectations. If it is expected, it makes less of an impact. If fate and similar religiously based mechanisms are used to account for it, the individual may take it to be normal and expected.

Some of the distress in life occurs not because negative life events impinge on the individual, but because they affect others in one's social network. Collectivists, who are more emotionally close to their extended family than individualists, will statistically have more opportunities to become distressed because some negative life event happens to one of their ingroup members. Conversely, individualists should experience less distress, both because they are emotionally detached (Triandis et al., 1988) and because they are affluent and can control negative life events better than collectivists can. This is one possible interpretation of the finding by Gudykunst and Ting-Toomey (1988) that individualists experience less anger than collectivists. Thus the links are by no means simple. Yet the literature reviewed by Triandis et al. (1988), particularly with respect to the lower heart attack rates among Japanese than among Americans, even when diet, cholesterol levels, weight, exercise levels, and other variables are statistically controlled, suggest that collectivists may have some advantages when compared with individualist populations that are equally affluent.

Bond (1988) found that values related to collectivism and individualism are correlated with health indexes such as the incidence of cardiovascular disease and arteriosclerosis. Johnson, Johnson, and Krotee (1986) found that cooperatively oriented athletes were higher in psychological adjustment and health, whereas individualistically oriented athletes were less healthy; however, athletic performance favored the individualists. McDermott (personal communication, 1986) discovered that individualistic high-school students were more likely to be absent from school without excuse, were more likely to be referred to the authorities for disciplinary problems, and had poorer academic achievement than students who were not high on this trait. On the whole there seems a cluster of individualism associated with "naughtiness, creativity, and achievement" and another of collectivism associated with "good adjustment and resistance to stress." However, much more research is needed in this area before we can be sure about the complex relationships.

Also, the impact of a negative life event depends on its duration, intensity, and the extent to which the individual feels able to control it. Thus the complexity of the relationship between collectivism/individualism and mental health is too great for us to be able to say much about it that is definitive at this time. However, it seems clear that the relationship deserves a great deal of research.

Already in studies done in Greece by Georgas and Dragonas (personal communication, 1988), many of the United States findings about the relationship of collectivism/individualism (traditional Greece vs. cities in Greece) and social support, as well as social support and mental health, have been replicated. Specifically, it has been found that frequent contact with parents and relatives is characteristic of collectivists, and collectivism is related to social support.

The more people who are available to provide support, the lower the subjects' level of anxiety. They found that the greater the level of satisfaction with social support the less the stress ($r < -.17$, $p < .01$); the highest levels of stress were observed among collectivists living in individualist environments; the greater satisfaction with social support, the less the frequency of reported psychosomatic symptoms.

INTERGROUP RELATIONS

The earlier discussion of the attributes of collectivism included the observation that collectivists are specially concerned with maintaining the integrity of their ingroups, are more likely to define the self in terms of ingroup memberships, and are more emotionally attached to their ingroups than are individualists. The intensity of identification with the ingroup increases with the extent to which (a) ingroup membership is rewarding (e.g., confers high status, increases the chance of material benefits, makes more resources available to the individual); (b) ingroup attributes are distinctive (e.g., the ingroup is a minority); (c) there is a clear common fate, such as an external threat; (d) there is competition with other groups; (e) the ingroup is mentioned frequently during socialization, as when the country is frequently mentioned in school; (f) the ingroup is small, so that it has a definite character; and (g) the ingroup has clear norms and distinct values.

Collectivism is associated with homogeneity of affect (if ingroup members are sad, one is sad; if joyful, one is joyful), unquestioned acceptance of ingroup norms, and homogeneity of norms, attitudes, and values. Interpersonal relations within the ingroup are seen as an end in themselves; there is the concept of "limited good" (Foster, 1965), according to which if something good happens to an outgroup member it is bad for the ingroup, because "good" is limited and thus resources are always in a zero-sum distribution pattern; and the ingroup is responsible for the actions of its members. This has implications for intergroup relations. Specifically, in collectivism one expects solidarity in action toward other groups. Thus in race relations or relations among economic groups (management and labor, across social classes) there is a strong expectation of joint action. Authorities usually decide what is to be done, and the public must follow without question. Good outcomes for the other group are undesirable, even when they are in no way related to one's own out-comes. Each individual is responsible for the actions of all other in-group members, and the ingroup is responsible for the actions of each individual member. Thus, for instance, Middle Eastern terror-ists relate to Americans in response to American policies in Israel as if each American were the maker of these policies, and they inter-pret the actions of individual Americans, which fit their general ideological framework, as the actions of the United States.

By contrast, individualists are emotionally detached from their ingroups and do not always agree with their policies. They perceive their ingroups as highly heterogeneous. They experience little sense of a common fate with ingroup members. They often have large in-groups, with norms that are loosely imposed, boundaries that are not sharp and clear, and high permeability. Individual behavior is best explained by internal mechanisms rather than ingroup norms, goals, and values. People define themselves by what they do, not by their ingroup memberships. So individualists often find the behav-ior of collectivists in intergroup relations quite "irrational."

These arguments suggest that collectivists may not show some of the phenomena that have been established among individualists, for example, that the outgroup is perceived to be more homoge-neous than the ingroup. This could also be true because collectivists consider agreement within the ingroup of great importance and are likely to view any "good" groups as more homogeneous than "bad" groups. Also, they are likely to be emotionally more attached to their ingroups than are individualists. To check these ideas Triandis, Mc-Cusker, and Hui (submitted) administered two tasks to samples of students at the University of Hawaii (of both collectivist and individ-ualist cultural backgrounds), at the University of Illinois (mostly of individualist cultural background) and at a course given in Beijing, PRC: (1) Rate the perceived homogeneity ("how much agreement you think there is about what people ought to do, what goals people should have, what standards should be used to judge if a behavior is good or bad, among members of the following communities . . .") on a 0 = no agreement, total dissimilarity to 9 = tremendous agree-ment, total similarity. (2) Rate on a 9-point scale the extent to which you see yourself as "different" from these groups. The PRC sample responded to four groups who were residents of Chinese provinces and a sample of countries that included some disliked countries (e.g., Vietnam). The Hawaii samples responded to stimuli that represented the various ingroups and outgroups salient in Hawaii (e.g., Haoles, part-Hawaiians). The Illinois sample responded to several such groups commonly found in Illinois.

Quattrone (1986) has reviewed a substantial body of literature, generated in individualist cultures, indicating that ingroups are perceived to be more heterogeneous than outgroups. In our data, the number of outgroups perceived to be more homogeneous than the ingroups supported Quattrone's generalization in the case of the Illinois sample (11 out of 15 groups were in the expected direction) and the Hawaii sample of individualist background. However, that was not the case with the Hawaiians of collectivist cultural background. The Chinese-Hawaiians saw only one outgroup (the Japanese) as more homogeneous than themselves; the Japanese saw no outgroup as more homogeneous than themselves; the Filipinos saw only one outgroup as more homogeneous (also the Japanese, which may be a veridical perception). In the PRC also, *none* of the outgroups were perceived as more homogeneous than the ingroups. Table 2 shows the means of 39 subjects from the PRC.

Outgroups in the PRC were seen as rather different from the self (5.89), whereas ingroups were seen as rather similar to the self (3.21). The difference in these ratings (2.68) is very similar to the difference obtained from collectivist background subjects in Hawaii (2.72), whereas the individualist background subjects in Hawaii (2.3) and Illinois (2.6) saw slightly smaller differences between themselves and their outgroups as compared with their ingroups. Thus on the whole we found support for the prediction that among collectivists outgroups will be seen both as more heterogeneous than ingroups and as more distant from ingroups; the former is opposite to what occurs among individualists.

Intergroup contact can be desirable or undesirable for intergroup peace, depending on several moderating variables. First, the greater the similarity and opportunity for interaction, the more rewarding is the contact; rewards lead to more contact, and more contact leads to more similarity. Conversely, the greater the dissimilarity the more opportunities for contact will lead to punishment. This will reduce the frequency of contact and increase the dissimilarity. Thus a vicious cycle can operate when the initial level of dissimilarity is high.

Second, when ingroups and outgroups are clearly perceived as distinct, the operation of other variables (e.g., similarity) is made more powerful and significant. Third, when authorities approve of the contact this improves the probability that the contact will be perceived as rewarding. Fourth, when ingroup and outgroup are similar there is a higher probability that each will be able to predict the behavior of the other. Predictability leads to trust; unpredictability leads to distrust. The greater the distrust the greater the chances that the conflict will expand to include new areas of conflict. Also, the greater the level of abstraction of the issue under dispute, the more difficult it is to resolve the conflict. These propositions have received substantial levels of empirical support (e.g., Worchel & Austin, 1986).

Given that individualism is often associated with an emphasis on equality, there is a tendency for individualism to lead to less dissimilarity. Thus the propositions above suggest that individualism

Table 2
Ratings of Homogeneity and Distance from Various Groups

Group	Homogeneity	Difference
Japanese	6.02	4.09
Americans	4.89	4.56
Residents of Shanghai Province	7.07	2.61
West Germans	5.08	5.97
Residents of Shaan Xi Province	6.21	4.00
North Koreans	5.92	5.76
Filipinos	4.46	5.97
South Koreans	4.51	6.49
Tibetans	5.49	5.38
Vietnamese	3.10	7.56
Italians	4.59	6.51
Residents of He Long Jiang Province	6.41	3.15
British	4.59	5.79
Residents of Guang Tong Province	6.23	3.10

Source: Triandis, McCusker, and Hui (submitted).

Note: Means of ratings from 39 people taking a course in Beijing, PRC. Total Agreements = 9; distance, difference, dissimilarity = 9.

will be linked to less punishment in intergroup relations. Conversely, collectivism will lead to more punishment and harmful acts toward the outgroup.

Several additional attributes of individualist and collectivist exchanges are relevant to understanding intergroup relations. First, in individualism exchanges are agreed upon in advance (e.g., if I give you $5, you give me this); in collectivism more ingroup relationships are of a long-term nature, where explicit agreements of tit for tat are not used. Thus, if the situation is such that the exchanges are undetermined as to quantity and quality, timing, and the like, individualists will find the exchanges less satisfying than will collectivists, who are used to such exchanges. This perception may be especially important in the case of the timing of exchanges. Collectivists who deal with ingroup members are used to timings of several months or even years; individualists exchange in very short time frames. Thus, if the exchange requires the time to be extended, individualists will be much less satisfied than collectivists (e.g., note the long time perspectives of the PRC with respect to Hong Kong and Taiwan). On the other hand, when collectivists deal with outgroups they behave like individualists.

Second, individualists tend to exchange resources of equal value. The most characteristic individualist exchange is in the market. Collectivists tend to exchange resources of indeterminate value (e.g., status, love, services) and certainly not of strictly equal value (e.g., a dinner invitation may be exchanged for a letter of recommendation written ten years later). To the extent that intergroup exchanges are of equal value, individualists will be satisfied with the exchanges; they will be less satisfied with exchanges of unequal value than will collectivists. Furthermore, the value of exchanges is likely to differ between members of these types of cultures.

Collectivists exchange with a focus on the long-term relationship. They do not make prior agreements about the exchange and do not sign contracts. It is the sense of trust that develops between ingroup and outgroup that is all-important. For individualists it is the written contract and the specific agreement, rather than the long-term relationship, that are all-important.

Collectivists see all members of the ingroup as a unit. Thus exchanges that benefit one member and not the others are seen as improper, whereas individualists see an exchange in which a person who has contributed much receives much as quite appropriate.

POLITICAL SYSTEMS

Rokeach (1973) identified two interesting patterns of values: one may emphasize much or not at all the value of *equality*, and one can emphasize much or not at all the value of *freedom*. The importance of *freedom* is clearly linked with individualism. Collectivists do not emphasize it nearly as much as individualists do, because they believe that people should not be free to do as they wish, but should behave so as to benefit the collective. The large or small emphasis on *equality* can be observed among both individualists and collectivists. The 2 x 2 = 4 emphases that can be traced to high/low emphasis on *freedom* and *equality* result in four distinct political viewpoints. Political conservatives in the United States (for instance, President Reagan), emphasize *freedom* and do not emphasize equality. For example, content analyses of Reagan's speeches shows that the word *freedom* was used frequently and equality infrequently. In the case of Democrats (e.g., President Johnson) both *freedom* and *equality* were used frequently. In the case of communist leaders the word *equality* is used much and freedom very little (except in the sense of "freedom" from the exploitation of capitalists), and in the case of fascist leaders neither *freedom* nor *equality* is used much at all, whereas other concepts, such as *Lebensraum*, "racial purity," domination of the "incompetent" groups by the competent, and the like are used. In short, both types of totalitarian regimes are more closely linked to collectivism than to democracy.

Bell (1976) notes that individualism is an essential element of Western culture and of modernity: "The fundamental assumption of modernity, the thread that has run through Western Civilization since the 16th Century, is that social unit of society is not the group, the guild, the tribe, the city, but the person" (p. 16). Individualism works well in economics, but not as a philosophy of life. In the early years there was Puritan restraint and the Protestant ethic to emphasize community goals and hard work. Now all that remains is the hedonism and the competition. There is a disjunction between the concept of society and this narrow view of individualism that threatens the society. Substance abuse may be one of the consequences of this disjunction.

We must also examine the extent to which the individualist position fosters acceptance of the status quo in race relations. A case can be made that "the democracies have developed individualism and symbolic responsiveness as a means of diverting and muting the demands of subordinate groups" (Jackman & Muha, 1984, p. 765). Specifically, groups that dominate societies develop ideologies that legitimize and justify the status quo. By emphasizing qualification, self-reliance, and the American dream, males can dominate females, whites can dominate blacks, and the nonpoor can ignore the poor. In fact, the more individualist the person, the more that person perceives current government policies as "favoring the blacks" (Klugel & Smith, 1982). These researchers identified four factors through factor analysis of items from public opinion surveys: (1) structural reasons for poverty (e.g., failures of the social system), (2) personal reasons for poverty (e.g., lack of effort), (3) structural reasons for wealth (e.g., being born to rich parents, pull), and (4) individual reasons for wealth (e.g., talent). Those who emphasized Factor 1 saw little improvement in the position of blacks in the United States; those who emphasized Factor 2 saw considerable improvement in the economic position of blacks. Those who emphasized Factor 1 saw little "reverse discrimination," whereas those who emphasized Factor 2 saw a great deal. In short, the value structures (individualist vs. collectivist) that underlie the perceptions determine the extent to which individuals perceive black progress as "good" or "bad."

These observations are compatible with Sears's (1988) discussion of symbolic racism. He measured this attribute with items such as "Blacks are getting too demanding in their push for equal rights," "Over the years blacks have got more economically than they deserve," and "Blacks have it better than they ever had it before." He found that individualism, as measured by items reflecting self-reliance (e.g., "All people of whatever color have equal opportunity, and it is up to the individual to work hard enough to succeed" [p. 687]), predicted preference for Reagan over Mondale in the 1984 election. Even more important was the attitude toward *equality*. It predicted approval or disapproval of racial policies that aid minorities and voting for Jesse Jackson as well as preferences for Mondale over Reagan. However, Sears concludes (1988, p. 73) that attitudes toward *equality* are more powerful than individualism in predicting symbolic racism.

Hui (personal communication, 1989) proposes that individualists favor equality when dealing with members of their ingroups and tolerate some inequality when dealing with members of their outgroups, whereas collectivists favor extreme equality when dealing with ingroup members of equal status and tolerate considerable inequality when dealing with outgroup members of any status. Since there are in both cases many outgroup members and few ingroup members of equal status, collectivists show much more status consciousness and accept inequality to a greater extent than do individualists. It should be said, also, that individualists support equality of *opportunity*, not of *outcome*.

However, racial attitudes are determined by many historical factors, not least of which is the density of blacks in a particular country. We see the most extreme antiblack attitudes in those countries where blacks are a majority (South Africa) or have substantial presence (the United States) and the least extreme attitudes in countries where there are few blacks (Sweden, France, Finland, the Netherlands, Switzerland, Greece, Austria; see Pettigrew, 1988, p. 27).

Where antiblack feelings are not strong, other outgroups are often important. For example, anti-Semitism is still widely found in Eastern Europe, religion is often the basis of social distance (see Triandis & Triandis, 1960), and social class is a major determinant of intergroup conflict (Triandis, 1967b).

Worldwide it is clear that democracy is associated with individualism (Hofstede, 1980). It is not clear whether this is inevitable. Certainly in collectivist cultures political parties act like ingroups, fighting with other political parties that are seen as outgroups. Little cooperation or tolerance for other parties is allowed. However, this situation is also complicated by the fact that many collectivist countries are also highly ideological and consider the ingroup's truths as *the truth*. That is, there is an unstated, unchallenged assumption that there is such a thing as *truth*, and hence that the group that possesses the truth should run things. Whether the truth is Marxist-Leninist or derives from religion makes little difference. The point is that there is such a thing. In individualist countries each individual has his own truth. Since in many cases it cannot be determined whose truth is valid, we arrive at the conclusion that each person should have one vote. This is a very different conception of reality than one finds in some collectivist countries, where there is no debate about the widely shared truth.

Of course, not all collectivist countries are ideological. For example, China (and East Asia generally) has had little taste for religion, and its current Marxism is more pragmatic than that in the USSR, where the domination of Christianity for a thousand years has had a profound effect on ways of thinking. In the USSR the Communist party is assumed to have the *truth*, and so it makes no sense to tolerate any other party, which by definition does not have it. Voting has to occur within the party. So one can allow some deviations from truth, and even accept the presence of truth 1, truth 2 . . . truth *n*, as long as all these truths can be accommodated within the party. If they cannot be accommodated, one is expelled from the party.

Strengths and Weaknesses of Collectivism and Individualism

A major problem with collectivists is that they hoard information. This is an automatic response, because ingroups and outgroups are "obviously" always in conflict and one must not give the "enemy" any help. This becomes so exaggerated that members of the same corporation do not communicate with corporation members who belong to other ingroups, and thus there is poor coordination in many collectivist companies (Triandis, 1967a). However, this problem is not present when the corporation is the ingroup, as in Japan.

Lack of communication can have serious consequences in the functioning of the political system. For instance, Kaiser (1984, p. 225) tells how Nikita Khrushchev discovered that some Russian navy commanders did not know the USSR has missile-launching planes. They made their plans on the assumption that such missiles did not exist. When Khrushchev questioned their plans, it became clear that other groups in the Russian navy had not communicated to them that such missiles did exist, let alone that the Americans might also have them! Similarly, there is very little cooperation among groups unless it is mandated from the top. Leonid Brezhnev was exasperated with the Soviet bureaucracy for that very reason (Kaiser, 1984, p. 128). The same point was made by Triandis and Vassiliou (1972) concerning Greek traditional cooperation patterns.

On the other hand, the literature reviewed by Triandis et al. (1988) suggested that, other things being equal (e.g., controlling for GNP per capita), collectivism has an advantage in the areas of low crime, suicide, divorce, and child abuse, as well as in mental health.

Interpersonal competition is often counterproductive (Rosenbaum et al., 1980) and can lead to distress and aggression (Gorney & Long, 1980). Palmer (1972) finds individualism related to high competition, concern for status, and violence. People in individualist cultures often experience more conflict within their families than people in collectivist cultures (Katakis, 1978). The greater emphasis on achievement in individualist cultures threatens the ego (Katakis, 1976) and causes insecurity. Insecurity leads to excessive concern about national security and feeds the arms race (Hsu, 1981).

In conclusion, neither extreme collectivism nor extreme individualism seems to be desirable. Although we reject both extremes, we do not yet know how to direct our energies so as to structure a society in the optimal way. Going back to the analogy of collectivism as water and individualism as molecules of ice, we do not yet know how to make sure that those relationships that should be water are not frozen and those that should be ice are frozen. The best guide is provided by Schwartz (1986), who has emphasized that relationships that evolve production and distribution of exchangeable commodities should be regulated by individualist values, while relationships that involve enjoyment and consumption should be governed by collectivist values.

Foa and Foa (1974) focused on six kinds of resources that humans exchange. Collectivists exchange love, status, and services better than individualists do; individualists exchange information, money, and goods better than collectivists do. The problems of collectivists occur when they use their models of exchange when exchanging information, money, or goods—that is, in broad societal actions, as is the case on the level of national governments. The problems of individualists occur when they exchange services, love, and status—in intimate, face-to-face relationships. Better understanding of how these value-cultural patterns affect social behavior and social problems will perhaps help us create better societies that exchange optimally in all social situations.

To attain such a society we will need to refine our conceptions of individualism and collectivism. Specifically, we need to consider two types of individualism: narcissistic individualism and communitarian individualism. In the former only the individual's goals direct behavior; in the latter the individual's goals are integrated with the goals of the community. In the early stages of American individualism, as described by Tocqueville, the latter kind of individualism operated. In recent years, however, the former has become more common.

Similarly, when discussing collectivism it is desirable to distinguish familism, such as described by Banfield (1958), which is inward looking and concerned only with the goals of the family, and communitarian collectivism, which is concerned with the goals of the community defined more broadly. Communitarian collectivism appears similar to Bond's (1988) "social integration" (vs. cultural inwardness). Pareek (1968) provided a formula for development that suggests that the communitarian forms of individualism and collectivism are required for development. He suggested that development depends on need for achievement (linked to individualism and competition) times the need for extension (linked to concern for the broader community) minus the need for affiliation (linked to narrow interpersonal concerns, such as occur in the family). A study by Gorney and Long (1980), though using different terminology, found support for Pareek's notions. They had the ethnographies of 58 cultures rated by 10 cultural experts on the dimensions of competition within the culture (related to individualism), interpersonal attachment—that is, passionate attachment to others (related to affiliation)—amount of aggression, and the extent of "synergy," the actions of individuals simultaneously benefiting society (an idea linked to Pareek's need for extension and to communitarianism, as outlined above). They found social development was proportional to competition and interpersonal attachment, but that the most development occurred where there was high competition (need for achievement), high synergy (need for extension), and low interpersonal intensity (need affiliation), just as Pareek specified. In other words, development occurs when communitarian individualism is high.

Conclusion

It seems clear from the discussion above that both narcissistic individualism and familism are detrimental to societal development; on the other hand, communitarian individualism should be most desirable if the criterion is economic development. If the criteria we wish to maximize are physical and mental health and those we wish to minimize are divorce rates, crime rates, and the like, then communitarian collectivism has much to recommend it. As societies evolve and become affluent, mobile, and the like, a shift from collectivism to individualism is inevitable. However, by emphasizing the communitarian aspects of these constructs we can maintain healthy cultural change.

It is unlikely that we can simultaneously maximize all desirable criteria and minimize all undesirable ones. It will still be the case that for family stability and for small-scale ingroups collectivism will have the advantage and for innovation and for large-scale ingroups, such as a state, individualism will have the advantage. In the final analysis one's evaluation of the constructs will depend on whether one has more collectivist or individualist values.

NOTES

1. The theoretical analysis provided by Deutsch (1949) discussed goals in terms of their being positively correlated (promotive interdependence), negatively correlated (contrient interdependence), and uncorrelated (no interdependence). If the structure of goals found most often in a society or a group is promotive for most individuals, one would have an "ideal" collectivist culture. Similarly, if the structure is uncorrelated one would have "ideal individualism." If a negatively correlated structure is found, then one has the "war of all against all" that was described by Hobbes (1651/1904).

The emphasis on cooperation, competition, and individualism is found in the writing of many authors. For example, Johnson and Johnson (1983) emphasized that classrooms can be organized according to these three principles. One can reward everyone when the group learns, one can use a competitive grading system, or one can make each person's rewards completely independent of the performance of others (individualism).

2. The factors were rotated orthogonally. An oblique rotation may have given a different result.

3. The contrast between Sparta and Athens is just about as great as that between East and West in modern times. There were also Korynth, Argos, Thebes, and Korcyra, and each island had a somewhat different viewpoint. If one could not get along in one city, one could migrate to another. Colonies were established all over the

Mediterranean. In such a complex intellectual environment, individualism did emerge for the first time.

4. The higher one's status, the more gifts one gives. That can lead to financial ruin.

5. Triandis et al. (1988) found that the meaning of self-reliance is different in collectivist and individualist cultures. In collectivist cultures people were found to be very high in self-reliance, but their concern was not to be a burden on their ingroup. In individualist cultures people were also high in self-reliance, but their concern was to be independent and able to "do their own thing." Another difference was that in individualist countries self-reliance was a very important idea. The attitude items that represented it loaded on the first factor in most factor analyses (this factor accounted for most of the variance of the responses to the attitude items). In the collectivist cultures the items that were related to self-reliance loaded on the second or third factor, suggesting that they were not the most important aspects of the self structure.

6. Tajfel (1982) has shown that minimum similarity is sufficient for a group to be perceived as a group. Similarly, minimum common fate (e.g., being in an elevator that stopped between floors), minimum stability, and minimum anonymity (e.g., five people who are anonymous in a room where the others are known) can result in the perception of a "group." Over time groups interact, developing common goals, norms, and values, and members become more similar. Thus, conceptually, we can think of a dimension from minimal to maximal group, with Tajfel providing a minimal group example and a small theocratic tribe providing an example of maximal groupness.

7. Following these studies a questionnaire that included the best items of the previous studies was administered to samples of about 100 men and 100 women students in Hong Kong, Indonesia, India, Greece, France, the Netherlands, Chile, Costa Rica, and several sites in the United States (Triandis et al., 1986). Family Integrity was the most important discriminant function, and it correlated .73 with Hofstede's (1980) individualism/collectivism scores. That was the only function that showed significant relationship with Hofstede's scores. However, the other factors (Interdependence and Sociability, Self-Reliance, and Separation from Ingroups) are also meaningfully related to the constructs. In general European and North American samples are low on Family Integrity, high on Interdepen-

dence and Sociability, high on Self-Reliance, and high on Separation from Ingroups. Samples from East Asia, South Asia, and Latin America are generally high on Family Integrity, moderately high on Interdependence and Sociability, moderately high on Self-Reliance, and low on Separation from Ingroups. In short, the Family Integrity and the Separation from Ingroups factors discriminate across the cultural areas. However, within cultures the other two factors are very important. They seem to contrast the allocentrics and the idiocentrics of each culture.

Hui (1984, 1988) emphasized that collectivists are more or less collectivist, depending on the ingroup. Some are family, some co-worker, some neighbor, and some country collectivists. Of course, the patriot is a country collectivist. It is possible for a person to be high in collectivism in one relationship and low in others. In fact, extreme family collectivism is often related to neglect of all other collectives. Thus Banfield (1958) found in southern Italy that there was extreme attachment to the family but very little support of community projects. Any action that did not benefit the family directly was opposed.

8. The empirical findings can be summarized as follows:

a. Szalay and Inn (1988) asked for free associations with the word "me" (*yo* in Spanish). The most frequent associations of me for mainstream Americans in both New York and Los Angeles were I, myself and good, loving, happy. For Hispanics the *I, myself* category (I, myself, self, my, mine, ego) was elicited much *less* frequently in response to me, but the *good, loving, happy* category occurred as frequently as for the mainstream. The category *love and friendship* (like, understand, friend, love, help, care, share), on the other hand, which is a relational version of "loving" and "good," occurred *more* frequently among Hispanics than among the mainstream. Thus the self-concepts of the two groups have common elements (person attributes such as good, loving, intelligent, kind, etc.) and unique elements, with the mainstream emphasizing individuality and the Hispanics emphasizing relationship.

b. When Hispanic high-school students were asked whether they might join the navy, they expressed more concern that they would miss their families, and would be unable to meet their family obligations, if they did join the navy, than comparable samples of mainstream young adults (Triandis, 1981).

c. Intense family attachment was found among Hispanics in a

study of Hispanics who visited navy recruiting stations (Rojas, 1981). A navy career was often considered incompatible with family obligations.

d. Hispanics were found to be more willing than mainstream navy recruits to sacrifice themselves in order to attend family celebrations involving second- and third-degree relatives (Triandis, Marin, Betancourt, Lisansky, & Chang, 1982). This suggests a more extended family among Hispanics, which is compatible with collectivism (see above) and suggests familism. Further confidence in the results was obtained when it was found that the more acculturated Hispanics showed less familism (Triandis, Marin, Betancourt, & Chang, 1982).

e. Consistent with Shweder and Bourne's (1982) argument that in collectivist cultures people perceive the self as a bundle of roles rather than as a bundle of personal attributes was the finding that Hispanics have difficulty distinguishing the person from the role (Rojas, 1981).

f. Hispanics were found to experience an exceptionally strong pull toward their families and some ambivalence toward work environments (Triandis, Marin, Hui, Lisansky, & Ottati, 1984).

g. Hispanics expressed avoidance of interpersonal competition much more than mainstream recruits (Triandis, Ottati, & Marin, 1982). Consistent with that, similar samples of Hispanics emphasized personal cooperation and help more often than mainstream subjects (Ross, Triandis, Chang, & Marin, 1982).

h. Hispanics expect positive behaviors in positive interpersonal situations (e.g., in a cooperative relationship) to a *greater* degree than do mainstream subjects; Hispanics expect negative behavior in negative interpersonal situations (e.g., when someone criticizes another) to a *lesser* extent than do mainstream subjects (Triandis, Marin, Lisansky, & Betancourt, 1984). Furthermore, Hispanics expect higher probabilities of positive and lower probabilities of negative behaviors than do mainstream subjects in most role relationships (Triandis, Marin, Lisansky, & Betancourt, 1984).

i. The values of Hispanics are more collectivist: they emphasize being *sensitive, loyal, respected, dutiful, gracious,* and *conforming.* Mainstream subject values tend to be more individualist: they emphasize the elements *honest* and *moderate* (Triandis, Kashima, Lisansky, and Marin, 1982).

j. Hispanics have been found to be more tolerant than mainstream navy recruits of supervisors who are not very well organized, as long as they provide much social support and are highly considerate (Triandis, Hui, Lisansky, Ottati, Marin, & Betancourt, 1982).

An interesting difference between Hispanics and non-Hispanics, reflecting the difference between collectivism and individualism was reported by Marin, Marin, Otero-Sabogal, Sabogal, and Perez-Stable (1987). They studied the attitudes of 263 Hispanics and 150 white non-Hispanics toward smoking. They found that Hispanics were more concerned than non-Hispanics that smoking affected the health of others, set a bad example for their children, and harmed their children's health. On the other hand, non-Hispanics were more concerned than Hispanics about their personal suffering, such as withdrawal effects from cigarettes and saw quitting as especially hard to do.

Findings obtained with United States Hispanics are found in an even stronger form among a variety of Latin Americans (e.g., Diaz-Guerrero, 1984; Holtzman et al., 1975, concerning Mexicans; Gruenfeld, Weissenberg & Loh, 1973, among Peruvians; and Espinel, 1982, concerning all Latin Americans).

9. Among the contrasting patterns that have been identified are the following. Collectivists define themselves in terms of social categories to a greater extent than individualists do (e.g., Morsbach, 1980). In a study by Triandis, McCusker, and Hui (submitted), when asked to complete 20 sentences that start with "I am . . . ," about 29% of the answers referred to a social category among Hawaiian Americans of East Asian background, while only about 20% of the answers had a social category reference among Hawaiian Americans of North American or European origin. European and North American samples averaged 15% to 19%, while samples from the People's Republic of China averaged 52%.

"Who the other is" dominates the social perception of collectivists; "what the other does" dominates the perceptions of individualists. Collectivists have few ingroups and are strongly attached to them; individualists have many ingroups and are somewhat emotionally detached from them. Ingroups "control" a wide range of behaviors among collectivists but only a narrow range among individualists (e.g., pay $5 a year and meet once a month). Conformity to ingroup authorities is often unquestioned among collectivists but is calculated among individualists. Privacy is linked to individualism. Collectivists often use a language that can be understood only by the ingroup, and they use "context" more than content in their communications. Conversely, individualists depend on context very little and tend to be explicit when communicating. Collectivists value harmony within the ingroup, politeness, and security. Individualists value pragmatism, human rights, freedom, competence, enjoyment, and pleasure (Schwartz & Bilsky, 1987). Some collectivists stress filial piety, loyalty to superiors, observation of rites, ordering relationships by status, benevolent authority, reciprocity, shame, protecting face, and the like (Chinese Cultural Connection, 1987). Horizontal relationships (e.g., spouse-spouse, friend-friend) more frequently take precedence over vertical relationships (e.g., parent-child, boss-subordinate) when there is conflict between them in individualist than in collectivist cultures. Conversely, when there is such a conflict, collectivists are likely to side with the vertical rather than the horizontal relationship.

Feather (1986) found happiness to be a more important value in individualist than in collectivist cultures. Diaz-Guerrero (1984) emphasized the importance of cooperation, fatalism, pessimism, and family centeredness among collectivists. Collectivists are high in the needs for affiliation, succor, abasement, and nurture (Hui & Villareal, 1987); they are inclined toward nurture, acquiescence, and dependency and are high in both superordination and subordination, particularly when they are also high on the F-Scale (Yang, 1970). By contrast, individualists are high in competition (Diaz-Guerrero, 1984), autonomy, and self-reliance (Hui & Villareal, 1989).

10. Studies reviewed by Triandis et al. (1988) suggest that collectivism is associated with low rates of heart attack per capita, high rates of social support when unpleasant life events occur, but also poor functioning of the society in the political realm. It is as if there is a trade-off between the quality of private and public life.

A most important American value is *freedom*. This value is ranked third, after *peace* and *family security*, by United States samples (Rokeach, 1973). It occurs very frequently in the speeches of politicians (Remember Barry Goldwater's acceptance of the presidential nomination?), academics, the press, and so on. It can be seen in a number of institutional patterns that distinguish the United States

from European countries, individualism is also high but some of the institutions were established when the countries were collectivist. It is manifested in economics, where there is very little central planning, in education (each school district establishing its own standards), in public behavior (e.g., very little punishment for littering, relative to most European countries), in freedom of the press (more extreme than in most European countries), in aesthetics (any style is socially acceptable), and even in the use of language (people are free to define terms as they wish; there is no French Academy to define words). The large number of homeless people is tolerated because they are "free" to do as they wish. Blacks are expected to share in the American dream, and are assumed to be "free" to do so (while the cultural influences of slavery are ignored, because most people do not understand how pervasive and long-term cultural influences are).

Americans find it difficult to believe that some people are made uncomfortable by too much freedom. Fromm's *Escape from Freedom*, or the return of some former Soviets to the USSR because they could not cope with so much freedom, tells us that even a good thing can be too much for some people under some conditions.

The linking of individualism with selfishness and narcissism, reflected in such popular books as *The Art of Being Selfish, How to Be Your Own Best Friend, Looking Out for Number One*, has raised questions about the desirability of extreme forms of individualism. Some (e.g., Kanfer, 1979) have attempted to find a cultural pattern that will preserve the desirable features of individualism and suppress the undesirable ones. Both the defenders of individualism (e.g., Waterman, 1981) and its attackers (e.g., Hogan, 1975; Lasch, 1978; Sampson, 1977; and Smith, 1978) have debated what elements are essential for the definition of the construct.

However, though philosophical analyses are interesting, it seems to me far more useful to examine the co-occurrence of elements in real data. It is in this specific realm that cross-cultural studies have made their major contribution. They tell us that ideas such as *self-reliance* are not the defining attributes of individualism. The defining attributes are *distance from ingroups, emotional detachment*, and *competition*. Conversely, *conformity* is not the defining aspect of collectivism, but *family integrity*, keeping the ingroup in "good health," and *solidarity*.

An examination of the way the various elements that enter the constructs are interrelated in various cultural contexts is especially instructive. Triandis et al. (submitted) examined the factor structures among items that are relevant to these constructs in three collectivist cultures (Indonesia, India, People's Republic of China) and two individualist cultures (United States and France). They found that subjects in collectivist countries pay more attention to the views of others than subjects in individualist countries, but that all over the world university student samples report not paying attention to the views of others. Thus, what we have is a case of extreme nonattention among the individualists and moderate nonattention among the collectivists. *Self-reliance, sociability, concern for the nuclear family,* and *interdependence with relatives* did *not* discriminate the collectivist from the individualist cultures. However, other dimensions did discriminate. Specifically, collectivists show relatively *small distances* and *little emotional detachment from their relatives, broad family concerns,* and more emphasis on *family integrity* and on *cooperation* than individualists do. Thus the defining attributes of collectivism appear to be *relative moderation in not paying attention to the views of others, little emotional detachment from others, broad concerns for family,* and *greater tendency toward cooperation.* Conversely, the defining attributes of individualism seem to be *much emotional detachment from others, extreme lack of attention to the views of others, relatively little concern for family and relatives,* and *tendency toward competition.*

11. *Other observations.* People walk more in Greece than in the United States. During the 100 minutes of my observations in each site, I observed 842 Greek pedestrians versus 137 United States pedestrians, 343 Greek car riders versus 705 American car riders. In sum, in about an equal number of observations, 1,185 Greeks and 842 Americans, the majority of Greeks walked (71%) and the majority of the Americans rode (84%).

The density of pedestrians in the pedestrian mall was greater in Greece. In a 10-minute period at about the same time of day, on an equivalent corner (Lincoln Square mall in Urbana, corner of Broadway and Green), I saw 94 people in Urbana (69 alone and 25 together, a ratio of 2.76) and 280 people (18 alone and 94 together) in Kozane, or a ratio of 1.97. That difference (2.8 vs. 2) in ratios may suggest more sociability in Greece, but I have no way of getting an error of measurement short of doing this work ten times or more.

An obvious difference that looks very promising is the *number* of people in the group. I did repeated observations at 8:00 P.M. in Kozane. There was a reliable tendency for groups to form according to sex and age. There were some young groups (age 15 to 25) and some old groups (over 60). (In other words, middle-aged people do not socialize in the public squares.) The typical distribution was young = 15 men, 3 women; old = 5 men, 1 woman. The size of these groups differed from 3 to 8, but they were *mostly* on the high side (6, 7, 8). All those observations were made in the main square of Kozane.

There is an interesting cultural difference. Those less than 18 years old are by law not allowed into a *coffeehouse* in Kozane (because there is gambling in those places), much as those of that age are not allowed in *bars* in Urbana. Coffeehouses are full of males in Kozane, and it is difficult to see that the alone/together measure means anything there. I also gave up on restaurants. Most of those eating at restaurants in Kozane were bachelors, civil servants, and the like, away from home. They ate alone. Most of my observations of randomly selected restaurants in Urbana showed people eating together. The A/T ratio is 0.375 in Urbana, a reversal of expectations.

Similarly, movie attendance was not useful, because the A/T ratio reflects the *kind* of movie it is. The Greeks go alone to sex films, but they go together to family films. The A/T ration is 0.29 in Urbana, but I suspect a similar sensitivity to the type of movie is applicable. It does not seem a useful index.

The sensitivity of the A/T ratio to other variables also occurs for cars and pedestrians. Although this is at first glance undesirable, it may turn out to be a useful feature. Here is what I observed:

a. In a location that had an A/T ratio of 7.7 in the *morning* for pedestrians in Kozane, in the *evening* I observed a ratio of 0.5. For cars the same location went from 2.1 to 0.65. Both indexes, then, show greater "sociability" in the evening.

b. The indexes of 0.5 and 0.65 just mentioned were not observed when I went to the same place at the same time next day. The indexes then were 0.95 and 1.5, and 15 minutes later they were 0.08 and 1.25. Thus this index shows stability over 15 minutes, but not over 24 hours. It seems to me that the 0.65 and 0.5 were atypical. Also, people looked much better dressed that day, as if they were going to a wedding or some other event. The second day of observations seemed more "normal." In any case, the large change from morning (say 7.7) to evening (say 1.5) is suggestive.

At the promenade, at 8:00 p.m. in Kozane, the ratio was 0.71, not that different from the "unusual day." The location of the promenade during the *day's* observations gave a ratio of 1.98. I repeated the observations next day. The promenade in the *evening* ratio was 0.50.

In short, we can measure sociability all right, but this is only partially related to collectivism.

c. I also did some observations in Alexandroupolis (in Greece, next to Turkey). It is also a city of 35,000 people.

I sat at a central location and observed that the A/T ratios for cars and pedestrians were 1.5 and 1.0, respectively.

The interesting thing is that the street becomes a pedestrian mall at 8:00 p.m. A policeman went by, calling on the motorists to leave.

So here are the observations over time:

In Cars

Time	Ratio	
7:40	1.50	($n=30$)
8:00	1.50	($n=5$)
8:25	1.00	*($n=1$)

*(one car, driving very slowly, policeman in hot pursuit to chase him out)

Pedestrians

Time	Ratio	
7:40	1.00	($n=45$)
8:00	0.87	($n=73$)
8:25	0.51	($n=131$)

The street that was available for cars at 8:40 p.m. had 32 alone and 20 together at 8:40 p.m., or a ratio of 1.6. So it seems the same traffic went to the other street (parallel to the pedestrian mall).

12. Food accumulation allows specialization of function. Not everyone has to be a farmer. The greater the specialization, the greater the complexity of the culture. As complexity increases one can find more conflict among the norms of various groups. Migration to other places is one way to reduce conflict, but migration has the effect of weakening the control of the ingroup. Thus we see individualism in those settings in which people faced a complex environment and where some population movements were probable. In England, primogeniture meant that most of the family moved away from the father's land, which was inherited by the oldest son. Such moves make individualism more likely.

Finding one's fortune in other places, including cities, resulted in more affluence, and affluence, as we saw above, results in more individualism. Financial independence means freedom to do one's own thing. But those who were artists, scientists, or merchants in the cities found that in some cases their own thing also brought more income. They experimented with new activities, and some of these activities brought affluence. The greater the affluence, the more people became free from their ingroups and the more they experimented with new ways of making money.

As people became more and more independent of their ingroups, they became emotionally detached from them and began competing as individuals rather than as groups. Competition in some cases resulted in innovations, and some of the innovations were successful, leading to more affluence. It is only in the middle of the 20th century that people have realized excessive competition is dysfunctional. Drug abuse, crime, and poor mental health may well be linked to excesses in competition in particular cultures. Some people "dropped out," joined communes, formed cooperatives.

In some cases, as in Greece, the shift from collectivism to individualism occurred in the cities between 1963 and 1988 (when we have measurements). By studying samples from the rural districts and islands, where collectivism is still high, from among the newcomers in large cities, where it is much lower, and from among the old-timers (more than 20 years in the city) in the cities where high levels of individualism have already been found (see Georgas, 1989; Katakis, 1976, 1978), we can obtain the whole transition from collectivism to individualism in one data set. Similarly, as samples of Hispanics become acculturated to the mainstream American culture we see a marked drop in collectivism (Sabogal, Marin, Otero-Sabogal, Marin, & Perez-Stable, 1987).

From the discussion above it is easy to understand the correlation between individualism, as measured by Hofstede (1980), and gross national product per capita. Depending on what GNP per capita data one uses, one obtains correlations from .72 to .87, when the N is 40–50 countries. The correlation is lower with 1980 data than with 1970 data because of the recent improvement in the status of Japan, a relatively collectivist country, and the large devaluation of the United States dollar.

I have argued already that cultural complexity is a determinant of individualism. The more complex the culture, the more an individual has to make choices—what ingroups to belong to and how much effort to invest in each. Thus simple societies, such as the early agriculturalists of China, could control the behavior of their members in ways that were impossible in more complex societies, such as the Roman Empire or the China of the early 20th century. Complexity is also greater in urban than in rural environments, and greater in open frontier situations, such as the American West, than in static, enclosed situations such as Swiss cantons of the 16th century. Mohan and Sharma (1985) found more individualism in urban than in rural samples; it is also higher in cultures where education levels are higher. Inkeles and Smith (1974) showed that modernity is related to education.

Cultural complexity has been found to be related to linguistic factors. Bernstein (1971) has argued that the upper classes use more complex, elaborate linguistic codes than the lower classes. It is also related to musical patterns (e.g., Lomax, 1968). Billings (1987) points out that individualism is linked to more complexity in language and song styles even in two relatively simple Melanesian societies. The Tikana are collectivists and rely on simple, repetitive forms, with few words and simple songs; the Lavongai, who tend toward individualism, shout out their discoveries to their fellows "in spontaneously composed forms and many words which other individuals nearby may, or may not, apprehend" (p. 496).

Changes in affluence are related to changes from collectivism to individualism. Empirical support can be found in a study by Herzog and Shapira (1986). They examined 4,131 entries in 130 autograph books, written by 12- to 14-year-olds during the period 1925 to 1980.

Of course that 55-year period is characterized by increased afflu-ence, particularly in the 1960s. They found an increase of individualist themes and a corresponding decrease in collectivist themes.

Taiwan has undergone substantial changes toward affluence in recent years. Corresponding to these changes, Hwang (1982) shows shifts away from conforming, self-restraint, humility, and a group orientation, and toward gender equality, internal locus of control, future orientation, tolerance for differences, and emphasis on action and achievement.

Social mobility is also linked to individualism, and men have somewhat more individualist attributes than women do (Eagly, 1987). Using data from the National Longitudinal Survey of Young Men and Women, Waite, Goldscheider, and Witsberger (1986) found that living away from home increases individualism. In short, several demographic attributes influence a person's position on the collectivism/individualism continuum.

Simple cultures have few ingroups and few ingroup goals; indi-viduals also have simple and limited goals. Thus the ingroup/person overlap in goals can be substantial (e.g., to survive, have enough food, have a good house). As societies become more complex ingroup and individual goals diverge, for many reasons, including the increased availability of goals. Individuals may want to take trips, acquire cars that seat only one or two passengers, learn things that others do not know, and so on, all of which are clearly individual rather than group goals. The nature of goals changes, as does their number.

Ingroup and personal goals are more likely to overlap when in-group members are similar. In individualist cultures ingroups are large (e.g., the nation) and obviously heterogeneous, so overlap is small. Also, when interdependence is high, goal overlap is high. But individualist cultures have members who are less interdependent and more self-reliant.

Goal overlap is more likely when there is common fate, when in-group authorities reward the internalization of ingroup norms, when "success" is defined by the ingroup rather than by personal conceptions, and when there are few ingroups (e.g., survivors on a desert island). It is also likely when population density is high, so that it is more functional to obey ingroup norms than to do one's own thing, which may lead to conflict; when resources are limited and survival is more probable if they are shared; when survival depends on unpredictable events (e.g., good weather); and when conformity to ingroup authorities is rewarding. The last is most likely when ingroup authorities control many resources, such as food or information, can defend against enemies, or can provide status.

By contrast, lack of overlap of ingroup/personal goals is likely when there is great affluence, when children are exposed to diverse information in socialization, when people have many diverse experiences (e.g., travel to foreign countries), and when there are many potential ingroups (high societal complexity).

Collectivism also involves control by the ingroup of more areas of social life than individualism. For example, the collective in China decides a wide range of matters, from one's education to the kind of medical care one will receive, where one is to live, how many children one can have, and so on.

When the ingroup is small (e.g., the nuclear family) treatment of the individual can be very personalized. That leads to more individualism. The nuclear family is linked to individualism via circular causation: the more individualist the culture, the more likely it is to limit the size of the family; the more the family size is limited, the more individualist the offspring. Individualists who grow up in collectivist cultures often are not accepted by the larger society. Current family policy in China is leading the one-child family toward individualism, but the attributes of the individualist child are perceived by the Chinese as "maladaptive."

Migrations and social mobility uproot the individual from the ingroup, so one can expect greater individualism among immigrant populations. Thus it is not surprising that the United States is the most individualist country in Hofstede's survey. It is populated by former immigrants, has open frontiers, is influenced by Protestantism, and has much social mobility. The population is largely urban and of better than average education.

The kind of identity that is found in a population closely reflects these patterns, from the protoindividualism of the food-gathering societies to the collectivism of the agricultural to the neoindividualism of the mercantile/industrial societies. One can guess that the identity of hunters was linked to individual attributes. But later identity, of agriculturalists, was linked to where one was born, one's family, marital family connections, occupation, social class, gender, age, and religion. Each of these demographic attributes specified patterns of behavior, and the individual's behavior was a kind of resolution of the conflicts across these role profiles. In a well-integrated society, the roles derived from these identities were more or less consistent. But as societies became more complex, some of the roles became inconsistent. One way for the individual to avoid role conflict is to reduce the importance of the role senders who are disagreeing among themselves. So the individual "escapes" from group influences and determines a course of action that maximizes self-interest.

As individualism increased rapidly in Europe after the 16th century, the importance of demographic attributes as determinants of social behavior was reduced. It was no longer the case that women acted one way and men a different way, that Catholics acted one way and Protestants another, and so on. People of any age could act young or old. Women could act like men, and men could act like women. The demographic attributes became trivial in their importance as determinants of identity (Baumeister, 1986). The self changed from a collective self, where a person was defined in terms of demographic attributes, to a personal self, where one was defined in terms of personality traits.

REFERENCES

Adamopoulos, J., & Bontempo, R. (1986). Diachronic universals in interpersonal structures. *Journal of Cross Cultural Psychology, 17*, 169–189.
Adelman, I., & Morris, C. T. (1967). *Society, political and economic development: A quantitative approach.* Baltimore: Johns Hopkins University Press.
Argyle, M., Henderson, M., Bond, M., Iizuka, Y., & Contarello, A. (1986). Cross-cultural variations in relationships rules. *International Journal of Psychology, 21*, 287–315.
Atsumi, R. (1980). Patterns of personal relationships: A key to understanding Japanese thought and behavior. *Social Analysis, 5–6*, 63–78.
Bakan, D. (1966). *The duality of human existence.* Chicago: Rand McNally.
Banfield, E. (1958). *The moral basis of a backward society.* Glencoe, IL: Free Press.
Barry, H. (1980). Description and uses of the Human Relations Area Files. In H. C. Triandis & J. W. Berry (Eds.), *Handbook of cross-cultural psychology* (Vol. 2, pp. 445–478). Boston: Allyn and Bacon.
Barry, H., Child, I., & Bacon, M. (1959). Relation of child training to subsistence economy. *American Anthropologist, 61*, 51–63.

Baumeister, R. F. (1986). *Identity: Cultural change and the struggle for self*. New York: Oxford University Press.

Bell, D. (1976). *The cultural contradictions of capitalism*. New York: Basic Books.

Bell, D. (1987). The world and the United States in 2013. *Daedalus, 116*, 1–31.

Bellah, R. N., Madsen, R., Sullivan, W. M., Swindler, A., & Tipton, S. M. (1985). *Habits of the heart: Individualism and commitment in American life*. Berkeley: University of California Press.

Bernstein, B. (1971). *Class, codes and control*. London: Routledge and Kegan Paul.

Berry, J. W. (1979). A cultural ecology of social behavior. In L. Berkowitz (Ed.), *Advances in experimental social psychology* (Vol. 12, pp. 177–207). New York: Academic Press.

Billings, D. K. (1987). Expressive style and culture: Individualism and group orientation contrasted. *Language Science, 16*, 475–497.

Blumberg, L., & Winch, R. F. (1972). Societal complexity and familial complexity: Evidence for the curvilinear hypothesis. *American Journal of Sociology, 77*, 896–920.

Bochner, S. (1980). Unobtrusive methods in cross-cultural experimentation. In H. C. Triandis & J. W. Berry (Eds.), *Handbook of cross-cultural psychology*, (Vol. 2, pp. 319–388). Boston: Allyn and Bacon.

Bond M. (1988). Invitation to a wedding: Chinese values and global economic growth. In D. Sinha & H. S. R. Kao (Eds.), *Social values and development* (pp. 197–209). New Delhi: Sage India.

Bond, M. (in press). Finding universal dimensions of individual variation in multi-cultural studies of values: The Rokeach and Chinese Value Surveys. *Journal of Personality and Social Psychology*.

Bond, M., & Forgas, J. P. (1984). Linking person perception to behavioral intentions across cultures: The role of cultural collectivism. *Journal of Cross Cultural Psychology, 15*, 337–352.

Bond, M., Leung, K., & Wan, K. C. (1982). How does cultural collectivism operate? *Journal of Cross Cultural Psychology, 13*, 186–200.

Bond, M., Wan, K., Leung, K., & Giacalone, R. A. (1985). How are responses to verbal insult related to cultural collectivism and power distance? *Journal of Cross Cultural Psychology, 16*, 111–127.

Boyd, R., & Richardson, P. J. (1985). *Culture and the evolutionary process*. Chicago: University of Chicago Press.

Brodbar, N., & Jay, Y. (1986). Divorce and group commitment: The case of the Jews. *Journal of Marriage and the Family, 48*, 329–340.

Brown, E. D., & Secrest, L. (1980). Experiments in cross-cultural research. H. C. Triandis & J. W. Berry (Eds.), *Handbook of cross-cultural psychology*. (Vol. 2, pp. 297–318). Boston: Allyn and Bacon.

Buss, David M., et al. (1990). International preferences in selecting mates: *A study of 37 cultures. Journal of Cross Cultural Psychology, 21*, 5–47.

Campbell, D. T. (1964). Distinguishing differences of perception from failures of communication in cross-cultural studies. In F. S. C. Northrop &

H. H. Livingston (Eds.), *Cross-cultural understanding*: Epistemology in anthropology. New York: Harper and Row.

Campbell, D. T. (1983). The two distinct routes beyond kin selection to ultrasociality: Implications for the humanities and social sciences. In D. Bridgman (Ed.), *The nature of prosocial development*: Theories and strategies (pp. 11–41). New York Academic Press.

Campbell, D. T. (1986). Science's social system of validity-enhancing collective belief change and the problems of the social sciences. In D. W. Fiske & R. A. Shweder (Eds.), *Metatheory in social science*. Chicago: University of Chicago Press.

Centre National de la Recherche Scientifique. (1973). *La notion de personne en Afrique noire*. Publication No. 544. Paris: Editions du Centre National de la Recherche Scientifique.

Chency, D., Seyforth, R., & Smuts, B. (1986). Social relationships and social cognition in nonhuman primates. *Science, 234*, 1361–1366.

Chinese Cultural Connection. (1987). Chinese values and the search for a culture-free dimension of culture. *Journal of Cross Cultural Psychology, 18*, 143–164.

Church, T. A. (1987). Personality research in a non-Western culture: The Philippines. *Psychological Bulletin, 102*, 272–292.

Ciborowski, T. (1980). The role of context, skill, and transfer in cross-cultural experimentation. In H. C. Triandis & J. W. Berry (Eds.), *Handbook of cross-cultural psychology* (Vol. 2, pp. 279–296). Boston: Allyn and Bacon.

Clark, M., Ouellette, R., Powell, M. C., & Milberg, S. (1987). Recipient's mood, relationship type and helping. *Journal of Personality and Social Psychology, 53*, 94–103.

Crandall, J. E. (1980). Adler's concept of social interest: Theory, measurement and implications for adjustment. *Journal of Personality and Social Psychology, 39*, 481–495.

Davidson, A. E., Jaccard, J. J., Triandis, H. C., Morales, M. L., & Diaz-Guerrero, R. (1976). Cross-cultural model testing: Toward a solution of the etic-emic dilemma. *International Journal of Psychology, 11*, 1–13.

Deutsch, M. (1949). An experimental study of the effects of cooperation and competition upon group process. *Human Relations, 2*, 199–232.

Diaz-Guerrero, R. (1979). The development of coping style. *Human Development, 22*, 320–331.

Diaz-Guerrero, R. (1984). La psicología de los Mexicanos: Un paradigma. *Revista Mexicana de Psicología, 1*, 95–104.

Dion, K. L., & Dion, K. K. (1988). Romantic love: Individual and cultural perspectives. In R. J. Sternberg & M. L. Barnes (Eds.), *The psychology of love*. New Haven: Yale University Press.

Doi, T. (1986). *The anatomy of conformity: The individual versus society*. Tokyo: Kodansha.

Doumanis, M. (1983). *Mothering in Greece: From collectivism to individualism*. New York: Academic Press.

Eagly, A. H. (1987). *Sex differences in social behavior: A social-role interpretation*. Hillsdale, NJ: Erlbaum.

Espinel, N. A. (1982). Criterios y valores de la cultura Anglo-Saxo-Americana y de la cultura Latina: Sus implicaciones para la psicología transcultural. *Revista Latinoamericana de Psicología, 14*, 63–79.

Espinoza, J. A., & Garza, R. T. (1985). Social group salience and interethnic cooperation. *Journal of Experimental Social Psychology, 21*, 697–715.

Evans-Pritchard, E. E. (1940). *The Nuer*. London: Oxford University Press.

Feather, N. T. (1986). Value systems across cultures: Australia and China. *International Journal of Psychology, 21*, 697–715.

Fiske, D. (1986). Specificity of method and knowledge in social science. In D. Fiske & R. Shweder (Eds.), *Metatheory in social science* (pp. 61–82). Chicago: University of Chicago Press.

Foa, U., & Foa, E. (1974). *Societal structures of the mind*. Springfield, IL: Thomas.

Forgas, J. P., & Bond, M. H. (1985). Cultural influences on the perception of interaction episodes. *Personality and Social Psychology Bulletin, 11*, 75–88.

Foster, G. (1965). Peasant society and the image of limited good. *American Anthropologist, 67*, 293–315.

Frager, C. (1970). Conformity and anti-conformity in Japan. *Journal of Personality and Social Psychology, 15*, 203–210.

Gabrenya, W. K., & Barba, L. (1987, March). *Cultural differences in social interaction during group problem solving*. Paper presented at the meetings of the Southeastern Psychological Association, Miami, FL.

Gaenslen, F. (1986). Culture and decision making in China, Japan, Russia and the United States. *World Politics, 39*, 78–103.

Geertz, C. (1963). *Peddlers and princes: Social change and economic modernization in two Indonesian towns*. Chicago: University of Chicago Press.

Geertz, C. (1983). *Local knowledge: Further essays in interpretive anthropology*. New York: Basic Books.

Georgas, J. (1986). *Social psychology*. Athens: University of Athens Press.

Georgas, J. (1989). Changing family values in Greece: From collectivistic to individualistic. *Journal of Cross Cultural Psychology, 20*, 80–91.

Gilligan, C. (1982). *In a different voice: Psychological theory and women's development*. Cambridge: Harvard University Press.

Gorney, R., & Long, J. M. (1980). Cultural determinants of achievement, aggression and psychological distress. *Archives of General Psychiatry, 37*, 452–459.

Gould, J., & Kolb, W. L. (1964). *A dictionary of the social sciences*. Glencoe, IL: Free Press.

Greenwald, A. G., & Pratkanis, A. R. (1984). The self. In R. S. Wyer & T. K. Srull (Eds.), *Handbook of social cognition* (Vol. 3, pp. 129–178). Hillsdale, NJ: Erlbaum.

Gruenfeld, L., Weissenberg, P., & Loh, W. (1973). Achievement values, cognitive style and social class. *International Journal of Psychology, 8*, 41–49.

Gudykunst, W. B. (Ed.). (1983). *Intercultural communication theory*. Beverly Hills, CA: Sage.

Gudykunst, W. B., & Nishida, T. (1986). The influence of cultural variability on perceptions of communication behavior associated with relationship terms. *Human Communication Research, 13,* 147–166.

Gudykunst, W. B., Nishida, T., & Schmidt, K. L. (1989). The influence of cultural variability and uncertainty reduction in ingroup vs. outgroup and same vs. opposite sex relationships. *Western Journal of Speech Communication, 53,* 13–29.

Gudykunst, W. B., Ting-Toomy, S. (1988). Culture and affective communication. *American Behavioral Scientist, 33,* 147–166.

Gudykunst, W. B., Yoon, Y., & Nishida, T. (1987). The influence of individualism-collectivism on perceptions of communication in ingroup and outgroup relationships. *Communication Monographs, 54,* 295–306.

Guthrie, G. M. (1961). *The Filipino child and the Philippine society*. Manila: Philippine Normal College Press.

Hamilton, V. L., & Sanders, J. (1983). Universals in judging wrongdoing: Japanese and Americans compared. *American Sociological Review, 48,* 199–211.

Hazard, P. (1953). *The European mind: The crucial years (1680–1715)*. New Haven: Yale University Press.

Henderson, G. E., & Cohen, M. S. (1984). *The Chinese hospital: A socialist work unit*. New Haven: Yale University Press.

Herzog, H., & Shapira, R. (1986). Will you sign my autograph book? Using autograph books for a sociohistorical study of youth and social frameworks. *Qualitative Sociology, 9,* 109–125.

Hobbes, T. (1904). *Leviathan*. Cambridge: Cambridge University Press. (Original work published 1651)

Hoffman, L. (1987). The value of children to parents and childrearing patterns. In C. Kağitçibaşi (Ed.), *Growth and progress in cross-cultural psychology* (pp. 159–170). Lisse: Swets and Zeiglinger.

Hofstede, G. (1980). *Culture's consequences*. Beverly Hills, CA: Sage.

Hofstede, G., & Bond, M. (1984). Hofstede's culture dimensions: An independent validation using Rokeach's Value Survey. *Journal of Cross Cultural Psychology, 15,* 417–433.

Hogan, R. (1973). Moral conduct and moral character: A psychological perspective. *Psychological Bulletin, 33,* 307–316.

Hogan, R. (1975). Theoretical ethnocentrism and the problem of compliance. *American Psychologist, 30,* 533–540.

Holtzman, W. H., Diaz-Guerrero, R., & Swartz, J. D. (1975). *Personality development in two cultures*. Austin: University of Texas Press.

Holzberg, C. S. (1981). Anthropology and industry: Reappraisal and new directions. *Annual Review of Anthropology, 10,* 317–360.

Hsu, F. L. K. (1971). *Kinship and culture*. Chicago: Aldine.

Hsu, F. L. K. (1981). *American and Chinese: Passage to differences* (3rd ed.). Honolulu: University of Hawaii Press.

126

Hsu, F. L. K. (1983). *Rugged individualism reconsidered*. Knoxville: University of Tennessee Press.

Hui, C. H. (1984). *Individualism-collectivism: Theory, measurement and its relation to reward allocation.* Unpublished doctoral dissertation, Department of Psychology, University of Illinois at Champaign–Urbana.

Hui, C. H. (1988). Measurement of individualism-collectivism. *Journal of Research on Personality, 22,* 17–36.

Hui, C. H., & Triandis, H. C. (1986). Individualism-collectivism: A study of cross-cultural researchers. *Journal of Cross Cultural Psychology, 17,* 225–248.

Hui, C. H., & Triandis, H. C. (submitted). Collectivism and reward allocation.

Hui, C. H., & Villareal, M. (1989). Individualism-collectivism and psychological needs: their relationships in two cultures. *Journal of Cross Cultural Psychology, 20,* 310–323.

Hwang, C. H. (1982). Studies of Chinese personality: A critical review. *Bulletin of Educational Psychology, 15,* 227–241.

Inkeles, A., & Smith, D. H. (1974). *Becoming modern.* Cambridge: Harvard University Press.

Iwao, S. (1988). Invited address to International Congress of Scientific Psychology, Sydney, Australia.

Jackman, M. R., & Muha, M. (1984). Education and intergroup attitudes: Moral enlightenment, superficial democratic commitment or ideological refinement? *American Sociological Review, 49,* 751–769.

Jensen, D. D. (1970). Polythetic biopsychology: An alternative to behaviorism. In J. H. Reynierse (Ed.), *Current issues in animal learning* (pp.1–31). Lincoln: University of Nebraska Press.

Johnson, D. W., & Johnson, R. T. (1983). The socialization and achievement crises: Are cooperative learning experiences the solution? In L. Bickman (Ed.), *Applied social psychology annual* (pp. 119–164). Beverly Hills, CA: Sage.

Johnson, D. W., Johnson, R. T., & Krotee, M. L. (1986). The relation between social interdependence and psychological health on the 1980 U.S. Olympic ice hockey team. *Journal of Psychology, 120,* 279–291.

Johnson, D. W., & Norem-Hebeisen, A. A. (1979). A measure of cooperative, competitive and individualistic attitudes. *Journal of Social Psychology, 109,* 253–261.

Jones, L., & Bock, R. D. (1960). Multiple discriminant analysis applied to "Ways to Live" ratings from six cultural groups. *Sociometry, 23,* 162–176.

Kaiser, R. G. (1984). *Russia: The people and the power.* New York: Washington Square Press.

Kanfer, F. (1979). Personal control, social control and altruism: Can society survive the age of ego-centrism? *American Psychologist, 34,* 231–239.

Kashima, Y. (1988, August). *Cultural conceptions of the person, and individualism-collectivism: A semiotic framework.* Paper presented at International Congress of Cross-Cultural Psychology, Newcastle, Australia.

Katakis, C. D. (1976). An exploratory multilevel attempt to investigate inter-personal and intrapersonal patterns of 20 Athenian families. *Mental Health and Society, 3,* 1–9.

Katakis, C. D. (1978). On the transaction of social change processes and the perception of self in relation to others. *Mental Health and Society, 5,* 275–283.

Katakis, C. D. (1984). *The three identities of the Greek family.* Athens: Kevdros. (In Greek)

Kerlinger, F. (1984). *Liberalism and conservatism: The nature and structure of social attitudes.* Hillsdale, NJ: Erlbaum.

Klugel, J. R., & Smith, E. R. (1982). Whites' beliefs about blacks' opportunity. *American Sociological Review, 47,* 518–532.

Knight, G. P. (1981). Behavioral and sociometric methods of identifying co-operators, competitors and individualists: Support for the validity of the social orientation construct. *Developmental Psychology, 17,* 430–433.

Kohlberg, L. (1976). Moral stages and moralization: The cognitive-developmental approach. In T. Lickona (Ed.), *Moral development and behavior: Theory, research and social issues.* New York: Holt, Rinehart and Winston.

Kohlberg, L. (1981). *Essays in moral development.* New York: Harper and Row.

Kohn, M. L. (1969). *Class and conformity.* Homewood, IL: Dorsey.

Kohn, M. L. (1987). Cross-national research as an analytic strategy. *American Sociological Review, 52,* 713–731.

Kuhn, M. H., & McPartland, T. (1954). An empirical investigation of self-attitudes. *American Sociological Review, 19,* 68–76.

Lambert, W. E., Hammers, J. F., & Frasure-Smith, N. (1979). *Child-rearing values: A cross national study.* New York: Praeger.

Lasch, C. (1978). *The culture of narcissism: American life in an age of diminishing expectations.* New York: Norton.

Lebra, T. S. (1976). *Japanese patterns of behavior.* Honolulu: East-West Center.

Leung, F. T. L., & Sedlacek, W. E. (1986). A comparison of international and U.S. students' preferences for help sources. *Journal of College Student Personnel, 27,* 426–430.

Leung, K. (1987). Some determinants of reactions to procedural models for conflict resolution: A cross national study. *Journal of Personality and Social Psychology, 53,* 898–908.

Leung, K. (1988). Some determinants of conflict avoidance. *Journal of Cross Cultural Psychology, 19,* 125–136.

Leung, K., & Bond, M. (1984). The impact of cultural collectivism on reward allocation. *Journal of Personality and Social Psychology, 47,* 793–804.

Leung, K., & Iwawaki, S. (1988). Cultural collectivism and distributive behavior. *Journal of Cross Cultural Psychology, 19,* 35–49.

Leung, K., & Lind, E. A. (1986). Procedural justice and culture: Effects of culture, gender and investigator status on procedural preferences. *Journal of Personality and Social Psychology, 50,* 1134–1140.

Lomax, A. (1968). *Folk song style and culture.* Publication No. 88. Washington, DC: American Association for the Advancement of Science.

Lukes, S. (1973). *Individualism*. Oxford: Basil Blackwell.

Ma, H. K. (1988). The Chinese perspective on moral judgment development. *International Journal of Psychology, 23*, 201–227.

MacFarlane, A. (1978). *The origins of English individualism: The family, property and social transition*. New York: Cambridge University Press.

Marin, G. (1985). Validez transcultural del principio de equidad: El colectivismo-individualismo como una variable moderatora. *Revista Interamericana de Psicología Occupational, 4*, 7–20.

Marin, G., & Triandis, H. C. (1985). Allocentrism as an important characteristic of the behavior of Latin Americans and Hispanics. In R. Diaz-Guerrero (Ed.), *Cross-cultural and national studies in social psychology* (pp. 69–80). Amsterdam: North-Holland.

Marin, G. V., Marin, G., Otero-Sabogal, R., Sabogal, F., & Perez-Stable, E. (1987). *Cultural differences in attitudes toward smoking: Developing messages using the theory of reasoned action*. Technical Report. San Francisco, 400 Parnasus Avenue.

Massimini, F., & Calegari, P. (1979). *Il contesto normativo sociale*. Milan: Angeli.

Mead, M. (1967). *Cooperation and competition among primitive people*. Boston: Beacon Press.

Mills, J., & Clark, M. S. (1982). Exchange and communal relationships. In L. Wheeler (Ed.), *Review of personality and social psychology* (Vol. 3). Beverly Hills, CA: Sage.

Mohan, J., & Sharma, N. K. (1985). A study of urban youth problems. *Indian Psychological Review, 28*, 1–28.

Moreland, R. L., & Levine, J. M. (1982). Socialization in small groups: Temporal changes in individual-group relations. In L. Berkowitz (Ed.), *Advances in experimental social psychology* (Vol. 15, pp. 137–192). New York: Academic Press.

Morsbach, H. (1980). Major psychological factors influencing Japanese interpersonal relations. In N. Warren (Ed.), *Studies in cross-cultural psychology* (Vol. 2). London: Academic Press.

Murphy-Berman, V., Berman, J. J., Singh, P., Pachauri, A., & Kumar, P. (1984). Factors affecting allocation to needy and meritorious recipients: A cross-cultural comparison. *Journal of Personality and Social Psychology, 46*, 1267–1272.

Naroll, R. (1983). *The moral order*. Beverly Hills, CA: Sage.

Noesjirwan, J., Gault, U., & Crawford, J. (1983). Beliefs about memory in the aged. *Journal of Cross Cultural Psychology, 14*, 455–468.

Northrop, F. S. C. (1949). *Ideological differences and world order*. New Haven: Yale University Press.

Palmer, S. (1972). *The violent society*. New Haven, CT: College and University Press.

Pandey, J. (1986). Sociocultural perspectives on ingratiation. In *Progress in experimental personality research* (Vol. 14, 205–229). New York: Academic Press.

Pareek, U. (1968). A motivational paradigm of development. *Journal of Social Issues, 24,* 115–122.

Pearson, H. W. (Ed.). (1977). *The livelihood of man: Karl Polanyi.* New York: Academic Press.

Perloff, R. (1987). Self-interest and personal responsibility redux. *American Psychologist, 42,* 3–11.

Pettigrew, T. F. (1988). Integration and pluralism. In P. A. Katz & D. A. Taylor (Eds.), *Eliminating racism: Profiles in controversy* (pp. 19–52). New York: Plenum.

Pilisuk, M., & Parks, S. (1985). *The healing web.* Hanover, NH: University Press of New England.

Quattrone, G. A. (1986). On the perception of a group's variability. In S. Worchel & W. G. Austin (Eds.), *The psychology of intergroup relations* (pp. 25–48). Chicago: Nelson-Hall.

Rakoff, V. (1978). The illusion of detachment. *Adolescent Psychiatry, 6,* 119–129.

Riesman, D. (1954). *Individualism reconsidered.* New York: Free Press.

Riesman, D. (1966). *Individualism reconsidered.* (2nd ed.). New York: Free Press.

Rojas, L. (1981). *An anthropologist examines the navy's recruiting process.* Technical Report No. 4. Champaign: University of Illinois, Department of Psychology.

Rokeach, M. (1960). *The open and closed mind.* New York: Basic Books.

Rokeach, M. (1973). *The nature of human values.* New York: Free Press.

Rosenbaum, M. E., Moore, D. L., Cotton, J. L., Cook, M. S., Hieser, R. A., Shovar, N. M., & Gray, M. J. (1980). Group productivity and process: Pure and mixed reward structures and task interdependence. *Journal of Personality and Social Psychology, 39,* 626–642.

Rosenthal, D., & Bornholt, L. (1988). Expectations about development in Greek- and Anglo-Australian families. *Journal of Cross Cultural Psychology, 19,* 19–34.

Ross, W., Triandis, H. C., Chang, B., & Marin, G. (1982). *Work values of Hispanic and mainstream navy recruits.* Technical Report No. 8. Champaign: University of Illinois, Psychology Department.

Rotenberg, M. (1977). Alienating individualism and reciprocal individualism: A cross-cultural conceptualization. *Journal of Humanistic Psychology, 17,* 3–17.

Rugh, A. (1985). *Family in contemporary Egypt.* Cairo: American University Press.

Sabogal, F., Marin, G., Otero-Sabogal, R., Marin, B., & Perez-Stable, E. J. (1987). *Changes in Hispanic familism with acculturation.* Technical Report No. 1. San Francisco: University of California, Department of Psychology.

Sampson, E. E. (1977). Psychology and the American ideal. *Journal of Personality and Social Psychology, 35,* 767–782.

Schmidt, N., & Sermat, V. (1983). Measuring loneliness in different relationships. *Journal of Personality and Social Psychology, 44,* 1038–1047.

Schwartz, B. (1986). *The battle for human nature: Science, morality and modern life.* New York: Norton.

Schwartz, S. (1988, August). *Values and individualism collectivism.* Paper presented at the meetings of the International Association of Cross-Cultural Psychology, Newcastle, Australia.

Schwartz, S., & Bilsky, W. (1987). Toward a universal psychological structure of human values. *Journal of Personality and Social Psychology, 53,* 550–562.

Sears, D. O. (1986). College sophomores in the laboratory: Influence of a narrow data base on social psychology's view of human nature. *Journal of Personality and Social Psychology, 51,* 515–530.

Setiadi, B. N. (1984). *Schooling, age, and culture as moderators of role perceptions.* Unpublished doctoral dissertation. University of Illinois, Champaign–Urbana.

Shannon, P. (1986). Hidden within the pages: A study of social perspective in young children's favorite books. *Reading Teacher, 39,* 656–663.

Shouval, R., Kav, V. S., Bronfenbrenner, U., Devereux, E. C., & Kiely, E. (1975). Anomalous reactions to social pressure of Israeli and Soviet children raised in family vs. collective settings. *Journal of Personality and Social Psychology, 32,* 477–489.

Shweder, R. A. (1982). Beyond self-constructed knowledge: The study of culture and morality. *Merrill-Palmer Quarterly, 28,* 41–69.

Shweder, R. A., & Bourne, E. J. (1982). Does the concept of person vary cross-culturally? In A. J. Marsella & G. M. White, (Eds.), *Cultural conceptions of mental health and therapy* (pp. 97–137). Boston: Reidel.

Sinha, D. (1988). The family scenario in a developing country and its implications for mental health: The case of India. In P. Dasen, J. Berry, & N. Sartorius (Eds.), *Health and cross-cultural psychology: Toward applications.* Newbury Park, CA: Sage.

Sinha, J. B. P. (1982). The Hindu (Indian) identity. *Dynamische Psychiatrie, 15,* 148–160.

Smith, M. B. (1978). Perspectives on selfhood. *American Psychologist, 33,* 1053–1063.

Spence, J. T. (1985). Achievement American style: The rewards and cost of individualism. *American Psychologist, 40,* 1285–1295.

Strodtbeck, F. L. (1958). Family interaction, values, and achievement. In D. McClelland (Ed.), *Talent and society* (pp. 135–195). New York: Van Nostrand.

Swap, W. C., & Rubin, J. Z. (1983). Measurement of interpersonal orientation. *Journal of Personality and Social Psychology, 44,* 208–219.

Szalay, L. B., & Inn, A. (1988). Cross-cultural adaptation and diversity: Hispanic Americans. In Y. Y. Kim & W. B. Gudykunst (Eds.), *Cross-cultural adaptation* (pp. 212–232). Newbury Park, CA: Sage.

Tajfel, H. (1982). *Social identity and intergroup relations.* Cambridge: Cambridge University Press.

Tallman, I., Marotz-Baden, R., & Pindas, P. (1983). *Adolescent socialization in cross-cultural perspective*. New York: Academic Press.

Tanaka, Y. (1978). The analysis of subjective political culture. *Gakushin Review of Law and Politics, 13*, 1–93.

Tesser, A., & Moore, J. (1986). On the convergence of public and private aspects of self. In R. Baumeister (Ed.), *Public and private self*. New York: Springer.

Thibaut, J., & Kelley, H. H. (1959). *The social psychology of groups*. New York: Wiley.

Ting-Toomey, S. (1988, May). *Intercultural conflict styles: A face-negotiation theory*. Paper presented at the meetings of the International Communications Association, New Orleans, LA.

Tocqueville, A. de. (1946). *Democracy in America*. New York: Knopf. (Original work published 1840)

Toennies, F. (1957). *Community and society* (C. P. Loomis, Trans.). East Lansing: Michigan State University Press.

Triandis, H. C. (1964). Exploratory factor analyses of the behavioral component of social attitudes. *Journal of Abnormal and Social Psychology, 68*, 420–430.

Triandis, H. C. (1967a). Interpersonal relations in international organizations. *Journal of Organizational Behavior and Human Performance, 2*, 26–55.

Triandis, H. C. (1967b). Toward an analysis of the components of interpersonal attitudes. In Carolyn Sherif & Muzafer Sherif (Eds.), *Attitudes, ego-involvement, and change* (pp. 227–270). New York: Wiley.

Triandis, H. C. (1972). *The analysis of subjective culture*. New York: Wiley.

Triandis, H. C. (1980a). Introduction. In H. C. Triandis & W. W. Lambert (Eds.), *Handbook of cross-cultural psychology* (Vol. 1). Boston: Allyn and Bacon.

Triandis, H. C. (1980b). Values, attitudes and interpersonal behavior. In H. Howe, & M. Page (Eds.), *Nebraska Symposium on Motivation, 1979*. Lincoln: University of Nebraska Press.

Triandis, H. C. (1981). *Hispanic concerns about the U.S. Navy*. Technical Report No. 1. Champaign: University of Illinois, Department of Psychology.

Triandis, H. C. (1984). A theoretical framework for the more efficient construction of culture assimilators. *International Journal of Intercultural Relations, 8*, 301–330.

Triandis, H. C. (1988). Collectivism v. individualism: A reconceptualization of a basic concept of cross-cultural psychology. In G. K. Verma & C. Bagley (Eds.), *Cross-cultural studies of personality, attitudes and cognition* (pp. 60–95). London: Macmillian.

Triandis, H. C., Bontempo, R., Betancourt, H., Bond, M., Leung, K., Brenes, A., Georgas, J., Hui, C. H., Marin, G., Setiadi, B., Sinha, J. B. P., Verman, J., Spangenberg, J., Touzard, H., & de Montmollin, G. (1986). The measurement of the etic aspects of individualism and collectivism across cultures. *Australian Journal of Psychology, 38*, 257–267.

Triandis, H. C., Bontempo, R., Villareal, M., Asai, M., & Lucca, N. (1988). Individualism-collectivism: Cross-cultural perspectives on self–ingroup relationships. *Journal of Personality and Social Psychology, 54*, 323–338.

Triandis, H. C., Hui, C. H., Lisansky, J., Ottati, V., Marin, G., & Bettancourt, H. (1982). *Perceptions of supervisor-subordinate relations among Hispanic and mainstream recruits*. Technical Report No. 11. Champaign: University of Illinois, Department of Psychology.

Triandis, H. C., Kashima, Y., Lisansky, J., & Marin, G. (1982). *Self-concept and values among Hispanic and mainstream navy recruits*. Technical Report No. 7. Champaign: University of Illinois, Department of Psychology.

Triandis, H. C., Leung, K., Villareal, M., & Clack, F. L. (1985). Allocentric vs. idiocentric tendencies: Convergent and discriminant validation. *Journal of Research in Personality, 19,* 395–415.

Triandis, H. C., Marin, G., & Betancourt, H. (1982). *Acculturation and acceptance of contact among Hispanic and mainstream navy recruits*. Technical Report No. 20. Champaign: University of Illinois, Department of Psychology.

Triandis, H. C., Marin, G., Betancourt, H., & Chang, B. (1982). *Acculturation, biculturalism and familism among Hispanic and mainstream navy recruits*. Technical Report No. 15. Champaign: University of Illinois, Department of Psychology.

Triandis, H. C., Marin, G., Betancourt, H., Lisansky, J., & Chang, B. (1982). *Simpatía as a cultural script of Hispanics*. Technical Report No. 19. Champaign: University of Illinois, Department of Psychology.

Triandis, H. C., Marin, G., Hui, C. H., Lisansky, J., & Ottati, V. (1984). Role perceptions of Hispanic young adults. *Journal of Cross Cultural Psychology, 15,* 297–320.

Triandis, H. C., Marin, G., Lisansky, J., & Betancourt, H. (1984). *Simpatía as a cultural script of Hispanics*. *Journal of Personality and Social Psychology, 47,* 1363–1375.

Triandis, H. C., Marin, G., et al. (1982). *Dimensions of familism among Hispanic and mainstream navy recruits*. Technical Report No. 14. Champaign: University of Illinois, Department of Psychology.

Triandis, H. C., McCusker, C., Betancourt, H., Iwao, S., Leung, K., Salazar, J. M., Setiadi, B., Sinha, J. B. P., Touzard, H., Wang, D., & Zaleski, Z. (submitted). An etic-emic analysis of individualism and collectivism.

Triandis, H. C., McCusker, C., & Hui, C. H. (submitted). Multimethod probes of individualism and collectivism.

Triandis, H. C., Ottati, V., & Marin, G. (1982). *Achievement motives of Hispanic and mainstream navy recruits*. Technical Report No. 5. Champaign: University of Illinois, Department of Psychology.

Triandis, H. C., & Triandis, L. M. (1960). Race, social class, religion and nationality as determinants of social distance. *Journal of Abnormal and Social Psychology, 61,* 110–118.

Triandis, H. C., & Vassiliou, V. (1972). A comparative analysis of subjective culture. In H. C. Triandis, *The analysis of subjective culture*. New York: Wiley.

Triandis, H. C., Vassiliou, V., & Nassiakou, M. (1968). Three cross-culture studies of subjective culture. *Journal of Personality and Social Psychology Monograph Supplement, 8,* 1–42.

Verma, J. (1985). The ingroup and its relevance to individual behavior: A study of collectivism and individualism. *Psychologia, 28,* 173–181.

Waite, L. J., Goldscheider, F. K., & Witsberger, C. (1986). *American Sociological Review, 51,* 541–554.

Waterman, A. S. (1981). Individualism and interdependence. *American Psychologist, 36,* 762–773.

Waterman, A. S. (1984). *The psychology of individualism.* New York: Praeger.

Weldon, E. (1984). Deindividuation, interpersonal affect and productivity in laboratory task groups. *Journal of Applied Social Psychology, 14,* 469–485.

Wheeler, L., Reis, H., & Bond, M. (1989). Collectivism-individualism in everyday social life: The Middle Kingdom and the melting pot. *Journal of Personality & Social Psychology 57,* 79–86.

Whiting, B. B., & Whiting, J. W. M. (1975). *Children of six cultures.* Cambridge: Harvard University Press.

Witkin, H. A., & Berry, J. W. (1975). Psychological differentiation in cross-cultural perspective. *Journal of Cross Cultural Psychology, 6,* 4–87.

Worchel, S., & Austin, W. G. (1986). *Psychology of intergroup relations.* Chicago: Nelson-Hall.

Wu, D. Y. H. (1985). Child rearing in Chinese culture. In D. Y. H. Wu & W. S. Tseng (Eds.), *Chinese culture and mental health* (pp. 113–134). New York: Academic Press.

Yang, K. S. (1970). Authoritarianism and evaluation of appropriateness of role behavior. *Journal of Social Psychology, 80,* 171–181.

Yang, K. S. (1986). Chinese personality and its change. In M. H. Bond (Ed.), *The psychology of the Chinese people* (pp. 106–170). Hong Kong: Oxford University Press.

Zern, D. S. (1982). The impact of values on development in a cross-cultural sample. *Genetic Psychology Monographs, 106,* 179–197.

Zern, D. S. (1983). The relationship of certain group-oriented and individualistically oriented child-rearing dimensions of cultural complexity in a cross-cultural sample. *Genetic Psychology Monographs, 108,* 3–20.

Ziller, R. C. (1965). Toward a theory of open and closed groups. *Psychological Bulletin, 64,* 164–182.

Family and Socialization in Cross-Cultural Perspective: A Model of Change

Çiğdem Kağıtçıbaşı
Boğaziçi University
Istanbul, Turkey

Approaches to Studying the Family and Socialization

PSYCHOLOGY AND THE FAMILY

Although it is of crucial importance for human development, the family is not commonly considered a topic of study for psychology. If we go through college catalogs, we find courses on the family listed under the sociology and anthropology departments, but rarely under psychology. This is because the family, as a unit of analysis, is not studied directly by psychologists; rather, they touch upon it in dealing with topics such as child development, life-span development, and psychology of gender. Similarly, to find scholarly books on the family in a bookstore, one must go to the sociology and anthropology sections. Books about the family on the psychology shelves are usually semipopular or deal with applied areas such as family therapy and counseling.

Academic psychology's apparent lack of involvement with the family is probably due to the discipline's general individualist orientation. For psychologists the "proper" unit of analysis is the individual, and they are better equipped to deal with individual-level data. This is the case even in social psychology, which has progressively become a "cognitive social psychology of the individual" and has moved

Special thanks are due to John Berman, Diane Sunar and Ayhan Koç, who provided helpful comments on the first draft. Preparation of this chapter was partially supported by Boğaziçi University Research Fund.

away from its holistic interpersonal, interactional beginnings as exemplified in the early work of Lewin (1936, 1948, 1951) on group dynamics and field theory and of Sherif on social norms and intergroup relations (1936, 1961) (see Taylor & Brown, 1979). Even an inherently interpersonal, interactional theory such as social exchange theory must be stretched to apply to collectivities larger than a dyad.

Thus, though human development almost always occurs in the family and always involves a process of socialization into family and society, the developmental psychologist typically focuses on child development (or the development of the individual), not on socialization or the family. This is a noncontextual, analytical approach rather than a synthetic, holistic one.

The noncontextual orientation of mainstream psychology is at least partially explained by its ambitious goal of developing universal laws of behavior. In accordance with this goal, the physical science model was adopted and commonalities in behavior have been emphasized. Abstraction of behavior from its natural total environment has been the rule in attempting to render the environment manageable for experimental control. Thus, to avoid the effects of "extraneous variables," a narrow definition of the environment has been adapted, stressing uniformity rather than diversity. Even social psychology, despite its name, has stuck to this simple model (Taylor & Brown, 1979).

When one considers the basic environmentalist thrust of 20th-century psychology, stemming from its behavioristic background, this limited conceptualization of the environment is ironic. It makes sense, nevertheless, in terms of the methodological concern of experimental design to hold "everything" constant in order to establish the causal relation between the independent and dependent variables. Contextualism, on the other hand, brings in diversity and therefore uncontrolled variation, which is not acceptable for a science claiming to uncover universal causal laws. The price of adhering to a mechanistic, positivistic physical science model has been giving up some of the potential richness and complexity that psychology could include.

Obviously, such a narrow definition of the environment does not do justice to the complex contexts in which human behavior actually takes place. In attempting to abstract behavior from its context and to establish generality in experimental research, psychology has in fact ignored the potentially different contextual factors that, if studied, would point to diversity. It has then come full circle and declared the limited generalities it has artificially created to be universal truths. One most serious outcome of this self-imposed limitation of behavioral domain has been the culture-bound nature of the discipline, noted by many (e.g., Jahoda, 1986a, 1986b; Pepitone, 1987) and to be taken up later in this chapter.

Another serious outcome of the noncontextual study of behavior at the individual level has been the failure to treat the family as a unit of analysis. The great complexity of the family as an intergenerational system moving through time also makes it difficult to think of it as a whole (McGoldrick & Carter, 1982). Since recognition of the different family patterns would point to a great deal of diversity, unwelcome for purposes of generalization, the "prototypical" Western nuclear family has been adopted as "the" family context. Psychology has thus "constructed" "the family" in the image of the Western middle-class nuclear family.

Here we see a clear example of misfit between theory and reality. Family is an integral part of society and is inherently tied to its social structure, values, norms, and so on. With variations in these societal and cultural factors, families differ greatly. Such variation is profound and cannot be legitimately ignored by assuming uniformity along the lines of the prototypical Western nuclear family. Yet psychology has not typically concerned itself with family diversity, regarding it rather as a topic appropriate for sociology or anthropology.

SOCIALIZATION

In accordance with the noncontextual approach undermining our understanding of family complexity and diversity, human development has typically also been studied at the individual level of analysis rather than as an interactional socialization process. In my understanding, socialization refers to the inherently complex process of becoming a socially competent being. It therefore necessarily involves the interaction of the human being's natural (biological) potential and the total of environmental influences, including ecology and society. This definition goes beyond the narrower definition of "deliberate shaping" of children by parents. It includes both intentional "socialization" and the unintentional process of "enculturation." It is the overall process of learning culture and becoming social.

Psychology has again chosen not to deal with this "amorphous" process. It has instead traditionally concerned itself with child psychology and more recently with life-span developmental psychology. In both cases the unit of analysis has been the individual. As with the "family," very few courses in psychology departments on socialization are given. In sociological social psychology socialization has traditionally been an important topic, but not in psychological social psychology. An exception was Brown's (1965) textbook, which examined such diverse topics as the development of intelligence, language, and morality under the general concept of socialization. This novel approach, however, is not repeated in the second edition (1986).

One factor underlying psychologists' lack of interest in the concept of socialization is its close association with late 19th-century sociology and especially with Durkheim. In his "social mold" theory Durkheim stressed the "exteriority" of social norms that restricted the individual while at the same time being internalized, thus molding the person in terms of society's needs and goals. This unidirectional conceptualization of socialization regarding the individual as a passive recipient of influence has been rejected. Such sociologistic concepts are no longer being used (Wentworth, 1980), and interactional models, as originally proposed by symbolic interactionists (Cooley, 1902; Mead, 1934) are preferred. According to Hurrelmann (1988, p. 1), the term "socialization" has been enjoying an increasing interest and acceptance in psychology in recent years. Whether this is a correct observation is hard to judge at this point. It may be reflecting a European rather than an American trend.

In any case, however, I strongly believe it is time for psychology to expand its boundaries to include more contextual approaches involving the family and the socialization process. In the face of the vast diversity and complexity of human experience, psychology can no longer afford the luxury of its methodologically dictated positivistic, mechanistic physical science model with its individual level of analysis. One may argue that such self-imposed limitation was necessary for launching psychology as a science and for separating it effectively from its philosophical/mentalist background. For whatever it was worth, however, the function of limitation has long been fulfilled. More contextual approaches involving the total environment and focusing on the dynamic interaction of the person and the environment would do better justice to human reality. Clearly there is a need for a comprehensive conceptualization of the socialization-family totality. An individualist approach is necessarily reductionist, since it attempts to reduce the multidimensional interactional entity to the individual level of analysis.

As psychology ventures into cross-cultural comparisons and strives to account for cultural diversity while claiming generality (Dasen & Jahoda, 1986, p. 413), it is in fact bound to expand into the "sociological" realms of the family and socialization. This is because the sociocultural context figures more centrally in cross-cultural inquiry. This is indeed an underlying theme of this chapter.

The process of socialization comprises both the individual (organismic and psychological) and the societal (environmental) aspects in interaction with each other. Thus any theory of socialization cannot build upon one of these aspects while ignoring the other. Nevertheless, psychological theories of human development have typically tended to stress the organismic-psychological aspects, and sociological theories of socialization have stressed the societal aspects of the process. Some rapprochement of the two disciplinary approaches may be in sight as theories developed within each discipline are increasingly cognizant of the "other approach" and willing to incorporate it (e.g., Baltes & Brim, 1979; Clausen, 1986; Elder, 1979, 1985; Hurrelmann, 1988; Hurrelmann & Ulich, 1982; Wentworth, 1980). This is a healthy development that should be encouraged through interdisciplinary research.

MODELS OF PERSON-ENVIRONMENT RELATION

It may be informative at this point to consider briefly some basic models of the person-environment relation that psychological theories of human development use, in terms of whether they can deal with the complex socialization process, and to what extent. I will make extensive use of Hurrelmann's (1988) treatment of the topic in this section. A similar treatment was used earlier by Eckensberger (1979).

The mechanistic model. Espoused by behaviorism, this model looks at human development as the sum of responses to environmental stimuli. As I mentioned before, this is a limited conceptualization of the environment as proximal surroundings, and the larger sociocultural context is ignored. Organismic factors are also ignored, and the environment is seen as the cause of behavioral development.

Classical learning theory adhered to this mechanistic view of stimulus-response connections (Skinner, 1938). In the more recent social learning formulations, however, extensions are seen on the one hand into social influences and relationships, and on the other into cognitive structuring of the environment in terms of role models (Bandura, 1977, 1986). Even though the model basically works at the dyadic level, through imitation, it can account for more complex contextual influences through these extensions. Similarly, since through cognitive structuring the developing individual is no longer seen as a passive recipient of stimuli (Bandura & Walters, 1963) but is considered an active processor of information, the theory can also account for a more interactional process of socialization. Thus, by distancing itself from its underlying mechanistic model, social learning theory can in fact contribute to an understanding of the complex socialization process as I have defined it.

The organismic model. This is a second model used extensively in theories of human development where the maturational causes of development are stressed at the expense of environmental causes. Qualitatively progressing sequential stages of development are postulated as leading toward a well-defined optimal stage of growth inherent in the maturational potential of the organism. Psychoanalysis and the Piagetian theory of cognitive development both adhere to the organismic model. In psychoanalysis early relations and interactions with significant others are clearly of key importance for personality development. The theory, therefore, can potentially account for the socialization process, especially through such concepts as identification, object relations, narcissism, and narcissistic forms of incorporation and attachment. However, the emphasis has been put more on the intrapsychic dynamics and biologically based drives than on the social relational aspects of personality development. Furthermore, the potentially important conflict between biological drives and social norms has not been developed adequately to contribute significantly to a theory of socialization (Hurrelmann, 1988, p. 13).

As for Piagetian developmental theory, it clearly focuses on the maturational processes of *cognitive* development, though it also deals with development in general as a process of active adaptation to the environment. It thus has the potential for dealing with socialization. Nevertheless, the theory is heavily biased toward the organismic rather than the environmental aspects of the adaptation process. The role assigned to the environment is as an accelerating or inhibiting influence on the "natural" maturational unfolding. Even such a rather limited role, however, can help explain, for example, what kinds of environments are supportive of development (Hurrelmann, 1988, p. 18). Kohlbergian moral development theory (Kohlberg, 1963) although basically Piagetian, has had to take into consideration sociocultural factors, which in turn has led to modifications of the theory. Specifically, alternative principled morality criteria have been formulated, based on collective solidarity-relatedness or other indigenous themes, representing a clear shift away from the absolutist universal criteria of reasoning and an extension into sociocultural analysis (LeVine, Kohlberg, & Hewer, 1985; Snarey, 1985).

The systemic model. This is a general orientation to understanding development or change within an entity (system) or between interrelated entities (systems) (Bertalanffy, 1968). From this perspective, human development is seen to be the result of the interpenetration of the psychological (person) and the social (environment) systems. This interpenetration through the reciprocal relation between person and environment strives to achieve a balanced state. In this model there is no fixed end state of human development. Theories as different as ecological theory in psychology (Bronfenbrenner, 1979) and systems theory in sociology (Parsons, 1964) share this basic orientation.

Ecological theory looks into the "dynamic interplay between the developing person and the environment" (Bronfenbrenner, 1977, 1979). Both the person and the environment are seen to be active; thus a balanced reciprocal accommodation takes place between them (Bronfenbrenner, 1977). Starting with the immediate environment, the microsystem, the developing person moves out into the larger sociocultural context through the meso-, exo-, and macro-

systems, "a complex of nested, interconnected systems" (Bronfenbrenner, 1978, p. 8). This is a theory that overcomes the limitations of the organismic model and combines some of its elements
with a systems model. Ecological theory is well suited to study the
complex socialization process, as I have defined it, since it focuses
on the dynamic interaction of the individual with the *total* sociocultural milieu.

Ecological theory has also been used by Berry in cross-cultural
psychology to study perceptual development and cognitive style
and to build a general model of person-environment relationships
(1966, 1976, 1980). In this model systematic relationships among ecological, cultural, acculturational, and behavioral variables are studied (Berry, 1980, p. 177).

The historical antecedents of the holistic ecological approach
can be traced back to Lewin's (1936) topological psychology,
Brunswik's (1955) "E-O-E arc" (environment-organism-environ-
ment), and Barker's (1968) environmental or ecological psychology.
In spite of this history covering half a century, however, the ecological approach has remained somewhat marginal in general psychology in the face of the latter's heavy reductionistic, laboratory-based
orientation. Nevertheless, it has paved the way for truly contextual
approaches.

The contextual model. This model considers human development
as a lifelong process of interaction between the human being and the
environment. It has provided a general framework for sociological
theories ranging from symbolic interactionism (Mead, 1934) to recent theories of social structure (Habermas, 1984). From the perspective of the contextual model the individual is "in a permanent process of acquisition from and confrontation with the social
environment" (Hurrelmann, 1988, p. 7), a dynamic process where
one is active in choosing contexts, which in turn shape one's behavior.

The contextual model of the relation between person and environment is very close to the systemic model, although interacting
entities are not necessarily defined as systems. To my understanding the ecological, systems, and contextual orientations are interchangeable as long as they focus on both the person and the environment in their reciprocal interaction and as long as they extend

the environment beyond the immediate (family) surroundings to encompass the larger sociocultural-historical context. Their differences may be more in focus or in temporal emphasis. I will be using the term "contextual approach" in a general sense to refer to one or more of these models.

This brief overview of some main models and corresponding psychological theories of the person-environment relation shows, in general, that they are all, at least to some degree, able to deal with the socialization process. Some of them, such as the organismic model, are less well suited for this task than others; nevertheless, they all contain some elements that would be relevant for understanding this complex process. Given this general theoretical capacity to deal with socialization, it is ironic that socialization as such has not traditionally been considered a topic of psychology.

Especially with the recent impetus provided by Bronfenbrenner's (1979) ecological theory and by the life-span developmental approaches (e.g., Baltes & Brim, 1979; Baltes, Reese, & Lipsitt, 1980) there appears to be a trend in psychological theories of human development toward more systemic-contextual models. Ecological models are also currently being used extensively in intervention work with the family (e.g., Bronfenbrenner & Weiss, 1983; Dym, 1988; Weiss & Jacobs, 1988). On the other hand, these models have been more commonly used in sociological approaches to explain person-environment relations. Thus Hurrelmann (1988, p. 22) notes the beginnings of some rapprochement between psychology and sociology as exemplified in the concept of "dynamic interactionism" (Lerner & Busch-Rossnagel, 1981), where biological, psychological, and societal factors are seen to interact within a systems-theory framework, and in the work of Riegel (1975) and Magnusson and Allen (1983), who attempt to combine learning theory, ecological theory, systems theory, and interaction theory. Along the same lines, Featherman and Lerner (1985) propose a metatheoretical perspective, "developmental contextualism," as an integrating framework for the interacting biological, psychological, and sociocultural changes. From such a perspective, development is seen as a "bi-directional person-population process" (p. 659).

Converging orientations thus call for multilevel, multidisciplinary study of person-environment relations and the complex socialization process. The Zeitgeist may now be ready for contextualism and for culture to be seen as context. This is the task that cross-cultural psychology has set for itself.

Socially Defined Meaning

A contextual approach to the person-environment relation that focuses on culture considers culture as a source of meaning. This view underlies, for example, the social-constructionist position, deriving basically from Berger and Luckmann (1967), which "is principally concerned with elucidating the processes by which people come to describe, explain, or otherwise account for the world in which they live" (Gergen, 1985, p. 3). Interpretive anthropologists who have a "symbols and meanings" approach to cultural analysis (e.g., Kirkpatrick & White, 1985; Marsella, DeVos, & Hsu, 1985; Marsella & White, 1984; Shweder & LeVine, 1984; Simons & Hughes, 1985) also provide important insights into the social and cultural construction of "reality."

The main point of social constructionism is that since any concept, even basic psychological concepts such as the person or mental health and illness, is socially defined, it is a cultural product that shows cross-cultural variation. For example, Shweder and Bourne (1984), in an insightful study of person descriptions, showed that the Oriyas in India described a person in terms of relations with others rather than in terms of enduring abstract traits, whereas Americans showed the opposite tendency. This difference held even when socioeconomic factors such as education, income, and caste or class standing were controlled. Similar relational and contextual concepts of the person are widely reported (Geertz, 1975; Ito, 1985; Lebra, 1984; White & Marsella, 1984), where "units" (persons) are believed to be necessarily altered by the relations they enter into (Shweder & Bourne, 1984, p. 110). These constructions result in situational thinking, which is also labeled "concrete" because person descriptions are made in terms not of abstract traits but of context-bound behaviors. Similarly, Marsella (1985) asserts that culture, self, and mental disorder are interdependent. Meanings attributed to self and to normality/abnormality are culturally constructed, and behavior is interpreted according to these cultural meanings. Ethnopsychology and ethnomedicine are based on this contextual hermeneutic (interpretive) premise (White & Marsella, 1984, pp. 14–16).

These examples show that "reality" is contextual in nature, and thus that events, people, and their behaviors are understood according to socially constructed meaning systems. Such systems can penetrate into basic psychological realities such as person definitions, judgments of normality/abnormality, attributions made about others' behaviors (J. Miller, 1984; Pepitone, 1987), and even the perception of one's own emotions (Schachter, 1964). Given such powerful sociocultural influence on the definition of "reality," cultural and cross-cultural analysis assumes great importance for the study of psychological phenomena.

Cross-cultural analysis is particularly relevant for the study of the family and family socialization. Precisely because socialization is human development within a sociocultural context, this context has to figure in the study of socialization. Family itself is both the context and also a part of the larger sociocultural context of socialization. Basic family processes acquire meaning within the particular sociocultural context in which the family is embedded. Much diversity exists in family processes, paralleling diversity in the larger environment.

As an example of culturally determined shifts in the *meaning* of family processes, I shall refer to cross-cultural studies on the concept of perceived parental control and acceptance. Research in North America and Germany showed that parental control was perceived by children as associated with perceived parental hostility and rejection (Rohner & Rohner, 1978; Saavedra, 1980; Trommsdorf, 1985). It thus appears that where permissive, nonrestrictive discipline in the family is the cultural norm and autonomy is emphasized in child rearing, children perceive restrictive control as reflecting hostility. However, in a different sociocultural context the same process of family control can have a different meaning. Thus Rohner and Pettengill (1985) in Korea and Kornadt (1987, also cited in Trommsdorff, 1985) in Japan found that perceived parental control is positively associated with perceived acceptance and warmth, so much so that "Japanese adolescents even feel *rejected* by their parents when they experience only little parental control and a broader range of autonomy" (Trommsdorff, 1985, p. 238; emphasis in original).

Note that I am using "permissive" in relative terms. Compared with the prevalent norms of family discipline in many non-Western societies, especially in Asia and the Middle East, Euro-American families are permissive. Neither permissive nor restrictive parental control is used in a pejorative sense here, though both have acquired such meaning in popular usage as well as in psychology. I see permissive/restrictive control as a bipolar dimension and families as showing more or less permissiveness (restrictiveness) in terms of the *extent* of control they have on children's behavior. The cultural differences above become particularly clear with respect to adolescents, who have greater freedom of action, without surveillance, in the Western countries. Some striking examples of differences, which appear "strange" from "the other side," are late adolescents leaving home to live "on their own" in "the West" (e.g., Young, 1987) and arranged marriages in the "East."

Differences become quite apparent in the context of international migration. Much research refers to the greater family control in ethnic groups compared with the host society (Storer, 1985). A subsequent study with Korean American adolescents (Pettengill & Rohner, 1985) showed patterns of adolescent perception similar to that of the dominant host culture (American adolescents) rather than the culture of origin (Korean adolescents). Clearly it is the *relevant* sociocultural context that influences psychological processes. Social comparison processes (Festinger, 1954; Gerard & Rabbie, 1961) and the reference group individuals compare themselves with are important in how they will interpret their situation.

Different social definitions of what is "normal" or "abnormal" can cause conflict in culture-contact situations, where customary child-rearing behaviors of immigrant parents may be considered wrong or abusive by the majority culture. When children and adolescents also assimilate the perceptions and values of the majority culture, intergenerational conflicts emerge, as Pettengill and Rohner (1985) found among Korean Americans and other researchers observed in immigration contexts (e.g., Storer, 1985). Thus the behavior and expectations of significant others, socially approved ways of doing things, and cultural ideals all form a nebulous context in which any event or behavior is embedded and according to which it acquires meaning.

The findings above are in line with those of an earlier cross-cultural study I conducted where I found that Turkish adolescents perceived more parental control than did American adolescents, but there was no difference between the two groups in their perception of parental affection (Kağıtçıbaşı, 1970). The study was mainly a critique of the authoritarian personality theory (Adorno, Frenkel-Brunswik, Levinson, & Sanford, 1950), which assumed that parental hostility went together with restrictive discipline. That I found the two dimensions of parental affection and control to be unrelated provided a critical test of the cross-cultural generality of the theory (other aspects of the theory also failed to hold cross culturally).

Many Western studies have also found warmth and control to be essentially orthogonal dimensions; nevertheless, much thinking in child development still assumes that strict parental control and hostility are associated. Together with the influence of early psycho-analytic teaching (and possibly of the authoritarian personality theory), a main reason behind this assumption is theorizing on the basis of a specifically Western experience. Where individual decision making, self-reliance, and autonomy are culturally valued goals, permissive family discipline becomes the norm in a society, and deviations from this norm are perceived as aberrations, even as reflecting pathology. Indeed, such deviant child-rearing behavior can *function* as pathology if for no other reason than that the children and adolescents exposed to it would also interpret it as "not normal" and therefore as reflecting hostility. Furthermore, in such a cultural context restriction may *actually* reflect hostility.

An important exception to this tendency to overcollapse affection and control is Baumrind's work (1971, 1980), where authoritarian, permissive, and authoritative parenting styles are differentiated. Authoritative parenting combines warmth and control, whereas authoritarian parenting focuses on discipline (and involves less warmth and nurturance). Some permissive parents are warm, while others are detached. Baumrind also found that authoritative parents valued both autonomy and discipline and had the most socially competent and self-reliant children. This conceptualization has implications for the cross-cultural study of socialization and will be referred to again later on.

Family Diversity

The previous discussion focused on contextual/cultural meaning and especially on its relevance for family processes and socialization. Now I want to consider some comparative studies of the family to work toward an understanding of both cross-cultural family diversity and the important variables along which diversity is seen—specifically parental beliefs and values, family interaction, social class, and family type. I will present research on these topics to exemplify the diversity in some basic family characteristics and processes, without making any attempt at comprehensiveness.

PARENTAL BELIEFS AND VALUES

A consideration of parental values is in line with the previous discussion of socially defined meaning. Basic parental beliefs and values related to children and the family and parents' perceptions of themselves and their roles constitute the basic context in which family processes and child socialization acquire meaning.

Although it may appear common sense that parents have beliefs about children, and though much lip service is given to the importance of parents' beliefs, not much systematic study has been done on this topic until rather recently (Miller, 1988). This is probably because it was assumed among professionals that "parents do not have systematic, logical beliefs about the child's development" (Sutherland, 1983, p. 138). However, a series of studies carried out by the Educational Testing Service (ETS) researchers with black, Anglo, and Mexican American parents clearly showed that parents have complex belief systems about how children develop and even have "theories" of children's learning (McGillicuddy-DeLisi, 1982a, 1982b; Sigel, 1985, 1986). Sutherland (1983) calls such a theory a "parenting model, the most essential ingredient of which is the parent's view of the nature of the child" (p. 139). Ethnic differences emerged in the ETS research, challenging the view that standard parent education can be used with any ethnic group. Social-class differences in beliefs about development also emerged, with higher SES beliefs' being more adaptive for the child's development on theoretical grounds (Miller, 1988, p. 273).

Goodnow's work has also focused on parents' beliefs about children (1984, 1985, 1988). In line with the anthropological and social constructionist viewpoints, Goodnow emphasizes the cultural construction rather than the self-construction of parental beliefs, since the former model has enjoyed much greater empirical support. In general, greater differences are found between groups than within groups (Goodnow, 1988, p. 297) across cultural, ethnic, and social-class groups. Similarly, in a comparison of German and Costa Rican mothers, important differences in "naive" theories of child development were found, with parental experience as measured by parity (number of children) having a negligible effect (Keller, Miranda, & Gauda, 1984).

Clearly, parents' beliefs about child development and socialization are powerful contextual meaning systems that influence the process by directly guiding child-rearing behaviors, expectations from children, and so on. Super and Harkness (1986) consider the "psychology of the caretaker" as one of the three components of the "developmental niche" (the others being the physical and social setting and child care and child rearing). Dasen (1988) shows how this parental psychology in the form of "ethnotheories" (Super & Harkness, 1986), indigenous theories (Chamoux, 1986), or "naive theories" (Sabatier, 1986) affects cognitive and social development. If, for example, a people's definition of intelligence includes a primarily social dimension and manual dexterity, as among the Baoule in Africa, then child rearing and socialization will stress the development of social-relational and manual skills rather than abstract reasoning.

Similarly, perceptions of parental roles, and values associated with these role perceptions, are important aspects of the socialization context. For example, cross-cultural comparisons of Japanese and American mothers' maternal role perceptions point to temporal differences in the definition of the role and the responsibilities it involves (Shand, 1985). The American mothers envision a short-term maternal involvement until children reach adolescence, and their responsibilities are physical care (with the husband's help) and loving the child, with no duties toward the patrilineage. For the Japanese mother, on the other hand, motherhood is a lifelong role embedded in her husband's patrilineal (corporate) structure, where she is responsible for bringing up a cooperative and respectful child who is also highly achievement oriented.

The contrasting familial-parental meaning systems in Japan and in the West, especially in the United States, have been the focus of much recent comparative research, mainly with regard to their impact on mother-child and mother-infant interaction outcomes (e.g.,

Durrett, Richards, Otaki, Pennebaker, & Nyquist, 1986; Otaki, Durrett, Richards, Nyquist, & Pennebaker, 1986; Shand & Kosawa, 1985; Takahashi, 1986). Much of this work benefits from earlier anthropological research that provided insights into the distinct familial-societal values in Japan. The basic social, rather than individual, orientation in Japanese child-rearing values is well established (e.g., Caudill & Frost, 1973; DeVos, 1973; Doi, 1973; Iwasaki-Mass, 1984; Kornadt, 1987).

FAMILY (PARENT-CHILD) INTERACTION

This discussion of parental values has already touched upon parent-child interaction in the family. It is to be noted, however, that the belief-behavior relationship is rather complicated, as reviewed by Miller (1988). Starting with the classic work of Barry, Child, and Bacon (1959) and further elaborated in Pelto's (1968) characterization of "tight" and "loose" societies, two contrasting socialization patterns have been proposed. In preindustrial societies with ecological conditions involving sedentary agrarian life-styles, high food accumulation, and complex hierarchical social structure, socialization tends to encourage obedience and compliance in children, whereas in hunting, nomadic, low food accumulating societies with simpler social structures, more individual freedom is fostered. Furthermore, these two contrasting emphases are also found to relate to field dependence (low psychological differentiation) and field independence (high psychological differentiation), respectively (Berry, 1967, 1976, 1980; Witkin & Berry, 1975; Witkin, Dyk, Faterson, Goodenow, & Karp, 1962).

Extensions to modern societies have been attempted, focusing on the degree of individual autonomy versus group orientation and dependency stressed in child socialization. Bagley, Iwawaki, and Young (1983) compared Japanese children with American, English, and Jamaican children and found the Japanese children more differentiating and disembedding (field independent) than the others, notwithstanding the "tighter" socialization environment in Japan, which would call for the contrary prediction. It appears that an "unpackaging" of tight environments is needed. There may be a difference between tight socialization environments based on "authoritarian obedience" and the "use of sociability and group experience" in the degree to which they promote field dependence. Indeed, in a study on maternal strategies for regulating children's behavior by Conroy, Hess, Azuma, and Kashiwagi (1980) in Japan and the United States and replicated in India (Sinha, 1985), appeal to feelings was seen more among Japanese and Indian mothers, and there was a greater use of authority by American mothers. Kornadt (1987) also emphasizes the basic empathic harmony between the Japanese mother and child, which enables the mother to regulate the child's behavior without escalation of conflict, confrontation, and depreciation of the child's self-esteem (p. 133). He also explains the lower aggression found among the Japanese mainly in terms of the "strong emotional, nonverbally-transmitted togetherness and probably a strong empathy" (p. 135) between mother and child. The resultant specific behaviors on the part of the mother (and the child) do not lead to aggression.

A common theme underlying these observations and research findings is the relative importance of expectations of autonomy or dependency from children. These expectations are inherently related to the interdependence or independence of family members—a basic dimension to be taken up later.

SOCIAL CLASS AND FAMILY TYPE

Variations in socioeconomic status emerge as social-class differences, rural/urban differences, and even ethnic differences, since (low) social-class standing and ethnicity (or minority status) often overlap. When ethnic or cross-cultural comparisons are made it is important to isolate the possible confounding effects of social class. Some studies show, in fact, that ethnic variations in socialization values initially obtained among different ethnic groups either disappear or are substantially reduced when socioeconomic status is controlled (Cashmore & Goodnow, 1986; Lambert, 1987). Similarly, socioeconomic status can override the effects of family size on children's cognitive performance (Marjoribanks & Walberg, 1976), the effects of ethnic/cultural differences on maternal behavior (Podmore & St. George, 1986), and even racial and national differences in ego development (Ciaccio, 1976). Therefore, if relative social class standing is not known, differences obtained in comparative studies cannot be attributed to ethnic or cultural differences (Kağıtçıbaşı & Berry, 1989).

This does not mean we should embark upon simplistic social-class comparisons or return to the class-specific socialization research of the 1960s and 1970s. It is more important to show why and how social-class standing makes a difference rather than to show that it does. For example, in his classic social-class analysis of parental values and child-rearing orientations, Kohn (1969) proposed that social-class difference is due to anticipatory socialization of children to develop orientations adaptive to the different future environmental (especially occupational) demands, as perceived by parents. Thus middle-class child-rearing orientations stress autonomy, which is adaptive for future middle-class occupational requirements of individual decision making, whereas working-class parents emphasize obedience and conformity to external constraints, in anticipation of such occupational contexts for their children.

Both groups also reflect their own current occupational experiences. Negative occupational experience lowers self-esteem and engenders feelings of powerlessness that affect people's lives in general (Kohn & Schooler, 1983), Taking Kohn's (1969) analysis one step further, Bernstein (1971, 1975) studied the complex relations among lower social class (restrictive work experiences and unfavorable living conditions), status-oriented family role structures, and restricted verbalization leading to lower cognitive abilities in children. In this model, class-related living conditions and family communication structure are as important as the socialization environment.

Extensions beyond social-class variation are seen in ecological orientations in cross-cultural comparison. For example, LeVine (1974) proposes that socialization that encourages compliant behavior in children is adaptive for survival in hazardous environments, and therefore in such contexts compliance constitutes a basic "parental goal" for children. The same line of structural-functional theorizing is also seen in the aforementioned work on different ecological contexts in subsistence-level economies (Barry, Child, & Bacon, 1959; Berry, 1967, 1976) and in extended or joint families in traditional society (Bisht & Sinha, 1981; Kağıtçıbaşı, 1984). It thus becomes important both to assess the relative influence of social class and other environmental variables and also to understand how social class influences socialization and family interactions, beyond other (ecological, ethnic, cultural) factors.

Together with social-class variations in family interactions, the effects of family type (mainly extended vs. nuclear) have also been studied, at times overlapping with rural/urban and social-class distinctions. The question of change in family interactions through social change has come to the fore in these studies, sometimes with conflicting findings. For example, a number of studies (Bisht & Sinha, 1981; Harrington & Whiting, 1972; Holtzman, Diaz-Guerrero, & Swartz, 1975; LeVine, Kline, & Owen, 1967) found less restrictive discipline and greater autonomy in child socialization with a shift from extended to nuclear families and with modernization in several sociocultural contexts. However, just the opposite trend is also observed (Sinha, 1988, pp. 59–60). Various factors undoubtedly account for the different findings, such as time of the investigation, sampling, and assessment techniques. Also, social class and family structure may be confounded. For example, Rohner and Chakı-Sircar (1987) found less maternal warmth in high-caste families, which are also extended, compared with the untouchables, which are nuclear households. It is not clear whether the difference is due to social class (caste) or family structure, to both, or to some other cause, such as the higher stress the researchers found among the high-caste families.

Other research shows decreasing extended family values with education (K. A. Miller, 1984) and urbanization but increased valuation with age (Gutman, 1976) among men. Although some aspects of extended family ideology are found to be weakened (such as obligations for the education of extended family members), it is still highly cherished in Africa (Obikeze, 1987) and is found to provide a favorable environment for the adjustment of children whose parents separate (Fine, 1986) in Africa and India.

It is important to understand the complex relations between social-class standing, family structure, and values, as well as changes in these through social change. It is commonly assumed, for example, that there is a general shift from extended to nuclear families with modernization, with corresponding changes in family ideologies and interaction patterns to resemble those of the Western middle classes. Assumptions like these are effective in undermining our understanding of the diversity existing in family structures and values by considering them "transitional," as I will discuss later on. These considerations lead us to take a closer look at some key underlying themes in the study of the family through time and space (across cultures). The following section on dependence/independence also reflects family diversity. However, since this is a dimension that is basic to the model of family change to be proposed, it is treated in a separate section rather than as an instance of family diversity.

Dependence/Independence: A Basic Dimension

A common theme underlying the discussions up to now has been the dependence-independence dimension. How much dependence or independence exists or is valued in family relations is a key to understanding both the socialization process and family functioning. This dimension can be conceptualized at both the individual and family levels, as the degree of "intrapsychic autonomy" or "interpersonal autonomy" (Cohler & Geyer, 1982).

The dependence/independence dimension has to do with basic human merging and separation. At the individual level it derives from the "resolution" of the issue of "individuation/separation" as proposed by the object-relations theory, based on the psychoanalytic perspective (e.g., Mahler, 1972; Mahler, Pine, & Bergman, 1975; Panel, 1973a, 1973b). As I mentioned before, in the discussion of family interactions, the degree of separation and individual autonomy induced in child socialization is a key factor that shows cross-cultural variability.

The separation/individuation hypothesis assumes this process is a natural (organismic) developmental sequence involving the attainment of object constancy, which allows mental representations of objects in their absence (mainly of people who are comforting) and thus autonomy from environment. This was also posited as the development of the rational autonomous ego by ego psychologists (Hartman, 1939/1958). Thus separation and individuation are considered to constitute the basic developmental process of early childhood. From a rather different perspective, family-systems theory proposes a similar model of family interactions. A basic structural factor underlying these interactions is the boundary separating the parent and the child. With a general systemic orientation, this theory (Guerin, 1976; Minuchin, 1974) emphasizes the boundaries separating the subsystems (selves) within the family system. Individual autonomy and separation of self from others with clear boundaries are considered necessary for healthy family interactions. "Enmeshed" families with unclear and overlapping boundaries are considered pathological (Minuchin, Rosman, & Baker, 1978).

Clearly, some early cognitive process of selfhood differentiation must take place for the identity formation of an individual, and every person in every society is aware of being a separate entity from others, even from those who are closest. At this absolute existential level the process of separation/individuation is obvious. Psychological theory goes far beyond this level, however, and explains healthy and pathological personality development and family functioning in terms of psychological (not philosophical or logical) interpretations and extensions of the concepts of symbiotic versus individuated and dependent versus independent interpersonal relations throughout the life-span development.

Indeed, individual autonomy and independence constitute the cornerstones of the psychology of personality—the model of man in the Western world. The related concepts of self-reliance and self-sufficiency, privacy, individual achievement, and freedom are stressed. For example, Kagan (1984) states that "in American families, the primary loyalty is to self—its values, autonomy, pleasure, virtue and actualization," and Spence (1985) notes, "At least since the time of Alexis de Tocqueville, observers have recognized that individualism is central to the American character." Individual autonomy is a cherished value, and it is well integrated into both theory and application: the latter is seen, for example, in parent education programs where mothers are taught to "let go" of their young children. Thus individualist independence is a part of the Western (and especially American) value system.

At this level the issue becomes wide open for alternative interpretations in accordance with different cultural values and meaning systems. To illustrate the point, I shall refer to the maternal regulation strategies of the Japanese mother, which I mentioned in the section on family interaction. Here is a contrast between two different meaning systems that render the same pattern of family relations normal or abnormal. The Japanese mother's message to the child, "I am one with you, we can be and will be of the same mind" (Azuma, 1984, reported in Kornadt, 1987, p. 133), is exactly the definition of a "symbiotic" relationship, an expression of pathological "enmeshment" in the Western family, as interpreted by Western psychology.[1]

Thus some concepts that are presumed to be structural universals, either from an organismic/maturational perspective or as inherent to functioning systems, emerge as culture-specific meanings when subjected to cross-cultural scrutiny. Psychological conceptualizations of individuation and personal boundaries do not appear to be universally invariant, since different conceptualizations of person-environment relations abound in different cultures. As described before, under "Socially Defined Meaning," contextual and relational definitions of the person are reported that do not stress psychological boundaries and separation/individuation. Accordingly, a great deal of research from non-Western family contexts that show "sociocentric" rather than "idiocentric" orientations in socialization in "tight" (i.e., close-knit) environments demanding conformity and obedience from children can also be explained by this basic relational concept of the person.

In the sections on family interaction and social class and family type, a functional explanation was provided for the findings of conformity and dependence orientation in socialization (e.g., Barry, Child, & Bacon, 1959; Berry, 1967; Kohn, 1969; LeVine, 1974). It now appears that an additional explanation is needed, in terms of basic family meaning systems of relatedness and interdependence. Expectations of dependency and close-knit family relations are seen even when dependency (and obedience) do not have a survival value, as is amply demonstrated by research, for example, in urban, developed contexts in Japan, China, Hong Kong, Singapore, Taiwan, Turkey, Mexico, and India as well as among ethnic minorities and working-class families in the United States (e.g., Bond & Hwang, 1986; Caudill & Frost, 1973; Hayashi & Suzuki, 1984; Holtzman et al., 1975; Iwasaki-Mass, 1984; Kagan & Madsen, 1971;

---

1. It is interesting to note here the use of an almost identical "symbiotic" phrase—"Mommy and I are one"—by subliminal exposure for therapeutic purposes in a study by Silverman and Weinberger (1985). These researchers found that gratification of such unconscious wishes for a state of oneness with the good mother has ameliorative effects. This may be seen as psychodynamic evidence of a basic need for relatedness.

Kağıtçıbaşı, 1985; Morsbach, 1980; Neki, 1976; Roland, 1980; Sinha & Kao, 1988; Sussman & Burchinal, 1971; Yang, 1988).

I started this section with the recognition of a basic dimension of human dependence/independence. The following discussion, however, has mainly shown the cross-cultural inadequacy of formulations focusing on one pole of this dimension—independence. This is because most psychological theorizing has stressed this pole almost exclusively. Thus critics of Western psychology's one-sided view and those from different sociocultural contexts find themselves stressing the other pole of human interdependence to make their point (e.g., Kağıtçıbaşı, 1987; Sampson, 1977, 1987). Yet we need to recognize that this dimension reflects a basic duality in human needs—for dependence *and* for independence. The parallel concepts of relatedness versus individuation/separation/autonomy, to my mind, reflect the same basic duality. It may be claimed that relatedness/separation dimension, meaning blurring of boundaries versus clearly defined boundaries of individuals, is different from dependence/independence dimension. If so, are these overlapping dimensions or are they in a reciprocal relation to one another? I believe they are reflections of the same dual needs and are sufficiently close to be used interchangeably. Nevertheless, these are matters for theorizing and empirical research and therefore will not be pursued here.

These two basic needs or opposing forces have been well recognized in personality theories, especially those of Rank (1929, 1945), Angyal (1951), and Bakan (1966, 1968). For Rank the core tendencies are to minimize the fears of life (the inevitable process of separation and individualization) and of death (the inherent tendency toward union, fusion, and dependency); Angyal uses the expressions "autonomy" and "surrender" and Bakan uses "agency" and "communion." These conflict theories of personality recognize the simultaneous process of differentiation and integration toward a compromise solution of the two opposing forces. When a disproportionate amount of one of the two forces is expressed to the detriment of the other, this is seen as a failure or malady. This is different from the view of the existentialists, who advocate achieving individuation at any cost (reviewed in Maddi, 1980). Yet Angyal and especially Bakan (1966, 1968) mainly stress the dangers of denying union, probably in reaction to the dominant individualist ethos of the Western world.

Similar themes are seen in others' formulations, ranging from Deutsch's (1962) promotive interdependence (cooperation)/contrient interdependence (competition) to Benedict's (1970) high- or low-synergy societies. Following up on Bakan's work, Block (1973) has examined the usefulness of agency and communion for studying male and female sex-role ideals, respectively, and the concepts have been important in theories of sex-role development (Chodorow, 1974, 1978; Gilligan, 1982).

Despite this theorizing and research, however, the two basic needs for autonomy and relatedness, for independence and dependence, are rarely recognized as equally important. The heavy individualist bias appears to be enduring in the face of opposing evidence. The recognition of these two human needs is important for the model of family change I shall propose later.

ASSUMPTION OF CHANGE

The organismic model of the psychoanalytic orientation (as elaborated in object relations theory) and even the systemic model as used in family systems theory are inadequate in dealing with cross-cultural family diversity. What are posited as basic universal structures in the development of human relations turn out to be Western social constructs. As a consequence, cross-cultural psychological study of the family finds itself in a theoretical vacuum. Cross-cultural research has seriously challenged the claim to universality of a psychology based on the Euro-American experience. However, neither mainstream psychology nor cross-cultural psychology has yet met the challenge in developing a cross-cultural theory of the family to deal with cross-cultural diversity.

In the absence of challenging theory, a common response of mainstream psychology to family diversity in the world is to depreciate it by considering it temporary. The assumption is that the cross-cultural variation in family and socialization values is bound to decrease with modernization, showing unidirectional change toward the Western model. This is the basic assumption of modernization theory (e.g., Inkeles, 1969, 1977; Inkeles & Smith, 1974).

As briefly discussed before, this assumption is common even though general modernization theory has lost the popularity it enjoyed in 1960s and early 1970s (Dawson, 1967; Doob, 1967; Kahl, 1968; Suzman, 1973). The implicit assumption of unidirectional change is shared by the psychologists of both Western and Third World countries, and the "changing" societies are considered "transitional." Through this change, the close-knit (extended) family structure is expected to go through a process of nucleation to end up resembling the Western nuclear family (e.g., Caldwell, 1977; Goode, 1963). With the structural nucleation, psychological nucleation or individuation is expected to occur, in the sense discussed earlier.

Underlying this expectation of unidirectional change is the evolutionary model of progressive improvement toward a fixed goal—the Western prototype, considered by some (Mazrui, 1968) to be in the tradition of social Darwinism. Thus what is different from this prototype is considered "deficient" and is expected to "improve" with modernization and social change. To understand the existing diversity therefore is not of much theoretical interest for the mainstream psychologist.

A second notion underlying the expectation of unidirectional change is that the Western family itself has evolved through the process of nucleation because of industrialization. Though widely assumed, this view is being challenged today by historical evidence of individualism and the nuclear family predating the industrial revolution in western Europe and especially in England (Laslett, 1971, pp. 93–95, 1977, pp. 14–25, 1977; Lesthaeghe, 1983; Lesthaeghe & Surkyn, 1988; Thadani, 1978; Thornton, 1984), even predating the rise of Protestantism (Hanawalt, 1986; MacFarlane, 1978, 1987). The evidence refers to many Western family patterns that have been assumed to be the result of modernization. For example, individual ownership and inheritance of property existed in England all the way back into the Middle Ages; secular individualism, individual interests, and rationality underlay the marital fertility decline of the eighteenth and nineteenth centuries; individual control of sexuality and of age at marriage dated as far back as the late Middle Ages (Ariès, 1980). Historical evidence in the United States also points to continuities and family patterns similar to current ones in preindustrial America (1800–1850) as reflected in travelers' observations (Furstenberg, 1966) and magazine articles of the period (Lantz, Keyes, & Schultz, 1975).

Given the historical evidence to the contrary, it is difficult to claim any longer that it was industrialization that "necessitated" family nucleation and individuation in western Europe and that the same process will "inevitably" take place in the rest of the world as it industrializes (Thornton, 1984). It appears, rather, that the present structure of the Western family derives from an individualist culture base and that industrialization capitalized on this individualist culture. It may even be speculated that the basic individualist elements existing in the western European culture paved the way for the rise of Protestantism and capitalism rather than the other way around. A reinterpretation of Weber's thesis (1958) is not being attempted here. The point is that the historical causal sequence accepted for western Europe may be open to alternative interpretations and in any case may not generalize to the rest of the world. If, as I have argued, individualism was not a necessary outcome of industrialization in the West, then the argument by analogy predicting that individualism will follow industrialization in the Third World is not warranted.

It is true that through industrialization and economic development similar demands are made on the family, such as for greater mobility, but it is conceivable that different elements of the non-Western cultural and familial context can be mobilized for industrialization and economic growth. Close-knit family ties may be such an element, which if utilized effectively may promote economic growth rather than hinder it, as is usually assumed. This brings us to the example of East Asia, especially Japan, which challenges the evolutionary model and the assumption of "deficiency" of everything different from the Western prototype.

There is an assumption that collectivist dependent orientations are "deficient" in the sense that they are not compatible with economic development (e.g., Kapp, 1963; Minturn & Hitchcock, 1966; Weber, 1958; as discussed by Sinha, 1988). Indeed, Hofstede (1980) found a close association between individualism and economic affluence in the world. The case of Japan, and to a lesser extent those of the newly industrialized East Asian societies, presents a real challenge to this view, since collectivist orientations and close-knit interpersonal and family ties are continuing and are obviously not incompatible with economic-industrial growth. They do not fit the unidirectional evolutionary model toward the end point of psychologyical individuation and family nucleation.

There is a great deal of evidence, some of it reviewed before, showing the continuity of the basic family culture in East Asia as well as in the developed metropolitan centers in the developing world (e.g., Bond, 1986; Duben, 1982; Hayashi & Suzuki, 1984; Iwawaki, 1986; Kağıtçıbaşı, 1988; Sinha & Kao, 1988; Yang, 1988). Thus, referring to survey results conducted by the Japanese government on the "national Japanese character" over more than two decades (Hayashi, Nishira, Suzuki, Mizuno, & Sakamoko, 1977; Suzuki, 1984), Trommsdorf concludes that no change in basic values has occurred in Japan (1985, p. 232). All this evidence challenges the evolutionary view with the Western pattern as the end point. Alternative patterns of family and human relations appear to be enduring rather than "transitional."

Nevertheless, convergence toward the Western pattern may in fact happen as a result of cultural diffusion. The mass media and communications in the world are very much dominated by Western and especially American programs that provide role models, particularly for the young. However, if it were to materialize, this would be a different kind of change than that necessitated by industrialization, as predicted by modernization theory.

THE AMERICAN FAMILY

I have already referred to a great deal of research comparing the Western, mainly American, family with the non-Western family. Differences in the patterns of independence versus dependence, individual versus group orientation (individuation and separation versus overlapping personal boundaries) have been noted. Individualist independence and autonomy and the emphasis put on these in psychology have been severely criticized by Sampson as "self-contained individualism" "undermining the social bond" (1977, 1987) and by other social critics (e.g., Gergen, 1973; Pepitone, 1976), or by feminists as imposing a masculine mode of thinking characterized by competitive separateness prevailing over a feminine orientation of relatedness (Chodorow, 1974; Gilligan, 1982). Nevertheless, the individualist ideology continues to be strong, and such criticisms point up its pervasiveness.

When discussing the dependence/independence dimension, I referred to Cohler and Geyer's (1982) conceptualization of these characteristics at the individual level as "intrapsychic autonomy" and at the family level as "interpersonal autonomy." In line with the individualist ideology, just as the person is to be separated from others with clear-cut boundaries, so too the conjugal nuclear family is to be separated from kin. Thus, for example, frequent contact between relatives has been seen to undermine the solidarity and autonomy of the nuclear family in American society (Blood, 1972, p. 214), and the extended family and collectivist orientations have been considered to hinder innovation and the formation of intrapersonal sources of security, since they provide "ready-made forms of security" (Gutman, 1976).

More recently, quite different views are being voiced in research (e.g., Fu, Hinkle, & Hanna, 1986) that consider dependency a valued trait in adulthood, since it helps maintain close family ties. Nevertheless, insightful observations of the American family note an ambivalance in basic values (Bellah, Madsen, Sullivan, Swindler, & Tipton, 1985, p. 144) or a conflict between professed ideology and observed behavior. While on one hand commitment to individualism, independence, and self-sufficiency is prevalent (Berger & Berger, 1984), on the other hand a great deal of interdependence actually exists among generations, kin, and families (e.g., Bronfenbrenner & Weiss, 1983; Cohler & Grunebaum, 1981; Fu et al., 1986; Keniston, 1985; Sussman, 1974; Sussman & Burchinal, 1971). The ambivalence is between the needs for dependency and for autonomy and is reflected in the discrepancy between the "myth of family independence" (Keniston, 1985) and the reality of interdependence. Cohler and Geyer (1982) review a great deal of evidence for mutual support between generations (adults and their parents) and among relatives or nonkin functioning as kin, extending over the family life cycle and covering such areas as economic help, help with child care, health care, and moral support. This is especially strong among women and among low-income families, mainly because women are more socialized to interdependence (Chodorow, 1978) and are more in charge of homemaking, and because low-income families often lack other sources of support.

It is precisely because self-sufficiency is a cultural ideal, however, that this interdependence is problematic. The ambivalence can even result in family pathology (Boszormenyi-Nagy & Spark, 1973). But in any case, actual relationships show much interdependence.

That the continuing use of "affectional dependence" (Parens & Saul, 1971) among adults in the United States evokes great discomfort for members of each generation (Boszormenyi-Nagy & Spark, 1973; Cohler & Geyer, 1982) contrasts sharply with other cultural contexts where the same interdependencies exist without any apparent ambivalence. For example, Yang (1988) reports the continuing importance of "familism" in China, in spite of policies undermining its role (p. 94), and of close networks among the elderly and their offspring, as evidenced by recent surveys (Lin, 1985; Pan, 1985). This interdependence continues even though the elderly do not have to depend on their offspring financially; in fact they may continue contributing to their offspring, a situation "indicative of the traditional parental protection of children until their death" (Yang, 1988, p. 109), which evokes no discomfort for anyone involved. Similar family interdependencies are reported for other cultural contexts— for example, Indian (Neki, 1976; Sinha, 1981, 1988; Sinha & Kao, 1988), Turkish (Kağıtçıbaşı, 1982c, 1985), Chinese (Bond, 1986), and various Asian societies (Sinha & Kao, 1988) as well as for ethnic groups in the posttechnological society, such as Asian American (Iwasaki-Mass, 1984; Suzuki, 1985) and Hispanic families in the United States (Mirande, 1985), and various ethnic groups in Australia (Storer, 1985).

Furthermore, family interdependence, both psychological and material, appears to be independent of household structure. It is not an exclusive characteristic of extended households but exists among families that are constituted of nuclear households but function as extended families in mutually supportive networks—the "functionally extended" (Kağıtçıbaşı, 1985, p. 133) or "modified extended" family (Cohler & Geyer, 1982, p. 197). In fact a great deal of research shows that in many parts of the Third World where interdependent family patterns prevail, most families are and have been nuclear for a long time, extended household structures being characteristic mostly of wealthy families that have enough land to support a large family (Drinkwater, 1985; Duben, 1982; McCarthy, 1979; Timur, 1972; Yang, 1988). The common assumption about the prevalence of the extended family appears to derive mainly from the observation and interdependent family *functioning*, that is, proximal nuclear households that are "functionally extended," as well as from prevalent extended family *ideals* that people have, since it represents an affluent life-style.

COMMONALITY ISSUE

The discussion above has questioned some common assumptions about the family both in the Western (American) and non-Western contexts. It has pointed to the interdependencies among American families, notwithstanding the commitment to individualism and self-sufficiency. Given these similarities, then, what is the difference between the Western (especially American) and the non-Western family? Is it only a difference of degree? And how is it to be explained? A claim of no difference would violate the extensive research findings and observations, some of which have been discussed before, as well as the personal impressions of cross-cultural psychologists, anthropologists, and laymen experiencing both cultures. It can be claimed here that the basic needs of dependence and independence are shared by both individuals and families to a greater or lesser extent in line with cultural values. Factors of a different order of existence, such as economic development or industrialization, are apparently not adequate to explain the observed commonalities and differences.

A problem in this discussion is lumping together many different cultural contexts and relevant variables when making comparisons between the Western and non-Western patterns. The same holds true for comparisons of loose versus tight or individualist versus collectivist societies. Even though this is disturbing, empirical evidence does point to greater commonalities within the Western societies and also within the Third World countries than between these two groups, such that almost all Third World countries are collectivist (Hofstede, 1980; Triandis, 1988, p. 293). Thus description of these common patterns, as well as differences, makes heuristic sense, even though some elements of the descriptive patterns may not be logical requisites of these cultural patterns. Instead, they may be more the result of such factors as poverty, low levels of education, and agrarian economy. It is important, therefore, to go beyond the descriptive characteristics into psychologically basic relational patterns to understand the commonalities and differences in family patterns. We need a more analytic psychological approach to the conceptualization of the self and the family in terms of separateness/independence versus relatedness/interdependence.

I have attempted this in the previous discussion. To go beyond description, however, we need to understand the structural-functional antecedents of the behavioral patterns under study. It appears that these antecedents are common among many societies rather than being unique features of any one culture. This brings us to a consideration of some of the relevant findings of what is called the Value of Children Study. Together with other research I have reviewed, it will form the basis of a model of family change that I will propose next.

The Value of Children Study

The nine-country Value of Children Study was conducted in the mid 1970s in Indonesia, the Federal Republic of Germany, Korea, the Philippines, Singapore, Taiwan, Thailand, Turkey, and the United States with nationally representative samples, except in Germany and Indonesia, totaling 20,000 married respondents (only women in Germany) (see Bulatao, 1979; Darroch, Meyer, & Singarimbun, 1981; Fawcett, 1983; Hoffman, 1987; Kağıtçıbaşı, 1982a, 1982b, 1982c). The study focused on motivations for childbearing and the values parents attributed to children, using a common core interview schedule. Two main value types attributed to children came to the fore—psychological and economic. The latter included children's material contribution to the family both when they are young and when they grow up, especially as a source of old-age security to their parents. The values attributed to children and the expectations from them reflect the very functioning of the family. Where utilitarian/ economic values are attributed to the child, the child's actual material contribution to the family is also found to be substantial, a situation that still prevails in many parts of the Third World, especially in rural agrarian contexts.

In reexaming the demographic transition theory, Caldwell (1977) proposed the concept of "the great divide," which is the point in historical time when the net wealth flows from the child to the parents are replaced by those from the parents to the child. This is the shift from high to low fertility, since with urbanization and economic development children become an economic burden rather than an economic asset. Together with this shift in wealth flows, according to Caldwell, go family nucleation and the shifting of young

Table 1
Old-Age Security as Reason for Childbearing and Expectation of Future Support from Sons or Daughters

	Germany	Indonesia		Korea	Philippines	Singapore	Taiwan	Thailand	Turkey	United States
		Javanese	Sundanese							
"To have someone to depend on when you are old" (as reason for having a child)										
Not important										
Women	68	1	0	19	2	13	7	3	8	73
Men	—	2	1	33	3	17	11	6	8	75
Somewhat important										
Women	24	6	2	27	9	36	14	18	15	19
Men	—	9	5	27	11	39	17	23	15	18
Very important										
Women	8	93	98	54	89	51	79	79	77	8
Men	—	89	94	40	86	44	72	71	77	7
"To be sure that in your old age you will have someone to help you" (as reason for wanting another child)										
Not important										
Women	79	8	6	64	10	15	37	5	38	73
Men	—	15	23	74	10	18	33	10	50	75

	Germany	Indonesia Javanese	Indonesia Sundanese	Korea	Philippines	Singapore	Taiwan	Thailand	Turkey	United States
Somewhat important										
Women	17	10	9	18	12	37	15	24	14	18
Men	—	12	13	13	12	39	15	24	14	17
Very important										
Women	3	82	84	18	78	48	48	71	48	9
Men	—	73	64	12	77	43	53	67	37	7

"Would you expect your son(s)/daughter(s) to support you financially when you grow old?"

	Germany S	Germany D	Javanese S	Javanese D	Sundanese S	Sundanese D	Korea S	Korea D	Philippines S	Philippines D	Singapore S	Singapore D	Taiwan S	Taiwan D	Thailand S	Thailand D	Turkey S	Turkey D	United States S	United States D
No																				
Women	—	—	6	7	9	10	9	45	6	7	5	8	12	56	8	9	9	22	86	87
Men	—	—	9	10	6	6	17	52	8	10	7	9	19	67	16	19	16	36	85	88
Depends																				
Women	—	—	9	9	12	20	6	9	8	7	55	61	3	5	4	4	0	0	2	2
Men	—	—	13	13	8	9	5	7	10	10	62	66	5	4	6	6	0	0	3	2
Yes																				
Women	—	—	85	83	76	69	85	46	86	85	39	31	85	39	86	87	91	78	12	11
Men	—	—	79	77	86	85	78	42	82	80	31	25	76	29	78	75	84	64	12	11

Note: All figures are percentages. S = son; D = daughter.

married couples' material/emotional investments from their elderly parents to their children. This is a demographic concept in line with modernization theory and fitting with Ariès's (1980) analysis of motivations for the declining birthrate in western Europe starting at the end of the eighteenth century (p. 649).

As I said before, generalizations of such complete family nucleation to the Third World are highly problematic. Nevertheless, in a comparative analysis of some of the Value of Children (VOC) Study findings I found evidence for a systematic variation of the old-age security value of children and expectations of material help from grown-up offspring with economic development (Table 1).

Clearly the American and German responses (where available) contrast with those from the other countries. The American and German respondents found the questions regarding help expected from offspring in old age rather offensive and denied being dependent on anyone, especially their children. Responses such as "I don't want anything from my children; if they can take care of themselves, I'll be glad" were common. By contrast, the Turkish respondents were offended that we were even questioning the loyalty of their children. A common response was, "Of course a loyal child [grown-up offspring] would never let down his parents." It is to be noted that the responses from Singapore and Korea, both going through rapid economic growth and decreased fertility, fell halfway between the extremes. The variations among the countries roughly parallel differences in their overall development levels. Thus, with low levels of economic/technological development and lack of widespread social welfare institutions such as social security systems and old-age pensions, their functions are undertaken by families, especially adult offspring. The opposite pattern is seen in the context of high economic development. Women stress the old-age security VOC more, except in the United States, reflecting their greater dependence on their children and more limited access to social welfare systems.

Within-country variations parallel the cross-cultural ones in terms of socioeconomic development, for example, in Turkey, as the development of the area of residence increased, the salience of the old-age security VOC decreased (100% in the least developed, 73% in medium developed, 61% in developed areas, and 40% in large metropolitan centers). Other utilitarian VOCs also decreased with socioeconomic development and education. For example, children's "help with household chores" and "material help" lost salience with education (28% and 56%, respectively, at no education level; 22% and 54% at primary-school level; 11% and 15% at high-school level; and 0% and 20% at university level). Similarly, the type of women's employment also relates to VOCs. For example, the old-age security VOC is stressed most strongly by unpaid (agricultural) family workers in rural areas (100%) and then by small shop owners and artisans (typically "traditional" groups) (91%) but is much less important for wage earners (50%) and least important for white-collar workers (19% to 37%). Thus, when employment provides old-age security benefits, the contribution of children to satisfy this need becomes less important. A similar pattern appears for men.

In addition to the general changes in VOCs, the importance of specific reasons for wanting to have sons, especially economic/utilitarian reasons, decreases with economic development. For example, "material help" reasons decrease from 100% to 56% from the least developed to the metropolitan areas. The "old-age security" reason shows a similar decrease with development, and both values also lose importance with education. These findings indicate decreased material interdependencies. Both men and women expect more economic help from their sons than from their daughters, especially in patriarchal contexts where there is a strong son preference, as found in Turkey and Korea in the VOC Study (Kağıtçıbaşı, 1982a).

Although I have not discussed horizontal interaction patterns in the family (spousal relations), I will briefly touch upon them with regard to the VOC findings; more detailed treatment of the topic is provided elsewhere (Kağıtçıbaşı, 1982a, 1982b, 1986). The Turkish VOC findings indicate negative correlations of woman's intrafamily status with economic/utilitarian VOC ($-.16$), son preference ($-.12$), and expectation of financial help from children ($-.19$). Increased role sharing between spouses (an indicator of increased female status) is negatively associated with son preference among men ($-.11$). Furthermore, with socioeconomic development, spouses' sex-role relations become more egalitarian, and both economic/utilitarian VOC and son preference decrease. Thus, important changes occur with development in intrafamily dynamics and VOCs. The opposite pattern, characterized by low woman's status, economic VOC, and strong son preference, is also associated with large number of children.

The last finding underlies the commonly observed relation between socioeconomic development and fertility decline—the so-called demographic transition theory. Economic VOC is associated with child numbers but psychological VOC is not. This is because the material contributions of children can be added to one another, yet psychological values such as love and pride are not cumulative in the same way and can be fully satisfied with one or two children. Thus in the VOC study women who had two children desired to have more if they stressed the economic VOC but did not want more if they stressed the psychological VOC (Kağıtçıbaşı, 1982a, 1982b). With socioeconomic development economic VOC decreases, and since it is associated with high child numbers, its reduction contributes to lower fertility. On the other hand, psychological VOC either does not change or may increase with development. Nevertheless, because it is not number based, such an increase does not contribute to fertility. Thus, at least to some degree it is because economic and psychological VOCs are differentially affected by development and are also differentially related to desired child numbers that a decrease in fertility is seen with development.

Thus a pattern of lower fertility, lower son preference, lower expectations of material contributions from children, and increased intrafamily status of the woman emerges with socioeconomic development. In terms of family interactions, the main finding is decreased intergenerational dependency with economic development. However, it is important to note that this is *material* dependency. With urbanization and economic development, compulsory education, child-labor laws, and nonagricultural urban living conditions, children cost more than they contribute to the family; institutional supports further replace children's contribution to the old-age security needs of their parents. Where living conditions undermine children's material contribution to the family, utilitarian/economic values are then not attributed to children.

These findings do *not* warrant concluding that family nucleation-separation is inevitable with economic growth or that there is a shift from the traditional interdependent interaction pattern to the independence of the Western nuclear family. This is because the two spheres of family interdependence—material and emotional (affectional, psychological)—need to be differentiated. The VOC Study findings refer to material interdependencies. Psychological family interdependencies can continue to be strong even in the absence of material interdependencies (e.g., Yang, 1988).

Evidence for decreased material dependencies without a corresponding decrease in emotional dependencies comes from a recent study by Erelçin (1988) comparing modern (young and urban) and traditional (old and rural) groups in Turkey. She found that though the modern groups were less willing to give material resources to significant others than were the traditional groups, there was no difference between them in their willingness to give emotional resources. Further evidence comes from other research in Turkey on migrants from rural to urban areas (Karpat, 1976; Kongar, 1976) and on urban family relations, including visiting patterns (Duben, 1982; Kongar, 1972; Olson, 1982). These studies point to the significance and prevalence of kinship-family relations in developed urban areas, among both former rural migrants and middle-class families, even of professionals, in metropolitan centers. Thus Duben (1982) concludes that "the significance of kin relations seems not to be fading with increased urbanization or industrialization" (p. 94). This is in line with family interdependencies and communal tendencies in the United States and other posttechnological societies reviewed earlier.

Continuing, perhaps increasing, emotional interdependencies are also evidenced by the VOC Study. Although economic VOCs decrease with socioeconomic development, psychological VOCs are found to not change (Fawcett, 1983) or even to increase (Kağıtçıbaşı, 1982a, 1982b). For example, the salience of the "companionship" value of children increases with the development level of the area of residence (20% in the least developed areas, 26% in medium developed, 32% in developed, and 51% in metropolitan areas) and with education in Turkey (from 33% to 43% from high-school to university level).

Child-rearing values also reflect family relations and the changes in them. In the VOC Study expectations of obedience (dependence) versus independence and self-reliance showed a systematic variance somewhat parallel to old-age security VOCs (Table 2). Among the characteristics most desired and second most desired in children, these two appear to be related to general development levels in opposite directions. The stress on independence in Korea and Singapore, newly industrialized countries, is notable. The findings from Indonesia and the Philippines and to a lesser extent from Turkey and Thailand point to expectations of dependence from children, this dependence to be reversed later on with the dependence of the elderly parents on their grown-up offspring—a pattern of family interdependence through generations.

In the context of material family interdependence, independence of a growing child is not functional and may even be a threat to the livelihood of the family, because independent offspring may look after their own self-interest rather than that of their family of origin. Thus qualities desired in children and future expectations from them fit together to form a general pattern of intergenerational family interactions (Tables 1 and 2). Socialization values are therefore related to socioeconomic development and are ingrained in family interaction patterns.

Together with the shift from material interdependencies to emotional interdependencies and from economic VOC to psychological

Table 2

Characteristics Most Desired and Second Most Desired in Children

	To Obey Their Parents		To Be Independent and Self-Reliant	
Country	Women	Men	Women	Men
Indonesia (Javanese)	88	85	17	23
Indonesia (Sundanese)	81	76	28	34
Korea	39	33	62	68
Philippines	81	83	15	13
Singapore	53	39	60	69
Taiwan	48	40	39	47
Thailand	59	55	17	24
Turkey	59	61	19	17
United States	35	43	51	43

Note: All figures are percentages.

VOC, modifications in child-rearing patterns can also be expected. When the material contribution of the offspring is no longer required, and thus their independence is not a threat to the family livelihood, autonomy would be allowed in child socialization. However, it would be limited so as not to lead to complete separation of children from the family, which would be a threat even for emotional interdependence. Thus socialization values and parent-child interaction would involve both control and autonomy. This pattern is closer to Baumrind's (1971, 1980) authoritative parenting than to authoritarian parenting, which is more in line with the obedience orientation in the context of material family interdependence.

A Model of Family Change

The discussions and review of research in this chapter and my analysis of the Value of Children Study findings have covered many basic characteristics differentiating family and socialization patterns across cultures. These characteristics also constitute the elements that may be expected to change through time with socioeconomic development. Here I will propose a general model of family change including three different patterns, based on the research results reviewed here as well as my own research. It incorporates the main lines of reasoning and evidence I have used up to now in a contextual model of change through space and time.

THREE PATTERNS

The context is conceptualized mainly in terms of objective living conditions surrounding the family interaction patterns and child socialization. Within this contextual model there is a systemic approach to the family, whose subsystems are socialization values and interaction patterns in child rearing and in self-other relations. Family structure can be seen both as a part of the family system and also as its context. Changes in context with social change and development result in corresponding changes in the family system, which in turn feed back into the context, modifying some of its elements. This occurs through modifications in family structure. Thus a dynamic interplay between the context and the family system occurs through time (Figs. 1, 2, and 3).

Before I describe what each one of the three patterns stands for, an explanation of the overall structure is needed. In each pattern the systems are interrelated in the same way. There is a recognition of the primacy of the context, though it can be modified through changes in family structure. The urban/rural, subsistence/affluence characteristics of the living conditions are differentiated mainly to refer to variations in socioeconomic development, with no attempt to be exhaustive. Such living conditions are seen to be causally related to family structure.

Family structures of the three patterns are significantly different from one another, though common characteristics exist between pattern Y and the other two, which do not overlap with one another. The structural aspects are those research has found to be basic to family functioning and to manifest systematic changes with socioeconomic development. They cohere to form systemic wholes within each pattern as the immediate context for family dynamics. That is why family structure is treated as context even though it is basically a part of the general family system.

The family system in each pattern comprises two interacting subsystems, socialization values and family interaction. The latter, in turn, is differentiated in terms of parenting/child rearing and the resultant self-other relations. Some of the main socialization values discussed in this chapter are included here—the ones that show variations along the individual/group, independence/interdependence dimensions and psychological/economic values of children. Baumrind's (1971, 1980) parenting terms are used under family interaction mainly with reference to the extent of control exercised and autonomy recognized in parents' orientation to children. The resulting familial/interpersonal, interdependence/independence, and relational/separated self characteristics can be seen as the final product of the overall system.

Pattern X. Pattern X refers mainly to rural/agrarian traditional societies with patrilineal family structures and to less developed areas in developing countries in general. Varieties of family structure, kinship, and descent systems involving matrilocal matrilineal structures, polygamous marriages, and so on, are not treated. I take up

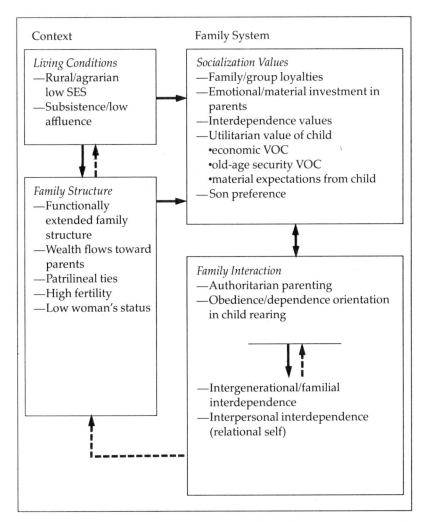

FIGURE 1. A model of family change: pattern X (interdependence): → causal relationship/influence; ↔ mutual causation; --➤ feedback.

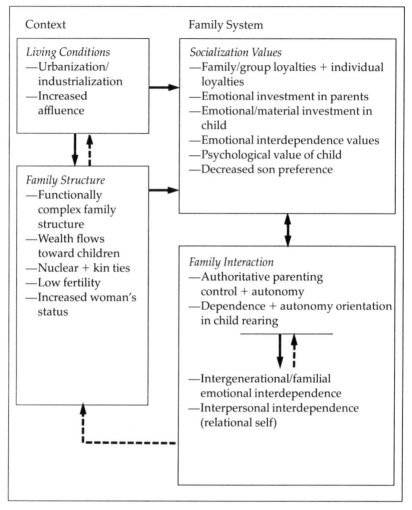

FIGURE 2. A model of family change: pattern Y (emotional interdependence).

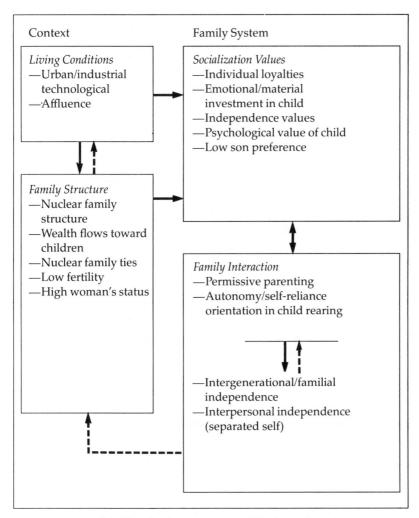

FIGURE 3. A model of family change: pattern Z (independence).

one common pattern, where a functionally extended family structure is prevalent. As I explained before, this is the type of family that often consists of nuclear household(s) but is in close proximity to immediate kin, especially the older generation. It operates as an extended family in carrying out such functions as home production of goods, child care, and agricultural production (Kağıtçıbaşı, 1985). With the importance of patrilineal ties, the woman, who is an outsider to the lineage, has low status.

Familism and group loyalties are stressed in socialization values; responsibilities of young adults toward their elderly parents and the flow of wealth toward parents highlight the importance of the old-age security and utilitarian values of children and son preference, in keeping with high fertility. Family interaction and child rearing revolve around parental control and obedience orientation—"authoritarian parenting" in Baumrind's terms (1971, 1980)—and result in intergenerational (familial) and interpersonal interdependence.

Pattern Y. This pattern differs from pattern X in significant ways, especially in terms of context, but they share basic characteristics, especially with regard to family interaction. The objective living conditions are different in this pattern and the previous one; this is the context of economic development and industrial/urban life-styles. The family structure is nuclear as a rule; however, again extension across generations and into kin renders it functionally complex. A functionally complex family means a family that has nuclear structure but is in complex interaction with immediate kin, extending into the communal environment for carrying out some functions, though not home production or consumption of goods, as may be the case for the functionally extended family (Kağıtçıbaşı, 1985). These extensions can occur bilaterally with less emphasis on the patrilineage and correspondingly increased woman's status, accompanied by women's education and gainful employment. With a shift from the utilitarian/economic value of children to the psychological value of children and decreased material contribution of children to their parents, there is decreased fertility and low son preference.

The main difference between pattern Y and pattern X in the family system is the nature of the interpersonal and interfamilial dependencies. Whereas in pattern X there are both material and emotional interdependencies, in pattern Y they are mainly of an emotional nature, as discussed before with regard to the VOC Study findings and other research results showing close ties among the generations even when not required for material well-being. Thus, emotional investment of young adults goes in both directions along the vertical axis, both toward their elderly parents and toward their children, but their material investment is directed mainly toward their children. Socialization values continue to stress group loyalties, in line with emotional interdependencies, but there is more room in this pattern for individual loyalties and autonomy.

Though these orientations may appear mutually exclusive, there is nothing illogical about their coexistence, as I argued earlier. A dialectical synthesis of the basic human needs for dependence and independence (autonomy) is postulated here. Though these needs are universal, one or the other may find greater expression in different contexts with different living conditions and ideologies (Spence, 1985, p. 1290). When economic/industrial development takes place in societies with a culture of relatedness, this type of a context probably allows both tendencies to be expressed in values and behavior more than the preindustrial collectivist or the industrial individualist cultural contexts.

In pattern Y family interaction and child rearing incorporate both dependence and autonomy, with parental control rather than permissiveness continuing to characterize family discipline. This is quite similar to Baumrind's (1971, 1980) authoritative parenting. Finally, the concept of self developing in such a family system is a relational self, for which interdependence with others is not a threat.

Pattern Z. This is the ideal-typical pattern for the industrialized Western family. It reflects the culture of separateness, at both the interpersonal and the interfamilial interaction levels, and the individualist ethos. As I said before, this pattern may be more of an ideal than a reality, given the recent evidence for the interdependence of the Western, even the American family (e.g., Cohler & Geyer, 1982). Nevertheless, the overall picture is obviously different from the other two, and both the Western individualist ethos and the psychological theorizing deriving from it shape this ideal-typical pattern.

Individuated nuclear family structure is the unit here for both emotional and material investments toward the child, discounting interspouse relations, which are not treated in this model. With lack of commitment to the patrilineage and affluence go low fertility, low son preference, and high woman's status. The last is a relative, not an absolute, level; it implies egalitarian spousal relations. Socialization values and interaction revolve around the individuated self, whose relations with others do not involve dependencies that blur the boundaries around the self. The family is also independent of other families, relations with them being those between separate entities, not overlapping ones. There is less parental control here ("permissive parenting" of Baumrind, 1971, 1980), and autonomy is valued in socialization.

Thus, three different patterns of contextual family systems are conceptualized. They should be seen not as absolutes but rather as approximations toward contextual wholes. Pattern X is the ideal-typical pattern for rural-agrarian-traditional society; pattern Z is the ideal-typical pattern for the Western middle-class family, characterized by individualism; and pattern Y is the ideal-typical pattern of the industrialized developed collectivist society. The characteristics of the patterns are based on research and thinking presented in this chapter. I am therefore not repeating them here for further elaboration. It is important to note that these patterns are approximations to cross-cultural diversity. The model should be seen as a heuristic device to understand this diversity.

Note that this model of family change is not a typology; rather, the three patterns form dimensions involving different combinations of characteristics. Pattern Y may not be at the midpoint between the other patterns on several of these characteristics. The three patterns are not mutually exclusive in all respects but share some characteristics; in some ways they are different in degree, not in kind. The model is not meant to be all-inclusive or to represent all aspects of the family system. For example, though woman's status is included, the horizontal (interspousal) family interaction pattern (Kağıtçıbaşı, 1985) is not covered, since that would entail a whole different array of research review, analysis, and conceptualization. (Change in woman's status in the model is only with regard to the change in the patrilineal family structure.) Only the vertical (intergenerational) family interaction pattern is presented in the figures in terms of child rearing and socialization values. The three patterns show variation mainly along the dependence/independence parameter. Pattern Z is clearly differentiated from the other two in this sense.

A MODEL OF CHANGE

The model of family change proposed here involves a shift from pattern X to pattern Y rather than to pattern Z as proposed by modernization theory. Pattern Y is not recognized by modernization theory or is seen only as a transitional stage in the progress toward pattern Z. The model of family change that is developed here, however, recognizes the existence of all three patterns of family and socialization but proposes that the main shift in the world is from pattern X to pattern Y, not pattern Z. In other words, pattern Y is proposed as an alternative end state of socioeconomic development. I have presented a great deal of evidence that does not fit the expectations of modernization theory. Pattern Y fits better than pattern Z with the current findings from Japan and other recently industrialized societies and the developed sectors of the developing countries characterized by cultures of relatedness (collectivist cultures).

Model Y can be seen as discordant, since it entails apparently contrasting elements such as individual and group loyalties. It may therefore be seen as an unstable state—a transition to something else. In fact this view is commonly held in analyzing conflicting influences on the family in conditions of rapid social change (e.g., Sinha, 1988).

Two arguments may be offered to deal with this criticism. First, as previously shown (Kağıtçıbaşı, 1987), some of these apparently contrasting elements may not be mutually exclusive polarities but may be compatible with one another. Incompatibility may be assumed rather than real and may derive from an imposed etic (Berry, 1978) (i.e., a view whose universality is assumed rather than demonstrated), based on a Western perspective contrasting the individual and group interests. Similarly, relatedness and autonomy can coexist in the same context, family or individual at different times or situations, with different tasks or people, and so on.

Second, one could view pattern Y not as an unstable discordant state but rather as a dynamic outcome or synthesis of a dialectic interplay of the basic needs for relatedness (and dependence) and autonomy (and separateness), doing more justice to these dual needs than the other two patterns. This dialectic conflict model is quite different from the equilibrium model underlying an assumption of unidirectional change. If pattern Y is indeed seen as a synthesis, then one could venture the prediction that there will possibly be a shift from pattern Z to pattern Y rather than the other way around, as commonly assumed. The recent evidence reviewed (e.g., Bronfenbrenner & Weiss, 1983; Cohler & Geyer, 1982; Cohler & Grunebaum, 1981; Fu et al., 1986; Keniston, 1985) regarding intergenerational dependence among American families, as well as other attempts at recreating the community such as seen in communal living arrangements, evangelistic movements, and so on, might be seen as indications of such a move arising from the human need for relatedness in the highly developed posttechnological society (Rotenberg, 1977).

Shifts from pattern Z to even more individualist nonfamily contexts may also result in a swing back toward pattern Y. Recent evidence points to the communal nature of alternative patterns of family life in modern societies. For example, in the Netherlands Saal (1987) describes such alternative housing and living arrangements as "additional group house," "chosen neighborhood relations," and "boarding community," and Jansen (1987) reports the "explosion" of communal living since the early 1980s. In Israel Weil (1987) shows how proximal households function as alternatives to joint families among the Bene Israel who migrated to Israel from India. In Sweden Ekstrand and Ekstrand (1987) find Swedish parents valuing group relations more than Indian parents because the former miss them more.

Whether there is such a shift in the Western world from pattern Z to pattern Y could be debated. However, there is no question that some synthesis like the one I have indicated, between individual autonomy/loyalties and group loyalties—merging of the individual self with the relational self—is being seriously searched for in the Third World (Holtzman et al., 1975; Kağıtçıbaşı, 1985a, 1987; Lenero-Otero, 1977; Sinha, 1985; Werner, 1979, p. 303; Yang, 1986, p. 168), which Yang (1988) has called "something creative that takes in the new element of individualism while keeping the old family tradition intact" (p. 117).

Implications for Application

The synthesis I have discussed at the level of theory also has implications for application, because development efforts and models, especially those directed to the Third World, utilize some "model of man." Even the more focused attempts at technology transfer and purely economic models of development base their feasibility expectations on assumed human factors. The latter, in turn, are formed by psychological theorizing of the kind discussed in this chapter, mainly deriving from Western experience. Expectations of unidirectional change in human behavioral patterns toward the Western model further reinforce the particular implicit models used in applications. If the synthesis I have been describing is taken seriously, then it needs to be pursued in applied work in Third World contexts, where assumptions of social change toward pattern Y rather than pattern Z would make more sense.

Any applied research involving intervention in a cultural context of relatedness has to be sensitive to this context. Such applied work benefits from capitalizing on the existing family culture and working through it; otherwise it may be doomed to fail. For example, if in an attempt to develop autonomy in the child, the individualist model is used and the family culture of relatedness is undermined by encouraging separation, competition, and individual loyalties, the intervention may not produce enduring results owing to the resistance of the indigenous culture.

Thus, in a recent applied research project I directed in low-income areas of Istanbul (Kağıtçıbaşı, Sunar, & Bekman, 1989) early enrichment was provided to children working through the existing environmental support systems. Specifically, in this research mothers were encouraged to develop a positive self-concept, feelings of competence, and efficacy as well as specific cognitive skills and positive orientations to provide their children with cognitive stimulation and enrichment at home. This was done by reinforcing the existing close mother-child relationship and also by capitalizing on the existing communal support systems. The latter were utilized in group meetings of mothers in the community and in paraprofessional home instruction. The effect of intervention on both the mothers and the children was found to be impressive (Kağıtçıbaşı et al., 1989).

Of special relevance to the present discussion are the findings regarding autonomy and dependence. Initial interviews with mothers revealed strong needs for close ties with their children. When asked what children's behavior pleased them most, they mentioned relational behavior, such as "being good to mother," most frequently. Together with "showing affection," "being obedient," and "getting along well with others," relational behavior accounted for almost 80% of desired behavior in children. Further probing for other things children do that please mothers brought forth more expressions of relational behavior. In contrast, autonomy, while having a low priority among desired behaviors in children, loomed large among behaviors that angered mothers. Taking the form of "self-assertion" or "not obeying," it accounted for more than half of the unacceptable behaviors. Almost all the other undesirable behaviors of children the mothers cited concerned interfering with good relations. In contrast, complaints about dependence (on mother) were strikingly low (1.2%). In describing a "good child," furthermore, the mothers in the Istanbul study stressed "being polite" (37%) and "obedient" (35%) more than any other characteristic; "being autonomous and self-sufficient" again was a negligible response (3.6% of the mothers mentioned it).

These findings are similar to earlier ones mentioned from similar close-knit societies with collective ecological settings (e.g., LeVine et al., 1967) and to those of the Value of Children Study. The emphasis on relatedness is striking; individualist separation and self-assertion are not valued by mothers.

After the initial interviewing to obtain baseline data, a randomly selected group of mothers participated in a two-year training program consisting of cognitive skills to teach their children and sensitization to the needs of the growing child. This extensive parent education was carried out through home instruction and supportive group discussions. In these group discussions the existing relatedness values and behaviors such as showing physical affection, being close, helping and supporting, and being good to and sensitive to the child were reinforced. However, new values were also introduced, encouraging autonomy, such as allowing children to make decisions and carry the responsibility for them and to do things on their own. Care was taken to show that these new values of autonomy are not incompatible with harmonious, close-knit human relatedness.

After the intervention, in the fourth year of the study reassessments were done of mothers' child-rearing attitudes. It was found that mothers who participated in the parent education intervention ($N = 90$) valued autonomous behavior in their children more than nontrained mothers ($N = 160$) ($F = 12.5$, $p = .02$). In describing a "good child," responses that could be classified as "autonomous" were again not frequent, but nearly all the mothers who gave this response were in the trained group (11% compared with only 2.6% of the nontrained mothers; $x^2 = 7.58$, $df = 1$, $p = .006$). Furthermore, more than twice as many trained as nontrained mothers mentioned autonomous child behavior as pleasing them (21% vs. 9.7%, $x^2 = 6.04$, $df = 1$, $p = .01$). Especially compared with the first-year baselines, this change is remarkable. Yet the great majority of mothers in both groups continued stressing affectionate and relational behavior in children as pleasing and otherwise demonstrated close-knit ties in their behaviors and values.

The few findings reported here constitute a very small part of this longitudinal study. They focus directly on autonomy. Some of the other findings have implications for individual autonomy and achievement also, such as the trained mothers' higher expectations that children could succeed without asking help from others (48.8% vs. 18.6% of the nontrained group). Thus the trained mothers acquired a new positive orientation toward their children's autonomy while remaining as close to them as the nontrained mothers. A synthesis of individualist and relational values appears to have been achieved. These findings show, on a small scale, that individualist and relational orientations can be compatible in application as well as in theory.

Summary and Conclusion

I have attempted to cover some aspects of the rather disjointed interdisciplinary field of family and socialization from a cross-cultural perspective. The coverage has necessarily been incomplete and selective, focusing mainly on intergenerational family interactions along the dependence/independence dimension, working toward a model of family change.

I started out with an observation that psychology has not concerned itself much with holistic study of the family or the complex socialization process, especially within a cross-cultural perspective, even though some of the main models of person-environment relations at its disposal are appropriate for such study. With the recently increasing acceptance and use of the ecological and contextual models in coverging interdisciplinary approaches, the time may be ripe for cross-cultural theorizing on the family and socialization. The contextual approach to socially defined meaning is a key in such an endeavor to develop a thorough understanding of family diversity. Such an approach goes beyond simple description of cross-cultural differences and explains what meanings are attributed to events and how similar behaviors may be given different meanings in different contexts or how apparently contrasting behaviors may carry common meanings and lead to common outcomes. Family diversity in parental beliefs and values, parent-child interactions, and social class and family types can be better understood with such a contextual approach, where structural-functional links between underlying causes and behavioral outcomes are sought.

Macro-level explanations such as industrialization, economic development models, and political/religious ideologies are often proposed to explain human diversity. What seem to be lacking are psychological models with cross-cultural validity that can tackle both human diversity and commonality. The (inter)dependence/independence dimension of human (family) relations is proposed as a psychological parameter that is independent of socioeconomic development levels and such and that has the potential to be the basis of a psychological explanation. There appears to be systematic cross-cultural variation along this dimension, and a number of assumptions prevail about shifts on this dimension through both time and space. The main assumption of unidirectional change toward the Western ideal-typical model of human (family) independence is challenged by much conflicting evidence, including that on the American family. Some of the findings of the cross-cultural Value of Children Study also throw light on this issue, so that material and emotional interdependencies can be differentiated.

I next proposed a heuristic model of family change comprising three ideal-typical patterns. The first (X) represents the "traditional" human/family interactions in the context of "underdevelopment," which are characterized by both material and emotional interdepen-

which are characterized by both material and emotional interdependencies. The second (Y) represents the "developed" or industrializing/urban non-Western context where human/family interactions are characterized by emotional interdependencies. The third (Z) represents the Western technological society where human/family interactions are based on independence. I further propose that the main shift in the world is from pattern X to Y, not to Z. One might even venture to speculate that there are forces for some shifts from Z to Y.

The model is thus based on the dimension of independence/interdependence, involving mutual dependence, but this mutuality may not be apparent at any one time because it emerges over the life span, with dependencies changing direction through time. Furthermore, dependence is used here not in the pejorative sense that it has acquired in (Western) psychology, but rather in terms of a non-Western socially defined meaning, as a process ideally moving toward the valued "dependability." The model deals with diversity, but not in a purely descriptive sense. It is a contextual model that attempts to establish the structural-functional links between context and behavior; and with different contextual links, different patterns emerge.

This is by no means an all-encompassing theory but rather is a heuristic device to throw light on some cross-cultural differences and similarities, their underlying causes, and some of the changes that take place in the family and socialization process with contextual changes. Pattern Y is the main thesis of this model, conceptualized as a dialectical synthesis of some apparently conflicting orientations seen in patterns X and Z. For example, autonomy and dependence (as conceptualized in a positive, not negative, sense) or individual and group loyalties are seen as compatible. This view is obviously open to debate and needs to be supported by more empirical evidence. Some evidence is provided here, also showing the implications of the model for application, but more work needs to be done especially toward refining the proposed causal relationships. Cross-cultural contextual studies that use multilevel interdisciplinary approaches and focus on the family and socialization process would contribute greatly to a better conceptualization of cross-cultural diversity and commonality on the one hand and of stability and change on the other.

REFERENCES

Adorno, T. W., Frenkel-Brunswik, E., Levinson, D. J., & Sanford, R. N. (1950). *The authoritarian personality.* New York: Harper.

Angyal, A. (1951). A theoretical model for personality studies. *Journal of Personality, 20,* 131–142.

Ariès, P. (1980). Two successive motivations for the declining birth rate in the West. *Population and Development Review, 6* (4), 645–650.

Bagley, C., Iwawaki, S., & Young, L. (1983). Japanese children: Group oriented but not field dependent? In C. Bagley & G. Verma (Eds.), *Multicultural childhood: Education, ethnicity and cognitive styles* (pp. 27–37). Hampshire: Gover.

Bakan, D. (1966). *The duality of human existence.* Chicago: Rand McNally.

Bakan, D. (1968). *Disease, pain, and sacrifice.* Chicago: University of Chicago Press.

Baltes, P. B., & Brim, O. (Eds.). (1979). *Life span development and behavior* (Vol. 2). New York: Academic Press.

Baltes, P. B., Reese, H. W., & Lipsitt, L. P. (1980). Life-span developmental psychology. *Annual review of Psychology, 31,* 65–110.

Bandura, A. (1977). *Social learning theory.* Englewood Cliffs, NJ: Prentice-Hall.

Bandura, A. (1986). *Social foundations of thought and action.* London: Allen and Unwin.

Bandura, A., & Walters, R. H. (1963). *Social learning and personality development.* New York: Holt, Rinehart and Winston.

Barker, R. G. (1968). *Ecological psychology.* Stanford: Stanford University Press.

Barry, H., Child, I., & Bacon, M. (1959). Relation of child training to subsistence economy. *American Anthropologist, 61,* 31–63.

Baumrind, D. (1971). Current patterns of parental authority. *Developmental Psychology Monographs, 4* (1, Part 2).

Baumrind, D. (1980). New directions in socialization research. *American Psychologist, 35,* 639–652.

Bellah, R. N., Madsen, R., Sullivan, W. M., Swindler, A., & Tipton, S. M. (1985). *Habits of the heart: Individualism and commitment in American life.* Berkeley: University of California Press.

Benedict, R. (1970). Patterns of the good culture. *Psychology Today, 4,* 53–55, 74–77.

Berger, B., & Berger, P. L. (1984). *The war over the family.* New York: Anchor Press.

Berger, P. L. & Luckmann, T. (1967). *The social construction of reality.* New York: Doubleday.

Bernstein, B. (1971). *Class, codes and control* (Vol. 1). London: Routledge and Kegan Paul.

Bernstein, B. (1975). *Class, codes and control* (Vol. 3). London: Routledge and Kegan Paul.

Berry, J. W. (1966). Temne and Eskimo perceptual skills. *International Journal of Psychology, 1*, 207–229.

Berry, J. W. (1967). Independence and conformity in subsistence-level societies. *Journal of Personality and Social Psychology, 7*, 415–418.

Berry, J. W. (1976). *Human ecology and cognitive style: Comparative studies in cultural and psychological adaptation*. Beverly Hills, CA: Sage-Halsted.

Berry, J. W. (1978). Social psychology: Comparative, societal and universal. *Canadian Psychological Review, 19*, 93–104.

Berry, J. W. (1980). Ecological analyses for cross-cultural psychology. In N. Warren (Ed.), *Studies in cross-cultural psychology* (Vol. 2, pp. 157–189). New York: Academic Press.

Bertalanffy, L. von. (1968). *General systems theory*. New York: Braziller.

Bisht, S., & Sinha, D. (1981). Socialization, family and psychological differentiation. In D. Sinha (Ed.), *Socialization of the Indian child*. New Delhi: Concept.

Block, J. H. (1973). Conceptions of sex role: Some cross-cultural and longitudinal perspectives. *American Psychologist, 28*, 512–526.

Blood, R. O. (1972). *The family*. New York: Free Press.

Bond, M. H. (Ed.). (1986). *The psychology of the Chinese people*. New York: Oxford University Press.

Bond, M. H., & Hwang, K. (1986). The social psychology of Chinese people. In M. H. Bond (Ed.), *The psychology of the Chinese people*. New York: Oxford University Press.

Boszormenyi-Nagy, I., & Spark, G. (1973). *Invisible loyalties: Reciprocity in intergenerational family therapy*. New York: Harper and Row.

Bronfenbrenner, U. (1977). Toward an experimental ecology of human development. *American Psychologist, 32*, 513–531.

Bronfenbrenner, U. (1979). *The ecology of human development: Experiments by nature and design*. Cambridge: Harvard University Press.

Bronfenbrenner, U., & Weiss, H. B. (1983). Beyond policies without people: An ecological perspective on child and family policy. In E. F. Zigler, S. L. Kagan, & E. Klugman (Eds.), *Children, families and government: Perspectives on American social policy* (pp. 393–414). New York: Cambridge University Press.

Brown, R. (1965). *Social psychology* (1st ed.). New York: Free Press.

Brown, R. (1986). *Social psychology* (2nd ed.). New York: Free Press.

Brunswik, E. (1955). Representative design and probabilistic theory. *Psychological review, 62*, 236–242.

Bulatao, R. A. (1979). *On the nature of the transition in the value of children*. Publ. No. 60-A. Honolulu: East-West Center.

Caldwell, J. A. (1977). Towards a restatement of demographic transition theory. In J. C. Caldwell (Ed.), *The persistence of high fertility* (Part 1). Canberra: Australian National University.

Cashmore, J. A., & Goodnow, J. J. (1986). Influences on Australian parents' values: Ethnicity versus socioeconomic status. *Journal of Cross Cultural Psychology, 17* (4), 441–454.

Caudill, W. A., & Frost, L. (1973). A comparison of maternal care and infant behavior in Japanese-American, American and Japanese families. In W. P. Lebra (Ed.), *Mental health research in Asia and the Pacific* (Vol. 3). Honolulu: University Press of Hawaii.

Chamoux, M. N. (1986). Apprendre autrement: Aspects des pédagogies dîtes informelles chex les Indiens du Méxique. In P. Rossel (Ed.), *Demain l'artisanat?* Paris: Cahiers IUED.

Chodorow, N. (1974). Family structure and feminine personality. In M. Z. Rosaldo & L. Lamphere (Eds.), *Women, culture and society.* Stanford: Stanford University Press.

Chodorow, N. (1978). *The reproduction of mothering: Psychoanalysis and the sociology of gender.* Berkeley: University of California Press.

Ciaccio, N. V. (1976). Erikson's theory in cross-cultural perspective: Social class and ethnicity in "Third World" communities. In K. F. Riegel & J. A. Meacham (Eds.), *The developing individual in a changing world* (Vol. 1). Chicago: Aldine.

Claussen, J. A. (1986). *The life course.* Englewood Cliffs, NJ: Prentice-Hall.

Cohler, B., & Geyer, S. (1982). Psychological autonomy and interdependence within the family. In F. Walsh (Ed.), *Normal family processes* (pp. 196–227). New York: Guilford Press.

Cohler, B., & Grunebaum, H. (1981). *Mothers, grandmothers, and daughters: Personality and child-care in three generation families.* New York: Wiley.

Conroy, M., Hess, R. D., Azuma, H., & Kashiwagi, K. (1980). Maternal strategies for regulating children's behavior: Japanese and American families. *Journal of Cross Cultural Psychology, 11* (2), 153–172.

Cooley, C. H. (1902). *Human nature and the social order.* New York: Scribner's.

Darroch, R. K., Meyer, P. A., & Singarimbun, M. (1981). *Two are not enough: The value of children to Javanese and Sundanese parents.* Publ. No. 60-D. Honolulu: East-West Center.

Dasen, P. R. (1988). Développement psychologique et activités quotidiennes chez des enfants africains. *Enfance, 41* (3–4), 3–24.

Dasen, P. R., & Jahoda, G. (1986). Cross-cultural human development. *International Journal of Behavioral Development, 9*, 413–416.

Dawson, J. L. M. (1967). Traditional versus Western attitudes in West Africa: The construction, validation and application of a measuring device. *British Journal of Social and Clinical Psychology, 6*, 81–96.

Deutsch, M. (1962). Cooperation and trust: Some theoretical notes. In M. R. Jones (Ed.), *Nebraska Symposium on Motivation.* Lincoln: University of Nebraska Press.

DeVos, G. A. (1973). *Socialization for achievement.* Berkeley: University of California Press.

Doi, T. (1973). *Anatomy of dependence.* Tokyo: Kodansha International.

Doob, L. W. (1967). Scales for assaying psychological modernization in Africa. *Public Opinion Quarterly, 31*, 414–421.

Drinkwater, B. A. (1985). Family size and influence in Italy and Australia. *Australian Journal of Sex, Marriage and Family, 6* (3), 163–167.

Duben, A. (1982). The significance of family and kinship in urban Turkey. In Ç. Kağıtçıbaşı (Ed.), *Sex roles, family and community in Turkey* (pp. 73–99). Bloomington: Indiana University Press.

Durrett, M. E., Richards, P., Otaki, M., Pennebaker, J. W., & Nyquist, L. (1986). Mother's involvement with infant and her perception of spousal support, Japan and America. *Journal of Marriage and the Family, 48*, 187–194

Dym, B. (1988). Ecological perspectives on change in families. In H. B. Weiss and F. H. Jacobs (Eds.), *Evaluating family programs*. New York: Aldine.

Eckensberger, L. (1979). A metamethodological evaluation of psychological theories from a cross-cultural perspective. In L. Eckensberger, W. Lonner, & Y. H. Poortinga (Eds.), *Cross-cultural contributions to psychology*. Lisse: Swets and Zeitlinger.

Ekstrand, L. H., & Ekstrand, G. (1987). Children's perceptions of norms and sanctions in two cultures. In Ç. Kağıtçıbaşı (Ed.), *Growth and progress in cross-cultural psychology*. Lisse: Swets and Zeitlinger.

Elder, G. H. (1979). Historical change in life patterns and personality. In P. H. Baltes & O. G. Brim (Eds.), *Life span development and behavior* (Vol. 2, pp. 117–159). New York: Academic Press.

Elder, G. H. (Ed.). (1985). *Life course dynamics*. Ithaca, NY: Cornell University Press.

Erelçin, F. G. (1988). *Collectivistic norms in Turkey: Tendency to give and receive support*. Unpublished master's thesis, Boğaziçi University, Istanbul.

Fawcett, J. T. (1983). Perceptions of the value of children: Satisfactions and costs. In R. Bulatao, R. D. Lee, P. E. Hollerbach, & J. Bongaarts (Eds.), *Determinants of fertility in developing countries* (Vol. 1). Washington, DC: National Academy Press.

Featherman, D. L., & Lerner, R. M. (1985). Ontogenesis and sociogenesis: Problematics for theory and research about development and socialization across the lifespan. *American Sociological Review, 50*, 659–676.

Festinger, L. (1954). A theory of social comparison processes. *Human Relations, 7*, 117–140.

Fine, S. (1986). Divorce: Cultural factors and kinship factors in the adjustment of children. *Child Psychiatry and Human Development, 17* (2), 121–128.

Fu, V. R., Hinkle, D. E., & Hanna, M. A. (1986). A three-generational study of the development of individual dependence and family interdependence. *Genetic, Social and General Psychology Monographs, 112* (2), 153–171.

Furstenberg, F. F., Jr. (1966). Industrialization and the American family: A look backward. *American Sociological Review, 31*, 326–337.

Geertz, C. (1975). On the nature of anthropological understanding. *American Scientist, 63*, 47–53.

Gerard, H. B., & Rabbie, J. M. (1961). Fear and social comparison. *Journal of Abnormal and Social Psychology, 62*, 586–592.

Gergen, K. J. (1973). Social psychology as history. *Journal of Personality and Social Psychology, 26* (2), 309–320.

Gergen, K. J. (1985). Social constructionist inquiry: Context and implications. In K. J. Gergen & K. E. Davis (Eds.), *The social construction of the person*. New York: Springer-Verlag.

Gilligan, C. (1982). *In a different voice*. Cambridge: Harvard University Press.

Goode, W. J. (1963). *World revolution and family patterns*. Glencoe, IL: Free Press.

Goodnow, J. J. (1984). Parents' ideas about parenting and development: A review of issues and recent work. In M. E. Lamb, A. L. Brown, & B. Rogoff (Eds.), *Advances in developmental psychology* (Vol. 3, pp. 193–242). Hillsdale, NJ: Erlbaum.

Goodnow, J. J. (1985). Change and variation in parents' ideas about childhood and parenting. In I. E. Siegel (Ed.), *Parental belief systems* (pp. 235–270). Hillsdale, NJ: Erlbaum.

Goodnow, J. J. (1988). Parents' ideas, actions, and feelings: Models and methods from developmental and social psychology. *Child development, 59*, 286–320.

Guerin, P. J. (1976). Family therapy: The first twenty-five years. In P. J. Guerin (Ed.), *Family therapy: Theory and practice* (pp. 2–22). New York: Gardner Press.

Gutman, D. (1976). A cross-cultural view of adult life in the extended family. In K. F. Riegel and I. A. Meacham (Eds.), *The developing individual in a changing world* (Vol. 1). Chicago: Aldine.

Habermas, J. (1984). *The theory of communicative action: Vol. 1. Reason and the rationalization of society*. Boston: Beacon Press.

Hanawalt, A. A. (1986). *The ties that bound: Peasant families in medieval England*. New York: Oxford University Press.

Harrington, C., & Whiting, J. W. M. (1972). Socialization process and personality. In F. L. K. Hsu (Ed.), *Psychological anthropology* (2nd ed.) (pp. 469–508). Cambridge, Mass.: Schenkman.

Hartman, H. (1958). *Ego psychology and the problem of adaptation* (D. Rapaport, Trans.). New York: International Universities Press. (Original work published 1939)

Hayashi, C., Nishira, S., Suzuki, T., Mizuno, K., & Sakamoko, Y. (Eds.). (1977). *Changing Japanese values: Statistical surveys and analyses*. Research Committee on the Study of Japanese National Character. Tokyo: Institute of Statistical Mathematics.

Hayashi, C., & Suzuki, T. (1984). Changes in belief systems, quality of life issues and social conditions over 25 years in post-war Japan. *Annals of the Institute of Statistical Mathematics, 36*, 135–161.

Hoffman, L. W. (1987). The value of children to parents and child rearing patterns. In Ç. Kağıtçıbaşı (Ed.), *Growth and progress in cross-cultural psychology*. Lisse: Swets and Zeitlinger.

Hoftstede, G. (1980). *Culture's consequences*. Beverly Hills, CA: Sage.

Holtzman, W. H., Diaz-Guerrero, R., & Swartz, J. D. (1975). *Personality development in two cultures: A cross-cultural longitudinal study of school children in Mexico and the United States*. Austin: University of Texas Press.

Hurrelmann, K. (1988). *Social structure and personality development*. Cambridge: Cambridge University Press.

Hurrelmann, K., & Ulich, D. (Eds.). (1982). *Handbuch der Sozialisationsforschung* (2nd ed.). Weinheim: Beltz.

Inkeles, A. (1969). Making men modern: On the causes and consequences of individual change in six developing countries. *American Journal of Sociology, 75*, 208–225.

Inkeles, A. (1977). Understanding and misunderstanding individual modernity. *Journal of Cross Cultural Psychology, 8*, 135–176.

Inkeles, A., & Smith, D. H. (1974). *Becoming modern: Individual changes in six developing countries*. Cambridge: Harvard University Press.

Ito, K. L. (1985). Affective bonds: Hawaiian interrelationships of self. In G. M. White & J. Kirkpatrick (Eds.), *Person, self and experience: Exploring Pacific ethnopsychologies*. Berkeley: University of California Press.

Iwasaki-Mass, A. (1984). *"Amae" in Japanese Americans*. Unpublished doctoral dissertation. UCLA, School of Social Welfare.

Iwawaki, S. (1986). Achievement motivation and socialization. In S. E. Newstead, S. M. Irvine, & P. L. Dann (Eds.), *Human assessment: Cognition and motivation*. Boston: Martinus Nijhoff.

Jahoda, G. (1986a). A cross-cultural perspective on developmental psychology. *International Journal of Behavioral Development, 9*, 417–437.

Jahoda, G. (1986b). Nature, culture and social psychology. *European Journal of Social Psychology, 16*, 17–30.

Jansen, H. A. M. (1987). The development of communal living in the Netherlands. In L. Shamgar-Handelman & R. Palomba (Eds.), *Alternative patterns of family life in modern societies*. Rome: Collana Monografie.

Kagan, J. (1984). *Nature of the child*. New York: Basic Books.

Kagan, S., & Madsen, M. C. (1971). Cooperation and competition of Mexican, Mexican-American and Anglo-American children at two ages under four instructional sets. *Developmental Psychology, 5*, 37–39.

Kağıtçıbaşı, Ç. (1970). Social norms and authoritarianism: A challenge to psychology. *International Journal of Psychology, 19*, 145–157.

Kağıtçıbaşı, Ç. (1982a). *The changing value of children in Turkey*. Publ. No. 60-E. Honolulu: East-West Center.

Kağıtçıbaşı, Ç. (1982b). Sex roles, value of children and fertility in Turkey. In Ç. Kağıtçıbaşı (Ed.), *Sex roles, family and community in Turkey*. Bloomington: Indiana University Press.

Kağıtçıbaşı, Ç. (1982c). Old-age security value of children and development. *Journal of Cross Cultural Psychology, 13*, 29–42.

Kağıtçıbaşı, Ç. (1984). Socialization in traditional society: A challenge to psychology. *International Journal of Psychology, 19*, 145–157.

Kağıtçıbaşı, Ç. (1985a). A model of family change through development:

The Turkish family in comparative perspective. In I. R. Lagunes & Y. H. Poortinga (Eds.), *From a different perspective: Studies of behavior across cultures*. Lisse: Swets and Zeitlinger.

Kağıtçıbaşı, Ç. (1985b). Culture of separateness—culture of relatedness. In *1984, Vision and reality: Papers in Comparative Studies* (4:91–99). Columbus: Ohio State University.

Kağıtçıbaşı, Ç. (1986). Status of women in Turkey: Cross-cultural perspectives. *International Journal of Middle East Studies, 18* (4), 485–499.

Kağıtçıbaşı, Ç. (1987). Individual and group loyalties: Are they compatible? In Ç. Kağıtçıbaşı, (Ed.), *Growth and progress in cross-cultural psychology*. Lisse: Swets and Zeitlinger.

Kağıtçıbaşı, Ç. (1988). Diversity of socialization and social change. In P. R. Dasen, J. W. Berry, & N. Sartorius (Eds.), *Health and cross-cultural psychology*. New Delhi: Sage India.

Kağıtçıbaşı, Ç., & Berry, J. W. (1989). Cross-cultural psychology: Current research and trends. In *Annual review of psychology* (pp. 493–531). Palo Alto, CA: Annual Reviews.

Kağıtçıbaşı, Ç., Sunar, D., & Bekman, S. (1989). *Early Enrichment Project.* Ottawa: IDRC. Manuscript Report.

Kahl, J. A. (1968). *The measurement of modernism: Study of values in Brazil and Mexico.* Austin: University of Texas Press.

Kapp, W. K. (1963). *Hindu culture, economic development and economic planning in India.* Bombay: Asia Publishing House.

Karpat, K. (1976). *The Gecekondu: Rural migration and urbanization.* London: Cambridge University Press.

Keller, H., Miranda, D., & Gauda, G. (1984). The naive theory of the infant and some maternal attitudes: A two country study. *Journal of Cross Cultural Psychology, 15* (2), 165–179.

Keniston, K. (1985). The myth of family independence. In J. M. Henslin (Ed.), *Marriage and family in a changing society* (2nd ed.) (pp. 27–33). New York: Free Press.

Kirkpatrick, J., & White, G. M. (1985). Exploring ethnopsychologies. In G. M. White & J. Kirkpatrick (Eds.), *Person, self and experience: Exploring Pacific ethnopsychologies.* Berkeley: University of California Press.

Kohlberg, L. (1963). Stage and sequence: The cognitive-developmental approach to socialization. In D. A. Goslin (Ed.), *Handbook of socialization theory and research* (pp. 347–480). Chicago: Rand McNally.

Kohn, M. L. (1969). *Class and conformity: A study in values.* New York: Dorsey.

Kohn, M. L., & Schooler, C. (Eds.). (1983). *Work and personality.* Norwood, NJ: Ablex.

Kongar, E. (1972). *İzmir'de kentsel aile* (The urban family in İzmir). Ankara: Turkish Social Science Association.

Kongar, E. (1976). Changing roles of mothers: Changing intra-family relations in a Turkish town. In P. Peristany (Ed.), *Mediterranean family structure.* Cambridge: Cambridge University Press.

Kornadt, H. J. (1987). The aggression motive and personality development: Japan and Germany. In F. Halisch & J. Kuhl (Eds.), *Motivation, intention and volition*. Berlin: Springer-Verlag.

Lamb, M. E. (1982). On the familial origins of personality and social style. In L. M. Laosa & I. E. Sigel (Eds.), *Families as learning environments for children*. New York: Plenum Press.

Lambert, W. E. (1987). The fate of old-country values in a new land: A cross-national study of childrearing. *Canadian Psychology, 28* (1), 9–20.

Lantz, H. R., Keyes, J., & Schultz, M. (1975). The American family in the preindustrial period: From base lines in history to change. *American Sociological Review, 40*, 21–36.

Laslett, P. (1971). *The world we have lost*. New York: Scribner and Sons.

Laslett, P. (1977). Characteristics of the Western family considered over time. In *Family and illicit love in earlier generations*. London: Cambridge University Press.

Lebra, T. S. (1984). Self-reconstruction in Japanese religious psychotherapy. In A. J. Marsella & G. M. White (Eds.), *Cultural conceptions of mental health and therapy*. Boston: Reider.

Lenero-Otero, L. (Ed.). (1977). *Beyond the nuclear family model: Cross-cultural perspectives*. Beverly Hills, CA: Sage.

Lerner, R. M., & Busch-Rossnagel, N. A. (1981). *Individuals as producers of their development: A life span perspective*. New York: Academic Press.

Lesthaeghe, R. (1983). A century of demographic and cultural change in Western Europe: An exploration of underlying dimensions. *Population and Development Review, 9* (3), 411–437.

Lesthaeghe, R., & Surkyn, J. (1988). Cultural dynamics and economic theories of fertility change. *Population and Development Review, 14* (1), 1–47.

LeVine, R. A. (1974). Parental goals. A cross-cultural view. *Teachers College Record, 76*, 226–239.

LeVine, R. A., Kline, N. H., & Owen, C. R. (1967). Father-child relationships and changing life-styles in Ibadan, Nigeria. In H. Miner (Ed.), *The city in modern Africa*. New York: Praeger.

LeVine, C., Kohlberg, L., & Hewer, A. (1985). The current formulation of Kohlberg's theory and a response to critics. *Human Development, 28*, 94–100.

Lewin, K. (1936). *Principles of topological psychology*. New York: McGraw-Hill.

Lewin, K. (1948). *Resolving social conflicts*. New York: Harper.

Lewin, K. (1951). *Field theory in social science*. New York: Harper.

Lin, I. (1985, November). *Family development and its change in urban cities in PRC*. Paper presented at the Second International Conference on Modernization and Chinese Culture, Hong Kong. (In Chinese)

MacFarlane, A. (1978). *The origins of English individualism*. Oxford: Blackwell.

MacFarlane, A. (1987). *The culture of capitalism*. New York: Oxford.

Maddi, S. R. (1980). *Personality theories* (4th ed.). Homewood, IL: Dorsey.

Magnusson, D., & Allen, V. L. (Eds.). (1983). *Human development: An interactional perspective*. New York: Academic Press.

Mahler, M. (1972). On the first three phases of the separation-individuation process. *International Journal of Psychoanalysis, 53*, 333–338.

Mahler, M., Pine, F., & Bergman, A. (1975). *The psychological birth of the human infant*. New York: Basic Books.

Marjoribanks, K., & Walberg, H. J. (1976). Social class, family size and cognitive performance. In K. Riegel & J. A. Meacham (Eds.). *The developing individual in a changing world* (Vol. 2, pp. 723–727). The Hague: Mouton.

Marsella, A. J. (1984). Culture and mental health: An overview. In A. J. Marsella & G. M. White (Eds.), *Cultural conceptions of mental health and therapy*. Boston: Reider.

Marsella, A. J. (1985). Culture, self and mental disorder. In A. J. Marsella, G. DeVos, & L. K. Hsu (Eds.), *Culture and self*. New York: Tavistock.

Marsella, A. J., DeVos, G., & Hsu, F. L. K. (Eds.). (1985). *Culture and self: Asian and Western perspectives*. New York: Tavistock.

Marsella, A. J., & White, G. M. (Eds.). (1984). *Cultural conceptions of mental health and therapy*. Boston: Reider.

Mazrui, A. (1968). From social Darwinism to current theories of modernization. *World Politics, 21*, 69–83.

McCarthy, J. (1979). Age, family, and migration in nineteenth-century Black Sea provinces of the Ottoman Empire. *International Journal of Middle East Studies, 10*, 309–323.

McGillicuddy-DeLisi, A. V. (1982a). Parental beliefs about developmental processes. *Human Development, 25*, 192–200.

McGillicuddy-DeLisi, A. V. (1982b). The relationship between parents' beliefs about development and family constellation, socioeconomic status, and parents' teaching strategies. In L. M. Laosa & I. E. Sigel (Eds.), *Families as learning environments for children* (pp. 261–299). New York: Plenum.

McGoldrick, M., & Carter, E. A. (1982). The family life cycle. In F. Walsh (Ed.), *Normal family processes*. New York: Guilford Press.

Mead, G. H. (1934). *The social psychology of George Herbert Mead* (A. Strauss, Ed.). Chicago: University of Chicago Press.

Miller, J. (1984). Culture and the development of everyday social explanation. *Journal of Personality and Social Psychology, 5*, 961–978.

Miller, K. A. (1984). The effects of industrialization on men's attitudes toward the extended family and women's rights: A cross-national study. *Journal of Marriage and the Family*, 153–160.

Miller, S. (1988). Parents' beliefs about children's cognitive development. *Child Development, 59*, 259–285.

Minturn, L., & Hitchcock, J. T. (1966). *The Rajputs of Khalapur, India*. Six Cultures Series, Vol. 3. New York: Wiley.

Minuchin, S. (1974). *Families and family therapy*. Cambridge: Harvard University Press.

Minuchin, S., Rosman, B., & Baker, L. (1978). *Psychosomatic families: Anorexia nervosa in context*. Cambridge: Harvard University Press.

Mirande, A. (1985). Chicano families. In J. M. Henslin (Ed.), *Marriage and family in a changing society* (2nd ed.) (pp. 133–138). New York: Free Press.

Morsbach, H. (1980). Major psychological factors influencing Japanese interpersonal relations. In N. Warren (Ed.), *Studies in cross-cultural psychology* (Vol. 2). London: Academic Press.

Neki, J. S. (1976). An examination of the cultural relativism of dependence as a dynamic of social and therapeutic relationships. *British Journal of Medical Psychology, 49*, 1–10.

Obikeze, D. S. (1987). Education and the extended family ideology: The case of Nigeria. *Journal of Comparative Family Studies, 18* (1), 25–45.

Olson, E. (1982). Duofocal family structure and an alternative model of husband-wife relationship. In Ç. Kağıtçıbaşı (Ed.), *Sex roles, family and community in Turkey*. Bloomington: Indiana University Press.

Otaki, M., Durrett, M. E., Richards, P., Nyquist, L., & Pennebaker, J. W. (1986). Maternal and infant behavior in Japan and America: A partial replication. *Journal of Cross Cultural Psychology, 17*, 251–268.

Pan, Y. K. (1985, November). *Nuclear families in PRC cities*. Paper presented at the Second International Conference on Modernisation and Chinese Culture, Hong Kong. (In Chinese)

Panel. (1973a). The experience of separation-individuation in infancy and its reverberations through the course of life: 1. Infancy and childhood. *Journal of the American Psychoanalytic Association, 21*, 135–154.

Panel. (1973b). The experience of separation-individuation in infancy and its reverberations through the course of life: 2. Adolescence and maturity. *Journal of the American Psychoanalytic Association, 21*, 155–167.

Parens, H., & Saul, L. (1971). *Dependence in man: A psychoanalytic study*. New York: International Universities Press.

Parsons, T. (1964). *Social structure and personality*. New York: Free Press.

Pelto, O. (1968). The difference between "tight" and "loose" societies. *Transaction*, April, pp. 37–40.

Pepitone, A. (1976). Toward a normative and comparative biocultural social psychology. *Journal of Personality and Social Psychology, 34*, 641–653.

Pepitone, A. (1987). The role of culture in theories of social psychology. In Ç. Kağıtçıbaşı (Ed.), *Growth and progress in cross-cultural psychology* (pp. 12–21). Lisse: Swets and Zeitlinger.

Pettengill, S. M., & Rohner, R. P. (1985). Korean-American adolescents' perceptions of parental control, parental acceptance-rejection and parent-adolescent conflict. In I. R. Lagunes & Y. H. Poortinga (Eds.), *From a different perspective: Studies of behavior across cultures*. Lisse: Swets and Zeitlinger.

Podmore, V. N., & St. George, R. (1986). New Zealand Maori and European mothers and their 3-year-old children: Interactive behaviors in pre-school settings. *Journal of Applied Developmental Psychology, 7*, 373–382.

Rank, O. (1929). *The trauma of birth*. New York: Harcourt, Brace.

Rank, O. (1945). *Will therapy and Truth and reality*. New York: Knopf.

Riegel, K. (1975). Towards a dialectical theory of development. *Human Development, 18*, 50–64.

Rohner, R. P., & Chakı-Sırcar, M. (1987). Caste differences in perceived maternal acceptance in West Bengal, India. *Ethos, 15* (4), 406–453.

Rohner, R. P., & Pettengill, S. M. (1985). Perceived parental acceptance-rejection and parental control among Korean adolescents. *Child Development, 56*, 524–528.

Rohner, R. P., & Rohner, E. C. (1978). Unpublished research data, Center for the Study of Parental Acceptance and Rejection, University of Connecticut.

Roland, A. (1980). Psychoanalytic perspectives on personality development in India. *International Review of Psychoanalysis, 7*, 73–87.

Rotenberg, M. (1977). "Alienating-individualism" and "reciprocal-individualism": A cross-cultural conceptualization. *Journal of Humanistic Psychology, 17*, 3–17.

Saal, C. D. (1987). Alternative forms of living and housing. In L. Shamgar-Handelman & R. Palomba (Eds.), *Alternative patterns of family life in modern societies*. Rome: Collana Monografie.

Saavedra, J. M. (1980). Effects of perceived parental warmth and control on the self-evaluation of Puerto Rican adolescent males. *Behavior Science Research, 15*, 41–54.

Sabatier, C. (1986). La mère et son bébé: Variations culturelles: Analyse critique de la littérature. *Journal of International Psychology, 21*, 513–553.

Sampson, E. E. (1977). Psychology and the American ideal. *Journal of Personality and Social Psychology, 35* (11), 767–782.

Sampson, E. E. (1987). Individualization and domination: Undermining the social bond. In Ç. Kağıtçıbaşı (Ed.), *Growth and progress in cross-cultural psychology* (pp. 12–21). Lisse: Swets and Zeitlinger.

Schachter, S. (1964). The interaction of cognitive and physiological determinants of emotional state. In L. Berkowitz (Ed.), *Advances in experimental social psychology* (Vol. 1). New York: Academic Press.

Shand, N. (1985). Culture's influence in Japanese and American maternal role perception and confidence. *Psychiatry, 48*, 52–67.

Shand, N., & Kosawa, Y. (1985). Culture transmission: Caudill's model and an alternative hypothesis. *American Anthropologist, 87*, 862–871.

Sherif, M. (1936). *The psychology of social norms*. New York: Harper.

Sherif, M. (1961). *Intergroup conflict and cooperation: The Robbers' Cave Experiment*. Norman: University of Oklahoma, Institute of Group Relations.

Shweder, R. A., & Bourne, E. J. (1984). Does the concept of the person vary cross-culturally? In R. A. Shweder & R. Levine (Eds.), *Culture theory*. New York: Cambridge University Press.

Shweder, R. A., & LeVine, R. (1984). *Culture theory*. New York: Cambridge University Press.

Sigel, I. E. (1985). A conceptual analysis of beliefs. In I. E. Sigel (Ed.), *Parental belief systems* (pp. 345–371). Hillsdale, NJ: Erlbaum.

Sigel, I. E. (1986). Reflections on the belief-behavior connection: Lessons learned from a research program on parental belief systems and teaching strategies. In R. D. Ashmore & D. M. Brodzinsky (Eds.), *Thinking about the family: Views of parents and children* (pp. 35–65). Hillsdale, NJ: Erlbaum.

Silverman, L. H., & Weinberger, J. (1985). Mommy and I are one: Implications for psychotherapy. *American Psychologist, 40* (12), 1296–1308.

Simons, R. C., & Hughes, C. C. (Eds.). (1985). *The culture-bound syndrome: Folk illnesses of psychiatric and anthropological interest.* Boston: Reider.

Sinha, D. (1981). *Socialization of the Indian child.* New Delhi: Concept.

Sinha, D. (1988). The family scenario in a developing country and its implications for mental health: The case of India. In P. R. Dasen, J. W. Berry, & N. Sartorius (Eds.), *Health and cross-cultural psychology: Toward applications.* Beverly Hills, CA: Sage.

Sinha, D., & Kao, H. S. R. (1988). *Social values and development: Asian perspectives.* New Delhi: Sage India.

Sinha, S. R. (1985). Maternal strategies for regulating children's behavior. *Journal of Cross Cultural Psychology, 16,* 27–40.

Skinner, B. F. (1938). *The behavior of organisms.* New York: Appleton.

Snarey, J. R. (1985). Cross-cultural universality of social-moral development: A critical review of Kohlbergian research. *Psychological Bulletin, 97,* 202–232.

Spence, J. T. (1985). Achievement American style. *American Psychologist, 40* (12), 1285–1295.

Storer, D. (Ed.). (1985). *Ethnic family values in Australia.* Sydney: Prentice-Hall.

Super, C. M., & Harkness, S. (1986). The developmental niche: A conceptualization at the interface of child and culture. *International Journal of Behavioral Development, 9,* 545–570.

Sussman, M. B. (1974). The isolated nuclear family: Fact or fiction? In M. B. Sussman (Ed.), *Sourcebook in marriage and the family.* Boston: Houghton Mifflin.

Sussman, M. B., & Burchinal, L. G. (1971). The kin family network in urban-industrial America. In M. Anderson (Ed.), *Sociology of the family.* London: Penguin Books.

Sutherland, K. (1983). Parents' beliefs about child socialization: A study of parenting models. In I. E. Sigel & L. M. Laosa (Eds.), *Changing families.* New York: Plenum Press.

Suzman, R. M. (1973). Psychological modernity. *International Journal of Comparative Sociology, 14* (3–4), 273–287.

Suzuki, B. H. (1985). Asian-American families. In J. M. Henslin (Ed.), *Marriage and family in a changing society* (2nd ed.) (pp. 104–118). New York: Free Press.

Suzuki, T. (1984). Ways of life and social milieus in Japan and the United States: A comparative study. *Behaviormetrika, 15,* 77–108.

Takahashi, K. (1986). Examining the Strange Situation procedure with Japanese mothers and 12-month old infants. *Developmental Psychology, 22,* 265–270.

Taylor, D. M., & Brown, R. J. (1979). Towards a more social psychology? *British Journal of Social and Clinical Psychology, 18*, 173–180.

Thadani, V. N. (1978). The logic of sentiment: The family and social change. *Population and Development Review, 4* (3), 457–499.

Thornton, A. (1984). Modernization and family change. In *Social change and family policies*. Proceedings of the 20th International CFR Seminar. Melbourne: Australian Institute of Family Studies.

Timur, S. (1972). *Türkiye'de aile yapısı* (Family structure in Turkey). Ankara: Hacettepe University Press.

Triandis, H. C. (1988). Collectivism and development. In D. Sinha & H. S. R. Kao (Eds.), *Social values and development: Asian perspectives*. New Delhi: Sage India.

Trommsdorf, G. (1985). Some comparative aspects of socialization in Japan and Germany. In I. R. Lagunes & Y. H. Poortinga (Eds.), *From a different perspective: Studies of behavior across cultures*. Lisse: Swets and Zeitlinger.

Weber, M. (1958). *The Protestant ethic and the spirit of capitalism* (Talcott Parsons, Trans.). New York: Charles Scribner's Sons.

Weil, S. (1987). Proximal households as alternatives to joint families in Israel. In L. Shamgar-Handelman & R. Palomba (Eds.), *Alternative patterns of family life in modern societies*. Rome: Collana Monografie.

Weiss, H. B., & Jacobs, F. H. (1988). Family support and education programs: Challenges and opportunities. In H. B. Weiss & F. H. Jacobs (Eds.), *Evaluating family programs*. New York: Aldine.

Wentworth, W. M. (1980). *Context and understanding: An inquiry into socialization theory*. New York: Elsevier.

Werner, E. E. (1979). *Cross-cultural child development: A view from the planet Earth*. Monterey, CA: Brooks/Cole.

White, G. M., & Marsella, A. J. (1984). Introduction: Cultural conceptions in mental health research and practice. In A. J. Marsella & G. M. White (Eds.), *Cultural conceptions of mental health and therapy*. Boston: Reider.

Witkin, H. A., & Berry, J. W. (1975). Psychological differentiation in cross-cultural perspective. *Journal of Cross Cultural Psychology, 6*, 14–87.

Witkin, H. A., Dyk, R. B., Faterson, H. F., Goodenough, D. R., & Karp, S. (1962). *Psychological differentiation*. New York: Wiley.

Yang, C. (1988). Familism and development: An examination of the role of family in contemporary China Mainland, Hong Kong, and Taiwan. In D. Sinha & H. S. R. Kao (Eds.), *Social values and development: Asian perspectives* (pp. 93–124). New Delhi: Sage India.

Yang, K. S. (1986). Chinese personality and its change. In M. H. Bond (Ed.), *The psychology of the Chinese people*. New York: Oxford University Press.

Young, C. (1987). *Young people leaving home in Australia*. Australian Family Formation Project, Monograph No. 9. Canberra: Australian Institute of Family Studies.

Psychology of Acculturation

J. W. Berry
Queen's University

Introduction

Within cross-cultural psychology there is an interest in two broad domains: the comparative examination of psychological similarities and differences across broad ranges of cultures, and the psychological adaptations individuals make when they move between cultures. The former is the preeminent line of enquiry in cross-cultural psychology and attempts to link variations in individual behavior to cultural and ecological contexts by way of general enculturation and specific socialization; the latter is a relatively new area and seeks to understand continuities and changes in individual behavior that are related to the experience of two cultures through the process of acculturation. It is with this latter domain that this chapter is concerned.

Psychological studies of acculturation are particularly relevant at present, in a variety of cultures. International migration, major refugee upheavals, and the painful process of decolonization have all increased intercultural contact, as have tourism and telecommunications. Previously culturally isolated and homogeneous peoples now rub shoulders daily with persons, ideas, and products from scattered parts of the globe, setting afoot a process of cultural and psychological adaptation to their new circumstances. How individuals negotiate their course through this process of acculturation is the focus here. I begin by outlining the process at both the cultural and the psychological levels, then consider variations in acculturating groups and strategies, and finally review a number of specific acculturation phenomena, including acculturation attitudes, behavioral changes during acculturation, and the stresses associated with the process.

Within anthropology the first major studies of *acculturation* were done in the 1930s. The two classic definitions of acculturation are contained in related publications:

Acculturation comprehends those phenomena which result when groups of individuals having different cultures come into continuous first-hand contact, with subsequent changes in the original culture patterns of either or both groups . . . under this definition acculturation is to be distinguished from culture change, of which it is but one aspect, and assimilation, which is at times a phase of acculturation. It is also to be differentiated from diffusion, which while occurring in all instances of acculturation, is not only a phenomenon which frequently takes place without the occurrence of the types of contact between peoples specified in the definition above, but also constitutes only one aspect of the process of acculturation. (Redfield, Linton, & Herskovits, 1936, pp. 149–152)

In another formulation, acculturation was defined as

culture change that is initiated by the conjunction of two or more autonomous cultural systems. Acculturative change may be the consequence of direct cultural transmission; it may be derived from noncultural causes, such as ecological or demographic modification induced by an impinging culture; it may be delayed, as with internal adjustments following upon the acceptance of alien traits or patterns; or it may be a reactive adaptation of traditional modes of life. Its dynamics can be seen as the selective adaptation of value systems, the processes of integration and differentiation, the generation of developmental sequences, and the operation of role determinants and personality factors. (Social Science Research Council, 1954, p. 974)

The implications of these definitions for research on acculturation will be examined later, in the section dealing with acculturation research.

Acculturation Framework

The framework presented in Figure 1 draws our attention to some of the key issues to be discussed in this chapter. The framework makes a distinction, first of all, between two levels: the *population* (ecological, cultural, social, and institutional, at the left) and the *individual* (the behaviors and traits of persons, at the right). Although this distinction has not usually been made by workers in anthropology, it has become of major importance for studies of individual acculturation. Graves (1967) coined the term *psychological acculturation* to refer to the changes an individual experiences as a result of being in contact with other cultures and participating in the process of acculturation that one's cultural or ethnic group is undergoing. The distinction between acculturation and psychological acculturation is important for two reasons. The phenomena are different at the two levels, as we shall see later in the chapter: for example, at the population level changes in social structure, economic base, and political organization frequently occur, whereas at the individual level the changes are in such areas as behavior, identity, values, and attitudes. Also, not every acculturating individual participates in the collective changes that are under way in the group to the same

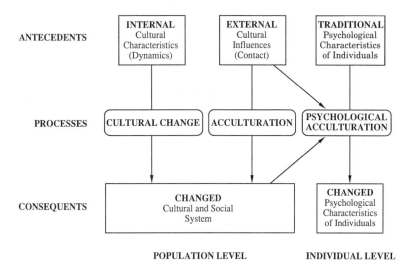

FIGURE 1. Model of key variables and relationships in the study of culture change and acculturation (modified from Berry, 1980).

extent or in the same way. Thus, if we want to eventually understand the relationships between culture contact and psychological outcomes for individuals, we will need to assess (using separate measures) changes at the population level and individuals' participation in these changes, then relate both of these measures to the psychological consequences for the individual.

This discussion of the need for two levels brings us to the second major distinction, between the antecedents to change and the consequents of change. In Figure 1 antecedents are placed at the top, while consequents are placed below. Generally speaking, the flow of events is from antecedents to consequents, and the goal is to understand the population- and individual-level consequents in relation to the antecedents. Reverse influences do occur, but return arrows are not illustrated in the figure, since our focus in this chapter is on the eventual psychological outcomes, at the lower right.

The third distinction in Figure 1 is between external and internal sources of change. As noted in the definitions I quoted at the outset, change can come about by events that impinge on a group or an individual from outside the culture: both diffusion and acculturation are examples of this source of change and include the introduction both of single innovations such as the plow, writing, and firearms (all examples of diffusion) and of whole institutions such as education, colonial government, and industrialization (all examples of acculturation). Internal sources of change are those that do not come from outside contact; they include forces such as invention, discovery, and innovation (ongoing dynamics at the population level) and insight, creativity, and drive (at the individual level).

A fourth feature of Figure 1 is that of the *processes* involved in change. The term *culture change* refers to the process that results in population-level changes that are due to dynamic internal events. The term *acculturation* refers to the process that results in population-level changes that are due to contact with other cultures. Finally, the term *psychological acculturation* refers to the process by which individuals change, both by being influenced by contact with another culture and by being participants in the general acculturative changes under way in their own culture. This process necessarily involves some degree of input from, and continuity with, an individual's traditional psychological characteristics.

Although many disciplines have been working for a long time at the population level of Figure 1 (including anthropology, international development studies, rural sociology, economics, and political science), the task has fallen mainly to cross-cultural psychology to study the individual level and its relationships with the population level.

To illustrate Figure 1, we may consider two concrete cases of individuals experiencing psychological change as a result of their membership in a changing cultural group. Although there are many categories of such individuals, we may take first an immigrant moving to set up a new life in another country; this would be an example of acculturation, since external culture contact is involved, followed by both cultural and individual changes. First, the decision to emigrate is often based upon some prior contact, knowledge, and influence. Perhaps other individuals, even members of one's own family, have already settled in the new country, and this has led to some changes in one's home culture. Perhaps the foreign language is being taught in the schools, new industries are being established, and the mass media are showing the way of life in the new country. On immigration to the new country, there can be some dramatic and sometimes overwhelming contact experiences followed by psychological reactions: differences in climate, language, work habits, religion and dress, for example, can all challenge the immigrant, and some response is required. These cultural differences may be accepted, interpreted, or denied, and the individual may ride with them or be run over by them.

For a second example, we may take a person whose country and culture have been colonized. In this case there is no choice made to enter into culture contact, since dominant cultures have a history of entering, uninvited, into many parts of the world, especially in Africa, Asia, and the Americas. Precontact experiences and positive motivation to acculturate are therefore lacking; however, once the process has started, individuals and communities may vary greatly in how they deal with the acculturative influences. Some may turn their backs, others may embrace them, while yet others may selectively engage the new while merging it with the old. Many options are possible (as we shall see later in this chapter), but in all cases the intercultural contact and the individual psychological response will be related to each other. It is the task of cross-cultural psychology to examine these relationships, to understand them, and finally to at-

tempt to find systematic features in order to produce some generalizations about the processes involved in psychological responses to
culture contact and change.

The Acculturation Process

From the definitions of acculturation presented earlier we may identify some key elements that are usually studied in cross-cultural psychology. First there needs to be *contact* or interaction between cultures that is continuous and firsthand; this rules out short-term,
accidental contact, as well as diffusion of single cultural practices
over long distances. Second, the result is some *change* in the cultural
or psychological phenomena among the people in contact, usually
continuing for generations down the line. Third, taking these first
two aspects together, we can distinguish between a *process* and a
state: there is activity during and after contact that is dynamic, and
there is a result of the process that may be relatively stable; this outcome may include not only changes to existing phenomena, but also
some novel effects generated by the process of cultural interaction.

Considering these distinctions as part of a general system of acculturation, the framework in Figure 2 can be proposed (cf. Berry,
Trimble, & Olmeda, 1986). It depicts two cultures (A and B) in contact. In principle each could influence the other equally (in a form of
symbiosis), but in practice one tends to dominate the other; in this
framework the "dominant group" (or "donor") is Culture A and the
"acculturating group" (or "receptor") is Culture B. For complete-
ness, mutual influence is depicted by the two arrows between Cultures A and B, as is the influence of Culture A directly on individuals
in Culture B. However, the consequences for culture group A are
not represented, and for the balance of this chapter I will focus on a
single culture (B), the one receiving the greater influence. This is not
to say that changes in the dominant culture are uninteresting or unimportant: acculturation often brings about population expansion,
greater cultural diversification, attitudinal reaction (prejudice and
discrimination), and policy development (for example, in the areas
of immigration, cultural pluralism, bilingualism, and schooling).
But these changes, however significant, have generally fallen outside the competence of cross-cultural psychology.

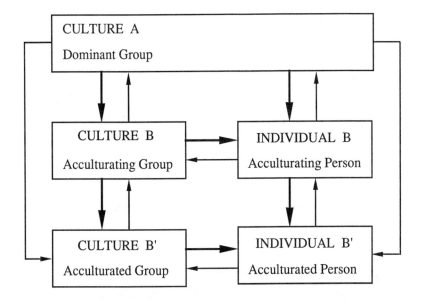

FIGURE 2. Framework for identifying variables and relationships in acculturation research (fig. 10.1 from Berry, Trimble, & Olmeda, 1986). Reprinted by permission of Sage Publications, Inc.

One result of the contact and influence is that aspects of group B become transformed so that cultural features of the acculturated group (B¹) are not identical to those in the original group at the time of first contact. Of course, if contact is still maintained, further influence from Culture A is experienced. A parallel effect is that individuals in group B undergo psychological changes (as a result of influences both from their own group and from group A), and again, if there is continuing contact further psychological changes may take place.

What characteristics of the dominant group is it important to examine? The essential ones are as follows. *Purpose*: Why is the contact taking place? What are its goals? Clearly acculturation effects will vary according to whether the purpose is colonization, enslavement, trade, military control, evangelization, education, and so on. *Length*: How long has the contact been taking place? Does it occur daily, seasonally, or annually? *Permanence*: Is the dominant group here to stay? Have they settled in, or is it a passing venture? *Population size*: How many are there? Do they form a majority, or are there only a few? *Policy*: What policies are being exercised toward acculturating groups—assimilation, eventual extermination, indirect rule, ghettoization, dispersion? *Cultural qualities*: Does the dominant group possess cultural qualities that can meet specific needs or improve the quality of life of the acculturating group? Potentially desirable cultural artifacts such as medicines, guns, and traps (for hunter populations), seeds, plows, and irrigation techniques (for agricultural populations) will obviously lead to acculturative changes more than will unwanted or nonfunctional cultural contributions. Without some indication of the nature of these variables, no account of acculturation would be complete.

A parallel account is needed of the characteristics of Culture B. *Purpose*: Is the group in contact voluntarily (e.g., immigrants) or under duress (e.g., native peoples)? *Location*: Is the group in its traditional location, with its land and other resources available, or displaced to some new environment (e.g., reservation, refugee camp)? *Length and permanence*: these variables are much the same as for the description of Culture A. In particular, the phase of acculturation needs to be specified: Has contact only begun? Have acculturative pressures been building up? Has a conflict or crisis appeared? *Population size*: How many are there? Are they a majority or a minority? Is the population vital (sustaining or increasing in number) or declining? *Policy*: To what extent does the group have an organized response to acculturation? If there is a policy orientation, is it one of resistance or exclusion (get rid of acculturative influence), of inclusion (accepting the influence), or of control (selective inclusion according to some scale of acceptability)? *Cultural qualities*: Do certain aspects of the traditional culture affect the acculturation process? For example hunter-gatherers are susceptible to habitat destruction due to war, forest reduction, or mineral exploration, and agricultural peoples may be dispossessed of their land by permanent settlers from Culture A. More complex societies may be better able to organize politically and militarily than less complex societies in order to alter the course of acculturation, while nomads may be in a position to disperse to avoid major acculturative influences.

In addition to these specific characteristics that may be discerned in particular groups, it is also important to consider how the cultural-level effects listed above for Culture B are distributed across individuals in the group: Do they vary according to age, sex, family position, and personal abilities? As I noted earlier, the crucial point is that not every person in the acculturating group will necessarily enter into the acculturation process in the same way or to the same degree. Hence, assessment of individual experience is an important aspect of the study of psychological acculturation.

At this point let us turn to the changes that have actually taken place (Culture B[1]) as a result of the acculturation process (recognizing, of course, that in many cases the acculturative influences continue to affect the group). These general consequences of acculturation have received considerable attention in the literature (see Berry, 1980, for a review of some general trends) and include such global descriptors as westernization, modernization, industrialization, and Americanization. Some specific consequences follow. *Political*: Have there been changes in political characteristics as a result of acculturation? For example, has independence been lost, have previously unrelated (even warring) groups been placed within a common framework, have new authority systems (e.g., chiefs, mayors, governors) been added, have people with regional similarities been categorized as "tribes" or "provinces"? *Economic*: Has the subsistence base been changed or the distribution of wealth been altered? For example, have hunter-gatherers been converted into herders or farmers, others into industrial or wage workers? Have previous concentrations of wealth in certain families or regions been eliminated or, conversely, has a new wealthy class emerged from a previously uniform system? Have new economic activities been introduced such as mining, forestry, game management, tourism, manufacturing? *Demographic*: Has there been a change in population size, its urban/rural distribution, its age or sex profile, or its regional dispersion? *Cultural*: To what extent are there new languages, religions, modes of dress, schooling, transportation, housing, and forms of social organization and social relations in the acculturated group? How do these relate to the previous norms? Do they conflict with them, partially displace them, or merge (as in some forms of Creole, or of African Christian churches)? All of these, and possibly many more depending on one's particular field site, are important markers of the extent to which acculturation has taken place in the group.

As I noted previously, there are very likely to be individual differences in the psychological characteristics people bring to the acculturation process, and not every person will necessarily participate in the process to the same extent. Taken together, this means that we need to shift our focus away from general characterizations of acculturation phenomena to a concern for variation among individuals in the group undergoing acculturation.

We also need to be aware that individual acculturation (as well as group-level effects) do not cohere as a neat package. Not only will groups and individuals vary in their participation and in their response to acculturative influences, but some domains of culture and behavior may become altered without comparable changes in other domains. For example, attitudes toward the value of traditional technology may change without a parallel change in beliefs and behaviors associated with it. That is, the process of acculturation is an uneven one and does not affect all cultural and psychological characteristics in a uniform manner.

Acculturation Research Designs

Turning to some actual research designs, we have noted that acculturation is a process that takes place over time and changes both the culture and the individual. The measurement of change between two or more points in time has a considerable literature in developmental and educational psychology, but not much in anthropology or in cross-cultural psychology. This lack has recently been highlighted for anthropology by a volume devoted to conducting long-term, even continuous, fieldwork (Foster, Scudder, Colson, & Kemper, 1978), but no similar treatment exists for cross-cultural psychology.

Culture change per se can be noted and assessed only when sets of data collected at different points in time (from Cultures B and B^1) are compared. Although this is ideal, in practice such longitudinal research is difficult and time consuming. A more usual practice is that many of the features of Culture B are identified from other sources (e.g., earlier ethnographic accounts) or are partially reconstructed from reports of the older or less acculturated members of the community. Similarly, longitudinal research is often plagued with problems of loss through death or out-migration, and by problems of the changing relevance of theoretical conceptions and the associated research instruments.

A common alternative to longitudinal research is cross-sectional research employing a time-related variable such as length of residence or generational status. For example, among immigrants, those who have resided longer in Culture A may experience more acculturation than those residing for a shorter period (usually controlling for present age and age of arrival). Similarly, it is common to classify group members by their generation (the first generation comprises the immigrants themselves, the second generation their immediate offspring, etc.). An assumption here is that acculturation is a linear process over time, an assumption we will consider later.

One longitudinal study (Berry, Wintrob, Sindell, & Mawhinney, 1982), which employed both a longitudinal and a cross-sectional design, was concerned with how the Cree Indian communities and individuals of James Bay (northern Canada) would respond to a large-scale hydroelectric project constructed in their midst. Initial fieldwork with adults and teenagers was carried out before construction began. Eight years later (after construction), about half the original sample was studied again; this sample was supplemented by an equal number of new individuals who were the same ages as the original sample had been eight years earlier. This provided a longitudinal analysis for one group (who were compared at two points in time) and a cross-sectional analysis to maintain an age control.

In this study we found evidence of both continuity and change in cultural and psychological characteristics. Although there was major upheaval in the political and economic life of the Crees, there was clear evidence that, collectively, they remained (and wanted to remain) a Cree nation. In the midst of such large-scale community and regional change, moreover, there was broad-ranging evidence for psychological continuity in abilities, attitudes, and behaviors. And though the *mean* scores on these variables changed little, there was evidence for *individual flux*, with both acculturation attitudes and acculturative stress (to be discussed later) showing a rise or a fall over time, depending on the individuals and their personal acculturation experiences. This latter finding, of course, could be uncovered only with a longitudinal design.

Other designs may be needed in other acculturation arenas. For example, where longitudinal work is not done, a respondent's age may be a suitable surrogate, since the younger are usually more exposed to acculturative influences from Culture A, while the older have a longer history of enculturation in Culture B and hence may be more resistive. The essential issue, though, is to ensure that both the design and the measures match as well as possible the local acculturation conditions.

Contact and Participation

The central issue here is the extent to which a particular individual has engaged in the acculturation process. Numerous indicators may be sought, from a variety of sources (the individual, an informant, or direct observation).

I approach the topic in two ways: first I list (and briefly comment on) many of the variables that appear in the literature; second, I present illustrative measures to show how the variables have actually been employed in fieldwork. The list includes the following. *Education*: How far has an individual gone in the formal schooling that has been introduced from outside? If one single indicator of individual contact and participation is to be taken in the field, previous research suggests that this is likely to be the most fruitful. *Wage employment*: To what extent has an individual entered the work force for wages, as opposed to remaining with traditional economic activity? *Urbanization*: In predominantly rural societies, to what extent has the individual migrated to, and lived in, a new urban agglomeration? To what extent has he traveled to or visited these urban areas? *Media*: To what extent does the individual listen to radio, watch television, and read newspapers and magazines that introduce him to Culture A? *Political participation*: To what extent does the individual involve himself in the new political structures, including voting, running for office, or volunteering for boards? *Religion*: Has the individual changed his religion to one introduced by Culture A, and to what extent does he practice it? *Language*: What is the extent of knowledge and use of the language(s) introduced by Culture A? *Daily practices*: To what extent is there a change in personal dress, housing and furniture styles, food habits, and so on? *Social relations*: To what extent does the individual relate to (marry, play with, work with, reside with) those of Culture A as opposed to those of his own group?

These numerous variables are likely to be interrelated; thus we find in the literature attempts to develop scales or indexes of contact and participation that sum across these various experiences. Two examples of these follow.

An index of contact (de Lacey, 1970) was developed as a general contact index for Australian Aboriginal children with white Australian society. It contains two sections: *exposure variables* (which include some cultural-level as well as individual-level variables) and *adaptation variables*. Exposure was assessed by the proportion of the schoolgoing population—and of the whole community—that is Euro-Australian, visits to Euro-Australian houses, shopping experiences of children, travel to Euro-Australian centers, use of English, and access to mass media and to Euro-Australian artifacts. Adaptation was assessed by ratings of persistence of Aboriginal culture, use of Euro-Australian games and hobbies, consumption of Euro-Australian food, home physical environment (Euro-Australian vs. Aboriginal), and community organization (primarily tribal vs. virtually Euro-Australian). Total scores were then calculated for each child. This index illustrates how acculturation may be assessed at the individual level, but of course the actual items will vary depending on population and research goals.

Another contact scale (Berry et al., 1986) was developed for use in central Africa with Biaka Pygmy and Bangandu villagers. It consists of eight variables: number of local languages spoken; knowledge of French; knowledge of Sango (the national lingua franca); ownership (cf. below, with items for knives, pottery, ornaments, outside goods); employment and technology (scaled from traditional hunter or farmer through to wage earner); religion (animism through to Islam); adoption of clothing (in European style), and travel (to towns and cities). All these variables were positively and (in most cases) significantly correlated and were used to create a single standardized index for each person.

An ownership index was developed (Berry & Annis, 1974a) for use among the James Bay Crees. The scale was such that participation at the "high end" of the scale usually included activities at the "low end," but not vice versa. The items in the scale (low to high) were ownership of radio, outboard motor, snowmobile, washing machine, freezer, bank account, and life insurance. The intention was to obtain objective evidence of the extent to which an individual had "bought into" Euro-Canadian society. Once again, this illus-

trates how to assess one aspect of acculturation rather than suggesting a standard instrument that can be used in all field settings.

It should be emphasized that these scales and indexes are not
universally valid, ready made, or standard instruments that can be
taken "as is" for use in any field setting. Some variables are clearly
more relevant to Pygmies than to a community of Italian-Americans
(e.g., adoption of clothing), while others may be more relevant to an
ethnic group undergoing acculturation (such as the language spoken in the family) than to a linguistically homogeneous community
in central Africa.

Acculturating Groups

Although many of the generalities found in the literature about the
effects of acculturation have been based on a single type of group, it
is clear that there are numerous types, and adaptations may vary depending upon this factor.

In the review by Berry and Kim (1988), five different groups
were identified, including immigrants, refugees, native peoples,
ethnic groups, and sojourners (see Figure 3). This classification into
five groups represents a view from Canada, where in principle all
people are thought to be attached in some way to a particular cultural heritage. The generic term "ethnic group" is most frequently
used to refer to people who identify with, and exhibit, a common
heritage in the second or subsequent generations after immigration.
By convention and by political ideology, the term "native peoples" is
used to refer to those indigenous or aboriginal groups that were resi-
dent before European colonization and who remain as nations (in the
cultural sense) within the larger society. "Immigrants" and "refugees"
are both first-generation arrivals into the population by way of migration from some other part of the world, while "sojourners" are temporary immigrants who reside for a specific purpose and time period and
intend to return eventually to their country of origin.

In other countries, the classification of groups may take different forms, based upon different histories and ideologies; however,
this classification derives also from three distinctions that have im-
port for psychological acculturation. There are variations in the degree of voluntariness, movement, and permanence of contact, all

factors that might affect the health of members of the group. Those who are voluntarily involved in the acculturation process (e.g., immigrants) may experience less difficulty than those with little choice in the matter (e.g., refugees and native peoples), since their initial attitudes toward contact and change may be more positive. Further, those only temporarily in contact and who are without permanent social supports (e.g., sojourners) may experience more health problems than those who are more permanently settled and established (e.g., ethnic groups). These distinctions suggest some important variations in outcomes that are subject to empirical verifications during the course of research.

Acculturation Attitudes

The valued goals of acculturation are not necessarily modernity or any other single alternative. Moreover, the goal as articulated by Culture A in its policy statements may not be the preferred course among the leaders or individuals of Culture B. In Australia (Sommerlad & Berry, 1970) an attempt was made to discover the attitudes of Aborig-

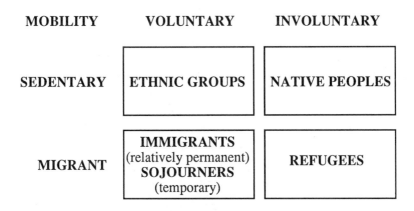

FIGURE 3. Five types of acculturating groups (fig. II from Berry, Kim, Minde, & Mok, 1987). Reprinted by permission of the Center for Migration Studies of New York, Inc.

ines toward their future in Australia; the Commonwealth government proposed assimilation, but others were not so sure. Since then the argument has been made (Berry, 1980) that acculturation can be viewed as multilinear—as a set of alternatives rather than a single dimension ending in assimilation or absorption into a "modern" society.

The ways an individual (or a group) of Culture B wishes to relate to Culture A have been termed "acculturation attitudes" (see Berry, Kim, Power, Young, & Bujaki, 1989, for a review of the reliability, validity, and correlates of these attitudes). In a sense they are conceptually the result of an interaction between ideas deriving from the modernity literature and the intergroup relations literature. In the former, the central issue is the degree to which one wishes to remain culturally as one has been (e.g., in terms of identity, language, way of life) as opposed to giving it all up to become part of a larger society; in the latter, the central issue is the extent to which one wishes to have day-to-day interactions with members of other groups in society, as opposed to turning away from them and relating only one's own group.

When these two central issues are posed simultaneously, a conceptual framework (Figure 4) is generated that posits four varieties of acculturation. It is, of course, recognized that each issue can be responded to on an attitudinal dimension, but for purposes of conceptual presentation, a dichotomous response (yes or no) is shown. When an individual in Culture B does not wish to maintain his identity (etc.) and seeks daily interaction with Culture A, then the assim-

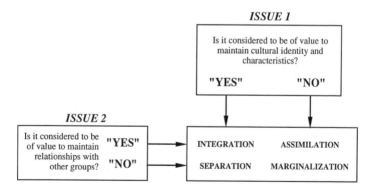

FIGURE 4. Four varieties of acculturation, based upon orientations to two basic issues (fig. 3 from Berry, Kim, Minde, & Mok, 1987). Reprinted by permission of the Center for Migration Studies of New York, Inc.

ilation path or mode is defined. In contrast, when one values holding onto one's original culture and at the same time wishes to avoid interaction with others, then the separation alternative is defined. When there is interest both in maintaining one's original culture and in daily interactions with others, integration is the option; here some degree of cultural integrity is maintained while one moves to participate as an integral part of the larger social network. Finally, when there is little possibility or interest in cultural maintenance (often for reasons of enforced cultural loss) and little interest in relations with others (often for reasons of exclusion or discrimination), then marginalization is defined. Note that the term *integration* as used here is clearly distinct from the term *assimilation* (although the two sometimes appear in the literature as synonyms); cultural maintenance is sought in the former case, whereas in the latter there is little or no interest in such continuity. Note also that acculturation may be "uneven" across domains of behavior and social life; for example, one may seek economic assimilation (in work), linguistic integration (by way of bilingualism), and marital separation (by endogamy).

To exemplify these four acculturation strategies, we may consider a hypothetical family that has migrated from Italy to Canada. The father may lean toward integration, wanting to get involved in the economics and politics of his new society, and learning English and French, in order to obtain the benefits that motivated his migration in the first place; at the same time he may be a leader in the Italian-Canadian community association, spending much of his leisure and recreation time in social interaction with other Italian-Canadians. In contrast, the mother may hold completely to Italian language use and social interactions, feeling that she cannot get involved in the work or cultural activities of the host society; she employs the separation strategy, having virtually all her personal, social, and cultural life within the Italian world. In further contrast, the teenage daughter is annoyed by hearing the Italian language in the home, by her mother's serving only Italian food, and by being required to spend most of her leisure time with her extended Italian family. She much prefers the assimilation option: to speak English, participate in her school activities, and generally be with her Canadian age-mates. Finally, the son doesn't particularly want to recognize or accept his Italian heritage ("What use is it here in my new country?") but is rejected by his schoolmates because he speaks with an Italian accent and often smells of garlic; he feels trapped between his two possible identity groups, neither accepting nor being accepted by them. As a result he retreats into the social and behavioral sink of marginalization, experiencing social and academic difficulties and eventually coming into conflict with his parents and the police.

Each of these four conceptual alternatives has been assessed with individuals in a variety of groups that are experiencing acculturation. The original study (Sommerlad & Berry, 1970) primarily sought to measure attitudes to assimilation and integration; other studies (e.g., Berry et al., 1982) assessed all four attitudes among James Bay Cree Indians, while work with other groups (such as French-, Portuguese-, Korean- and Hungarian-Canadians, see Berry et al., 1989) has demonstrated the usefulness of the approach not only with native peoples, but also with acculturating ethnic groups.

The four scales are developed by selecting a number of topics (e.g., endogamy, ethnic media) that are relevant to acculturation in the particular group (see Table 1 for some examples of these scales). Then four statements (one for each alternative) are generated with the help of informants. Usually it is possible to establish face validity for the statements by asking judges who are familiar with the model (as depicted in Figure 4) to sort them into the four alternatives; those statements with good interrater agreement are then kept. Administration involves either a Likert scale response to each statement or a statement of preference for one of the four statements within a topic. Four scores are then calculated for each person by summing across topics within each alternative. Reliability (internal consistency) is enhanced by item selection, and validity is checked against behavioral measures (e.g., high separation scorers read only ethnic newspapers, high assimilation scorers read only newspapers in the language of Culture A, high integration scorers read both).

Further work will be necessary to bring the various measures together conceptually and empirically. In particular, the political and cultural context in which acculturation is taking place (usually determined by the power of Culture A) will almost certainly affect the topics chosen and the options or alternatives that are conceivable. However, in any specific setting, the most important issue is whether the scales developed are modeled in the appropriate way so that they match the actual situation in which the research is being conducted.

Table 1
Sample Items from Acculturation Attitudes Scale

Friendship

S   Most of my friends are Koreans because I feel very comfortable around them, but I don't feel as comfortable around Canadians.

I   The kind of relationships that I have with Koreans are valuable while the kind of relationships with Canadians are also worthwhile.

M   These days it's hard to find someone you can really relate to and share your inner feelings and thoughts.

A   Most of my friends are Canadians because they are enjoyable and I feel comfortable around them, but I don't feel the same way with Koreans.

Canadian Society

A   We're living in Canada, and that means giving up our traditional way of life and adopting a Canadian life-style, thinking and acting like Canadians.

I   While living in Canada we can retain our Korean cultural heritage and life-style and yet participate fully in various aspects of Canadian society.

S   Because we live in Canada, we are always pressured to assimilate to Canadian life-style. Thus we must emphasize our distinct Korean identity and restrict our association with Canadian society.

M   Politicians use national pride to exploit and to deceive the public.

Note: A = assimilation; I = integration; S = separation; M = marginalization. From Berry, et al., 1989.

Behavior Changes

In this section I want to focus on what happens to individuals as a result of acculturation. As we saw in the last section, it is not always possible to maintain a clear separation between contact measures and attitude measures when we examine a particular acculturation study. Similarly, we will see here that not all observed changes can be linked directly to acculturation; some effects may be delayed in time, and some may even bring about acculturation in a continuing antecedent-consequent chain. For example, more contact often results in a more positive attitude to assimilation; thus the attitude could be classified as a "consequence of acculturation." Conversely, an initially positive attitude toward assimilation may result in a person's seeking out more contact; here the contact could just as well be classified as a consequence. Despite these qualifications, a number of studies have attempted to comprehend the results of acculturation and have developed instruments specifically designed to measure them.

Another distinction can be found in the literature between two kinds of consequences (Berry, 1976). One refers to the relatively conflict-free changes in behavior, such as an individual's gradually taking on wage employment and giving up another economic role; these have been termed *behavioral shifts* and are characterized by a continuity in quality but a change in quantity (e.g., from a pattern of 20% wage employment/80% farming at Time 1 to 90% wage employment/10% farming at Time 2). The other refers to new circumstances that often accompany acculturation, which appear to result from psychological conflict and social disintegration, such as an increase in homicide, spouse abuse, or a decline in mental health status; this type of consequence has been termed *acculturative stress*, and is characterized by a qualitative change in the life of an individual or community. Once again it is possible to challenge the distinction; after all, homicide, aggression, and neglect are present in most societies before acculturation, but we frequently encounter new forms as well as new rates, so that rather than being regarded as deviant and sanctioned (in Culture B) they become common in Culture B[1] and people learn to live with them.

As the definitions of acculturation presented earlier suggested, there can also be novel conditions stimulated or even created by the process of acculturation. These are not just shifts in previous behaviors or problematic stress effects; they are new cultural and behaviors that arise by way of social and political movements, themselves stimulated by acculturative contact.

Virtually any behavior studied by psychology is a candidate for a shift during acculturation. Of course this challenges the basic notions of the personality trait and behavioral stability, which posit continuity over time and across situations. However, the field of cross-cultural psychology has established fairly solid linkages between how an individual acts (including thoughts, feelings, and motives) and the culture that nurtured him; it should not be difficult to accept, then, that when the culture changes the individual may change as well. What may be stable over time is the culture-behavior linkage rather than the behavior itself.

The amount of behavior change with acculturation, and the way it relates to the two cultures, can vary a great deal. Figure 5 presents a general framework for examining behavior change (vertical axis) as a function of the phase or time period of acculturation (horizontal axis) and as a function of the variety or mode of acculturation (as defined in the previous section on attitudes) an individual engages in.

On the vertical axis, greater change is higher on the dimension, while little or no change is lower. Along the horizontal axis, the phase moves from precontact, through initial contact, often through a period of rising conflict (both psychological and cultural) between the two groups, sometimes resulting in a crisis, followed by three possible acculturation outcomes or forms of adaptation. In the *assim-*

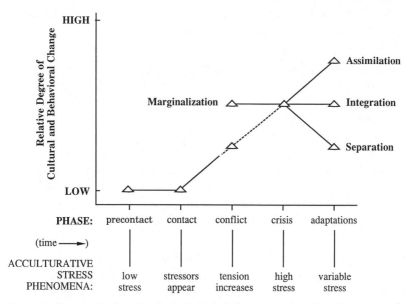

FIGURE 5. Degree of cultural and psychological change as a function of phases and varieties of acculturation (fig. 9.2 from Berry & Kim, 1988). Reprinted by permission of Sage Publications, Inc.

ilation outcome, behavioral change is maximal, whereas in the *separation* mode there is a return to more traditional (similar to minimally changed) behaviors; *integration* represents an outcome on which there is a relatively stable balance between behavioral continuity with one's traditional culture and change toward the new culture. In *marginalization* the individual is suspended between the two cultures, often in a state of personal and social conflict. It is in this last situation that greatest levels of acculturative stress are to be found; it will be considered in detail in the next section.

Among the many behaviors that could be considered in this examination of change, only a few can be presented. I will begin with identity, move to aspects of cognition, then to personality, and finally (to come full circle) consider attitudes and contact as psychological characteristics that themselves shift as a result of acculturation.

Identity (how one usually thinks of oneself) can be seen in terms of cultural (including ethnic and racial) or other factors (e.g., age, sex, location; Aboud, 1981). Here we are primarily interested in ethnic identity and how it may change over the course of acculturation. There is widespread evidence (e.g., De Vos, 1980) that cultural identities do change. At the beginning of contact there is usually little question: one thinks of oneself as a member of the group into which one was enculturated, be it small in scale (a village or a band) or large (a state or country). As contact continues, identity changes may be monitored by a variety of techniques that can provide evidence for simple shifts and for identity conflict and confusion (at the crisis stage, related to acculturative stress).

Cognitive shifts are also frequently observed in studies of acculturation. Indeed, cognitive shifts are often the goal of acculturation, as in the case of educational or religious missions in many parts of the world. Here we are primarily interested in the intellectual changes that may occur with acculturation. A major focus (e.g., Rogoff, 1981; Scribner & Cole, 1973) has been on the cognitive consequences of formal education, with an associated interest in the consequences of literacy (Scribner & Cole, 1981). Cognitive qualities that have been assessed are general intelligence (e.g., Vernon, 1969), cognitive style (e.g., Berry, 1976), memory (e.g., Wagner, 1981), and classification (e.g., Scribner & Cole, 1981), as well as some of the more overt consequences such as success at school.

Perhaps the most common (and ambiguous) finding is that performance on cognitive tests becomes "better" (more like the expectations of the test maker or test administrator) as the test taker becomes more acculturated to the society of origin of the tests. Phrased in this way, the finding is obvious and perhaps meaningless. The use of such tests among cultural groups in various parts of the world and among ethnic groups in plural societies continues, and continues to be criticized (e.g., Samuda, 1983), and the results continue to be open to numerous interpretations. One point of view about such results is that there is no substantive shift in cognitive functioning, only a superficial change in performance due to learning some "test taking tricks"(e.g., familiarity with the language of the test and with testlike situations). Another point of view is that new cognitive qualities or operations may indeed develop with acculturative influences such as literacy or industrialization. Although this view is held by many who carry on modernization research (e.g., Inkeles & Smith, 1974), and in literacy (e.g., Goody, 1968), the evidence for such fundamental changes is rather sparse. For example, the study by Scribner and Cole (1981) revealed very little in the way of general cognitive consequences of literacy—only a few changes that are more specific to skills directly related to the practice of literacy.

The evident conclusion to be drawn is that the search for cognitive consequences of acculturation is methodologically very difficult if one wants unambiguous results. If the point is to demonstrate that over time or over generations beliefs, abilities, or even general intelligence (as defined and measured by the larger society culture) change in the acculturating group in the direction of the norms in the larger society, then the task is rather easy. But the meaning (or "depth") of these changes is much more difficult to specify.

Personality shifts have also been observed during acculturation (which may appear to be a contradiction in terms). In one classical study by Hallowell (1955), three groups of Ojibwa Indians were administered the Rorschach test. One sample was close to Euro-Canadian influence, one was in the remote hinterland, and the third was geographically in between, with an intermediate degree of contact. Hallowell interpreted his results as showing a continuity of a modal Ojibwa personality, but with differences from one sample to another such that the most remote was most intact, the higher-contact sample had shifted more toward Euro-Canadian personality, and the middle community was in between. However, such a "linear gradient" may not always be evident. Peck et al. (1976) found that some individuals may show this pattern but others may not change at all or indeed may reverse the process. One way of interpreting these variations is to argue that those who are in the "assimilation mode" may show a linear gradient, whereas those who are separating or integrating may not exhibit the pattern.

Acculturation attitudes, as we have seen, may predispose contact and hence lead to acculturative change. To come full circle, then, we should remind ourselves that the consequences of acculturation can be changes in acculturation attitudes and changes in contact participation. Evidence does indeed show that there is a complex interrelationship among many variables; for example, a preference for assimilation has often been observed to increase as a result of acculturation experience, and it leads in turn to even more contact and participation by individuals of Culture B in the life of Culture A (Berry et al., 1989). However, lest I leave the impression that there is a continuous linear skid toward assimilation and cultural and psychological homogeneity, we may remind ourselves that conflict, reaction, and other resistive strategies also frequently occur during acculturation; these are important factors in acculturative stress phenomena, to which I now turn.

Acculturative Stress

One of the most obvious and frequently reported consequences of acculturation is societal disintegration accompanied by personal crisis. The old social order and cultural norms often disappear, and individuals may be lost in the change. At the group level, previous patterns of authority, civility, and welfare no longer operate; and at the individual level, hostility, uncertainty, identity confusion, and depression may set in. Taken together these changes constitute the negative side of acculturation, changes that are frequently, but not inevitably, present. The opposite, successful *adaptation*, may also take place; as we shall see, the outcome appears to vary as a function of a number of variables.

The concept of *acculturative stress* (Berry & Annis, 1974b) refers to one kind of stress, in which the stressors are identified as having their source in the process of acculturation; in addition, there is often a particular set of stress behaviors that occur during acculturation, such as lowered mental health status (especially confusion, anxiety, depression), feelings of marginality and alienation, heightened psychosomatic symptoms, and identity confusion. Acculturative stress thus may underlie a reduction in the health status of individuals (including physical, psychological, and social aspects). To qualify as *acculturative* stress, these changes should be related in a systematic way to known features of the acculturation process as experienced by the individual.

In a recent review and integration of the literature, Berry and Kim (1988) attempted to identify the cultural and psychological factors that govern the relationship between acculturation and mental health. We concluded that mental health problems clearly often do arise during acculturation; however, these problems are not inevitable and seem to depend on a variety of group and individual characteristics that enter into the acculturation process. That is, acculturation sometimes enhances one's life chances and mental health and sometimes virtually destroys one's ability to carry on; the eventual outcome for any particular individual is affected by other variables that govern the relationship between acculturation and stress.

This conception is illustrated in Figure 6. On the left of the figure, *acculturation* occurs in a particular situation (e.g., migrant com-

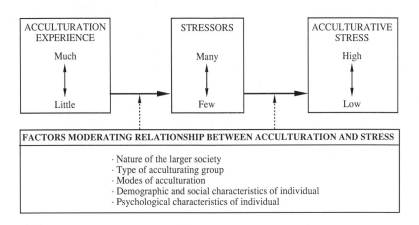

FIGURE 6. Relationships between acculturation and stress, as modified by other factors (fig. I from Berry, Kim, Minde, & Mok, 1987). Reprinted by permission of the Center for Migration Studies of New York, Inc.

munity or native settlement), and individuals participate in and experience these changes to varying degrees; thus individual acculturation experience may vary from a great deal to rather little. In the middle, *stressors* may result from this varying experience of acculturation; for some people acculturative changes may all be in the form of stressors, while for others they may be benign or even be seen as opportunities. On the right, varying levels of *acculturative stress* may become manifest as a result of acculturation experience and stressors.

The first crucial point to note is that relationships among these three concepts (indicated by the solid horizontal arrows) are probabilistic rather than deterministic; the relationships all depend upon a number of moderating factors (indicated in the lower box), including the nature of the larger society, the type of acculturating group, the mode of acculturation being experienced, and a number of demographic, social, and psychological characteristics (including coping abilities) of the group and individual members. That is, each of these factors can influence the degree and direction of the relationships between the three variables at the top of Figure 6. This influence is indicated by the broken vertical arrows drawn between this set of moderating factors and the horizontal arrows.

Archival, observational, and interview methods have been employed to assess acculturative stress. Archival approaches can provide collective data for the society or community as a whole: rates of suicide, homicide, family and substance abuse, and so on, can provide important information about the acculturation context in which an individual is operating. In particular, rates of psychiatric attention have often been employed in the literature. However, all these archival records require an organized social system with equal access to all members of society. The system may itself be suffering from disintegration; thus such macroindicators may not always be available or reliable.

Survey studies have typically employed third-party sources of information about, or direct observations of, more specific research subjects. For example, number of court appearances, alcohol consumption, or work and school absenteeism for specific individuals or target communities can provide, over time, a reasonable indicator of problem behaviors during acculturation.

Interviewing samples of individuals in acculturating communities has been a particularly important source of evidence about stress both in Western urban groups undergoing change (e.g., Srole, Langer, & Michael, 1962) and in specific cultural groups experiencing acculturation (e.g., Wintrob & Sindell, 1972). Because of the popularity of this approach, some fairly concise self-report measures have been developed, of which we will consider two.

One scale has been developed in a number of versions from the Cornell Medical Index (Brodman et al., 1952). The full scale consists of 195 items concerned with somatic functioning and 51 items concerned with psychological life, arranged into six subscales (Inadequacy, Depression, Anxiety, Sensitivity, Anger, and Tension). Work in Alaska by Chance (1965) revealed somewhat heightened levels of psychological problems among acculturating Inuit. A 20-item version was developed by Cawte, Bianchi, and Kiloh (1968) containing 10 somatic items and 10 psychological items. This version was employed with an Australian Aborigine group that had experienced both relocation and acculturation. Berry (1976) later used the scale with various acculturating Canadian Indian groups, and Blue and Blue (1983) have employed it with Canadian Indian university students. The full 51-item psychological scales have also been used with various groups, including Vietnamese refugees (Masuda, Lin, & Tazuma, 1979–1980; Berry & Blondel, 1982), and foreign students (Berry et al., 1987).

A second scale was devised by Mann (1958) to assess the concept of marginality. The essence of being marginal is being "poised in psychological uncertainty between two worlds" (Stonequist, 1935), unable to participate fully in either culture. The scale consists of 14 items, such as "I feel that I don't belong anywhere" and "I feel that nobody really understands me." Respondents indicate which statements they agree with, and the total score is the number of items agreed with.

A major problem with these scales is that all the items are phrased in a positive direction; thus those with a tendency to agree will score higher than others. Another problem is that self-reports of these disorders may not bear any relationship to their actual presence. However, cross-validation with other tests, and with observational data, tends to support their continued use in studies of acculturation as indicators of the stresses and strains individuals experience.

Results of studies of acculturative stress have varied widely in the level of difficulties found in acculturating groups. Early views were that culture contact and change inevitably led to stress; however, current views are that stress is linked to acculturation in a probablistic way, and the level of stress experienced will depend on a number of factors.

There is evidence (Berry & Kim, 1988) that mode of acculturation is one important factor: those who feel marginal tend to be highly stressed, and those who maintain a separation goal are also stressed; in contrast, those who pursue integration are minimally stressed, with assimilation leading to intermediate levels.

Similarly, the phase of acculturation (see Figure 5) is also important: those in first contact and those who have achieved some long term adaptation tend to be less stressed than those caught in the conflict or crisis phase, especially, as I have noted, if they also feel marginal.

Another factor is the way the host society exerts its acculturative influences. One important distinction is the degree of pluralism extant (Murphy, 1965). Culturally plural societies, in contrast to culturally monistic ones, are likely to be characterized by two important factors: one is the availability of a network of social and cultural groups that may provide support for those entering into the experience of acculturation (i.e., provide a protective cocoon); the other is a greater tolerance for or acceptance of cultural diversity (termed "multicultural ideology" by Berry, Kalin, & Taylor, 1977). Related to this general tolerance for ethnic diversity (which is usually found in plural societies) is the pattern of specific ethnic and racial attitudes in the larger society: some acculturating groups may be more accepted and placed higher in the prestige hierarchy, while others may occupy the lower ranks in the societies' prejudice system. Taken together, one might reasonably expect the stress of persons experiencing acculturation in plural societies to be less than in monistic societies that pursue a forced inclusion or assimilationist ideology.

A related factor, paradoxically, is the existence of policies designed to *exclude* acculturating groups from full participation in the larger society; to the extent that acculturating people wish to participate in the desirable features of the larger society (such as adequate housing, medical care, and political rights), the denial of these may increase acculturative stress.

There are also many social and cultural qualities of the acculturating group that may affect the degree to which its members experience acculturative stress. The list of possible factors identified in the literature is extremely long; thus I attempt only a selective overview. It is useful to distinguish between original (precontact) cultural characteristics and those that evolve during the process of acculturation; however, some factors involve the interaction of variables from these two sets (pre- and postcontact).

One basic cultural factor that appears in the literature is the traditional settlement pattern of the group: nomadic peoples, who are usually hunters, gatherers, or pastoralists, may suffer more negative consequences of acculturation than peoples who were sedentary before contact. A complex of factors has been suggested to account for this proposal: nomadic peoples are used to relatively large territories, small population densities, and unstructured sociopolitical systems; acculturation, typically requires sedentarization into relatively dense communities with new authority systems, and this induces relatively greater tension among nomadic peoples than among others.

Status is also a factor even when one's origin is in a relatively stratified society. For example, one's "entry status" into the larger society is often lower than one's "departure status" from the home society; this relative loss of status may result in stress and poor mental health. One's status mobility in the larger society, whether to regain one's original status or just to keep up with other groups, may also be a factor. In addition, some specific features of status (such as education and employment) provide one with resources for dealing with the larger society, and these are likely to affect one's ability to function effectively in the new circumstances.

Some standard indicators, such as age and gender, may also play a role: relatively older persons, and often females, have frequently been noted to experience more stress, as have those who are unmarried, either because of loss or because no partner is available.

Perhaps the most comprehensive variable in the literature is social support—the presence of social and cultural institutions that support the acculturating individual. Included here are such factors as ethnic associations (national or local), residential enclaves ("ghetto"), extended families (including endogamy), availability of one's original group (visits to, vitality of, alienation from the culture), and more formal institutions such as agencies and clinics devoted to providing support.

A final set of social variables refers to the acceptance or prestige of one's group in the acculturation setting. Some groups are more acceptable than others on grounds of ethnicity, race, or religion; those less acceptable run into barriers (prejudice, discrimination, exclusion) that may lead to marginalization of the group and are likely to induce greater stress. The point here is that even in plural societies (those societies that may be generally more tolerant of differences) there are still relative degrees of social acceptability of the various acculturating groups.

Beyond these social factors numerous psychological variables may play a role in the mental health of persons experiencing acculturation. Here again a distinction is useful between those characteristics that were present before contact and those that developed during acculturation. The precontact set of variables includes certain experiences that may predispose one to function more effectively under acculturative pressures. These are prior knowledge of the new language and culture, prior intercultural encounters of any kind, motives for the contact (voluntary vs. involuntary contact), and attitudes toward acculturation (positive or negative). Other prior attributes that have been suggested in the literature are level of education and employment, values, self-esteem, identity confusion, rigidity/flexibility, and cognitive style.

Contact experiences may also account for variations in acculturative stress. Whether one has a lot of contacts with the larger society (or few), whether they are pleasant (or unpleasant), whether they meet current needs (or not), and in particular whether the first encounters are viewed positively (or not) may set the stage for all subsequent ones and may affect mental health.

Among factors that appear during acculturation are the attitudes toward the various modes of acculturation: as I noted in the previous section, individuals within a group do vary in their preference for assimilating, integrating, or rejecting. These variations, along with experiences of marginalization, are known to affect mental health (Berry, Kim, Minde, & Mok, 1987). Another variable, an individual's sense of cognitive control over the acculturation process, also seems to play a role; those who perceive that the changes are opportunities they can manage may have better mental health than those who feel overwhelmed. In essence, then, the attitudinal and cognitive perspectives propose that it is not the acculturative changes themselves that are important, but how one sees them and what one makes of them.

Finally, a recurring idea is that the congruity between expectations and actualities will affect mental health; individuals for whom there is a discrepancy—who aspire to or expect more than they actually obtain during acculturation—may have greater acculturative stress than those who achieve some reasonable match between them. That is, expectations and goals (and whether they can be met) appear to be major predictors of how individuals and groups will fare during the course of acculturation. Recent work (reviewed in Beiser, Barwick, Berry, et al., 1988) indicates that a desire to participate in the larger society, or a desire for cultural maintenance, if thwarted, can lead to a serious decline in the mental health of acculturating individuals. Policies or attitudes in the larger society that are discriminatory (not permitting participation, and leading to marginalization or segregation) or assimilationist (leading to enforced cultural loss) are all predictors of psychological problems. In my view, acculturative stress is always a possible concomitant of acculturation, but the probability can be much reduced if both participation in the larger society and maintenance of one's heritage culture are welcomed by policy and practice in the larger acculturative arena.

Conclusion

Applications of findings reported in this chapter, especially if done with continuing evaluation and validation, should go a long way to helping the millions who find themselves in a situation of culture contact and change. Refugees, immigrants, and guest workers can all be provided with information, counseling, and other forms of psychological assistance based on these data. Receiving countries can also develop policies and programs based on these findings, and public education of the host population may also be attempted. Enough information is now available about the process of acculturation, and about factors affecting various psychological outcomes, that there could, with better programs, be a significant reduction in the problems acculturating peoples experience. However, with the possibility that there will be increasing numbers of refugees in the world, and perhaps increasing numbers of temporary migrants (out-migration followed by return migration), the problem potential is not likely to diminish. Hence the findings reported in this chapter, and the basic principles they point to, urgently require interpretation and transfer to those responsible for managing acculturation, in both the donor and receiving countries.

REFERENCES

Aboud, F. (1981). Ethnic self identity. In R. C. Gardner & R. Kalin (Eds.), *A Canadian social psychology of ethnic relations*. Toronto: Methuen.

Beiser, M., Barwick, C., Berry, J. W., et al. (1988). *After the door has been opened: Mental health issues affecting immigrants and refugees in Canada*. Ottawa: Ministries of Multiculturalism and Health and Welfare.

Berry, J. W. (1976). *Human ecology and cognitive style: Comparative studies in cultural and psychological adaptation*. London: Sage.

Berry, J. W. (1980). Social and cultural change. In H. C. Triandis & R. Brislin (Eds.), *Handbook of cross-cultural psychology: Vol. 5. Social Psychology*. Boston: Allyn and Bacon.

Berry, J. W., & Annis, R. C. (1974a). Acculturative stress: The role of ecology, culture and differentiation. *Journal of Cross Cultural Psychology, 5*, 382–406.

Berry, J. W., & Annis, R. C. (1974b). Ecology, cultural and psychological differentiation. *International Journal of Psychology, 9*, 173–193.

Berry, J. W., & Blondel, T. (1982). Psychological adaptation of Vietnamese refugees in Canada. *Canadian Journal of Community Mental Health, 1*, 81–88.

Berry, J. W., Kalin, R., & Taylor, D. M. (1977). *Multiculturalism and ethnic attitudes in Canada*. Ottawa: Supply and Services.

Berry, J. W., & Kim, U. (1988). Acculturation and mental health. In P. Dasen, J. W. Berry, & N. Sartorius (Eds.), *Health and cross-cultural psychology* (pp. 207–236). London: Sage.

Berry, J. W., Kim, U., Minde, T., & Mok, D. (1987). Comparative studies of acculturative stress. *International Migration Review, 21*, 491–511.

Berry, J. W., Kim, U., Power, S., Young, M., & Bujaki, M. (1989). Acculturation attitudes in plural societies. *Applied Psychology, 38*, 185–206.

Berry, J. W., Trimble, J., & Olmeda, E. (1986). The assessment of acculturation. In W. J. Lonner & J. W. Berry (Eds.), *Field methods in cross-cultural research*. London: Sage.

Berry, J. W., van de Koppel, J. M. H., Sénéchal, C., Annis, R. C., Bahuchet, S., Cavalli-Sforza, L. L., & Witkin, H. A. (1986). *On the edge of the forest: Cultural adaptation and cognitive development in Central Africa*. Lisse: Swets and Zeitlinger.

Berry, J. W., Wintrob, R. M., Sindell, P. S., & Mawhinney, T. A. (1982). Psychological adaptation to culture change among the James Bay Cree. *Naturaliste Canadien, 109*, 965–975.

Blue, A., & Blue, M. (1983). The trail of stress. In R. Samuda, J. W. Berry, & M. Laferriere (Eds.), *Multiculturalism in Canada: Social and educational perspectives*. Toronto: Allyn and Bacon.

Brodman, K., et al. (1952). The Cornell Medical Index health questionnaire: 3. The evaluation of emotional disturbances. *Journal of Clinical Psychology, 8*, 119–124.

Cawte, J., Bianchi, G. N., & Kiloh, L. G. (1968). Personal discomfort in Australian Aborigines. *Australian and New Zealand Journal of Psychiatry, 2*, 69–79.

Chance, N. A. (1965). Acculturation, self-identification, and personality adjustment. *American Anthropologist, 67*, 372–393.

de Lacey, P. R. (1970). An index of contact. *Australian Journal of Social Issues, 5*, 219–223.

De Vos, G. (1980). Ethnic adaptation and minority status. *Journal of Cross-Cultural Psychology, 11*, 101–124.

Foster, G. M., Scudder, T., Colson, E., & Kemper, R. V. (Eds.). (1978). *Long-term field research in social anthropology*. Orlando, FL: Academic Press.

Goody, J. (1968). *Literacy in traditional societies*. New York: Cambridge University Press.

Graves, T. D. (1967). Psychological acculturation in a tri-ethnic community. *South-western Journal of Anthropology, 23*, 337–350.

Hallowell, A. I. (1955). Sociopsychological aspects of acculturation. In A. I. Hallowell, *Culture and experience*. Philadelphia: University of Pennsylvania Press.

Inkeles, A., & Smith, D. (1974). *Becoming modern*. Cambridge: Harvard University Press.

Mann, J. (1958). Group relations and the marginal man. *Human Relations, 11*, 77–92.

Masuda, M., Lin, K., & Tazuma, L. (1979–1980). Adaptation problems of Vietnamese refugees. *Archives of General Psychiatry, 36–37*, 955–961, 447–450.

Murphy, H. B. M. (1965). Migration and the major mental disorders. In M. B. Kantor (Ed.), *Mobility and mental health*. Springfield, IL: Thomas.

Peck, R., et al. (1976). A test of the universality of an acculturation gradient in three-culture triads. In K. Riegel & J. Meacham (Eds.), *The developing individual in a changing world*. The Hague: Mouton.

Redfield, R., Linton, R., & Herskovits, M. J. (1936). Memorandum on the study of acculturation. *American Anthropologist, 38*, 149–152.

Rogoff, B. (1981). Schooling and the development of cognitive skills. In H. C. Triandis & A. Heron (Eds.), *Handbook of cross-cultural psychology: Vol. 4. Development*. Boston: Allyn and Bacon.

Samuda, R. (1983). Cross-cultural testing within a multicultural society. In S. H. Irvine & J. W. Berry (Eds.), *Human assessment and cultural factors*. New York: Plenum.

Scribner, S., & Cole, M. (1973). Cognitive consequences of formal and informal education. *Science, 182*, 553–559.

Scribner, S., & Cole, M. (1981). *The psychology of literacy*. Cambridge: Harvard University Press.

Social Science Research Council. (1954). Acculturation: An exploratory formulation. *American Anthropologist, 56*, 973–1002.

Sommerlad, E. A., & Berry, J. W. (1970). The role of ethnic identification in distinguishing between attitudes towards assimilation and integration of a minority racial group. *Human Relations, 23*, 23–29.

Srole, L., Langer, T. S., & Michael, S. T. (1962). *Mental health in the metropolis*. New York: McGraw-Hill.

Stonequist, E. V. (1935). The problem of the marginal man. *American Journal of Sociology, 41*, 1–12.

Vernon, P. E. (1969). *Intelligence and cultural environment*. London: Methuen.

Wagner, D. A. (1981). Culture and memory development. In H. C. Triandis & A. Heron (Eds.), *Handbook of cross-cultural psychology: Vol. 4. Development*. Boston: Allyn and Bacon.

Wintrob, R. M., & Sindell, P. S. (1972). Culture change and psychopathology: The case of Cree adolescent students in Quebec. In J. W. Berry & G. J. S. Wilde (Eds.), *Social psychology: The Canadian context*. Toronto: McClelland and Stewart.

Normal and Abnormal Behavior in Cross-Cultural Perspective: Specifying the Nature of Their Relationship

Juris G. Draguns
Pennsylvania State University

Culture and Psychopathology: History and Current State

The comparison of abnormal behavior across cultures developed initially in virtual isolation from other areas of cross-cultural psychology. If Wilhelm Wundt is credited with being a remote forefather of cross-cultural psychology, on the basis of his 10-volume set of *Völkerpsychologie*, the founder of transcultural psychiatry is Emil Kraepelin (1904), who early in this century reported on his personal observations of depressive manifestations in Algeria and in Java, now a part of Indonesia. Kraepelin was probably the first to note differences in non-Western expressions of depression, and he commented on the rarity of expressions of guilt. After this early and prominent start, the description of psychiatric disturbance outside the European and North American cultures proceeded fitfully and erratically. For a rather long period, it failed to produce a systematic body of findings and remained on the fringes of its parent discipline of descriptive psychiatry. To a lesser degree still was it connected with the emerging data of psychology, including that of the psychology of abnormal behavior.

I express sincere appreciation to Jeffrey Packard for valuable bibliographic assistance. I am grateful to Geert Hofstede, who read an earlier draft of this chapter and contributed numerous constructive suggestions. His comments and proposals have been incorporated, but I remain responsible for the way these changes were made.

As cross-cultural psychology came into being as a systematic and continuous enterprise, roughly in the late 1960s, the cross-cultural study of psychological disturbance, by this time pursued by psychiatrists, psychologists, and anthropologists, continued to represent a rather specialized, even esoteric subject, little related to the major themes and concerns of the "mainstream" cross-cultural researchers in psychology, whose sights were focused upon such intensively investigated subjects as childhood development, cognition, perception, and social behavior. Over the past two decades this situation has been changing, but at a slow and uneven pace. The gap between the study of abnormal and normal patterns from a cross-cultural perspective still remains to be bridged. The object of this chapter is to forge links between some major themes that have emerged in the cross-cultural study of complex social behavior and the accumulated findings on the human universals and cultural particulars in the manifestations of psychological disorders. Specifically, I want to use some formulations derived within normal cross-cultural psychology in order to explicate the often atheoretical data of transcultural psychiatry and cross-cultural abnormal psychology. My objectives are threefold. First, I shall briefly review the current state of knowledge on the nature and extent of cultural influences on psychopathology or, conversely, document what is known about the universality of psychopathological manifestations. Second, I shall extract a number of general dimensions of abnormal behavior along which cultures around the world can plausibly be said to vary. Third, I shall refer these axes of variation to major variables of theoretical and empirical interest in cross-cultural psychology of normal experience and behavior, with particular reference to complex social human action. The final product will be, I hope, a clarification of the generic relationship between culture and psychopathology. As I intend to say more elaborately and in greater detail later, this relationship has all too frequently been invoked post hoc rather than being formulated prospectively and explicitly as an explanatory principle capable of generating new data and uncovering hitherto unknown phenomena.

Cultural Influences upon Psychopathology: Essential or Trivial?

Let me introduce my first objective with a question: How much of abnormal behavior can be said to vary as a result of cultural influences, and how much of it remains invariant regardless of geographic site and cultural milieu? Although virtually all observers and authorities pay lip service to the influence of cultural factors upon psychopathology, opinions differ dramatically on the weight assigned to such influences, which range from central to peripheral and from major to trivial. The positions of two major pioneering figures in this field illustrate this divergence of opinion.

The prominent anthropologist Ruth Benedict (1934) represented most articulately a cultural relativist point of view. According to this position, the social plasticity of psychopathology is virtually infinite. Although she allowed hypothetically for a common core of human disturbance, on the basis of anthropological fieldwork she was much more impressed with the range of variation in psychopathological expressions at various sites around the world. Such dramatic patterns of behavior as the paranoia of the Dobuans of New Guinea or the megalomania of the Kwakiutl potlatch in British Columbia—were these manifestations not equivalent to the symptoms observed in psychotics of our back wards? Lest Ruth Benedict be accused of ethnocentrism, let me hasten to add that she appended a ringing passage excoriating various socially pathological practices tolerated and even admired in our own society that, as she maintained, show no qualitative or intrinsic distinction from the properly labeled psychopathological behaviors of hospitalized psychiatric patients. As she put it:

> From the point of view of absolute categories of abnormal psychology, we must expect in any culture to find a large proportion of the most extreme abnormal types among those who from the local point of view are farthest from belonging to this category. The culture, according to its major preoccupations, will increase and intensify hysterical, epileptic, or paranoid symptoms, at the same time relying socially in a greater and greater degree upon these very individuals. . . . Such individuals are probably mentally warped to a greater degree than

many inmates of our institutions who are nonetheless socially unavailable. (Benedict, 1934, p. 75)

On the basis of the argument above, Benedict envisaged the future formulation of worldwide principles of abnormal behavior as follows:

Any conclusions about such behavior must await the collection of trained observers of psychiatric data from other cultures. . . . When data are available in psychiatry, this minimum definition of abnormal human tendencies will be probably quite unlike our culturally conditioned, highly elaborate psychoses such as those that are described, for instance, under the terms of schizophrenia and manic-depressive. (Benedict, 1934, p. 79)

Twenty-two years later Eric Berne, the founder of transactional analysis, offered an articulate version of the universalist view.

The major psychoses take the same form in many regions, regardless of race, physical environment, cultural background, and socio-economic situation in the sense that a well-trained clinician entering mental hospital in any one of a number of different countries scattered on all the continents can diagnose by inspection (say) 25% of the patients; can diagnose after a few moments of listening even to a language he does not understand (say) another 25%; and will have similar difficulties almost anywhere in diagnosing the remainder. This means that well developed catatonia, hebephrenia, mania, and melancholia are common afflictions in widely scattered countries. . . . In borderline cases and neuroses, a well-trained clinician with a command of the language can sometimes penetrate the veneer of even the most exotic culture in short time, say a quarter of an hour, sufficiently to proceed thenceforward as usual in constructing a working diagnosis and a preliminary treatment program. (Berne, 1956, pp. 198–199)

In another article Berne elaborated on this position as follows:

The differences between individuals in any culture seem to be greater than the differences between "cultures." Clinically, cultural differences can be effectively treated as mere dialects or accents of a common language: the Italian schizophrenic speaks schizophrenic with an Italian accent, and the Siamese manic speaks manic with a Siamese accent. The chronic female closed ward can be located from earshot on any continent. The interchangeability of clinicians is the most compelling single fact in comparative psychiatry: the migratory psychoanalyst, the transferred French colonial medical officer, the psycho-therapeutic approach which is as effective in the Fiji Islands as it is in Trinidad. (Berne, 1959, p. 108)

These two positions, so eloquently and outspokenly expressed, define the range of views about the scope of cultural variation in psychopathology. They hark back to what Kleinman (1988) has recently described as the anthropological and psychiatric traditions of cross-cultural investigation of mental disorder. The former tradition emphasizes cultural uniqueness and is focused upon and exemplified by the discovery and description of culture-bound syndromes of abnormal behavior such as *amok* or *latah*. The latter tradition stresses cultural similarity or even identity of the major psychological disorders and is concentrated on the clinical description and statistical comparison of such patterns of disturbance, often as they occur in institutional environments. And though the relevant data have proliferated, articulate proponents of the opposing views are still very much with us. Witness these two statements, both made in 1979, by more recent observers. The American cross-cultural psychologist Marsella persuasively argued for the weight of cultural factors, as follows:

Cultures do vary in the manifestation of mental disorders and this finding should not surprise even the most ardent supporters of the universalist position. To deny such a finding would not only be tantamount to rejecting the research that has been conducted, but also to denying that cultural differences exist in behavior. (Marsella, 1979, p. 251)

The Nigerian psychiatrist Odejide upheld the universalist position in the following words:

From the various reports cited on the universality of psychiatric disorders and their symptoms across cultures, the stable prevalence rate (0.3 percent) of schizophrenia across time and across space, and the similarities in the prescription practices of psychotropic drugs across cultures, it seems appropriate to conclude that cross-cultural psychiatry is real. There is little evidence in support of the theory of cultural relativity (violations of the social norm of particular groups) in the diagnosis of psychiatric disorders. (Odejide, 1979, p. 108)

Actually, the statements above are not necessarily incompatible. What they emphasize are two sides of the same coin. Odejide refers to the demonstrated existence of universal components of at least the major and most serious disorders, while Marsella argues for the pervasiveness of cultural differences that virtually suffuse the entire experience of a psychologically disturbed state. Many of the expectations and generalizations of their two distinguished predecessors have, however, been proved demonstrably wrong in light of the data accumulated in the intervening decades. This state of affairs does not necessarily vitiate their arguments. Actually, both Benedict's and Berne's articles are uncommonly insightful; they contain seminal ideas and anticipate findings that were to be empirically demonstrated many years later. But the points made in the statements quoted have been factually disproved. It is just not true that, as Benedict thought, schizophrenia and bipolar affective disorder are limited to Western cultures. By this time the occurrence of these disorders in all regions of the world has been extensively documented. Similarly, the statement—which, to be sure, Benedict never made, yet implied—to the effect that one culture's madmen are another culture's prophets and healers has received no support from the close scrutiny of shamans and other native therapists who have been clinically and empirically studied over the years (e.g., Fabrega & Silver, 1973; Jilek, 1982; Jilek & Jilek-Aal, 1978; Scharfetter, 1985; Trimble, Manson, Dinges, & Medicine, 1984). In light of these findings, the image of the shaman or culturally indigenous healer has shifted from that of a hallucinating psychotic to that of an intuitively sensitive and effective psychotherapist within his or her own cultural tradition. On the other hand, Berne's assertions about the interchangeability of therapists across cultures and about the uncanny acumen of itinerant diagnosticians even in cultures and language areas they are not familiar with flies by now in the face of the documented difficulties and pitfalls that diagnosis and therapy frequently experience as they are transplanted beyond the sites of their cultural origin (e.g., De Hoyos & De Hoyos, 1965; Egeland, Hofsteter, & Eshleman, 1983; Jewell, 1952; Tseng, Di, Ebrata, Hsu, & Yuhua, 1986). And most contemporary observers and investigators would react skeptically to the comparison of cultural factors in psychological disturbance to mere accents within a language. A major body of evidence has come into existence that points to substantial differences in the mode of expression and specific manifestations of psychopathology around the world (cf. Draguns, 1973, 1980, 1986; Marsella, 1979). Even in culturally distinctive groups living side by side in the same communities, noteworthy differences were discovered in the symptoms manifested (Jilek-Aal, Jilek, & Flynn, 1978). Yet the argument about the central versus peripheral role of culture in psychopathology continues. It is but a special case of a general controversy in cross-cultural psychology, extending across all domains of complex behavior: developmental, motivational, personality, social, organizational, and abnormal. The question is asked, Is the link between culture and complex human behavior an intimate relationship or a tenuous liaison (Draguns, 1988a)? In Benedict's or Berne's day, these two positions could be argued a priori and could be bolstered by incidental or casual observations. At this time, the cumulative results of systematic research can be brought to bear upon this controversy.

Culture and Psychopathology: The Current State of Knowledge

The World Health Organization has been engaged in ambitious projects concerned with the manifestations of the most serious variants of psychopathology around the world. Schizophrenia was studied at nine research sites representing developed and developing countries, most regions of the world, and the two major competing political systems. These research centers were in China (Taiwan), Colombia, Czechoslovakia, Denmark, India, Nigeria, the United Kingdom, the United States, and the USSR. At the later stages of this WHO-sponsored investigation, Taiwan was replaced by Japan and another American location, in Hawaii, was added to the original research center in Bethesda, Maryland. The best-known and the most widely publicized finding of this investigation was the high degree of uniformity of schizophrenic symptoms regardless of location (World Health Organization, 1973). A series of schizophrenic manifestations were identified that were observed at all nine sites of the investigation. This core syndrome of schizophrenia featured restricted affect, poor insight, thinking aloud, poor rapport, incoherent speech, unrealistic information, and bizarre and/or nihilistic delusions. The initial report by the WHO research team admittedly did not focus on national differences in schizophrenia that may have come to light in this study. The object of this investigation was to develop realistic yet flexible methods that would be appropriate for use at all the research centers. In the book-length follow-up report, however, the WHO investigators identified important cultural variations in the course of the disorder (WHO, 1979). Somewhat surprisingly and counterintuitively, it was found that schizophrenia followed a more benign course—toward remission if not recovery—in developing countries, exemplified by Nigeria and India, than in some of the most prosperous and advanced nations of the First World, such as the United States, Great Britain, and Denmark (WHO, 1979; Sartorius, Jablensky, Korten, & Ernberg, 1986). This unexpected finding was paralleled by the negative relation between educational level and the likelihood of remission, observed only in the developing world. This latter result appeared to contradict the conclusions of earlier investigations conducted for the most part in industrialized and technologically advanced countries, which pointed to a positive relation between educational and occupational attainment and the remission of serious mental disorder (Dohrenwend & Dohrenwend, 1969). Both of these results are unexpected and puzzling. A plausible, though not compelling, explanation of the favorable prognosis of schizophrenia in developing countries was provided by Cooper and Sartorius (1977) on both a historical and a cultural basis. These authors argued that though the symptoms of schizophrenia have always existed, they have become socially intolerable with the advent of the industrialized society, increasingly dominated by the clock and the machine. In the traditional social order of the preindustrial small town and village, a modest but acceptable niche was preserved within the family and the community for noncontributory members of society such as schizophrenics. Such niches continue to be available in the social settings of the developing world; they have virtually disappeared in the urbanized and industrialized modern West.

In the more recent extensions of the World Health Organization project (Sartorius, Jablensky, Korten, & Ernberg, 1986), a total of 1,300 cases of schizophrenia were examined in Colombia, Denmark, India, Great Britain, Japan and at two centers in the United States, in Honolulu, Hawaii, and in Rochester, New York. This study replicated the existence of the core syndrome of schizophrenia as identified in the earlier phases of the same research. It also brought to light, however, the much greater proportion of acute undifferentiated and catatonic cases in the developing countries as compared with the developed countries. The high incidence of these phases of the disorder may shed new light on the benign course of schizophrenia in the developing world. It is consistent with the reports from a variety of African, Asian, and Caribbean sites about the prevalence of a dramatic and reversible psychotic disorder that may overlap with schizophrenia, as diagnosed by the World Health Organization team of researchers (e.g., Bustamente, 1969; Collomb, 1965; Leff, 1981; Murphy, 1982). In any case, the World Health Organization investigators have demonstrated that a nucleus of schizophrenic symptoms occurs at a number of culturally diverse sites around the world. Although their emphasis was upon worldwide uniformities, the World Health Organization follow-up reports provide hints of cultural diversity in the manifestation of schizophrenia. The nature and effect of these cultural influences remain to be explored.

This task was in part undertaken by Leff (1973, 1981), who pursued the relation between the several emotional states on the basis of the data collected in the pilot phase of the World Health Organization survey. The emotions studied included anxiety, depression, and irritability. Leff was able to demonstrate higher correlations among these affects in Colombia, India, Nigeria, and Taiwan. He concluded that economic development promoted greater differentiation in affective expression. Conversely, in developing countries exemplified by the four nations above, emotional expression tended to be global.

Another World Health Organization project, more modest in scope, was concerned with depression. Four countries participated: Iran, Japan, Canada, and Switzerland. The two reports available on this research (Jablensky, Sartorius, Gulbinat, & Ernberg, 1981; WHO, 1983) bring to the fore the elements of depression common to these four different cultures: sad affect, loss of enjoyment, anxiety, tension, lack of energy, loss of interest, inability to concentrate, and ideas of insufficiency, inadequacy, and worthlessness. These findings extended and in part replicated the results of an earlier mail survey of practicing psychiatrists in over 30 countries from all continents and regions that was conducted by the staff of the Transcultural Psychiatric Research Centre at McGill University in Montreal (Murphy, Wittkower, & Chance, 1967). In that study vegetative symptoms, as exemplified by fatigue, loss of sexual interest, loss of appetite, and weight reduction, were among the cross-culturally typical manifestations of depression, together with self-accusatory ideas. Even this pattern of symptomatology was not present in all the cultures surveyed. In nine countries, all of them non-Western, depression tended to be expressed through excitement, ideas of influence, and partial mutism.

The second phase of the World Health Organization depression project identified a smaller number of symptoms that were present in more than three-fourths of the cases in one or more centers, but not in all four of them. Thus in Basel, Switzerland, most depressed patients complained of inability to fall asleep, lack of appetite, feelings of guilt and self-reproach, feeling worse in the morning than late in the day, and constipation. Their Canadian counterparts echoed feelings of guilt and self-reproach but added hopelessness, disruption of social functioning, and early awakening to their characteristic list of symptoms. The corresponding array of symptoms in Tehran included tension, somatic symptoms, psychomotor agitation, suicidal ideas, hopelessness, ideas of insufficiency, psychomotor retardation, and decrease in libido. At the two Japanese sites the characteristic expressions of depression featured tension, hypochondriasis, constipation, loss of interest, ideas of insufficiency, changes in time perception, and fitful, restless sleep. Somewhat embarrassingly for the culturalist hypothesis, a fair number of differences between Nagasaki and Tokyo were registered, suggesting that depressive manifestations are not uniform even within an unusually homogeneous culture.

Limiting ourselves for the moment to the two most disabling psychological disorders, schizophrenia and major depression, we can say with certainty only that they occur in widely separated parts of the world. The assertion that these two syndromes are present in all cultures remains vulnerable to the demonstration of a single dissenting instance. What can more cautiously be stated is that a culture free of schizophrenia and depression has not as yet been reliably identified or described. The old notion, however, that schizophrenia is a malady of complex, modern, or Western civilizations no longer has any scientific standing. We have seen, however, that technological, economic, and social advancement may affect how well schizophrenics are accepted in their customary family and community settings. Even here, however, it would be a mistake to assume a linear relationship between traditional culture and benevolence toward schizophrenia. Examples of rejecting and punitive attitudes in traditional cultures toward schizophrenics in their midst are plentiful (cf. Pfeiffer, 1970), and the inability of modern Western peoples to find a niche for schizophrenics in their homes and communities may not be entirely or mostly animated by rejection.

In relation to depression, likewise, the available findings easily put to rest the various rash statements, made not so long ago, about the nonexistence or rarity of depressive manifestations among the members of various non-Western groups: Africans south of the Sahara (Carothers, 1953), Arabs (Bazzoui, 1970), Indians, Chinese (Yap, 1965), Japanese, and even blacks in the American South (Prange & Vitols, 1962). At the same time, cross-cultural observations of depression provide a shift and correction in the Western culture-bound conceptions of depression. One of the findings of the WHO study on depression highlights the infrequency of feelings of guilt in the two non-Western cultures represented in this comparison, Iran and Japan. There are also numerous and consistent reports from Africa south of the Sahara that document the existence of depression but emphasize the absence of guilt in this experience or at most assign it a minor or subsidiary role (Binitie, 1975; Diop, 1967; German, 1972; Zeldine et al., 1975). Although some of the other comparative studies on the experience of guilt in Japan have yielded ambiguous or negative results (e.g., Kimura, 1965, 1967, 1972; Radford, 1989), a tentative conclusion is warranted that guilt feelings play a less central role in many non-Western cultures than has been expected on the basis of clinical, especially psychodynamic, formulations that have originated in the West.

When and how did this culturally characteristic intertwining of guilt and depression come about? Murphy attempted to answer this question on the basis of the available historical materials concerning the experience of depression in Western Europe in the seventeenth and eighteenth centuries. His conclusions are worth quoting:

The evidence presented here suggests that depressive patients exhibit excessive guilt feelings and self-accusations when they have become accustomed to thinking of pleasure and displeasure as arising from their own acts and, indirectly, their own volition, rather than by hazard, by reason of something happening within the body, or from the acts of others. The conceptual orientation, although so familiar to us today, is only likely to arise when external forces are reasonably predictable, when the individual is encouraged to act predictably himself, when he is not continuously interacting with other people and when he thinks of the mind or soul as considerably separate from the body. Without these conditions, the depressive's unhappiness can be attributed to luck, to the body, or to other people; and historical and cross-cultural studies suggest that this was often the case. (Murphy, 1978, p. 242)

The transition from depression without guilt to the same disorder dominated by self-castigation occurred in the eighteenth century. In addition to political and economic stability, it required individuation, a sense of an autonomous self divorced from both bodily constraint and social nexus. Thus, if Murphy's argument has merit, the birth of individualism and the advent of guilt are inextricably linked.

There is also some plausibility to the notion that the incidence of depression is lower in various non-Western cultures of Africa and Asia than it is in the West. However, no cross-cultural epidemiological studies with objective and comparable indicators of depression have been conducted (Marsella, 1980; Marsella, Sartorius, Jablensky, & Fenton, 1985). The task of providing such conclusive cross-cultural data is further complicated by the so-called depressive equivalents, which may also be subject to cultural shaping. Research by Kleinman and associates (Kleinman, 1982; Kleinman & Kleinman, 1985) in Mainland China has highlighted the possible role of neurasthenia, which involves fatigue and weakness, with multiple physical complaints, as a culturally sanctioned avenue for expressing depressive reactions. Neurasthenia frequently occurs in cultures such as the Chinese, where the threshold for the recognition of depressive affect as a signal of distress and for a social reaction to it is unusually high. Kleinman also entertains the possibility that focusing on somatic distress as a channel for expressing depression is not, as one would believe from the Western point of view, a "conversion" of personal experiences into somatic sensations. Rather, it may represent an enhanced sensitivity to the genuine bodily manifestations of depression that, because of our own cultural bias in favor of a psychological idiom of distress, are glossed over and overlooked in the West.

In contrast to China, somatization in the United States is little valued, although it is widely experienced (Kirmayer, 1984; Kleinman & Kleinman, 1985). It is associated with low educational level and social status, with rural or remote location, with membership in low-status ethnic groups, and in short, with low sophistication. In China bodily complaints are a socially sanctioned medium of communication of personal distress. The psychological aspects of depression may be experienced and even shared with a few trusted friends, but they are an inappropriate signal for initiating helpful action on the part of health professionals (Cheung, 1986; Kleinman, 1977; Tseng, 1975). There are also data, however, that suggest that both depressive and somatic complaints are reported more frequently by Taiwanese patients than by their American counterparts (Yamamoto, Yeh, Loya, Slawson, & Hurwicz, 1985). Although the presentation of depressive experience through a bodily medium of distress is amply documented in China by a number of observers, this apparently does not preclude the direct communication of depression, at least in some Chinese settings. It is also possible that in modern urban milieus in Taiwan depression is being accepted more readily than in the more traditional regions of China or in past periods. Prince (1968) documented a similar shift if Africa when many of the newly independent nations of that continent embarked upon a rapid course of modernization.

Finally, there is the observer's contribution to the detection and, in some cases, distortion of depressive and related manifestations across culture lines. In contrast to schizophrenia, which is obtrusive in its bizarreness, depression is all too easily overlooked, especially as it is observed across a culture gulf. Two examples will suffice to bring this point home. De Hoyos and De Hoyos (1965) documented the tendency of white middle-class clinicians to overlook depressive symptoms in lower-class blacks, a finding that has been extended more recently (Keisling, 1981). Additional confirmation of this tendency comes from a recent epidemiological study of the Amish in rural Pennsylvania, a fundamentalist and pacifist Protestant sect that has preserved its preindustrial life-style (Hostetler, 1980). In the course of this study, Egeland et al., (1983) reported that Amish psychiatric patients were typically misdiagnosed by local psychiatrists as schizophrenic when, in light of standardized psychiatric assessment procedures, they presented the manifestations of manic-depressive disorder. As one of the local psychiatric practitioners said incautiously to the members of the research group, "I know the diagnosis immediately, all our Amish patients are schizophrenic" (Egeland et al., p. 68).

On the basis of the cultural panorama of these two disorders, both of them consist of a pancultural nucleus plus a variety of culturally characteristic accretions and transformations. The question then arises, What is the nature of the relation of culture to the manifestations of the disorder. Earlier (Draguns, 1980), I identified three possibilities: the relationship is one of magnification or exaggeration, where a culturally characteristic behavior is caricatured and reduced to absurdity. A major axis of difference between Latin American and Anglo-American cultures, identified by Diaz-Guerrero (1967) and others, is activity/passivity. Normal Anglo-Americans and Latin Americans are, with due allowance for intragroup differences, respectively, *adaptively* active and passive. In Latin American and Anglo-American psychiatric patients, as Fundia, Draguns, and Phillips (1971), among others, have demonstrated, both passivity and activity assume grotesque and unrealistic forms, as a blanket cessation of activity or as an indiscriminate assault upon any obstacles and barriers to one's goals. The opposite idea is that of contrast in symptomatology to the culturally modal response. Often this takes the form of violating cultural norms and taboos and doing what is not culturally permissible. The incidence of physically aggressive acts by Japanese psychiatric patients is a case in point, which Schooler and Caudill (1964) demonstrated. Not only were Japanese patients aggressive in violation of an important cultural norm, but the objects of their aggression—mothers, for example—were chosen to augment and dramatize the effect of this violation. In addition to the two options above, there is also the residual possibility of the existence of cultural differences in symptomatology, but without a recognizable link to any modal cultural characteristics.

Beyond this generic relationship between culture and symptomatology, there is the question of the specific bridges between the symptoms and cultural or culturally shaped psychological characteristics. Elsewhere (Draguns, 1988b) I have enumerated a provisional list of such links on the planes of cognition, values, self-experience, optimal behavior, self-control, ego identity, and sense of belonging. Certainly this list is not exhaustive, and other connections between cultural characteristics and manifestations of psychopathology can be identified. I shall now proceed to identify a number of additional dimensions that may be heuristically useful in explaining the existing differences between cultures in psychopathology and in predicting differences yet to be discovered.

Hofstede's Worldwide Study of Work-Related Values

Hofstede (1980) identified four cultural characteristics that, on the basis of a multivariate analyses, enabled him to account for most of the cultural differences within a multinational corporation among the employees of over 40 nationalities and three more inclusive geographic regions. The unrepresentativeness of this unique pool of subjects was made up for by its size; Hofstede collected 116,000 questionnaires. Moreover, the bias due to any putative corporate culture would work against demonstrating cultural differences. That such differences did emerge argues all the more compellingly for their cogency. Hofstede (1980) labeled these four dimensions individualism/collectivism, uncertainty avoidance, power distance, and masculinity/femininity.

Of these four dimensions, individualism/collectivism is probably the most important in a conceptual sense, though not necessarily a statistical sense. Over the past decade it has been intensively investigated in a continuing series of studies (cf. Triandis et al., 1986). In the course of this research, the manifestations of individualism/collectivism in various domains of social behavior have been elucidated. In light of the results of this research and Hofstede's (1980, 1983a, 1983b, 1986) descriptions, individualists strive foremost for the attainment of their own goals. They experience themselves as autonomous units and are at most loosely integrated into a variety of supraordinate social entities. Members of their nuclear families may be included as objects of their care and responsibility. Beyond their family boundaries, altruism, selflessness, and even self-sacrifice may be practiced, but on the basis of an individual, deliberate, personal decision. By contrast, collectivistically oriented individuals or members of collectivist cultures experience themselves prominently in reference to the groups they are members of: family, community, nation. They seek and obtain fulfillment by maintaining and enhancing the harmony of the group, even at the expense of subordinating their goals and aspirations. The United States is an individualist culture par excellence, as are the English-speaking nations of the "old" Commonwealth of Nations and the countries of northern and western Europe. Southern Europe has been traditionally regarded as a collectivist region (Triandis, 1985). Hofstede's (1980) empirical results, however, provide a number of surprises in this respect. Italy emerged as more individualist than France, Belgium, Sweden, Germany, or Switzerland. In Greece Georgas (1989) has documented a recent shift toward individualism, more pronounced in urban than in rural settings. In Hofstede's analyses, such countries as Pakistan, Colombia, Venezuela, Peru, Taiwan, Thailand, and Singapore occupied slots near the collectivist pole.

The other three variables have seen less investigation except for Hofstede's (1980) own research and remain to be described.

Uncertainty avoidance, as described by Hofstede (1986, p. 308), "defines the extent to which people within a culture are made nervous by situations which they perceive as unstructured, unclear, and unpredictable, situations which they therefore try to avoid by maintaining strict codes of behavior and a belief in absolute truths. Cultures with a strong uncertainty avoidance are active, aggressive, emotional, compulsive, security-seeking, and intolerant; cultures with a weak uncertainty avoidance are contemplative, less aggressive, unemotional, relaxed, accepting personal risks, and relatively tolerant." Uncertainty avoidance is related to intolerance of ambiguity (Frenkel-Brunswik, 1949; Draguns, 1963), but transposed from the perceptual-cognitive to the social-organizational arena. In countries where uncertainty avoidance is high, improvisation is avoided and personal initiative is restricted. Rules are numerous, explicit, and complex. Rituals and ceremonies may be important and prominent. By contrast, low uncertainty avoidance cultures thrive on improvisation, prize initiative, and operate with few rules to be flexibly applied according to the demands of the situation and the judgment of individuals. In Hofstede's (1980) research, countries such as Portugal, Belgium, Japan, France, and Spain emerged as being high in uncertainty avoidance. At the low end of the same dimension were found Denmark, Sweden, Great Britain, Ireland, and India.

Power distance, in Hofstede's (1986, p. 307) words, refers to "the extent to which the less powerful persons in a society accept inequality in power and consider it as normal. Inequality exists within any culture, but the degree of it that is tolerated varies between one culture and another." Power distance also refers to the gulf between the leaders (e.g., industrial managers) and their subordinates (e.g., production workers). The degree and ease of personal contact and the absence of ritualistic barriers to free and open interchange are some of the indicators of power distance. In high power distance settings the decision-making power is concentrated in the person of the leader; the leader then bears the responsibility and shoulders the blame if anything goes wrong under his aegis. The subordinate is rarely included in decision making but is absolved from responsibility. Where power distance is low, contact between leaders and followers is frequent and spontaneous. Responsibility is diffused; blame and praise are shared by the group. The leader may be "one of the boys" (or girls); fraternization, camaraderie, and informality are highly valued. Among the high power distance countries one finds India, Brazil, France, Iran, and Japan; at or near the opposite pole are found Denmark, Sweden, Norway, Switzerland, Great Britain, and Germany.

Finally, we come to the bipolar dimension of masculinity/femininity. In Hofstede's (1986, p. 308) formulation, these two characteristics "differ in the social roles associated with the biological fact of the existence of two sexes, and in particular in the social roles attributed to *men*. . . . The cultures which I labelled as *masculine* strive for maximal distinction between what men are expected to do. . . . *Feminine* cultures, on the other hand, define relatively overlapping social roles for the sexes, in which, in particular, men need not be ambitious or competitive but may go for a different quality of life than material success; men may respect whatever is small, weak, and slow." One may quibble over how aptly the terms masculine and feminine describe this dimension. I would have called one of its poles androgynous rather than feminine. It also appears to have points of contact with the instrumental/expressive distinction proposed by Parsons and Bales (1956). In light of Hofstede's (1980) results, Japan, Austria, Venezuela, Italy, Switzerland, Mexico, Ireland, and Great Britain are among the "masculine" nations. The "feminine" countries include Sweden, Norway, the Netherlands, Denmark, Finland, Chile, Portugal, and Thailand.

Application of Hofstede's Data to Manifestations of Abnormal Behavior Across Cultures

It was necessary to present Hofstede's scheme in some detail as a prelude to applying it to the explanation of the existing cross-cultural differences in psychopathology. Let us remember that Hofstede's dimensions have originated in a very different domain, that of industrial-organizational behavior. Nonetheless a leap from its empirical origins to psychological disturbance appears to be worth undertaking. Values are implicated in organizational-industrial settings, educational activities, and also in psychopathological symptom choice and expression that some modern authorities (e.g., Kleinman, 1986; Wiener, 1989) conceptualize as social transactions. As Kleinman (1986, p. 1) put it, "Analyzing the relationship of depression (or any disorder) to society offers a glimpse of a sociosomatic reticulum (a symbolic bridge) that ties individuals to each other and to the local systems within which they live." Hofstede (1986) has shown the way by extending some of his variables to the educational setting and demonstrating empirically the differences between groups high and low on these dimensions in teaching and learning. What are then some of the plausible expressions of Hofstede's four dimensions in the manifestations of psychopathology? Optimally, to answer this question we would need parallel data on psychiatric symptoms prevalent in all the cultures Hofstede studied. But no one has as yet conducted such research, and the prospect of its ever being carried out is exceedingly slim. In the absence of such a study, I started out with the intention of updating the reviews of cross-cultural research on psychopathology I had completed at various times (Draguns, 1973, 1980, 1986, 1989) and referring the various cultural and national samples included to their respective spots in Hofstede's typology of cultures. However, cross-cultural studies on psychopathology are disproportionately concentrated upon a few cultures—for example, Japan (Caudill, 1973) and China (Draguns, 1985; Kleinman & Lin, 1981; Tseng & Wu, 1986); a great many other nations have been studied only minimally, if at all. Moreover, not all cultures that have been studied by cross-cultural investigators of psychopathology were included in Hofstede's research, which was limited to nation-states. Hofstede's equating nations with cultures poses few problems in the case of homogeneous states in which all or most of the residents speak the same language and share the same group identity. Such is the case with Japan, Norway, Austria, Portugal, and Taiwan. With nations that are pluralistic in culture or language, such as South Africa, Finland, Canada, Singapore, or India, equating nation with culture is more problematic and obscures major sources of within-country variance.

For all these reasons, filling in all eight cells for high and low in each of the four dimensions proved impossible to accomplish. Scaling down my aspirations, I decided to embark upon a preliminary comparison limited to those cultures or nations that presented a contrast on one or more dimensions. Optimally, one would wish for maximally related and contiguous nations that would vary on only one of Hofstede's dimensions, a true approximation of the experimental method of allowing one characteristic to vary and holding everything else constant. Alas, instances of such comparisons were almost impossible to find. Much more typically, one would encounter the situation in which the two cultures compared would vary on three or even all four dimensions, as in the case of the several comparisons involving the United States and Japan. The scheme, which at its inception seemed simple, elegant, even automatically applicable, was in the end only sketchily and incompletely realized. If it has any value, it is in the form of providing leads for future exploration and research, to fill the many gaps that have inevitably come about.

Most of the work I have been able to include pertains to individualism/collectivism, which is in any case the most intensively and successfully investigated of Hofstede's four dimensions. The extension of this variable to psychopathology was anticipated by Hofstede (1983b), who pointed out its relationship to Benedict's (1946) distinction between "guilt" and "shame" cultures. The former group corresponds to individualist and the latter to collectivist cultures. The country Benedict focused this distinction on was Japan. It has also been a major target of cross-cultural psychiatric symptomatology investigation. The manifestations of psychological disorder of the Japanese have been compared with corresponding behaviors in the United States, but also in Taiwan (Rin, Schooler, & Caudill, 1973), West Germany (Kimura, 1965, 1967, 1972), and Australia (Radford, 1989).

As all of us know, Japan is a highly economically successful nation that, in Hofstede's four-dimensional scheme, is high in collectivism, power distance, uncertainty avoidance, and masculinity. With the exception of the last variable, it is at the opposite end of these dimensions from the United States. In broad and general terms, the symptomatology of its psychiatric patients should be at the opposite extreme from that of their counterparts in the United States and similar Western nations. In an early comparison of symptom manifestation in hospitalized psychiatric patients in Munich and Kyoto, Kimura (1965, 1967), however, dispelled the notion that Japanese depressives do not experience guilt.

The differences that emerged in Kimura's comparison were subtle and required a thorough phenomenological analysis. Specifically, he contributed two kinds of findings that are potentially relevant to the Hofstede dimension. Japanese symptoms were found to be more concrete and socially oriented, especially in their expression of guilt. The referents of these symptom expressions were more specific and interpersonal than for psychiatrically hospitalized Germans. German patients tended to voice feelings of self-accusation and condemnation in absolute and abstract terms; they would castigate themselves for imaginary violations of religious and moral principles and would condemn themselves—anticipating Abramson, Seligman, and Teasdale (1980) in their well-known attributional model in depression—in global, stable, and internal terms. Depressed patients in Japan would turn against themselves for specific failings and transgressions, perhaps equally as fanciful as those of the patients in Bavaria, but very much tied to a personal relationship in a specific situation. The German patients were suffering from having violated in their own eyes immutable and timeless norms; the Japanese accused themselves of having let down important people in reference groups essential to them—the family, the school, and the work situation.

The other cultural difference in Kimura's comparisons was much more subtle. Upon an exhaustive phenomenological exploration, and an erudite linguistic scrutiny of Japanese and German vocabulary dealing with the self and with social relationships, Kimura (1972) concluded that the basic contrast in symptom expression was traceable to differences in *Mitmenschlichkeit,* literally the experience of being with people or, to coin a word, a sense of cohumanity that was far more pronounced in Japanese psychiatric patients than in their American counterparts. From another point of view, Doi's (1973) well-known concept of *amae* describes a lifelong web of dependent relationships and expectations that suffuse the experience of the normal Japanese. The flip side of this sense of sensitivity to and inextricable oneness with other people is that the autonomous, circumscribed self, so central in the subjective experience of Western individuals, whether adequately functioning or psychiatrically impaired, is less developed or, Kimura would go so far as to say, undeveloped in the Japanese patients observed in his studies. In Kimura's (1972, p. 7) words, "We have seen that in the mode of thought and experience of the Japanese there can be *no* question of a continuous identity, of a permanent sense of 'This is within me.' This, however, does not mean at all that the Japanese have no sense of the I or that they lack self-consciousness, only that in their experience of situations they do not habitually assign primary place to their selves" (my translation). To elaborate, the Japanese have a hard time imagining a constant core to their own being apart from the network of lifelong personal and group relationships that provide the context and the framework of their existence.

These empirical findings, supplemented to be sure by far-reaching theoretical analyses of their personal significance, fit in beautifully with the individualism/collectivism dimension brought to the fore in Hofstede's research over a decade later. They also fit closely the classic formulation on the situational and specific nature of self-experience by the prominent psychological anthropologist Francis Hsu (1971). If Hsu is correct, such a context-dependent interpersonal self is characteristic not only of the Japanese, but also of the other major East Asian civilizations, notably the Chinese. To the extent that the Japanese patients in Kimura's research focused on concrete events in their relationships, his findings are also relevant to uncertainty avoidance. This dimension is also implicated in the results of another study, by Draguns, Phillips, Broverman, Caudill, and Nishimae (1971), in which the Japanese patients were found to express their symptoms in the form of direct and immediate discharge of their affect and expression of their distress, whereas the American patients more prominently elaborated and embroidered their complaints and subjective experiences by relying on cognition. Even though this difference is clearly relevant to uncertainty avoidance, it is not quite clear whether the Japanese symptom data bespeak exaggeration of this culturally prevalent mode of response or whether they indicate its conversion into the opposite.

Is uncertainty more effectively reduced by giving expression to one's aversive feelings at the point of their experience or by providing some kind of a more focused and crystallized, apparently rational, account of its causes and reasons? This dilemma illustrates the old problem that the investigators of intolerance of ambiguity had to tackle (cf. Draguns, 1966). Does unease or discomfort in the face of unclear sensory stimulation lead to hasty and premature imposition of meaning, or does it result in waiting inordinately long before being satisfied with perceiving all features of the stimulus loud and clear? There are studies in the literature that have relied upon either of these two kinds of indicators to impute the same personality variable. Likewise with uncertainty avoidance. Post hoc it can be argued that what the Japanese did in our study "makes sense" as an uncertainty reduction technique, but it remains unclear whether it supports the exaggeration or the contrast version of continuity between normal and maladaptive manifestations within a culture.

In terms of social decorum, an important consideration in collectivist cultures, the data are unclear. As I mentioned, Schooler and Caudill (1964) observed a great deal of assaultiveness on psychiatric wards in Japan, clearly a violation of the norm of social harmony so important in all collectivist cultures. Yamamoto (1972), however, reported that, compared with their American counterparts, Japanese psychiatric patients desired more personal relationships with staff, which is exactly what one would expect in collectivist societies. The research by Rin, Schooler, and Caudill (1973) constitutes the only comparison of Japanese psychiatric patients with their counterparts in another East Asian culture, Taiwan. These two settings are similar in a great many respects. In light of Hofstede's (1980) research, they differ in uncertainty avoidance, in which the Taiwanese scored much lower. The differences between the two groups of patients, however, seem to be only tenuously relevant to this axis. Two contrasts emerged. Although members of both cultures reported a great many somatic symptoms, these manifestations among the Japanese were for the most part in the form of diffuse distress signals; among the Taiwanese they appeared as crystallized and specific signs of somatic illness. The other finding was the greater prominence of paranoid ideation in Taiwan.

A recent report about American and Japanese schizophrenics (Suzuki, Peters, Weibender, & Gillespie, 1987) based on Rorschach data may be more directly relevant to the vicissitudes of uncertainty reduction, in which, recall, Japan exceeded the United States. Several cross-cultural contrasts appeared, which Suzuki et al. presented as follows. American schizophrenics tended to proceed from details to wholes; their Japanese counterparts exhibited the opposite sequence. Japanese patients gave vent to primitive impulses and emotional reactivity; the mode of American impulse expression was described by the authors as controlled and sophisticated. Americans relied on repressing their primitive impulses; the Japanese accepted them. Finally, more directly relevant to individualism/collectivism, the Japanese not surprisingly were more conforming in their responses.

A major project just completed by Radford (1989) contributes a wealth of findings analyzed thoroughly and with sophistication. There are several innovative features of this study that may well make it a landmark. For one, it includes both normal and psychiatric patient samples, in Australia and in Japan. Moreover, it has a theoretically significant focus in that it is concerned with the model of decision making developed by Mann (1985) and systematically investigated by him over a great many years. In the course of this research program, Mann developed a taxonomy of self-reported decision-making styles, investigated them in a variety of age groups, such as children and adolescents, and applied the results of these studies to improve the effectiveness and efficiency of decision making. He also extended his research across cultures and identified a number of meaningful differences, for example, between the Australians and the Japanese. Mann's model has recently been extended to psychiatric disturbance, more specifically depression (Radford, Mann, & Kalucy, 1986).

The cross-cultural research by Radford represents the first attempt both to cross cultural barriers and to encompass normal and psychiatrically disturbed samples alike. It is of special interest in the present context because decision making may represent the missing link between values as investigated by Hofstede and the psychopathological symptoms observed in patient populations of various countries. Radford (1989) found that, in line with Hofstede's first dimension of individualism/collectivism, on which the two countries differed substantially, normal Australian subjects espoused an individualist decision-making style. By contrast, among Japanese normals, a "collateral" group-oriented mode of decision-making prevailed. The two patient groups exhibited a similar pattern of symptoms and relied upon a group-centered decision-making style, which in the case of Australians represented a breakdown of their characteristic autonomous pattern of decision making. For the Japanese depressives, however, this finding highlighted the continuity of their decision making from normality to psychopathology.

These results provide a fascinating and unexpected instance of psychopathology's reducing, if not obliterating, cultural differences. Whereas both Japanese groups acted as was expected of members of a collectivist society, the depressed Australian group found the challenge of individual decision making unbearable. The difficulties depressed individuals have in making independent decisions are proverbial; they are known to every clinician who has worked with depressives. Radford et al. (1986) have provided objective data that document this trait. Even though symptom differences between the two countries were few, Australian patients presented significantly more aggression and irritability, but they also showed greater frequency of memory loss, experience of time distortion, and hypochondriasis. Although the first two symptoms are in line with expectations for an individualist and hence active and expressive culture, the last three are puzzling and defy being fitted into Hofstede's scheme. Their value is in reminding us that not all symptom differences can be accommodated within Hofstede's four-dimensional system.

Turning to China, the two characteristic Chinese symptom patterns that have emerged from various international comparisons and other pertinent studies are somatization and interpersonal emphasis (cf. Draguns, 1985). Mainland China was not included in Hofstede's (1980) research study, although Hong Kong and Taiwan were. There is no doubt that all Chinese cultures are collectivist par excellence (cf. Bond, 1986). This dimension is directly reflected in the more social orientation of Chinese psychiatric patients, even in conditions generally characterized by social withdrawal and noncommunicativeness. There is even a study of a small number of autistic children in Hong Kong (Ney, Lieh-Mak, Cheng, & Collins, 1979) in which a somewhat higher degree of social interaction and responsiveness was recorded by comparison with the Western norms for this extremely asocial disorder. This finding, of course, should be replicated and extended to larger and more representative samples before it is definitively accepted. In my own observations of several psychiatric institutions in the People's Republic of China in 1985, I was struck by the unusually sociable behavior of patients in the form of greetings, smiles, conversation, and cooperative activity.

These observations, of course, are not data, but only impressions—and preliminary impressions at that. They are, however, backed by a solid body of empirically based writing, all of which suggests that the cycle of retreat and isolation from social contact, so characteristic of at least the traditional psychiatric hospitalization in the West, is not entirely completed in China and that psychiatric patients there are less socially withdrawn than is typical in Europe or America. Thus vestiges of collectivist social ties remain, while psychological distress is rarely fully and directly communicated. The personal experience of distress in psychological terms is there, according to modern Chinese psychiatric and psychological authorities, but its privacy is preserved. "Calls for help" in the Western manner, capitalizing upon the person's misery and the need to find a sympathetic ear, are rarely made and would probably elicit infrequent responses in China. Psychological distress remains a primarily internal, but not entirely intrapsychic, subject, with few if any outlets for social communication. The relief of anxiety positively through food and negatively through medicine, on the other hand, represents a culturally sanctioned avenue for responding to anxiety, tension, depression, and the more general needs for understanding, comfort, and acceptance. A widely understood code is developed for communicating these needs without putting them into words.

How does all of this relate to collectivism/individualism? One possible integration would suggest that collectivism is very much the prominent surface orientation governing overt social behavior. Individualism is not nonexistent, but submerged. The result is that personal communication of the kind expected among friends is rare in China, and psychotherapy as we know it our own milieu of necessity entails a steep and difficult climb. Do the Chinese really operate on these two planes, the public and the conventional on the one hand and the private and intimate on the other? There are suggestions that many of them do. If the Chinese on the mainland are as low in uncertainty avoidance as are their more intensively investigated compatriots on Taiwan, they may be able to tolerate the complexity of living in two worlds: conventionalized and social, private and personally unshared.

Also relevant in this connection is a series of studies conducted by Marsella and collaborators (Marsella, Kameoka, Shizuru, & Brennan, 1975; Marsella, Kinzie, & Gordon, 1973; Marsella, Shizuru, Brennan, & Kameoka, 1981; Marsella, Walker, & Johnson, 1973) with normal subjects of several ethnic groups in Hawaii. Consonant with the results already reported, these investigators were able to report that depression among Chinese Americans and Japanese Americans was experienced by means of bodily distress and existential symptoms rather than through self-reproach and guilt. These results are all the more remarkable because they were obtained with highly acculturated subjects, several generations removed from their ancestral cultures.

Only a few isolated studies are available about the other cultures of the East Asian region. In the Philippines, Sechrest (1969) found a minimum of guilt-related symptoms and low representation of depression generally in a group of hospitalized patients who were compared with their counterparts in Chicago. In normal Filipinos, Marsella, Escudero, and Gordon (1972) reported that depression was expressed mainly through agitation. In Hofstede's study, the Philippines were found to be low in individualism, high in power distance, low in uncertainty avoidance, and high in masculinity. Pfeiffer (1969) compared symptoms of depression in Indonesian and

German patients and found a predominance of vegetative symptoms among Indonesians, together with a near absence of feelings of guilt. Like the Philippines, Indonesia was found by Hofstede to be a culture low in individualism, high in power distance, weak in uncertainty avoidance, but somewhat feminine. In India, several studies (Davis, 1973; Gada, 1982; Rao, 1966, 1973; Teja, Narang, & Aggarwal, 1970) pertain to depression. By comparison with British and other Western depressives, Indian patients experienced guilt less frequently and more prominently reported somatic symptoms and hypochondriasis. Several of these studies (Gada, 1982; Teja et al., 1970) also emphasized the greater prominence of anxiety and agitation, which was often focused upon physical health. In Hofstede's analysis India was characterized by large power distance, weak uncertainty avoidance, below average individualism, and moderately strong masculinity. It remains to disentangle these four threads and relate them to the psychopathological findings for India, which in the present state of knowledge it is virtually impossible to do. Another complication is that India is very heterogeneous in language, history, economy, and culture. Gada (1982) has documented regional differences in psychiatric symptoms within India; these may very likely be paralleled on the plane of social values.

Another set of contrasts in individualism versus collectivism has come from the studies of Latin Americans and North or Anglo-Americans, either in the microcosm of the pluralistic culture of the United States or in the macrocosm of the Spanish-speaking and English-speaking countries of the Americas (Escobar, Randolph, & Hill, 1986; Fabrega, Schwartz, & Wallace, 1968; Fundia et al., 1971; Kolody, Vega, Meinhardt, & Bensussen, 1986; Mezzich & Raab, 1980; Stoker, Zurcher, & Fox, 1968; Zippin & Hough, 1985). The findings from this body of research provide a number of parallels to the normal expressions of these contrasts in the same cultural milieus as described by Diaz-Guerrero (1970), Holtzman, Diaz-Guerrero, and Swartz (1975), and Marin and Triandis (1985). These authors are in agreement in emphasizing a more sociocentric orientation among Latin Americans than among Anglo-Americans. In Hofstede's (1980) findings, the few Latin American countries represented in the study clustered toward low individualism, high power distance, strong uncertainty avoidance, and masculinity. In psychiatric symptomatology, three trends can be identified: (1) Social referents in symptoms are more prominent among Latin Americans, as opposed to their more cognitive, self-contained character among the Anglo-Americans. (2) A tendency is present toward passive symptomatology among Latin Americans and active symptom expression among North Americans, to which I alluded earlier. (3) Concentration upon the somatic and bodily experience prevails among Latin Americans, whereas emphasis upon the mental representation of problems is characteristic among North Americans. The social features of Latin American symptomatology parallel the prominence of social relations in normal Latin Americans' values, attitudes, and behaviors. Less directly, submission to fate, serenity and stoicism in accepting the vicissitudes of life, and the realization of one's limited power to change external circumstances appear to be compatible with a collectivist orientation. Implicitly, these beliefs appear to rest on the assumption of the futility of individual effort as opposed to collective action. The somatic orientation that, apparently, Latin Americans share with many Asians and Africans is more difficult to explain within Hofstede's scheme. Murphy's (1978) explanation cited earlier may be invoked as a plausible link. Unless the environment is predictable and the self stable, personal experience is not the focus of psychic distress. And a crystallized constant self is an attribute, if not a prerequisite, of individualism.

The preceding portions of the chapter have focused mainly on individualism/collectivism, which unquestionably, of the four Hofstede dimensions, lends itself best to the explication and integration of cultural differences in abnormal behavior. A promising lead, however, also links uncertainty avoidance with some of the features of psychopathology. In a series of studies, Lynn (1971, 1973, 1975) and Lynn and Hampson (1975, 1977) intercorrelated several available statistical indicators such as calorie intake, accidental death rate, alcohol and tobacco consumption, prevalence of coronary heart disease, number of prisoners, murder rate, divorce rate, and percentage of extramarital births in eighteen economically developed countries. These operations yielded two factors that Lynn (1971) labeled neuroticism and extroversion, to correspond to the two principal dimensions of Eysenck's (1970) personality theory. The first of these two factors can also without too much distortion be called anxiety. In Lynn's (1971) factor analysis, high loadings for this dimension were found for such indicators as low rate of psychiatric hospitalization (negative), high suicide, high alcoholism, and low coronary heart disease (negative). Clearly, this pattern of characteristics is relevant to psychopathology. It can be plausibly, though not compellingly, equated with manifestations of anxiety. It also has relevance to the experience of stress and its pathogenic effects. Proceeding from these considerations, Hofstede (1980) was able to relate Lynn and Hampson's (1975) neuroticism factor scores for the eighteen countries included in their research to the uncertainty avoidance index derived in the course of his international project. The size of the correlation obtained, .73, suggests that uncertainty avoidance is strongly related to at least some components of susceptibility to disruption by stress and the experience of anxiety. These findings strongly argue the need for further predictive studies of anxiety levels, more directly and specifically measured, in cultures contrasted in uncertainty avoidance and vice versa. This undertaking holds all the more promise since the older concept of intolerance of ambiguity has been repeatedly linked to anxiety and its avoidance (e.g., McReynolds, 1960; Smock, 1955). It is of interest in this connection that Hofstede and Bond (1988), in an analysis based on Chinese-derived, mainly Confucian, values in twenty-two countries, were unable to reproduce the dimension of uncertainty avoidance, whereas the other three Hofstede factors reemerged in this research. Hofstede and Bond interpreted this finding to mean that Western cultures, where uncertainty avoidance forms an autonomous dimension, concentrate on search for truth while the major civilizations of East Asia are centrally concerned with the nature of virtue. In any case, if uncertainty avoidance is less relevant in the East than in the West, the findings on its relationship with anxiety, based on seventeen Western countries plus Japan, are less than global in their applications and implications.

As yet there is little to be said about the relation of the power distance and psychopathological variables. Hofstede (1980, p. 130) suggested that, in combination with high uncertainty avoidance, low power distance is conducive to the development of strong moral self-control or superego. If this formulation is valid, it should lead to greater rates of depressive disorders in cultures characterized by this combination of these two variables. In light of the results recapitulated earlier in this chapter, however, one should keep in mind that the connection between guilt and depression is not as strong in many non-Western cultures as it is in the West. Depression without self-accusation has been described; it appears to be especially characteristic in settings characterized by a collectivist orientation.

Finally, let us look at a couple of comparisons that are relevant to masculinity/femininity. Hofstede (1980, p. 297) suggested that this dimension is relevant to the understanding of suicides engendered by performance failure, such as the much described self-inflicted deaths of Japanese students who have failed crucial university entrance examinations (e.g., Iga, 1971). In Germany, another highly masculine and performance-oriented country, such suicides are, according to Hofstede, reasonably frequent. They are, however, virtually unknown in similar economically developed countries, such as the Netherlands, that are characterized by a more feminine orientation. Clearly this is a promising lead that remains to be explored, optimally in a multinational study going beyond a standard comparison of suicide rates and taking into consideration types of suicide. Two of the available studies involving masculinity/femininity pertain to the Netherlands. The other sites of the comparisons were the United States and Great Britain. One of these reports by Saenger (1968) goes back twenty years ago and refers to clinical outpatient populations; the other one, by Bridges, Arindell, Pickersgill, Katsounis, and Mervyn-Smith (1988), is recent and involves the reports of personal fears in nonclinical populations. In Hofstede's project the Netherlands emerged as a clearly, though not extremely, "feminine" culture; both the United States and Great Britain were toward the opposite pole of the same axis. In the Saenger study, the Dutch outpatients were somewhat more depressed and anxious and less behaviorally disturbed than American patients in an analogous facility. This finding, then, broadly fits with the expectations for feminine and masculine psychopathology. The results by the trinational research team of Bridges et al. are less easily accommodated into this scheme. Their finding that fewer fears were reported by the Dutch students than by the British and American students appears to be paradoxical in reference to masculinity/femininity. The other results of this research can be more readily explained, though not on the basis of Hofstede's factors. British students exceeded the Americans in their fears of aggression and sexuality—fears that probably were not proportional to the actual danger of violence. Quite likely, though, they can be related to the threat of losing control over impulses, to which British students may be selectively sensitive. The more intensive agoraphobic fears in Great Britain curiously parallel the distinguished contributions of British clinicians and researchers to the understanding and treatment of this disorder (e.g., Hafner & Marks, 1976).

Two recent comparisons were conducted with psychiatric patients in Sweden and in Italy (Perris et al., 1981; Perris et al., 1985). In Hofstede's (1980, 1983a) research, these two countries were found to differ markedly in uncertainty avoidance, power distance, and masculinity, with Sweden scoring higher on all three dimensions. For individualism, Hofstede's results were counter to expectations, and Italy rather than Sweden emerged slightly higher on that dimension. However, there is still a question whether Hofstede's results are applicable to the interpretation of the two comparisons, which involved patients in southern Italy, a region long reputed to be traditionalist, sociocentric, and collectivist. Be that as it may, in one of the studies Perris et al. (1981) demonstrated that the symptoms of depressives in the two countries were generally similar. Moreover, the few cultural differences obtained were specific to patients' self-ratings and physicians' ratings. Swedish patients rated themselves higher in weight loss, tachycardia, and agitation than did Italians; the opposite pattern obtained for hopelessness, loss of interest, and dissatisfaction. In light of physicians' ratings, Italian depressives were higher in motor retardation and hypochondriasis, whereas Swedish patients obtained higher ratings in inability to feel and in agitation. The discrepancies between the clinicians' and patients' ratings introduce another source of complexity into the interpretation of these results.

The other study by Perris et al. (1985) compared involuntarily hospitalized patients in Sweden and Italy. The most frequent reason for the admission of Swedish patients was odd or improper behavior; in Italy dangerous behavior, actual or potential, was most frequently recorded as a justification for hospitalization. It is also worth noting that more patients lived alone before admission in Sweden than in Italy. Without referring these findings to Hofstede's four axes, it becomes apparent that, from the health professionals' point of view, involuntary admission was triggered by the prevalent social concerns—proper behavior in Sweden and loss of control in Italy— which in both cases appear to represent culturally prominent preoccupations. Contrast, however, was predominant in the case of the differentiating self-reported symptoms in the two countries, with the Italians reporting a pattern of withdrawal and resignation and the Swedes expressing their distress through agitation and psychophysiological reactivity. It is difficult, however, to relate any of these findings to Hofstede's four axes, except possibly to note, post hoc, that the Swedish pattern of internalized symptoms is consistent with individualism. In any case, the contrast between dramatic behavioral and elaborate ideational symptoms was also observed in the United States between the descendants of Irish and Italian immigrants. In a classical and frequently cited study, Opler and Singer (1959) identified these two symptom patterns and related them to the prevailing socialization experiences in these ethnic groups. Apparently these patterns of parent-child interaction survived one or more generations of residence in America. It is pointless, however, to relate them to Hofstede's values, which were recorded in the recent past.

Another cross-cultural comparison was undertaken between Germany and the United States (Townsend, 1975a, 1975b, 1978). Normal subjects, hospitalized patients, and mental health professionals were the participants, and the study focused on the attitudes of the three groups of subjects in the two countries rather than on symptoms. The results demonstrated the continuity within cultures of the beliefs of the three samples. Germans stressed the immutability of disturbed behavior, or at least the difficulty of bringing about change. They also expressed a belief in organic causes of mental disturbance. Americans, on the other hand, emphasized self-improvement, believed in responsibility for one's acts, and were optimistic about the solution of personal problems. These findings provide another instance of continuity between culture and psychopathology. They do not, however, help us bridge the gap between the experience of psychological disorder and the prevailing values of the cultures in question. Germany and the United States are, in any case, in the same quadrant on all four of Hofstede's dimensions, and it is idle to expect that these four axes exhaust the universe of cross-cultural differences in psychopathology.

Conclusions

The attempt to integrate Hofstede's four dimensions with the culturally characteristic modes of expressing psychopathology has yielded rather sketchy and fragmentary results. What can we conclude from these bits of data? Perhaps the following generalizations are in order.

1. On the most general plane, the accumulated data on psychopathology around the world document the existence of a universal core of manifestations of abnormal behavior. The nature of these universal symptoms is well documented for schizophrenia and major depression. It has been demonstrated that these two disorders are represented in all regions of the world. It may, however, be rash to assert at this point that they are present in all human cultures. A thorough anthropological or ethnographic study documenting the absence of either or both disorders in a specific culture would be a major addition to the present state of knowledge on the interplay of culture and psychopathology.

2. Around the panculturally constant nucleus of both schizophrenia and depression, culturally variable features of these two disorders have been identified and investigated. In particular, in reference to schizophrenia, the benign course and positive outcome of acute psychotic disorder, sometimes with conspicuous and dramatic symptoms, in developing countries is well established. The question is moot whether all the varieties of this disorder, described under different names in their respective locations, fall within the range of schizophrenia as restrictively defined in current American clinical practice.

3. In the case of depression, vegetative symptoms appear to be more constant across cultures than are the more cognitive and social expressions of this disorder. In particular, the experience of guilt does not appear to be a universal component of depression. The description of "depression without guilt" in a variety of non-Western locations may be a major contribution of cross-cultural psychology to the understanding of human maladaptation.

4. On the basis of historical considerations and cross-cultural data, the pivotal role of guilt in depression in the West has been linked with the development of a permanent and autonomous sense

of selfhood. Such an experience of the self, in turn, is intertwined with the advent of individualism.

5. Similarly, the chronicity of a substantial proportion of schizophrenic disorders in the West has been suggestively, though not conclusively, traced to the social isolation and separation under the impact of industrialization and the resulting separation of schizophrenics from their families and other primary groups. This kind of isolation is more likely to occur in individualist than in collectivist cultures.

6. In terms of direction of the relationship, most of the findings seem to favor the exaggeration or caricature theory of psychopathology in culture. There are clearly certain instances of contrast, but their total number appears to be small.

7. The caricature or exaggeration theory needs to be corrected and modified in this sense. The symptoms become exaggerated only in that they are inappropriate and rigid; they do not invariably become more intense.

8. There is at least one unanticipated instance in the body of findings reviewed—that of psychopathology's not accentuating, but obliterating, cultural differences (Radford, 1989); it remains to be seen whether this is a unique or at least an isolated occurrence or whether it represents a more prominent instance of psychopathology's impact on culture.

9. Of the four Hofstede dimensions, the only substantial amount of work done pertains to individualism/collectivism; it is indicative of some of the potential features of psychopathology associated with this dimension. The symptoms are typically cognitive, explicit, and intrapsychic. Self-blame and guilt are prominent.

10. There is only sketchy information on symptoms associated with power distance, uncertainty avoidance, and masculinity/femininity. Bicultural studies that vary one of these dimensions while holding the other three constant should be useful in filling the gaps in our present knowledge. Plausible leads, based largely upon Hofstede's own research and observations, are available for power distance, uncertainty avoidance, and masculinity/femininity in their relationship to psychopathological characteristics. They remain to be systematically investigated. The few documented findings in these areas must be replicated and extended.

11. Bicultural studies, however, are ill equipped to elucidate by themselves the connections between social behavior and psycho-

logical disorder. Multicultural or multinational studies are badly needed. These studies should be explicitly designed to relate to one or more relevant dimensions.

12. A study format should include both normal and abnormal samples and present theoretically relevant tasks that can be performed by clinical and control subjects alike, in addition to symptoms.

13. As this review demonstrates, the experience of psychopathology varies across cultures even when there is no substantial difference on any of Hofstede's four dimensions. Identifying and systematically investigating additional axes of variation and their relationships to normal experience should be given high priority.

14. The ultimate goal of this enterprise is the formulation of a functional relationship between cultural characteristics and psychopathology. Once such a relationship is specified, it should be possible to predict manifestations of abnormal behavior from cultural characteristics and to infer cultural characteristics from manifestations of psychopathology.

REFERENCES

Abramson, L. Y., Seligman, M. E. P., & Teasdale, J. D. (1980). Learned helplessness in humans: Critique and reformulation. *Journal of Abnormal Psychology, 87*, 49–74.
Bazzoui, W. (1970). Affective disorders in Iraq. *British Journal of Psychiatry, 117*, 195–203.
Benedict, R. (1934). Culture and the abnormal. *Journal of General Psychology, 10*, 59–82.
Benedict, R. (1946). *The chrysanthemum and the sword.* Boston: Houghton Mifflin.
Berne, E. (1956). Comparative psychiatry and tropical psychiatry. *American Journal of Psychiatry, 113*, 193–200.
Berne, E. (1959). Difficulties of comparative psychiatry. *American Journal of Psychiatry, 116*, 104–109.
Binitie, A. (1975). A factor-analytic study of depression across cultures. *British Journal of Psychiatry, 127*, 559–563.
Bond, M. H. (Ed.). (1986). *Psychology of the Chinese people.* Hong Kong: Oxford University Press.
Bridges, K. R., Arindell, W., Pickersgill, M. J., Katsounis, L. D., & Mervyn-Smith, J. (1988, April). *A cross-cultural comparative study of self-reported fears: The responses of American, British, and Dutch university students to the*

Fear Survey Schedule. Paper presented at the Eastern Psychological Association meeting. Buffalo, NY.

Bustamente, J. A. (1969). La réaction psychotique aiguë, la transculturation, le sous-développement et les changements sociaux. *Psychopathologie Africaine, 5*, 223–233.

Carothers, J. C. (1953). *The African mind in health and disease*. Geneva: World Health Organization.

Caudill, W. (1973). The influence of social structure and culture on human behavior in Japan. *Journal of Nervous and Mental Disease, 157*, 249–258.

Cheung, F. M. C. (1986). Psychopathology among Chinese people. In M. H. Bond (Ed.), *The psychology of the Chinese people*. Hong Kong: Oxford University Press.

Collomb, H. (1965). Bouffées délirantes en psychiatrie africaine. *Psychopathologie Africaine, 3*, 167–239.

Cooper, J. E., & Sartorius, N. (1977). Cultural and temporal variations in schizophrenia. *British Journal of Psychiatry, 130*, 50–55.

Davis, R. (1973). Special aspects of depression in Indian patients. In S. Arieti (Ed.), *World biennial of psychiatry and psychotherapy*, (Vol. 2). New York: Basic Books.

De Hoyos, A., & De Hoyos, G. (1965). Symptomatology differentials between Negro and white schizophrenics. *International Journal of Social Psychiatry, 11*, 245–255.

Diaz-Guerrero, R. (1967). Sociocultural premises, attitudes, and cross-cultural research. *International Journal of Psychology, 2*, 79–88.

Diaz-Guerrero, R. (1970). *Estudios de psicología del mexicano* (2nd ed.). Mexico: Trillas.

Diop, M. (1967). La dépression chez le noir africain. *Psychopathologie Africaine, 3*, 183–195.

Dohrenwend, B. P., & Dohrenwend, B. S. (1969). *Social status and psychological disorder*. New York: Wiley.

Doi, T. (1973). *The anatomy of dependence* (J. Bester, Trans.). Tokyo: Kodansha.

Draguns, J. G. (1963). Responses to cognitive and perceptual ambiguity in chronic and acute schizophrenia. *Journal of Abnormal and Social Psychology, 66*, 24–30.

Draguns, J. G. (1966). Affective meaning of reduced stimulus input: A study by means of the semantic differential. *Canadian Journal of Psychology, 21*, 231–241.

Draguns, J. G. (1973). Comparison of psychopathology across cultures: Issues, findings, directions. *Journal of Cross Cultural Psychology, 4*, 9–47.

Draguns, J. G. (1980). Disorders of clinical severity. In H. C. Triandis & J. G. Draguns (Eds.), *Handbook of cross-cultural psychology: Psychopathology* (Vol. 6, pp. 99–174). Boston: Allyn and Bacon.

Draguns, J. G. (1985). *Mental health characteristics of the Chinese in light of comparative cross-cultural research*. Paper presented at the World Psychiatric Association's Transcultural Psychiatry Section Regional Symposium for Asia and the Pacific, Nanjing, People's Republic of China.

Draguns, J. G. (1986). Culture and psychopathology: What is known about their relationship? *Australian Journal of Psychology, 38,* 329–338.

Draguns, J. G. (1988a). *Culture and complex human behavior: A close relationship or a tenuous connection?* Invited address, Eastern Psychological Association, Buffalo, NY.

Draguns, J. G. (1988b). Personality and culture: Are they relevant for the enhancement of quality of mental life? In P. R. Dasen, J. W. Berry, & N. Sartorius (Eds.), *Health and cross-cultural psychology: Toward applications* (pp. 141–161). Newbury Park, CA: Sage.

Draguns, J. G. (1989). La culture et le comportement anormal: L'état actuel de nos connaissances. [Culture and abnormal behavior: The present state of our knowledge]. In J. Retschitzry, M. Bossel-Lagos, & P. K. Dasen (Eds.), *La recherche interculturelle,* tome 1 (pp. 140–144). Paris: L'Harmattan.

Draguns, J. G., Phillips, L., Broverman, I. K., Caudill, W., & Nishimae, S. (1971). The symptomatology of hospitalized psychiatric patients in Japan and in the United States: A study of cultural differences. *Journal of Nervous and Mental Disease, 152,* 3–16.

Egeland, J. A., Hofstetter, A. M., & Eshleman, S. K. (1983). Amish study: 3. The impact of cultural factors on diagnosis of bipolar illness. *American Journal of Psychiatry, 140,* 67–71.

Escobar, J. I., Randolph, E. T., & Hill, M. (1986). Symptoms of schizophrenia in Hispanic and Anglo veterans. *Culture, Medicine and Psychiatry, 10,* 259–276.

Eysenck, H. J. (1970). *The structure of human personality.* London: Methuen.

Fabrega, H. J., & Silver, D. B. (1973). *Illness and shamanistic curing in Zinacantán: An ethnomedical analysis.* Stanford, CA: Stanford University Press.

Fabrega, H. J., Swartz, J. D., & Wallace, C. A. (1968). Ethnic differences in psychopathology: Clinical correlates under varying conditions. *Archives of General Psychiatry, 19,* 218–226.

Frenkel-Brunswik, E. (1949). Intolerance of ambiguity as an emotional and perceptual personality variable. *Journal of Personality, 18,* 104–141.

Fundia, T., Draguns, J. G., & Phillips, L. (1971). Culture and psychiatric symptomatology: A comparison of Argentine and United States patients. *Social Psychiatry, 6,* 11–20.

Gada, M. T. (1982). A cross-cultural study of symptomatology of depression: Eastern versus Western patients. *International Journal of Social Psychiatry, 28,* 195–202.

Georgas, J. (1989). Changing family values in Greece: From collectivist to individualist. *Journal of Cross Cultural Psychology, 20,* 80–91.

German, G. A. (1972). Aspects of clinical psychiatry in sub-Saharan Africa. *British Journal of Psychiatry, 121,* 461–479.

Hafner, R. J., & Marks, I. M. (1976). Exposure *in vivo* of agoraphobics: Contributions of Diazepam, group exposure, and anxiety evocation. *Psychological Medicine, 6,* 71–88.

Hofstede, G. (1980). *Culture's consequences: International differences in work-related values.* Beverly Hills, CA: Sage.

Hofstede, G. (1983a). Dimensions of national cultures in fifty countries and three regions. In J. B. Deregowski, S. Dziurawiec, & R. C. Annis (Eds.), *Expiscations in cross-cultural psychology* (pp. 335–355). Lisse: Swets and Zeitlinger.

Hofstede, G. (1983b). The cultural relativity of organizational practices and theories. *Journal of International Business Studies, 14,* 75–89.

Hofstede, G. (1986). Cultural differences in teaching and learning. *International Journal of Intercultural Relations, 10,* 301–320.

Hofstede, G., & Bond, M. H. (1988). The Confucius connection: From cultural roots to economic growth. *Organizational Dynamics, 16* (4), 4–21.

Holtzman, W. H., Diaz-Guerrero, R., & Swartz, J. D. (1975). *Personality development in two cultures.* Austin: University of Texas Press.

Hostetler, J. A. (1980). *The Amish society* (3rd ed.). Baltimore: Johns Hopkins University Press.

Hsu, F. L. K. (1971). Psychological homeostasis and *jen*: Conceptual tools for advancing psychological anthropology. *American Anthropologist, 73,* 23–44.

Iga, M. (1971). Kyoto and university student suicide. *Psychologia, 14,* 15–24.

Jablensky, A., Sartorius, N., Gulbinat, W., & Ernberg, G. (1981). Characteristics of depressive patients contacting psychiatric services in four cultures. *Acta Psychiatrica Scandinavica, 63,* 367–383.

Jewell, D. P. (1952). A case of a psychotic Navaho Indian male. *Human Organization, 11* (11), 32–36.

Jilek, W. (1982). *Indian healing: Shamanistic ceremonialism in the Pacific Northwest today.* Surrey, BC: Hancock House.

Jilek, W., & Jilek-Aal, L. (1978). The psychiatrist and his shaman colleague: Cross-cultural collaboration with traditional American therapists. *Journal of Operational Psychiatry, 9,* 32–39.

Jilek-Aal, L., Jilek, W., & Flynn, F. (1978). Sex role, culture, and psychopathology: A comparative study of three ethnic groups in western Canada. *Journal of Psychological Anthropology, 6,* 473–488.

Keisling, R. (1981). Underdiagnosis of manic-depressive illness on a hospital unit. *American Journal of Psychiatry, 138,* 672–673.

Kimura, B. (1965). Vergleichende Untersuchungen über depressive Erkrankungen in Japan und Deutschland. *Fortschritte der Psychiatrie und Neurologie, 33,* 202–215.

Kimura, B. (1967). Phänomenologie des Schulderlebnisses in einer vergleichenden psychiatrischen Sicht. *Aktuelle Fragen der Psychiatrie und Neurologie, 6,* 54–65.

Kimura, B. (1972). Mitmenschlichkeit in der Psychiatrie. *Zeitschrift für Klinische Psychologie, 20,* 3–13.

Kirmayer, L. (1984). Culture, affect, and somatization: Parts 1 and 2. *Transcultural Psychiatric Research Review, 21,* 159–188, 237–262.

Kleinman, A. (1977). Depression, somatization, and the "new cross-cultural psychiatry." *Social Science and Medicine, 11,* 3–9.

Kleinman, A. (1982). Neurasthenia and depression: A study of somatization and culture in China. *Culture, Medicine, and Psychiatry, 6,* 117–190.

Kleinman, A. (1986). *Social origins of distress and disease.* New Haven: Yale University Press.

Kleinman, A. (1988). *Rethinking psychiatry: From cultural category to personal experience.* New York: Free Press.

Kleinman, A., & Kleinman, J. (1985). Somatization. In A. Kleinman & B. Good (Eds.), *Culture and depression* (pp. 429–490). Berkeley: University of California Press.

Kleinman, A., & Lin, T. Y. (Eds.). (1981). *Normal and abnormal behavior in Chinese culture.* Dordrecht: Reidel.

Kolody, B., Vega, W., Meinhardt, K., & Bensussen, G. (1986). The correspondence of health complaints and depressive symptoms among Anglos and Mexican Americans. *Journal of Nervous and Mental Disease, 174,* 221–228.

Kraepelin, E. (1904). Vergleichende Psychiatrie. *Zentralblatt für Nervenheilkunde und Psychiatrie, 15,* 433–437.

Leff, J. (1973). Culture and the differentiation of emotional states. *British Journal of Psychiatry, 123,* 299–306.

Leff, J. (1981). *Psychiatry around the globe.* New York: Marcel Dekker.

Lynn, R. (1971). *Personality and national character.* Oxford: Pergamon.

Lynn, R. (1973). National differences in anxiety and the consumption of caffeine. *British Journal of Social and Clinical Psychology, 12,* 92–93.

Lynn, R. (1975). National differences in anxiety, 1935–1965. In I. G. Sarason & C. D. Spielberger (Eds.), *Stress and anxiety* (Vol. 2). Washington, DC: Hemisphere.

Lynn, R., & Hampson, S. L. (1975). National diffrences in extraversion and neuroticism. *British Journal of Social and Clinical Psychology, 14,* 223–240.

Lynn, R., & Hampson, S. L. (1977). Fluctuations in national level of neuroticism and extraversion, 1935–1970. *British Journal of Social and Clinical Psychology, 16,* 131–137.

Mann, L. (1985). Decision making. In N. T. Feather (Ed.), *Australian psychology: Review of research.* Sydney: Allen and Unwin.

Marin, G., & Triandis, H. C. (1985). Allocentrism as an important characteristic of the behavior of Latin Americans and Hispanics. In R. Diaz-Guerrero (Ed.), *Cross-cultural and national studies in social psychology* (pp. 85–104). Amsterdam: Elsevier.

Marsella, A. J. (1979). Cross-cultural studies of mental disorders. In A. J. Marsella, R. G. Thorp, & T. J. Ciborowski (Eds.), *Perspectives on cross-cultural psychology* (pp. 233–262). New York: Academic Press.

Marsella, A. J. (1980). Depressive experience and disorder across cultures. In H. C. Triandis & J. G. Draguns (Eds.), *Handbook of cross-cultural psychology: Vol. 6. Psychopathology* (pp. 237–289). Boston: Allyn and Bacon.

Marsella, A. J., Escudero, M., & Gordon, P. (1972). Stresses, resources, and symptom patterns in urban Filipino men. In W. Lebra (Ed.), *Transcultural* research in mental health (pp. 148–171). Honolulu: University Press of Hawaii.

Marsella, A. J., Kameoka, V., Shizuru, L., & Brennan, J. (1975). Cross-validation of self-report measures of depression among normal populations of Japanese, Chinese, and Caucasian ancestry. Journal of Clinical Psychology, 31, 281–287.

Marsella, A. J., Kinzie, D., & Gordon, P. (1973). Ethnic variations in the expression of depression. Journal of Cross Cultural Psychology, 4, 435–456.

Marsella, A. J., Sartorius, N., Jablensky, A., & Fenton, F. R. (1985). Cross-cultural studies of depressive disorders. In A. Kleinman & B. Good (Eds.), Culture and depression (pp. 299–324). Berkeley: University of California Press.

Marsella, A. J., Shizuru, L., Brennan, J., & Kameoka, V. (1981). Depression and body image satisfaction. Journal of Cross Cultural Psychology, 12, 360–371.

Marsella, A. J., Walker, E., & Johnson, F. (1973). Personality correlates of depression in college students from different ethnic groups. International Journal of Social Psychiatry, 19, 77–81.

McReynolds, P. (1960). Anxiety, perception, and schizophrenia. In D. D. Jackson (Ed.), The etiology of schizophrenia (pp. 248–292). New York: Basic Books.

Mezzich, J., & Raab, E. (1980). Depressive symptomatology across the Americas. Archives of General Psychiatry, 37, 818–823.

Murphy, H. B. M. (1978). The advent of guilt feelings as a common depressive symptom: A historical comparison on two continents. Psychiatry, 41, 229–242.

Murphy, H. B. M. (1982). Comparative psychiatry. Berlin: Springer-Verlag.

Murphy, H. B. M., Wittkower, E. W., & Chance, N. A. (1967). Cross-cultural inquiry into the symptomatology of depression: A preliminary report. International Journal of Psychiatry, 3, 6–15.

Ney, P., Lieh-Mak, F., Cheng, R., & Collins, W. (1979). Chinese autistic children. Social Psychiatry, 14, 147–150.

Odejide, A. O. (1979). Cross-cultural psychiatry: A myth or reality? Comprehensive Psychiatry, 20, 103–108.

Opler, M. K., & Singer, J. L. (1959). Ethnic differences in behavior and psychopathology: Italian and Irish. International Journal of Social Psychiatry, 2, 11–23.

Parsons, T., & Bales, R. F. (1956). Family, socialization, and interaction process. Chicago: Free Press.

Perris, C., Eisemann, M., Eriksson, V., Perris, H., Kemali, D., Amati, A., DelVecchio, M., & Vacca, L. (1981). Transcultural aspects of depressive symptomatology. Psychiatria Clinica, 14, 69–80.

Perris, C., Kemali, D., Dencker, S. J., Malm, U., Rutz, W., Amati, A., Stancati, G., Morandini, G., Minnai, G., Maj, M., & Gritti, P. (1985). Patients admitted for compulsory treatment to selected psychiatric units in Italy and in Sweden. Acta Psychiatrica Scandinavia, 71 (Suppl. 316), 135–149.

Pfeiffer, W. M. (1969). Die Symptomatik der Depression in transkultureller Sicht. In H. Hippius & W. Selbach (Eds.), *Das depressive Syndrom* (pp. 151–167). Berlin: Urban und Schwarzenberg.

Pfeiffer, W. M. (1970). *Transkulturelle Psychiatrie*. Stuttgart: Thieme.

Prange, A. J., & Vitols, M. M. (1962). Cultural aspects of the relatively low incidence of depression in southern Negroes. *International Journal of Social Psychiatry, 8,* 104–112.

Prince, R. (1968). The changing picture of depression syndromes in Africa: Is it fact or diagnostic fashion? *Canadian Journal of African Studies, 1,* 177–192.

Radford, M. H. B. (1989). *Culture, depression, and decision making behaviour: A study with Japanese and Australian clinical and non-clinical populations*. Unpublished doctoral dissertation, Flinders University of South Australia.

Radford, M. H. B., Mann, L., & Kalucy, R. S. (1986). Psychiatric disturbances and decision making. *Australian and New Zealand Journal of Psychiatry, 20,* 210–217.

Rao, A. (1966). Depression: A psychiatric analysis of thirty cases. *Indian Journal of Psychiatry, 8,* 143–154.

Rao, A. (1973). Depressive illness and guilt in Indian culture. *Indian Journal of Psychiatry, 15,* 231–236.

Rin, H., Schooler, C., & Caudill, W. A. (1973). Culture, social structure, and psychopathology in Taiwan and Japan. *Journal of Nervous and Mental Disease, 157,* 296–312.

Saenger, G. (1968). Psychiatric patients in America and the Netherlands: A transcultural comparison. *Social Psychiatry, 3,* 149–164.

Sartorius, N., Jablensky, A., Korten, A., & Ernberg, G. (1986). Early manifestation and first contact incidence of schizophrenia. *Psychological Medicine, 16,* 909–928.

Scharfetter, C. (1985). Der Schamane: Zeuge einer alten Kultur—wieder belebbar? *Schweizer Archiv der Neurologie und Psychiatrie, 136,* 81–95.

Schooler, C., & Caudill, W. (1964). Symptomatology in Japanese and American schizophrenics. *Ethnology, 3,* 172–178.

Sechrest, L. (1969). Philippine culture, stress, and psychopathology. In W. Caudill & T. Lin (Eds.), *Mental health research in Asia and the Pacific* (pp. 306–334). Honolulu: East-West Center Press.

Smock, C. D. (1955). The influence of psychological stress on the "intolerance of ambiguity." *Journal of Abnormal and Social Psychology, 50,* 177–182.

Stoker, D., Zurcher, L. A., & Fox, W. (1968). Women in psychotherapy: A cross-cultural comparison. *International Journal of Social Psychiatry, 15,* 5–22.

Suzuki, A., Peters, L., Weibender, L., & Gillespie, J. (1987). Characteristics of American and Japanese schizophrenic patients elicited by the Rorschach technique and demographic data. *International Journal of Social Psychiatry, 33,* 50–55.

Teja, J., Narang, R., & Aggarwal, A. (1970). Depression across cultures. *British Journal of Psychiatry, 119,* 253–260.

Townsend, J. M. (1975a). Cultural conceptions, mental disorders, and social roles: A comparison of Germany and America. *American Sociological Review, 40,* 739–752.

Townsend, J. M. (1975b). Cultural conceptions and mental illness: A controlled comparison of Germany and America. *Journal of Nervous and Mental Disease, 160,* 409–421.

Townsend, J. M. (1978). *Cultural conceptions of mental illness.* Chicago: University of Chicago Press.

Triandis, H. C. (1985). Some major dimensions of cultural variation in client populations. In P. Pedersen (Ed.), *Handbook of cross-cultural counseling and therapy* (pp. 21–28). Westport, CT: Greenwood.

Triandis, H. C., Bontempo, R., Betancourt, H., Bond, M., Leung, K., Brenes, A., Georgas, J., Hui, C. H., Marin, G., Setiadi, B., Sinha, J. B. P., Verma, J., Spangenberg, J., Touzard, H., & de Montmollin, G. (1986). The measurement of the etic aspects of collectivism and individualism across cultures. *Australian Journal of Psychology, 38,* 257–267.

Trimble, J. E., Manson, S., Dinges, N., & Medicine, B. (1984). American Indian concepts of mental health: Reflections and directions. In P. Pedersen, N. Sartorius, & A. J. Marsella (Eds.), *Mental health services: The cross-cultural context* (pp. 199–220). Beverly Hills, CA: Sage.

Tseng, W. S. (1975). The nature of somatic complaints among psychiatric patients: The Chinese case. *Comprehensive Psychiatry, 16,* 237–245.

Tseng, W. S., Di, X., Ebata, K., Hsu, J., & Yuhua, C. (1986). Diagnostic pattern for neuroses in China, Japan, and the U.S. *American Journal of Psychiatry, 143,* 1010–1014.

Tseng, W. S., & Wu, D. Y. H. (Eds.). (1986). *Chinese culture and mental health: An overview.* New York: Academic Press.

Wiener, M. (1989). Psychopathology reconsidered: Depressions interpreted as psychosocial transactions. *Clinical Psychology Review, 9,* 295–322.

World Health Organization. (1973). *Report of the international pilot study of schizophrenia.* Geneva: World Health Organization.

World Health Organization. (1979). *Schizophrenia: An international follow-up study.* New York: Wiley.

World Health Organization. (1983). *Depressive disorders in different cultures: Report of the WHO collaborative study of standardized assessment of depressive disorders.* Geneva: World Health Organization.

Yamamoto, J., Yeh, E.-K., Loya, F., Slawson, P., & Hurwicz, M. L. (1985). Are American outpatients more depressed than Chinese outpatients? *American Journal of Psychiatry, 142,* 1347–1351.

Yamamoto, K. (1972). A comparative study of "patienthood" in the Japanese and American mental hospital. In W. P. Lebra (Ed.), *Transcultural research in mental health* (Vol. 2, pp. 190–212). Honolulu: University Press of Hawaii.

Yap, P. M. (1965). Phenomenology of affective disorder in Chinese and other cultures. In A. deReuck & R. Porter (Eds.), *Transcultural psychiatry.* Boston: Little, Brown.

Zeldine, G., Ahvi, R., Leuckx, R., Boussat, M., Saibou, A., Hanck, C., Collignon, R., Tourame, G., & Collomb, H. (1975). A propos de l'utilisation d'une échelle d'évaluation en psychiatrie transculturelle. *L'Encéphale, 1*, 133–145.

Zippin, D. H., & Hough, R. L. (1985). Perceived self-other differences in life events and mental health among Mexicans and Americans. *Journal of Psychology, 119*, 143–155.

Cultural Psychology: A Once and Future Discipline?

Michael Cole
University of California, San Diego

It is the dilemma of psychology to deal as a natural science with an object that creates history.

—Ernst Boesch

Cultural psychology is different from specialized branches of psychology in that it did not evolve as a subdiscipline after the founding of experimental psychology; the idea of cultural psychology predates experimental psychology and was present at its birth (see Jahoda, this volume). It rests on the assumption that two closely related distinctive characteristics of human beings as a species are: (1) their special ability to modify their environment by creating artifacts and (2) their corresponding ability to transmit the accumulated modifications to subsequent generations through precept and procedure coded in human language.

Specifying the implications of these two characteristics for a full understanding of human psychological processes and the kind of science needed to study them is the task of cultural psychology.

The ideas contained in this essay have been developed over more than two decades of collaborative work. I wish to thank my colleagues for the opportunity to carry out the work it is based on, and for their forbearance at the slow pace of my thinking. Needless to say, they cannot be held responsible for the deficiencies of this chapter, which I hereby claim as my own.

Recent Proposals for Cultural Psychology

At a symposium reviewing the state of psychology over the previous 100 years, Steven Toulmin (1980) declared that it would be-
hoove the discipline to reconsider Wilhelm Wundt's (1916) conten-
tion that in addition to an experimental program of research,
psychologists also need to study those aspects of human psychological functioning that are shaped by the accumulated knowledge
of the cultural group into which individuals are born. The burden of
Toulmin's argument was that culture, as a historically accumulated
system of designs for living, had to be made a fundamental constitu-
ent of psychological theories of human nature. He pointed out that
Wundt had also advocated the study of cultural phenomena such as
language, myth, and custom as a necessary complement to his more
familiar studies of elementary psychological processes using experimental methods based on trained introspection. Wundt termed this
cultural-historical half of the discipline of scientific psychology *Volkerpsychologie*. Toulmin explicitly translated *Volkerpsychologie* using
the term "cultural psychology."

Douglas Price-Williams, the well-known cross-cultural developmental psychologist, writing in a volume about the perspectives
of cross-cultural psychology, suggested that psychologists should
recognize the existence of cultural psychology, which he defined as
"that branch of inquiry that delves into the contextual behavior of
psychological processes" (Price-Williams, 1979, p. 14). Shortly there-
after, Price-Williams (1980) enlarged upon the goal of creating a cultural psychology. In addition to urging that the category of culture
be made the centerpiece of such a discipline, he pointed to the great
relevance of closely related thinking in the semiotic and pragmatic
schools of linguistics and cultural studies and emphasized once
again the commitment to some form of contextualism that a move to
cultural psychology would entail.

A few years later, in what I am sure was an "independent invention," J. R. Kantor, the venerable behaviorist, wrote a volume entitled
Cultural Psychology. Kantor (1982) asserted that cultural psychology is
the study of human beings' responses to "institutional stimuli." By institutional stimuli, Kantor meant stimuli that have acquired meaning
as a consequence of their inclusion in prior meaningful human activity.
He gives as an example the contrasting responses of a Hindu and a

Christian to the sight of a cow. Both individuals share "noncultural" perceptual responses to the biological properties of cows, but they have different cultural responses, corresponding to the inclusion of cows in two quite different cultural meaning systems.

Quite recently, important papers proposing a cultural psychology have been written by two very disparate scholars who share a background in cross-cultural research. Richard Shweder, in a book entitled *Cultural Psychology: The Chicago Symposium on Culture and Human Development* (1990, p. 2), writes that the basic idea of cultural psychology is that "no socio-cultural environment exists or has identity independent of the way human beings seize meaning and resources from it, while every human being has her or his subjectivity and mental life altered through the processes of seizing meanings and resources from some socio-cultural environment and using them (p. 2, MS)." Shweder's suggestions for places to look for appropriate models of theory and practice include such diverse areas of scholarship as the study of expertise and event schemata in cognitive-developmental psychology, cognitive and symbolic anthropology, intentional worlds philosophy, discourse process studies in various disciplines, and many more.

Lutz Eckensberger (1988), who shares Shweder's interest in cross-cultural psychology, draws on quite different traditions of scholarly thought in arriving at his conception of cultural psychology. Eckensberger is a student of Ernst Boesch, a man whose career combines the German historical tradition (described in some detail by Jahoda in this volume) with a form of action theory and Piagetian constructivism. In elaborating on the consequences of a psychology that takes seriously the cultural-historical constitution of mind, Eckensberger also draws on Barker's (1978) ecological psychology, certain strains in German and American critical psychology, and anthropologically oriented developmental psychologists in the United States. Eckensberger, Krewer, and Kasper (1984) identify another central feature of cultural psychology: it implies a developmental approach to the study of human nature as a general methodological requirement. They assert that, if properly implemented, the action-theoretic approach to cultural psychology "offers at least theoretically the possibility of interrelating the three main levels of the concept of development within the same theoretical language: the actual genesis (microprocess), the ontogeny, and the historiogenesis; that is it allows linking historical change to individual change substantially" (1984, p. 97).

This sampling of modern views concerning cultural psychology is not intended to be exhaustive. But it *is* taken to be representative of a rather broad consensus that seems to be building about the key features of a cultural psychology among American and European social scientists.[1] There seems to be convergence on several distinctive concepts among these otherwise disparate authors: the importance of meaning and context and the centrality of methodological approaches that are broadly comparative and developmental.

I believe the core of cultural psychology that unites these somewhat different formulations and shapes the methods they adopt is a conception of culture as the unique *medium* of human existence, a medium that acts as both constraint and tool of human action. This medium has coevolved with the biological constitution of our species for hundreds of thousands of years. Although this conception of culture as the historically accumulating medium of human activity can be found in many scholarly traditions, as will become clear, my own work has been most heavily influenced by the sociohistorical school of psychology associated with the names of Lev S. Vygotsky, Alexander R. Luria, and Alexei N. Leontiev. Because this tradition of psychological theory is relatively unfamiliar to English-speaking psychologists and I plan to use its basic ideas to organize the empirical sections of this chapter, I will summarize it in somewhat greater detail than the other approaches mentioned above.

The Soviet Sociohistorical School

The sociohistorical school of psychology emerged in the 1920s as an explicit attempt to resolve the dilemma Boesch pointed to in the quotation I began with—the contradictions that arise because psychology uses the methods of the natural sciences in a search for universal explanatory laws of mind although its subject matter comprises

1. I do not want to give the impression that the views identified here are the only way to conceive of cultural psychology. For example, John Berry (1985, p. 3) defines cultural psychology as "an analogous term to social, industrial, developmental (etc.) psychology. That is, it identifies an area of study which seeks to discover systematic ʳelationships among cultural and behavioral variables."

organisms whose distinctive characteristics are associated with a historically contingent environment of their own making. As developed in the USSR, the sociohistorical view shares with German action theory its emphasis on the role of history in constituting development, but instead of combining action-theoretic ideas with Piagetian constructivism, the originators of the sociohistorical school proposed a cultural constructivism that drew its inspirations from the early writings of Karl Marx.

In A. R. Luria's (1979) account of the early work of this school, it arose as a principled solution to the "crisis in psychology" (much discussed by Western European psychologists) occasioned by Wundt's proposal for a dual psychology: an experimental psychology of "elementary psychological functions" distinct from an observational/descriptive psychology of "higher psychological functions" (Wundt, 1916; see also Jahoda, this volume).

The rudiments of this Soviet approach to the relation of culture to human mind first appeared in English in a series of remarkable publications in the late 1920s and 1930s (Leontiev, 1932; Luria, 1928, 1932; Vygotsky, 1929). Their fundamental postulates, which obviously resonate with the recent discussions about cultural psychology reviewed above, are that human psychological functions differ from the psychological processes of other animals because they are *culturally mediated*, are *historically developing*, and arise from *practical activity*. Each term in this formulation is linked to the other. Taken as a whole they provide a starting point for an approach to psychology that accords culture a central role in the constitution of mind. I will briefly characterize each of these postulates and some of their major implications before proceeding to describe the way my colleagues and I have combined them with ideas from Western European and American social sciences in the process of appropriating them in our own work.[2]

CULTURAL MEDIATION

The basic idea here, which can be traced back to antiquity and forms the basis for a good deal of anthropological theorizing, is the no-

2. For a more thorough treatment of the basic tenets and history of this school of psychology see Cole (1988), Kozulin (1984), Luria (1979), Valsiner (1988), and Wertsch (1985).

tion that human beings live in an environment transformed by the artifacts of prior generations, extending back to the beginning of the species (Geertz, 1973; Sahlins, 1976). The basic function of these artifacts is to coordinate human beings with the physical world and each other.

In that they mediate interaction with the world, cultural artifacts can also be considered tools. As Luria put the matter early on, "Man differs from animals in that he can make and use tools. [These tools] not only radically change his conditions of existence, they even react on him in that they effect a change in him and his psychic condition" (Luria, 1928, p. 493).

One standard example of this principle evoked by the Soviets included such artifacts as notched sticks and knotted strings. These "tool/artifacts" change the conditions of existence because they "off-load" a part of memory into the environment. They "react on" their makers in that they fundamentally reorganize the process of remembering.[3]

A crucial fact about the artifacts that constitute culture is that they are simultaneously ideational (symbolic, conceptual) *and* material. Thus, in acting on the world by first creating an artifact and then using that artifact, human beings simultaneously engage in a material act and a symbolic act.

Vygotsky (1966) expressed this idea when he pointed out that artifacts like a knotted string or hankerchief, which have the dual function of mastering the world and one's own behavior, are simultaneously signs.

> The behavior of man is distinguished by the fact that he creates artificial signalling stimuli, primarily a grand signal system of speech, and thereby masters the signalling activity of the cerebral hemispheres. Whereas the basic and most common activity of the cerebral hemispheres of animals and man is signalling, the basic and most common activity of man, which primarily distinguishes man from animals psychologically, is *signification*, i.e. creation and use of signals. (Vygotsky, 1966, p. 27)

---

3. Modern research has cautioned us not to claim too strong a discontinuity between *Homo sapiens* and other species. Rudimentary aspects of tool use and language clearly exist in other species, especially nonhuman primates. However, human beings are distinctive in their use of, and dependence on, culture as a mode of adaptation (Goodall, 1986; Tomasello, 1989).

This same point is made by the American anthropologist Leslie White in a slightly different way that helps to illuminate the notion of artifacts as simultaneously material and conceptual. "An axe has a subjective component; it would be meaningless without a concept and an attitude. On the other hand, a concept of attitude would be meaningless without overt expression, in behavior or in speech (which is a form of behavior). Every cultural element, every cultural trait, has a subjective and an objective aspect" (White, 1959, p. 236).

It is important to keep in mind, as the quotation from Vygotsky indicates, that this conception of culture as artifact applies with equal force whether one is considering language/speech or the more usually noted forms of artifacts that constitute material culture. Hence every word in a natural language must be considered an artifact in a manner analogous to an ax. This is relatively obvious when we consider the written word "ax," whose physical features are made up of a pattern of ink on paper (two other artifacts), but the spoken word "ax" is also an artifact with a material as well as conceptual side in that it is a culturally specific pattern of sound waves that is part of an intricate system including the syntax, the phonology, and the remainder of the lexicon of the English language.

As a consequence of the dual material/ideal nature of the systems of artifacts that constitute the cultural environment, human beings live in a "double world," simultaneously "natural" and "artificial."

HISTORICAL DEVELOPMENT

From the outset, proponents of the sociohistorical school have maintained that culturally mediated psychological functions are historical processes. In addition to individual human beings' creating and using artifacts like a notch in a stick or a knot in a handkerchief, they make these artifacts available to other human beings. Hence each generation develops in an environment that has been modified by the accumulated artifacts that mediated the successful adaptations of all prior generations of that particular human group. Echoing a widely held point of view concerning the historical origin of specifically human forms of activity and their psychological concomitants, A. A. Leontiev wrote, "Man learns from errors—and still more from the successes—of other people while each generation of animal can learn solely from its own. . . . It is mankind as a whole, but not a separate human being, who interacts with the biological environment; therefore such laws of evolution as, for example, the law of natural selection become invalid inside human society" (1970, p. 124). Stephen Jay Gould (1980) has adopted a similar position, pointing out that the process of cultural evolution is one in which the creation of variability for natural selection to operate on is directed, and in this sense, Lamarckian. However, Gould's formulation has the advantage of emphasizing that human society itself is inside phylogenetic history, a point that is very important for understanding human ontogeny.

An important consequence of these general principles for the conduct of cultural psychology is that investigators cannot restrict themselves to the study of people growing up in a particular historical era. If one wants to understand human memory or problem-solving processes, for example, it becomes necessary to examine also the history of the mediational means that play a role in the particular function in question. We will see the importance of this principle clearly when we inquire into such questions as whether a general shift occurring in the nature of human psychological processes is a universal accomplishment in the years from 5 to 7, or how and whether the acquisition of the ability to read and write influences the nature of cognitive processing.

PRACTICAL ACTIVITY: THE STARTING POINT FOR
THE STUDY OF PSYCHOLOGICAL PROCESSES

This idea, taken from Hegel by way of Marx and Engels, was expressed by Leontiev as follows:

Human psychology is concerned with the activity of concrete individuals, which takes place either in a collective—or in a situation in which the subject deals directly with the surrounding world of objects—i.e., at the potter's wheel or the writer's desk . . . if we removed human activity from the system of social relationships, it would not exist . . . the human individual's activity is a system in the system of social relations. It does not exist without these relations. (Leontiev, 1981, pp. 46–47)

At one level this kind of statement can be considered little more than common sense. Of course people's psychological functions are shaped by their experiences and their experiences occur as part of human activity. Considered within the context of psychology as a scientific discipline, however, this bit of common sense might be thought rather odd. After all, it is not human activity, but psychological processes like memory, perception, problem solving, anxiety, and so on that are the subject matter of psychology. Psychologists have long studied these processes by conducting experiments that expose people to highly controlled experiences in order to ascertain the basic workings of the mind without any specific grounding in people's everyday practical activities.

To be sure, if one believes that people "think through artifacts" and that the shape of this thinking is constrained by the way the particular set of artifacts is put together as part of a historical stream of human activity, the motives for which are survival and reproduction, then experimental procedures that grew out of late 19th-century science cease to be plausible as generally appropriate to the study of human thinking. An activity-centered approach to the study of psychology produces a narrow interpretation of results from experiments that (for example) study human memory by exposing people to a list of nonsense syllables to be remembered "for their own sake" or logical puzzles that were constructed purely to test alternative models of reasoning with no explicit reference to previous activities where remembering or reasoning played a leading role. The results of such experiments might, for example, be considered useful as models of the kind of thinking that goes on during a test in a school or as part of a game popular in the social group, but they are not likely to be taken as evidence about the operation of reified psychological process called "memory" or "problem solving."

In effect, when one starts from the perspective of culturally valued activities rather than presumed psychological processes, the entire nature of experiments as tools of psychological theorizing is transformed. Instead of representing priviliged settings for diagnosing the nature of psychological processes, they come to be viewed as historically specific forms of activity (the activity of a certain kind of scientist) that give shape to the very processes they are supposed to be diagnosing. Their full psychological significance cannot be ascertained unless one can, in a principled way, show how the specific practices of psychologists serve as model systems for particular (presumably significant) forms of culturally organized practical activity.

These basic postulates entail several consequences, the most important of which are the following:

1. The context specificity of mental processes. As Vygotsky put it, "the mind is not a complex network of *general* capabilities, but a set of specific capabilities. . . . Learning . . . is the acquisition of many specialized abilities for thinking" (Vygotsky, 1978, p. 83).

2. Social origins. This point, which is emphasized in Wertsch's thorough (1985) account of the ideas of Vygotsky and his colleagues, is summarized in what Vygotsky referred to as "the general genetic law of cultural development": "Any function in the child's cultural development appears twice, or on two planes. First, it appears on the social plane, and then on the psychological plane. First it appears as an interpsychological category, and then within the child as an intrapsychological category. . . . Social relations or relations among people genetically underlie all higher functions and their relationships" (quoted in Wentsch, 1985, pp. 60–61).

3. The need for a "genetic" analysis. This is really a generalization of the specific case of historical development to all "genetic" domains (Wertsch, 1985). Citing the maxim that "it is only in movement that we know what a body is," Vygotsky argued that a developmental approach is essential to understanding human mind. "By a developmental study of a problem," he wrote, "I mean the disclosure of its genesis, its causal dynamic basis."

I will return to discuss the implications of adopting this view of cultural psychology's key concepts, but first I want to summarize the way my colleagues and I have melded the basic propositions of the Soviet sociohistorical tradition with complementary scholarly traditions arising in the United States and Western Europe.

The Ecocultural Framework

A widely accepted way psychologists have conceived of how culture shapes human psychological functions is to formulate some version of the ecological framework depicted in Figure 1 (Berry, 1976; J. Whiting, 1969).

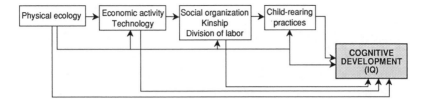

Figure 1. The normative ecological model. Culture is treated as a group's response to its physical ecology, in terms of which it evolves a technology and forms of economic activity, which shape social organization and division of labor, which in turn shape child-rearing practices, which are seen as the proximal "causes" of mental characteristics.

According to this view, the physical ecology sets up a "problem" or a set of constraints that a cultural group "solves" or responds to through its economic activities (mediated by its technologies of production); these activities involve a division of labor that is organized according to specially designed systems of social organization; within the constraints set up by the social organization, especially the kinship system, adults organize the upbringing of their children, "molding" their psychological characteristics as they move from one setting to another.

Conceived in this way, the ecocultural framework allows one to specify a set of ecological, technological, and social-organizational independent variables that can then be used to predict various psychological dependent variables.

When one adopts the kind of cultural psychological approach I am proposing here, certain difficulties with the ecocultural framework are highlighted (see Laboratory of Comparative Human Cognition [LCHC], 1983, for more extensive discussion). First, as Beatrice Whiting (1976) has emphasized, cultural variables are difficult to think of as independent. She uses the term "packaged" to refer to the fact that cultural systems represent unique configurations of adaptation in which economic activity, technology, social organization, and so on combine to determine the characteristics of members' experiences.

Second, as Beatrice Whiting has also pointed out, in addition to influencing cognitive development directly through the way they interact with their children, adults affect children's development by

assigning them to settings that have important socializing influences. Indeed, Whiting (1980) claims that the latter influence is more
important. Generalizing on the work of Whiting and LCHC, we can
redraw the ecocultural framework more in the spirit of Bronfenbrenner's (1979) ecological model, in which "culture," a group's entire
collection of artifacts for acting in the world accumulated from the
past is conceived of as nested sets of activities in their culturally appropriate contexts. This view, though consistent with other ecological approaches in some respects, entails a quite different way of
going about psychological analysis, since we now have to attend to
persons acting in contexts rather than psychological processes as-

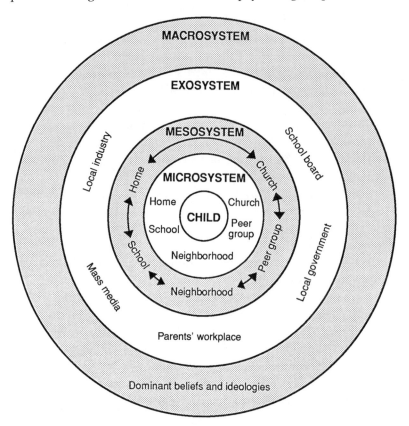

FIGURE 2. An embedded-context version of an ecocultural approach (in this case,
adapted from Bronfenbrenner) conceives of the child as the center of a nested set of
activities, united by a single worldview with its beliefs and a dominant ideology.

sessed by context-free tests and experimental procedures as a basic starting point for analysis. Moreover, the generality expected of particular psychological processes can be expected to be rather limited, or context bound; and when it appears that a particular mode of functioning is general across contexts, that generality will be looked for in the culturally organized connections between contexts in addition to such presumed psychological processes as "metacognition" and "context-free thinking" (LCHC, 1983).

Starting with Practical Activity

Perhaps the most radical departure from alternative psychology approaches entailed by cultural psychology is its commitment to begin analysis on the basis of mundane human activity as it is found in particular cultural-historical circumstances. Well before I began to appreciate the overall approach promoted by the Soviet sociohistorical theorists, I had hit upon practical activity as the starting point for psychological analysis as a consequence of cross-cultural research on culture and learning (see Cole, 1978, for a more detailed account).

Like many of those who have "discovered" the idea of cultural psychology, I found my thinking was enormously influenced by the experience of going to a radically different culture with the assignment of figuring out how growing up in cultural circumstances markedly different from my own influenced the mental processes of the local people. My assignment: to illuminate the sources of difficulty faced by Kpelle (Liberian) tribal children when they were confronted with mathematics in American-style schools built in the Liberian hinterlands.

Trained as an American learning theorist, I arrived in Liberia well schooled in the use of psychological testing and various experimental methods to assess learning and thought processes. In the spirit of the times, I came prepared to assess the development of mediated learning processes using one of several discrimination transfer designs; strategic thinking using probability learning; classification and abstract thinking abilities using a variety of concept formation tasks; logical remembering using free recall techniques; and so on. I was uncertain about just which of these analytic tools would come in handiest; that depended upon what psychological processes seemed most relevant to the problems that arose. But I was not uncertain about one thing: my analysis would proceed by making hypotheses about some kind of psychological process, and all I would need to do then would be to choose the appropriate tool from my tool chest.

At the beginning of my first visit to Liberia I spent a good deal of time traveling around the countryside, observing in schools, and talking with people who spent time with children (teachers, doctors, expatriate women who had observed Kpelle children playing with their offspring). My inquiries focused on, but were not restricted to, the difficulties in mathematics education and their presumed sources, which were the object of my visit. The set of difficulties I was told about was impressive. Tribal children, I was told, could not tell the difference between a triangle and a circle because they experienced severe perceptual problems. They had great trouble classifying because they lacked the essential vocabulary in their language. Their difficulties at math were a combination of an absence of numerical concepts in their culture and the legendary proclivity of African schoolchildren to learn by rote. And so on. Taken as a whole, these explanations fit well the common wisdom of the time (e.g., Riessman, 1962), according to which culturally disadvantaged children failed to perform well in school owing to deficient experience.

At this point John Gay and I made an assumption that was not really a part of my training as a psychologist, although it was a part of my commonsense heritage. We assumed that although Kpelle children might lack particular kinds of experiences routinely encountered by children in the United States, they were by no means lacking in experience. So we began with the assumption that in order to learn about their difficulties when confronted with mathematics in school, we needed to learn more about indigenous mathematics practices that might serve as a basis for instruction. Consequently we devoted a great deal of our research effort to discovering the situations in which Kpelle people measure, engage in arguments, and organize situations for the education of their children, along with the ways that numbers, geometric forms, and logical operations are expressed in the Kpelle language. Then, instead of restricting ourselves to the applications of experimental techniques developed in the United States to assess general cognitive abilities, we created experiments that modeled indigenous practices (Gay & Cole, 1967).

The Kpelle are rice farmers, and they have a rich vocabulary for discussing the amount of rice as it is harvested, stored in bags, and sold in the marketplace. They have a standard of measurement, a *kopi* (from the English "cup"), that corresponds to a United States tall number-one tin can, which they use for buying and selling rice in the market. Merchants use a tin can with the bottom pounded outward to buy rice from farmers and the same can with a flat bottom to sell it, suggesting that people will develop a highly elaborated concept of "amounts of rice." In one experiment subjects were asked to estimate the amount of rice contained in a large wooden bowl. When Kpelle adults were asked to estimate the amount of rice in each of several bowls whose contents varied from 1½ to 6 cups, their responses were virtually perfect, whereas a group of American adults increasingly erred as the quantity of rice increased.

In subsequent years the basic strategy involved in this research has been applied successfully in a number of instances. For example, Price-Williams, Gordon, and Ramirez (1969) demonstrated that children who grew up in a Mexican village where adults specialized in potting were precocious in their mastery of the principle of conservation of mass; Serpell (1979) showed that Zambian children, who make toys out of wire, could reproduce drawn patterns more effectively than Scottish children when asked to make wire models, whereas the Scottish children were more effective than the Zambians at reproducing patterns by drawing them; Jahoda (1983) found that fourth- to sixth-grade children from Zimbabwe, who had experience helping their parents in local markets, were well ahead of Scottish children the same age in understanding the concept of profit.

Such examples could be multiplied (see LCHC, 1983, for an extensive review and discussion), but here I have sought simply to establish that it is possible to take mundane cultural practices as an object of study, and that when one does so it can both influence one's estimation of the intellectual abilities of the people under study and change the ways one goes about the business of doing psychology.

During the subsequent 20 years, my colleagues and I have applied this line of thinking to both theoretical and practical problems of learning and development. Between 1967 and 1978 a good deal of this work was manifestly cross-cultural in nature, focusing on the special forms of activity involved in schooling. Beginning in the early 1970s our cross-cultural research was complemented, and eventually superseded, by research carried out exclusively in the United States. In the remainder of this chapter I will attempt both to summarize the general theoretical conclusions we have derived from our work and to illustrate the way we have applied our theoretical ideas to concrete areas of psychological research and social practice.

When we combine our own intuitively arrived at strategy for understanding Kpelle mathematical abilities with ideas from anthropology and cognitive psychology and the general principles of the sociohistorical school discussed earlier, we obtain the research enterprise I characterize as cultural psychology. It takes as its starting point the everyday activities of ordinary people. Rather quickly one is led both "inward" into an analysis of the within-context interactions that assemble the psychological processes in question and "outward" into the ecological constraints and cultural history of a people to seek the origins of their activities and the sources of regularities in their thought processes as they move from one context to another. The logic of this approach leads us simultaneously to study within-activity context patterns of interaction and the ways activities themselves are linked to form a people's overall "design for living."

As Gustav Jahoda has pointed out, this approach has an obvious shortcoming, for which he proposes a solution.

[It] appears to require extremely exhaustive, and in practice almost endless explorations of quite specific pieces of behavior, with no guarantee of decisive outcome. This might not be necessary if there were a workable "theory of situations" at our disposal, but as Cole admits, there is none. What is lacking in [the context-specific] approach are global theoretical constructs relating to cognitive processes of the kind that Piaget provides, and which save the researcher from becoming submerged in a mass of unmanageable material. (Jahoda, 1980, p. 126)

I have considerable sympathy for the problems Jahoda points out in a psychological research program that begins with everyday activity contexts. There *is* a certain degree of continuity in behavior across contexts considered both historically and synchronically, and it needs to be accounted for by any viable theory of culture and mind. And I find it plausible, as Piaget has argued, that there are universal modes of thought that develop among biologically normal people as a result of universal forms of interaction arising in conjunction with universal constraints on the kinds of environment-individual transactions that *Homo sapiens* is capable of by virtue of phylogenetic heritage. I find it equally plausible that there are culturewide constraints on activity that shape behavior in particular contexts, as John Berry (1976) has emphasized. However, as my discussion of the ecocultural model above indicates, my preference is to start with the actual activities of people as they are organized in a particular society and to discover the sources of generality in what are initially context-specific achievements. In adopting this approach I am siding with Vygotsky (see above) in viewing the mind not as a set of general capacities, but as a loosely coupled network of relatively specific abilities, the resolution of which in consciousness can be described, following Luria (1932), as a "non-accidental mosaic." When one adopts this view, it strongly biases one toward looking at historically situated systems of activity that adhere owing to a common structural role in mediating the activity of a society.

Rather than pursue the general intertheoretical dialogue here (see, for example, Berry, 1981; Dasen, 1980; Dasen, Berry, & Witkin, 1979), I will devote the rest of this chapter to illustrating the usefulness of an activity-centered, cultural practice approach to cultural psychology. Following the logic of this approach, I will focus on a domain of practice for which evidence is available at several levels of developmental analysis and which is important to contemporary science and society—the practice called reading/writing, or literacy. Although the principles I will apply to this domain of practice must in some respects be restricted to human activities mediated by writing, I hope readers will agree that the methods of analysis, as well as certain of the psychological principles I adduce, are of general significance for understanding the role of culture in the constitution of human mind.

Applying the Principles: The Acquisition of Literacy

Whether one draws one's inspiration from the sociohistorical school that originated in the Soviet Union, the action-theoretic approach proposed by Boesch and his students, or the cultural context approach my colleagues and I have developed, the basic logic of cultural psychology that results requires one to go beyond the study of children of a given age, or even longitudinal studies, to encompass change at each of the major levels that contributes to the structure of the psychological processes in question. Following the program laid out by Vygotsky and his colleagues, this means we must consider four "genetic domains" in our analysis of literacy (see Wertsch, 1985, for further discussion): phylogeny, history, ontogeny, and microgenesis. That is far too demanding a requirement for an essay of this length (and perhaps too demanding altogether), but I will at least attempt to show how such an analysis works. I have chosen to illustrate my view of cultural psychology using the topic of literacy because, aside from my personal involvement in this line of research, literacy is manifestly a form of activity that is unique to *Homo sapiens*, has evolved historically in different ways and to different degrees, and poses important problems of a very practical kind to contemporary societies around the world.

THE PHYLOGENETIC LEVEL

Although elements of tool use and language are found in other species, the particular form of signification we know as writing, in which one object (be it a letter of the alphabet, an arrow etched on a board, or a clay token) is used to stand for another object or a relationship between objects (a sound in a language, the direction in which something or someone is to be found, an amount of something) appears to be unique to human beings.

As discussed below, writing in the conventional sense of a system of signs that represent the sounds or concepts of a language is of very recent origin indeed, extending back in time no more than 6,000 years. Since no major phylogenetic change in *Homo sapiens* has occurred for more than 40,000 years, it must be that in some sense the potential for literacy existed at the dawn of our species but emerged as part of the process of cultural evolution. Although there is no way of knowing precisely (owing in no small measure to the absence of a writing system to record the facts), it is logical to assume that the core capacity that eventually gave rise to writing is precisely the ability to create artificial stimuli such as notched sticks and knotted ropes, which the Soviet sociohistorical psychologists identify as the central distinguishing phylogenetic feature of humankind.

THE HISTORICAL LEVEL

When we look into the archaeological record, we find that even the earliest precursors of literacy and numeracy (which were not clearly differentiated from each other) reveal the operation of the two most distinctive purposes of reading and writing: to regulate people's interactions with the physical world, and to regulate their interactions with each other. The first of these purposes is illustrated by remnants of bones discovered in the vicinity of Lascaux, in southern France, where people lived approximately 40,000 years ago. In the 1960s Alexander Marshack began to take an intense interest in these artifacts because of their patterned inscriptions (Marshack, 1972). Previous scholars had assumed they were used as decorations or perhaps represented no more than doodling by people inhabiting the caves. By sitting at the mouth of a cave evening after evening and observing the rising moon, Marshack discovered that the cave dwellers were not doodling; they were making calendars.

A calendar is an excellent example of the way written symbol systems can be used to regulate people's interactions with the physical environment. The key purpose of a calendar is prediction: How many days until winter? How many days until salmon return from the sea? Prediction is essential to control. Knowing when the salmon will come allows one to build fish traps and set them in time to catch the fish; knowing when winter will arrive provides time to lay in provisions that enable one to survive the winter. Marshack's discovery is not an isolated one. Throughout the world archaeologists have discovered a variety of sophisticated calendrical devices that were important for organizing people's activities thousands of years before a form of mediation recognizable as writing appeared.

A more immediate precursor of modern literacy, focused more on coordinating the activities of people than on discovering invariances in human beings' experience of the physical world, is to be found in what is now called the "Middle East," where farming and the domestication of animals began some 10,000 years ago (Harris,

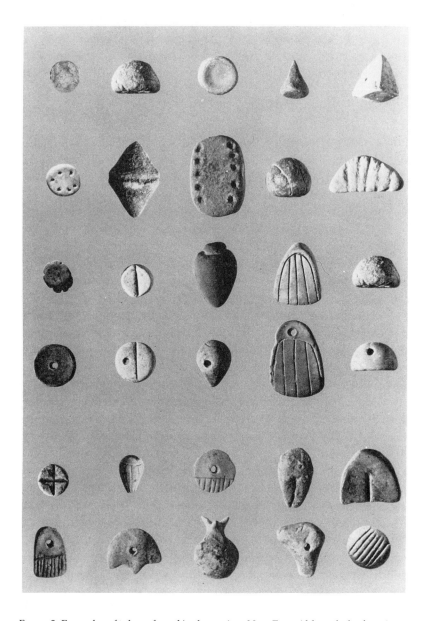

FIGURE 3. Examples of tokens found in the ancient Near East. Although the functions of the earliest tokens is in dispute, a number of shapes in these objects became symbols in the earliest writing systems and it appears that they filled representational functions that make them early precursors of writing.

1986; Pfeiffer, 1972; Schmandt-Besserat, 1978). Once people discovered that they could collect and raise the seeds of food-bearing plants, and that they could raise animals in captivity, they began to make permanent settlements where their new modes of production permitted them to accumulate surplus goods to use in trade for things they could not grow or make themselves. In the remains of these settlements, archaeologists discovered a variety of small clay objects, such as those shown in Figure 3.

These tokens illustrate both of the fundamental features of writing systems in their most primitive aspect. First, because they "stood for" the actual objects, they enabled people to keep track of their goods over time without having to count them over and over. Second, because they were small and sturdy, they could be carried from one place to another as a kind of "promissory note" for purposes of trade. In either case, they were artificial signs that represented natural objects, allowing people to regulate their economic and social activities more effectively.

What makes these tokens so important to understanding the role of literacy and numeracy in human development is evidence that they are the direct antecedents of our system of writing. Moreover, the conditions under which this crude system of marked tokens became a full-blown writing system are the same ones that eventually gave rise to schools as distinctive social institutions with their own special forms of activity.

The Origins of "Western" Formal Schooling

The system of tokens remained unchanged for several thousand years, during which people continued to live in small villages or as nomads.[4] Then, about 4,000 B.C., people discovered a means of smelting bronze that revolutionized their economic activities and their social lives. Plows could till the earth more deeply, extensive canals could be built to irrigate fields, and armies could be equipped with more effective weapons. For the first time, people could regu-

---

4. I am deliberately restricting my focus to the history of a single system of writing and the forms of schooling it was associated with. The important question of historical/cultural variability in both the technologies of representation and the social institutions of education will be touched upon slightly here owing to limited space.

larly grow substantially more food than they needed for their own use and compel large numbers of other people to work for them. City-states arose where large numbers of people lived in close proximity to each other and separate from their sources of food.

The new form of life that arose with cities required a substantially more complex division of labor. This made it impossible for everyone to interact face to face as they had when they lived in small, self-sufficient villages, and it greatly increased the importance of their primitive systems of record keeping.

Side by side with the development of these early cities, a token-based record-keeping system rapidly evolved, allowing kings to monitor the wealth of their lands, the size of their armies, and the tax payments of their subjects. Under these new conditions, the early token system expanded to keep pace with the variety of things to be counted. This increase in the number of tokens made the entire system cumbersome. As a solution, people began to make pictures of the tokens on clay tablets instead of using the tokens themselves. This practice gave rise to cuneiform ("cone-shaped") writing.

This transformation in the medium of recording permitted a crucial change in how people began to relate inscribed symbols to objects. Tokens literally "stood for" objects. But when complicated transactions began to occur in the newly complex political and economic arenas, the need arose to represent relationships among objects (such as "owe" or "paid") as well as objects themselves. A revolutionary discovery was made—that one could represent the sounds of language using marks in clay just as one could represent objects. (See Goody, 1987; Harris, 1986; Larsen, 1986, for more extended discussions of early writing systems, cuneiform in particular.)

The cuneiform writing that resulted from this discovery could not be mastered in a day. It required long and systematic study. Nevertheless, so important was the power associated with this new system of communication that societies began to support young men who otherwise might be engaged directly in a trade or farming with the explicit purpose of making them "scribes"—people who could write. The places where young men were brought together for this purpose were the earliest schools.

Fragmentary records show that though these early schools were very restricted and specialized in some ways, they were startlingly like modern ones in others (see Table 1). As in modern schools, students were asked to copy out lists of various objects deemed important by their teachers. In addition to learning the rudiments of writing and reading, early students were learning something about the basic contents of the records they were asked to keep so that they could act as civil servants once they graduated.

Children in elementary school in the 1980s still make lists, though they are more likely to be lists of the presidents of the United

Table 1
Ancient and Modern Lists

	Ancient		Modern	
Subject	Number of Items	Subject	Number of Items
Trees	84	Presidents	41
Stones	12	States of the Union	50
Gods	9	Capitals of the states	50
Officials	8	Elements in the periodic table	105
Cattle	8	Planets in the solar system	9
Reeds	8		
Personal names	6		
Animals	5		
Leather objects	4		
Fields	3		
Garments	3		
Words compounded with gar	3		
Chairs, etc.	3		

Source: Goody (1977, p. 95).

Note: One column shows lists memorized in ancient times, the other the kinds children memorize today. Students in ancient scribal schools spent a lot of time memorizing facts, which they copied out in lists. In addition to the financial benefits that derived from schooling, the ancients believed there was power to be had from the knowledge it produced. The basis of this knowledge is the ability to read, write, and solve problems in the economic and social spheres of life.

States or the spelling words in which "e" comes before "i." But the purposes to which this list making is to be put, and the presumed advantages to be gained from study, no matter how boring, remain much the same. As one father admonished his son several thousand years ago,

> I have seen how the belaboured man is belaboured—thou shouldst set thy heart in pursuit of writing . . . behold, there is nothing which surpasses writing. . . .
> I have seen the metalworker at his work at the mouth of his furnace. His fingers were somewhat like crocodiles; he stank more than fish-roe. . . .
> The small building contractor carries mud. . . . He is dirtier than vines or pigs from treading under his mud. His clothes are stiff with clay. . . .
> Behold, there is no profession free of a boss—except for the scribe: he is the boss. . . .
> Behold, there is no scribe who lacks food from property of the House of the King—life, prosperity, health! (Quoted in Donaldson, 1978, pp.84–85)

Having imbibed the value system of schooling, if not its intellectual content, high-school graduates in Liberia routinely refuse to engage in manual labor in their home villages (they are in fact legally excused from doing so). And it was common to see a slightly educated man walking emptyhanded while a small boy trotted after him, carrying his briefcase.

Restricting myself for the moment to the situation at hand, several points concerning the special organization of behavior peculiar to formal schooling stand out:

1. There is an intimate link between the development of schooling and the development of large urban centers engaged in trade and technologically sophisticated means of production.

2. There is a special mediational means—writing—that is essential to the activity of schooling. Writing is used to represent both language and physical systems (e.g., mathematics).

3. The settings where schooling occurs are distinctive in that they are removed from contexts of practical activity, and the behaviors engaged in there are valued less for their own sake than for their contribution to the goal of later economic productivity and civic participation.

4. There is a peculiar social structure to formal schooling in which a single adult interacts with many (often as many as 40 or 50, sometimes as many as 400) students at a time. Unlike most other settings for socialization, this adult is unlikely to have any family ties to the learner, rendering the social relationship relatively impersonal.

5. There is a peculiar value system associated with schooling that sets educated persons above their peers and that, in secular versions of formal education of the type I am focusing on, values change and discontinuity over tradition and community.

This characterization of the distinctive nature of the settings associated with formal schooling does not do justice to the full range of contexts that distinguish such schooling from other contexts of socialization that might be considered educational in the broad sense (for more extended discussions see Greenfield & Lave, 1982; Lave, 1987; Scribner & Cole, 1973). However, it is sufficient to permit me to pose more clearly the next level of analysis in this account of literacy and thought: How does schooling influence cognitive development at the level of ontogeny?

THE ONTOGENETIC LEVEL

To simplify drastically, we can distinguish two dominant views about the effect schooling may have on individual development. The first, which accords well with commonsense thinking during this century, is that education promotes intellectual development. According to this view (Inkeles & Smith, 1974; Lerner, 1957; UNESCO, 1970), schooling not only changes the content of people's knowledge, it increases the sophistication of the very process of thinking.

Second, there is the view, promoted by Piaget (1966), that schooling would have at best a very limited effect on cognitive development. The major reason for this belief was that too often interactions in school are structured so that children are required to submit to authority rather than work through problems for themselves. In such circumstances of "unauthentic interaction," accommodation overshadows assimilation, blocking the acquisition of genuine understanding.

A third position, which I have favored, is that the ontogenetic effect of formal education will be context specific, depending upon the particular activity and the way interactions are organized within it, leading to the acquisition of more powerful understanding in some domains and in some circumstances but not in others (LCHC, 1982a, 1983).

I will evaluate these alternative views of formal schooling with respect to two classes of cognitive functioning: logical thought operations and memory.

Note that schooling's effect on development is a question that clearly recommends the use of cross-cultural research methods. In the technologically advanced countries of the world, there is an almost perfect correlation between age and years of education, beginning at 5–7 years of age. This is the same age at which Piaget posits the emergence of concrete operations and American cognitive psychologists discern a qualitative shift in the forms of thought (White, 1965). Are such changes universal, or do they depend upon particular forms of culturally organized experience?

Schooling and the Development of Logical Operations

For discussion, I will assume that the logical operations in question are those that form the basis for Piagetian theory, in particular the well-known categories of concrete and formal operations. According to Inhelder and Piaget (1958), concrete operations consist of organized systems such as classification, serial ordering, and correspondences that children employ step by step in a broad range of problem-solving situations, without relating each partial link to all the others. With the advent of formal operations, the child is able to consider each partial link in relation to a structured whole.

CONSERVATION STUDIES

Addressing first the question of concrete operations as embodied in conservation tasks, it appears that schooling has no consistent influence on performance, although in a few well-publicized cases (e.g., Greenfield & Bruner, 1966) the steady development of conservation among schooled children and its absence among noneducated adults has led to speculation that schooling might do more than accelerate rates of development; it might actually be necessary for the development of concrete operations. This kind of result was picked up by Hallpike (1979), who claimed that adults in nonliterate societies, as a rule, fail to develop beyond preoperational thought (a conclusion hotly denied by, among others, Jahoda, 1980).

The crucial feature of the situations used to assess performance on concrete-operations tasks is that the subject understand the problem "in the way the experimenter intended" (Rogoff, 1981). This is easier said than done, especially when one is dealing with children from a very alien culture.

A number of years ago Dasen (1977) suggested that performance factors associated with interpretation of the experimenter's intentions might interfere with the expression of concrete operational competence among people from traditional, nonliterate societies, leading to misjudgment of their underlying competence. Evidence for the existence of such interference in cross-cultural studies and in support of the universality of concrete operations was obtained through training studies (Dasen, Ngini, & Lavallee, 1979). In many but not all cases, modest amounts of conservation training were sufficient to improve performance markedly among 7- to 8-year-old children, and such training was always effective with preadolescents. These results leave open the question whether different kinds of training or more training would reveal the hypothesized competence at the earlier age expected on the basis of European norms. But they also establish the universality of concrete operations by the end of childhood. Greenfield's own research also points to situational factors that interfere with conservation judgments; when Wolof children poured water themselves, conservation performance improved markedly (see also Irvine, 1978).

Further evidence that the failure of older children and adults in some studies to display concrete operational thinking results from relatively superficial aspects of the testing procedures has been obtained when university-trained African psychologists have conducted studies with Piagetian conservation tasks. The few studies of this kind have found rates of development to be similar for schooled and nonschooled populations (Kamara & Easley, 1977; Nyiti, 1976). Nyiti (1982) found a similar result when he contrasted the performance of Micmac (Canadian) children tested in English and in Micmac.

Although there is room for disagreement, I believe it is sensible to conclude that concrete operational thinking is not influenced by schooling; what is influenced is subjects' ability to understand the language of testing and the presuppositions of the testing situation itself.

At the level of formal operations, it is far more often concluded that schooling is a necessary, but not sufficient, condition for development. Even highly schooled subjects are none too proficient when presented standard Piagetian formal operations tasks (Neimark, 1975). On the other hand, as Jahoda (1980) points out, when one moves outside the narrow realm of the procedures used by Inhelder and Piaget (1958) in their monograph on formal operations, there is anecdotal but persuasive evidence of the use of formal operations.

My own belief appears to be close to that of Piaget (1972) (and, I believe, Jahoda, 1980). Formal operations are a universal achievement accompanying the change in social status from child to adult, but they will be manifest in specific domains of dense practice. As Jahoda notes, such practice is likely to be most dense in the domain of social relations. Consequently, it should come as no surprise that when Erik Erikson defines the process of identity formation, which is a hypothesized universal feature of the transition to adulthood, he seems to capture precisely the conception of a "structured whole" underpinning formal operations: "In psychological terms, identity formation employs a process of simultaneous reflection and observation, a process taking place on all levels of mental functioning, by which the individual judges himself in the light of what he perceives to be the way others judge him in comparison to themselves and to a typology significant to them; while he perceives himself in comparison to them and to types that have become relevant to him" (Erikson, 1969, pp. 22–23).

Although I have considerable doubts that identity formation— even successful identity formation—creates such a uniform cognitive integration, I am happy to grant that some such process is universal in human cultures and hence evidence of the universal acquisition of formal operations. However, outside contexts where individuals are actively thinking about their identities, in the absence of recording devices, full-blown formal operational thinking is probably a rarity in any culture. It will be associated with schooling as a normative part of scientific activities, but it almost certainly does not describe the actual thinking of trained scientists except in special circumstances where they need to check on their results or are working with auxiliary tools that help them to record information and keep it straight (Latour & Woolgar, 1986). In the special sense that schooling expands the contexts of its use, then, formal operational thinking can be said to be influenced by schooling.

SYLLOGISTIC REASONING

An interesting line of evidence in favor of this context-specific interpretation of formal logical skills comes from reasoning about logical syllogisms. In an early study, Luria (1934/1976) demonstrated what appeared to be a strong relationship between formal schooling and syllogistic reasoning. Nonschooled Central Asian peasants responded to the syllogisms he posed in terms of their everyday knowledge, not in the logical terms of the problem. To take a famous example, when presented with a syllogism of the form, "In Siberia all the bears are white; my friend Ivan was in Siberia and saw a bear: What color was it?" nonschooled subjects answered to the effect, "I have never been to Siberia, so I cannot say what color the bear was; Ivan is your friend, ask him." This kind of response has now been recorded in many cultures among nonschooled peoples and has been shown to diminish quickly with a few years of schooling in favor of a response based on the logical requirements of the task (Cole, Gay, Glick, & Sharp, 1971; Scribner, 1975; Tulviste, 1979). Judging from such evidence, it appears that formal schooling promotes a distinctive kind of theoretical thinking, a result consistent with expectations of the sociohistorical school as developed in the USSR. However, this achievement remains content specific. For example, Tulviste (1979) has shown that in societies where schooling is a recent cultural innovation, children first display theoretical thinking with respect to content that is the subject matter of the school, only later applying it to everyday concepts.

In addition, a substantial literature collected among college students in Great Britain and the United States shows that for slightly more complicated syllogisms, responses are highly content dependent. For example, Wason (1960) found that British college students could solve a particular syllogism when it was embodied in a realistic question about postage stamps and envelopes, but not when it was embodied in a hypothetical question about quality control at work. This same problem did not work for students in the United States, where one based on rules about the age of drinking worked quite well (D'Andrade, 1982).

Schooling and Memory

Speculations about the impact of schooling on the ontogeny of memory have differed sharply from those focused on logical thought. Some authors (e.g., Bartlett, 1932; Havelock, 1978) have argued that nonliterate peoples exhibit a way of remembering that adheres closely to the narrative structure of the events being remembered, a characteristic Bartlett called "rote recapitulation." Vygotsky (1978) referred to this same tendency as "natural remembering" based upon the retention of actual experiences. However, he believed that alongside this natural form of remembering there was a second, cultural form mediated by artifacts such as notched sticks and knotted ropes such as the Inca *quipu*. In his view, the consequence of schooling was to provide greatly expanded mediational means for this second kind of remembering.

A variety of evidence supports the generalization that schooling promotes the acquisition of specialized ways of remembering (Cole & Scribner, 1977; Stevenson, 1982; Wagner, 1982). For example:

1. In repeated trial free recall of common items that all fit into culturally recognized categories, children with six or more years of schooling (Cole et al., 1971) and adults with varying years of schooling (Scribner & Cole, 1981) remember more and cluster items in recall more than nonschooled comparison groups.

2. Short-term recall of item location increases as a function of schooling, but not age (Wagner, 1982).

3. Paired-associates learning of randomly paired items increases with schooling (Sharp, Cole, & Lave, 1979).

In addition, Stevenson (1982) reports a small positive effect of very small amounts of schooling on a battery of tasks that included various kinds of memory problems as well as visual analysis.

Evidence that these effects do not apply to "memory in general" but rather apply to particular ways of remembering for particular kinds of materials presented in particular ways comes from research showing that schooling effects are generally absent in cases of recall of well-structured stories (Mandler, Scribner, Cole, & DeForest, 1980). They are also absent when the items to be paired in a paired-associates task are strongly associated with each other (Sharp et al., 1979). Note too that very short-term memory also seems unaffected by schooling; in Wagner's studies, most recently probed locations show no education effects (Wagner, 1974, 1978).

LITERACY WITHOUT SCHOOLING

Although there is some ambiguity about the ontogenetic effect of schooling, because of the possibility that those who remain in school longer are cognitively more able to begin with and because the results are very specific to the particular tasks in question (see Cole, in press, or Sharp et al., 1979, for more extended discussion). For present purposes I am content to assume that several thousand hours spent in classrooms during middle childhood do result in measurable cognitive change in at least some cognitive domains. Such an assumption immediately raises the additional question of the precise mechanisms that produce such change.

This section will examine the possibility that the crucial feature of schooling is that it requires mastery of written language, a speculation that has enjoyed a good deal of support from antiquity to modern times. For example, the classicist Eric Havelock (1978), drawing on Plato's critique of written discourse, argued that oral language is "unfriendly" to the expression of analytic relationships, while written language by its very structure forces the writer to engage in abstract operations that bring about a change from narrative-based representation to true concepts. In a widely cited article, Jack Goody and Ian Watt (1968) made a very similar argument that the written record allows individuals to interact with information in qualitatively new ways that lead to the elimination of inconsistency and the elaboration of new tools of logical thinking such as the syllogism. Vygotsky (1978) made similar arguments.

In the 1970s Sylvia Scribner and I had the chance to test some of these notions through research in a culture that provided an unusual opportunity to disentangle literacy from schooling (Scribner & Cole, 1981). This work was conducted among the Vai people of northwestern Liberia, who have been employing a syllabic script of their own invention for the past 150 years or more. The Vai syllabary is known and used by approximately 20% of Vai men, primarily for letter writing and record keeping. Unlike literacy acquired in school, Vai literacy involves no mastery of esoteric knowledge or new forms of institutionalized social interaction. Nor does it prepare the learner for a variety of new kinds of economic and social activity. Learning is almost always a personal affair carried out in the course of daily activities (most often, when a friend or relative agrees to teach the learner to read and write letters). The Vai are primarily upland rice farmers, small entrepreneurs, and craftsmen. Their literacy skills play a useful role in those traditional occupations, but a more restricted role than we usually associate with school-based literacy. There is no tradition of text production for mass distribution, and no traditional occupations depend upon being literate. Nonliterates can engage in the same basic economic activities as literates. The contrast between Vai literacy and literacy acquired in school (some Vai have attended American-style schools) provided us with one line of evidence about the consequences of literacy independent of schooling.

Because the Vai have been influenced by Islam for about as long as the existence of the Vai script, a third kind of literacy also flourishes in Vai country, literacy in Arabic. Actually, Arabic literacy consists of two distinct skills. Most Vai who read Arabic do not understand the words they read. Rather, they have learned to decode the characters of the alphabet in order to help them recite the Qur'an at religious services. However, some Vai have mastered sufficient Arabic to keep records, and in some cases to write letters or read books such as commentaries on the Qur'an. I will distinguish these groups by referring to those who use Arabic only to recite the Qur'an as *Qur'anic literates*, reserving the term *Arabic literate* for those who write and read Arabic more generally.

Using these four groups (English, Vai, Arabic, and Qur'anic literates) to contrast with nonliterates and with one another, we conducted several series of studies to determine the nature and generality of cognitive skills generated by each kind of literacy.

In our initial investigations, we selected a variety of classification, memory, and logical reasoning tasks that had produced improved performance for *schooled* literates in previous research (Rogoff, 1981; Sharp et al., 1979). The results of this phase of the work were as clear as negative results can be. English schooling produced changes in many, but not all, of the tasks; the other literacies produced almost no changes. The most consistent effect of schooling was to improve individuals' abilities to explain the basis of performance on cognitive tasks.

Finding no measurable consequences of Vai literacy, we then narrowed our focus. Noting that a core of all speculations about literacy's impact is the notion that practice in reading and writing should change a person's knowledge of the properties of language, we designed a new series of tests to demonstrate *metalinguistic* consequences of becoming literate. These tasks included the ability to define words, to engage in syllogistic reasoning, and to distinguish between an object and its name. As an example of the latter task we used a classic problem employed by Piaget, who asked subjects,

> Suppose that everyone in the world got together and decided that from now on we will call the sun the moon and the moon will now be called the sun. All we are going to do is change the names. Could we do that if we wanted to?
>
> Now, when you go to bed at night what will you call the thing that you see up in the sky?
>
> What will the sky look like when you go to bed?

This kind of task seemed an appropriate way to test speculations such as those of Goody (1977), who conjectured that the acquisition of literacy meant words would no longer be fully fused with reality because "the written word becomes a separate thing abstracted to some extent from the flow of speech, shedding its close entailment to action" (p. 46). Unfortunately for this line of theorizing, very little evidence of cognitive effects for any of the literacies encountered in Vai country were found in this phase of the work. The strongest result to emerge was increased skill among schooled and Vai literates when they were asked to explain the basis for judgments of grammaticality, a result that seemed to fit more closely with the idea that the change was brought about by practice in analyzing the grammar of language when reading and writing letters than the notion that literacy changes broad understanding of language in general, as the notion of metalinguistic ability implies.

The combined results of these two lines of study failed to support the idea that literacy per se produces the cognitive changes associated with schooling. Indeed, although schooling produced changes in performance on many tasks, its effects were by no means uniform.

At this point we began designing studies that were intended to test very specific hypotheses about cognitive effects growing out of specific literate practices. From analysis of a large corpus of letters, we hypothesized that Vai literates ought to be able to communicate effectively with someone in a remote place, because writing letters seems to entail practice in formulating descriptions for someone who does not share one's knowledge of the events to be described. Vai literates ought to produce fuller, less egocentric descriptions. Utilizing the analysis of the reading and writing process used by Vai literates, Scribner constructed rebuslike tasks in which pictures of common objects had to be combined according to the way they are pronounced to make up a meaningful sentence, then asked people to code and decode these pictures to form propositions. To differentiate among the various groups (all of which engage in such activities in order to write), she constructed one task based on syllables (the unit of analysis central to Vai script, but only implicit in Arabic or English) and another based on words as the basic units.

These studies yielded clear-cut evidence of *function-specific* cognitive change, where functions were implemented within different, but overlapping, configurations of cultural practice. As hypothesized, the two literacies used widely for letter writing, Vai and English, both improved performance on the communication task. All the literacies in which understanding the text was important improved performance on the rebus tasks. However, only Vai literacy produced improved performance when the basic graphic units referred to *syllables*.

Completing the case for function-specific consequences of literacy were results from the only experiment designed to test a hypothesis favoring Qur'anic literacy. Using a memory procedure proposed by Mandler and Dean (1969), in which lists of words are built up by starting with a list length of one item and adding one item per trial (called the incremental recall task), we found that practice in reciting the

Qur'an (which was associated with both Qur'anic and Arabic literacy) was the literacy factor that improved serial recall performance.

The pattern of results obtained from this series of studies is shown in Figure 4. Figure 4 clearly displays the fact that schooling has more effect than any of the literacies. When tasks call for explaining the basis for performing a task, schooling is the *only* literacy contributor. The only significant exception was that Vai literacy enhances the descriptive communications at a distance and the ability to justify grammatical judgments. We attributed this result not to Vai reading and writing in general, but rather to the specific practice in

Broad category of effect		Type of literacy			
		English/ school	Vai script	Qur'anic	Arabic language
Categorizing	Form/number sort	▨	▨		▨
Memory	Incremental recall			▨	▨
	Free recall	▨			
Logical reasoning	Syllogisms	▨			
Encoding and decoding	Rebus reading	▨	▨		
	Rebus writing	▨	▨		▨
Semantic integration	Integrating words	▨	▨	▨	▨
	Integrating syllables		▨		
Verbal explanation	Communication game	▨	▨		
	Grammatical rules	▨	▨		
	Sorting geometric figures	▨			
	Logical syllogisms	▨			
	Sun-moon name-switching (Because of ambiguities in this task, we include only those literacy effects appearing in more than one administration.)	▨			

FIGURE 4. Summary chart of Vai literacy results. The consequences of literacy are shown to depend strongly on the cultural practices that they are a part of. (Hatched-in parts of the figure indicate a significantly higher level of performance when compared with a nonliterate control group.)

arguing the merits of various propositional forms that is common among Vai literates.

Overall, these results seem to fit most readily with an interpretation that emphasizes the fit between cognitive processing and the structure of activity within culturally organized contexts. Whenever there appears to be a cognitive effect attributable to reading/writing, analysis of the social organization and purposes of writing points at literacy-related *practice* as the crucial experience. Thus the increased ability to explain the basis of one's cognitive performance is an attribute of classroom discourse in the case of the schooled students, for whom questions and requests such as "How did you know that?" "Why did you say that?" "Go to the board and show us how you do that" are a ubiquitous accompaniment to becoming literate. The improved ability of Vai literates on the communication task has a straightforward interpretation based on the structure of Vai literacy practices. The ability of Vai literates to explain the basis of grammatical (but not other cognitive) judgments is attributable to the practice of discussing the properties of correct Vai speech on occasions when someone receives a letter containing unusual constructions. Finally, the evidence that English schooling and Qur'anic and Arabic literacy improve performance on memory tasks, although weak and spotty, is consistent with the fact that these three literacies, but not Vai, require practice in remembering large amounts of novel material, material that is often devoid of specific meaning for the rememberer.

Perhaps in some sociocultural circumstances involvement in literate practices outside formal school contexts may so pervade cultural practices that it will result in measurable, general increases in information processing skills or cognitive style. But at present it appears that those who look to literacy to bring about qualitative changes in cognitive functioning should rest content that literate people have at their disposal a new means of organizing their social activity. The conditions under which this form of mediated activity brings about cognitive change constitute an important topic for those who wish to promote literacy worldwide, for if our results (and those of Wagner and Spratt, 1987) are to be trusted, it would be an error to place much faith in the general transformative power of either literacy or modest amounts of schooling, so long as effects at the level of individual cognitive change are our focus.

From History and Ontogeny to Microgenesis

Thus far we have pursued the logic of cultural psychology applied to the psychological implications of literacy at the historical and ontogenetic levels. This inquiry has revealed how the form of literacy that arose in the ancient Middle East was intimately associated with the emergence of a new form of representation that occurred in intimate relationship to new forms of economic and social activity, one element of which was the invention of a new social institution for transmitting skills valued by segments of the adult community—formal schools. The "morphology of activity" in such institutions had a character quite distinct from other socialization settings that has remained strikingly similar up to the present day, despite enormous changes in the technological sophistication of civilization.

Those who participate in these activities acquire distinctive forms of intellectual behavior, including new forms of remembering and new conventions for reasoning, such as the syllogism. However, such schooling does not markedly affect the development of very general thought operations, and there is good reason to suspect that, even in those cognitive domains where it can be shown to exert an influence, that influence is context and activity dependent.

In societies that have invented serviceable writing systems without undergoing simultaneous massive changes in their economic and social lives, such as the Vai of Liberia, cognitive changes associated with literacy appear to be restricted to those cultural practices where literacy plays a direct role. (We might suspect that the same is true of schooling, but that possibility would take us beyond the limits of the current discussion.)

Yet to be addressed is the most intimate, most "psychological," level of analysis required by a cultural psychology—analysis of the within-context interactions that give rise to new cognitive abilities (in this case, literacy) in the first place. This is a vast topic to which we have devoted a great deal of our attention over the past decade (Cole, Dore, Hall, & Dowley, 1978; Griffin & Cole, 1984; King, Griffin, Diaz, and Cole, in press; Newman, Griffin, & Cole, 1989). Since space does not permit a proper review of this line of work, I will describe an example that illustrates both the process of mediated development involved in the acquisition of literacy and the intimate mechanisms by which culture enters into the development of specifically human psychological processes.

THE PROBLEM OF READING ACQUISITION

There is broad agreement that reading is "a complex skill requiring the coordination of a number of interrelated sources of information" (Anderson, Hiebert, Scott, & Wilkinson, 1985), and a great deal is known about how those who have acquired some degree of skill behave. But despite intensive research efforts throughout this century, especially over the past two decades, the process of acquisition remains disputed (see Foorman & Siegel, 1986, for a juxtaposition of conflicting views). The problem is important, because at present a great many children of normal intelligence fail to acquire reading skills deemed adequate for productive participation in modern societies (Miller, 1988).

Despite important differences among them, modern approaches to reading have distinguished two presumably distinct major components of the reading process: decoding (the process by which letters of the alphabet are associated with corresponding acoustic patterns) and comprehension (the process by which meaning is assigned to resulting visual/acoustic representation). Within this seemingly obvious dichotomy, theorists differ on how to sequence instruction (code emphasis first versus meaning emphasis first) and how best to help children "break the code" (by teaching phonetic analysis or by teaching whole words) (Chall, 1979).

An example of the "code emphasis first" approach can be found in the work of Jean Chall (1983) who proposes a stage theory of reading development.

> Stage 1: Decoding. The basic task of Stage 1 is to learn the arbitrary set of letters in the alphabet and to decode their correspondence to the sounds of spoken language.
> Stage 2: Confirmation, fluency, ungluing from print. New readers confirm and solidify the gains of the previous stage. To avoid confusion, they are given familiar texts that do not demand much mental effort to comprehend.
> Stage 3: Reading to learn something new. Instead of relating

print to speech, children now are asked to relate print to ideas. It is only at this stage, writes Chall, that "reading begins to compete with other means of knowing."

In the two remaining stages, children elaborate their comprehension skills, learning to juxtapose facts and theories and to construct complex ideas with the help of print.

Goodman and Goodman (1979) start from the assumption that children living in a literate society arrive at school with the rudiments of "reading as comprehending the world through print" already in their repertoires; for example, children can read various road signs, pick out the MacDonald's sign, and perhaps recognize their own names in print. Their model of acquisition is nondevelopmental in the sense that acquisition does not entail the emergence of any new process or the reorganization of old ones. All they need to do is expand from the beginning the repertoire of functions that they can accomplish with the aid of print. This expansion process occurs naturally with the accretion of experiences in comprehending the world through print.

OUR CULTURAL-MEDIATIONAL MODEL

Like Chall, we believe that reading is a developmental process and that the goal of reading instruction is to provide means for children to reorganize their interpretive activity using print. Like the Goodmans, we believe that reading text is an elaboration of the preexisting ability to "read the world" using signs of various kinds. We differ from both Chall and the Goodmans in three interrelated ways. First, we believe that reading instruction must emphasize *both* decoding *and* comprehension in a single integrated activity. Second, we believe that in ordinary circumstances adults play a crucial role in coordinating children's activity so that the development of reading becomes possible. Third, we believe that successful adult efforts depend crucially on the way they organize a "cultural medium for reading" that structures children's experience with various artifacts (most notably, but not only, the text) to coordinate the child in just the right way to make possible the necessary development.

Let me begin by modifying slightly the commonsense definition of reading. Reading, in a cultural-psychological perspective, is the process of *expanding the ability to mediate one's interactions with the environment by interpreting print*. There are two significant aspects of this definition. First, learning to read and reading proficiently are subsumed in the same definition. What one learns to do is expand; what one does, having learned, is to continue expanding (see Engestrom, 1987, for a general discussion of "learning by expanding"). Second, there is no dichotomy between decoding and comprehension, since comprehension is understood as the process of mediating one's interactions with the environment, including text processing (interpreting letter groups) as a condition.

Figure 5 presents a bare-bones representation of the idea that reading, in the broadest sense, requires the coordination of information from "two routes." Any reader must "see" the world as refracted through a text; but in order to do so, the reader's more direct access to the world, topicalized by the text, must be simultaneously engages. This figure may be familiar from Vygotsky's (1978) discussion of the fundamental mediational structure of higher psychological functions, of which reading is certainly a prime example.

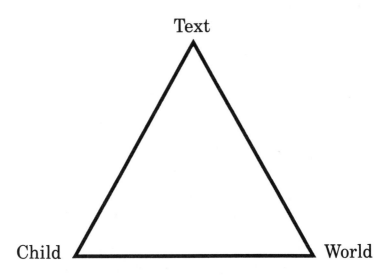

FIGURE 5. The basic structure of activity mediated by print. The child constructs an interpretation of the world through two routes, one "direct" (child-world) and one "indirect" (child-text-world).

Phrased in the currently fashionable vocabulary of cognitive psychology, Figure 5 can be said to represent the idea that reading requires the coordination of two routes in the construction of meaning, which results in the necessary interaction of "bottom up" (feature→ letter→ word→ phrase→ . . .) and "top down" (knowledge-based, comprehension-driven processes out of which new schemas emerge (McClelland & Rumelhart, 1981).

A first shortcoming of the mediational process depicted in Figure 5 is that it represents a timeless ideal. Even among skilled readers, coordinating the two routes may require adjustments in the representation of the "worlds" arrived at by either route to permit a new representation (expanded understanding) to emerge. The slight discoordination depicted in Figure 6 more accurately reflects the dynamic process I have in mind.

Figure 6 represents the fact that the child's prior knowledge and interpretations of the topic discussed in the text must be modified by whatever new information is derived from the text. In making an interpretation of the text, the child must always create a synthesis of the two sources of information—prior information and text-derived information. It is out of the synthesis of these two sources of knowledge that a new interpretation—new knowledge—emerges. Reading for meaning, according to this view, is unavoidably a creative, microgenetic process.

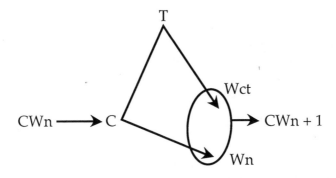

FIGURE 6. A dynamic version of the basic structure of activity mediated by print. At the start of any reading act, the child has an interpretation of the world (CWn). The child (C) must then reconcile the information derived from the child-world link (C-Wn) and the child-text-world link (C-T-Wct) to synthesize a new interpretation, CWn+1.

With this minimal structural apparatus in hand, we can turn to the crucial question: Assuming that children do not enter school already able to expand their ability to comprehend by reading alphabetic text, how can we arrange for them to develop this ability? In attempting to answer this question, we will simultaneously be tackling one of the crucial questions of modern developmental psychology: How is it possible to acquire a more powerful cognitive structure unless, in some sense, it is already present to begin with? This question, called the "paradox of development" by Fodor (1983) and the "learning paradox" by Bereiter (1985), calls into doubt any developmental account of reading that fails to specify the preexisting constraints that make development possible.

BRINGING THE END POINT "FORWARD" TO THE BEGINNING

From my perspective, developmental theories of reading such as Chall's are vulnerable to the learning paradox. Since I share with her a belief that the acquisition of reading is a developmental process requiring a qualitative reorganization of behavior, I must begin by showing in what sense the end point of development, the ability to mediate one's comprehension of the world through print, could in principle be shown to be present in embryonic form at the outset of instruction. The solution to this problem, following the principles of the sociohistorical version of cultural psychology, is to invoke Vygotsky's "general genetic law of cultural development": functions that initially appear on the interpsychological plane shared between people can then become intrapsychological functions of the individual. What we seek is a way to arrange the context of interaction such that the desired end point, the full act of mature reading, appears as an interpsychological process in the interaction between child and adult as a precondition for this new structure of activity to appear at the level of individual psychological function in the child at the end of instruction.

Figure 7 shows in graphic form that at the beginning of instruction there are two preexisting mediational systems that can be used as resources for creating the necessary structural constraints to permit the development of reading in the child. The far left of the figure illustrates the commonsense fact that children enter reading instruction with years of experience in mediating their interactions through the world via adults. The center represents the equally commonsense fact that literate adults routinely mediate their interactions through text. Finally, on the far right of the figure is the to-be-developed system of mediation that is our target.

Figure 8 shows the next stage in the analytic/instructional strategy: the given and to-be-developed systems of child mediations are juxtaposed (A), and the given adult system is then superimposed (B) to reveal the skeletal structure of an "interpsychological" system of mediation that, indirectly, establishes a dual system of mediation for the child, which permits the coordination of text-based information and information based on prior knowledge of the world that is involved in the whole act of reading.

The instructional/developmental task is now better specified: we must somehow create a system of interpersonal interaction so that the combined child-adult system at the right of Figure 8 can coordinate children's acts of reading before they can accomplish this activity for themselves. Our strategy for accomplishing this goal was a modification of the reciprocal teaching procedure of Palinscar and Brown (1984), in which teacher and student silently read a passage of text and then engage in a dialogue about it that includes summarizing the text, clarifying comprehension problems that arise, asking questions about the main idea, and predicting the next part of the text. For a number of reasons (see King et al., in press, and LCHC, 1982b, for additional details), our modification of reciprocal teaching

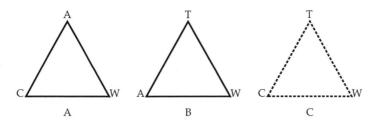

FIGURE 7. Given and to-be-developed mediations: (A) the previously existing mediation structure in which children mediate activity via adults; (B) the previously existing ability of adults to mediate activity in the world via print; (C) the to-be-developed system of mediation whereby the child mediates activity through print (identical to figure 5).

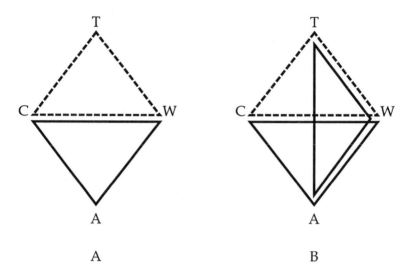

FIGURE 8. The given and to-be-developed systems are juxtaposed to show how they must be coordinated if the children's actions are to come under the constraints of the whole act of reading before they are able to read independently.

was conducted as a small-group reading activity with third- to sixth-grade children identified by their teachers as having extraordinary difficulty learning to read.

The core elements of the procedure are a set of roles (each corresponding to a different hypothetical part of the whole act of reading) and a set of role cards printed on 3" × 5" index cards. Each participant was responsible for fulfilling at least one role in the full activity of question-asking-reading. These cards specified the following roles:

The person who asks about words that are hard to say.

The person who asks about words that are hard to understand.

The person who picks the person to answer questions asked by others.

The person who identifies the main idea.

The person who asks what is going to happen next.

All participants including the instructor had a copy of the text to read, paper and pencil to jot down words, phrases, or notes (in order to answer questions implicit in the roles), and their cards to remind them of their roles. In light of the general principles of cultural psychology, we consider the role cards and the script within which they were sequenced to be cultural artifacts that could be used by the adults to create a structured medium for the development of reading. In order to move from the script to an appropriate medium of development, the procedural script was embedded in a more complex activity structure designed to make salient both the short-term and long-term goals of reading and to provide a means of coordinating around the script. It is in this embedding process that we make the transition from a focus on the structural model of reading depicted in Figures 5–8 to focus on the necessary transformation of the mediational structure of the child's interactions with print.

Recognizing the need to make the environment rich in goals that could be resources for organizing the transition from reading as a guided activity to independent, voluntary reading, we saturated the environment with talk and activities about growing up and the role of reading in a grown-up's life. This entire activity was conducted after school in a global activity structure we called "Field Growing up College" (it took place in the auditorium of the Field Elementary School). As part of their application to participate in Field College, of which question-asking-reading was a major activity, the children filled out applications that emphasized the relation between reading and growing up. They got involved with us in discussions about the difference between growing older and growing up as well as about how our activities related to their goal of growing up.

As shown in Figure 9, question-asking-reading began each session with such "goal talk," discussion about the various reasons children might have for wanting to learn to read. These included such poorly understood reasons (from the children's point of view) as the need to read in order to obtain an attractive job such as being an astronaut, intermediate-level goals such as graduating from question-asking-reading to assist adults with computer-based instruction to quite proximate goals—the desirability of getting correct answers on the quiz that came at the end of each reading session.

Joint work with the text began with a group discussion of the title or headline of the story to be read that day. Then, following the script outline provided in Figure 9, which was written on the blackboard, the role-bearing cards and the first paragraph of the text were

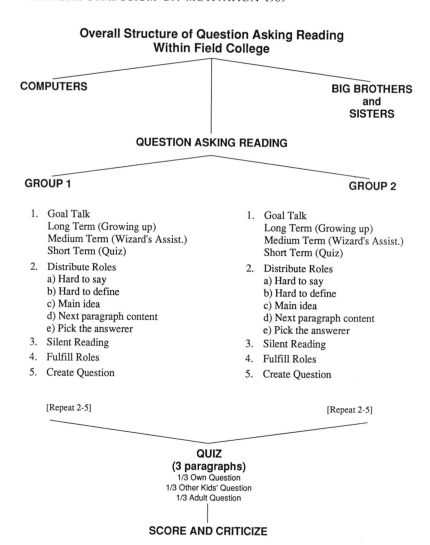

FIGURE 9.

passed around. A good deal of discussion usually ensued about who had gotten what roles; "pick the answerer" was an obvious favorite, whereas the card implicating the main idea was avoided like the plague. Once the role cards were distributed, the text for the day (usually taken from local newspapers with content of potential interest to the children) was distributed, one paragraph at a time. The participants (including the instructor and one competent reader, usually a UCSD undergraduate, and the children) then bent over their passages to engage in silent reading.

These and other procedural arrangements constituted our attempt to organize a medium that would repeatedly create moments when the three mediational triangles depicted in Figure 8 would be coordinated to create the conditions for "remediating" the children's prior systems of mediation.

Our evidence for the way this procedure worked is derived from several sources: videotaped recordings of the instructional sessions, the children's written work on the quizzes they completed each session, and various test results. Here I will concentrate on the in situ process of coordination and discoordination around the scripted activity as a key source of evidence about individual children's ability to internalize the scripted roles and the points where internalization fails, resulting in discoordination with the ongoing activity structure. In this example, two children, both of whom are failing in their reading classes, discoordinate with the publicly available scripted activity, permitting differential diagnosis of their particular difficulties. I will then briefly summarize the results of a study designed specifically to test the efficacy of these procedures at the level of group products in a controlled experiment.

In the transcripts that follow, the two boys, Billy and Armandito, are starting to read the second paragraph of the day with Katie as their teacher and Larry as an additional competent reader.

Evidence for internalization of the scripted activity is provided by instances in which the children's talk and actions presuppose a next step in the procedure with no overt provocation from the adults. For example:

1. Katie: OK, lets go on to the second paragraph then.
2. Billy: How did they find them?
3. Armandito: The Eskimos.
4. Katie: I think it was an accident (as she says this, she begins to pass out the role cards, face down).
5. Billy: (Taking a card from the stack) How come, what kind of accident?
6. Billy: (Looking at his card) That's the same card again.

In (2) Billy's question is an internalized version of the "what's going to happen next" role in the script that no one specifically stimulated. In (5) he takes the card handed to him and asks a relevant question about the text, and in (6) he comments on the relationship between his role in the previous segment of interaction and its relation to what he is about to do. Armandito's participation is problematic. His comment ("The Eskimos") is relevant to the topic at hand but opaque. He does not take one of the role cards and has to be stimulated by Katie while Billy continues to show evidence of coordination:

6. Katie: Armandito! (He looks up and takes a card).

7. Billy: We each get another one (referring to the cards; there are only four participants and Katie has not taken one, so someone will get an extra one).

In a number of places in the transcript we see Armandito discoordinating within the activity the other three participants maintain, permitting him to recoordinate from time to time. These discoordinations are of several types. The most obvious are such actions as drawing a picture instead of reading or pretending to abandon the activity altogether. But repeatedly, Armandito presupposes the scripted activity sufficiently to motivate quite specific analyses of his difficulties. The first example to follow illustrates his aversion to the question about the main idea:

8. Larry: (He has the card that says to pick the answerer) Armandito. What's the main idea?

9. Armandito: I want to ask mine. I want to ask what happens next.

10. Larry: No. I know what you want, but I am asking. I pick the answerer.

Armandito is both accepting the joint task of question-asking-reading and attempting to avoid the role that is at the heart of his problem by skipping that part of the scripted sequence. Now Armandito accepts his role and attempts to state the main idea, but his answer ("The main idea is . . . how these guys live") not only is vague, it is about the *previous* paragraph.

Through an accumulation of many such examples over several sessions, we were able to obtain a consistent pattern. This pattern showed that Billy experienced great difficulty with coming "unglued" from the letter-sound correspondences when he attempted to arrive at the main idea. When asked about the main idea, he repeatedly returned to the text and sought a "copy match" in which some word from the question appeared in the text, read the relevant sentence aloud, and then puzzled over meaning. Armandito's problem was of a quite different order: he continually lost track of the relevant context, importing information from his classroom activities that day or previous reading passages where they had no relevance.

The first conclusion I want to draw from this exercise is that we were in fact successful in creating a structured medium of activity that provided diagnostically useful information about which part of the structure depicted in Figures 5–8 was deficient in the children we worked with. However, we also wanted to establish that the question-asking-reading procedure is an effective procedure for acquiring reading. Both Billy and Armandito did in fact improve their reading ability, and Armandito's general behavior in the classroom changed so markedly that he won an award from the school recognizing his unusual progress. However, such individual change could not be attributed to question-asking-reading, both because it was part of the larger activity system of Field College and because we had no proper control group.

To remedy these shortcomings, King (1988) replicated the small-group reading procedures in a follow-up experiment that included appropriate control conditions, used more stringently quantified pre- and posttest measures, and was conducted as the sole activity in a school before the start of regular classes.

In addition to testing the effectiveness of question-asking-reading against a no-treatment control group, King included a group of children who were provided the kind of structured intervention that Scardamalia and Bereiter (1985) call "procedural facilitation" to assess whether the dynamic, dialogic characteristics of question-asking-reading were any more effective than workbook exercises that asked children to complete each of the tasks corresponding to the role cards individually in written form. Once again the children were selected from the upper elementary grades owing to their difficulty in learning to read.

King found that both question-asking-reading and her version of the procedural facilitation technique boosted children's reading performance. However, children in the question-asking-reading group retained significantly more material from the training passages than did the students in the procedural facilitation group. The students in the question-asking-reading group also spent more total time actively engaged with the task and demonstrated a greater interest in the content of the readings, indicating an intimate link between the motivational, social-interactional, and cognitive aspects of activity in context.

These results, although sketchily presented here owing limited space, support the theoretical approach developed in this chapter. Reading, we can conclude, is an emergent process of meaning making that occurs when information topicalized by the text is synthesized with prior knowledge as part of a general process of mediated interaction with the world. Moreover, it is useful to conceive of the process of acquisition as developmental in nature. Where this process differs from other developmental approaches to reading acquisition is in its emphasis on the special role of the teacher in arranging the conditions that coordinate preexisting systems of mediation in a single system of activity subordinated to the goal of comprehension.

Conclusion

It is time now to return to the quotation I began with and to consider once again the dilemmas confronting a science that seeks to explain a subject that creates history within the paradigmatic frame of scientific psychology. I fully recognize that my account has been fragmentary; it could not be otherwise considering the scope of the enterprise.

I commented at the outset that common to many of those calling for a *cultural* psychology has been the conviction that this kind of psychological analysis focuses on the meaningful, symbolic nature of humankind's special environment of adaptation and the closely related notion that meaning is historically, which is to say, contextually, dependent. As our German and Soviet colleagues have persistently pointed out, to take such a position commits one to research at several levels of analysis. In this chapter I have restricted myself to three of the requisite levels—history, ontogeny, and microgenesis—but full development of these ideas clearly also requires analysis of the phylogenetic continuities and discontinuities between *Homo sapiens* and other species. Even in the reduced manner presented here, in which I have restricted myself to the domain of literacy, my account has been fragmentary, despite its relative length compared with the norm for symposium contributions. I can well understand if after considering the methodological requirements of such a position, many readers feel the enterprise is not worth the effort and join with those who would seek to account for the same phenomena by applying natural scientific tools.

My own predilection, obviously, is to pursue the logic of cultural psychology, wherever that might lead. It is certainly true that, at our current state of understanding, an approach that begins its analysis with everyday human practices in their cultural-historical contexts experiences great difficulty in arriving at global characteristics of our mental lives that generalize broadly across contexts. Nevertheless, it is not the case that even in its still-embryonic state cultural psychology has nothing to offer the scientific community other than a critique of existing practices. We have been able to shed light on the nature of literacy and schooling at all three levels of analysis we have considered, as well as the links between levels that condition human performance. This approach has also allowed us to address important practical issues such as the diagnosis of children who fail to learn to read using methods derived from standard cognitive psychology and the creation of more powerful instructional procedures.

Our efforts thus far have been fragmentary. But if the ground swell of interest in creating a broad-based effort to understand human beings as creatures created in a cultural medium is any indication, the ranks of people who are willing to take on such a task is growing. Perhaps, when historians of psychology look back on the time of its second centennial, they will see in these efforts a fruitful return to the scientific aspirations of our forefathers in the late 19th and early 20th centuries. In such a case the title of this essay will have been justified, and cultural psychology will indeed turn out to be a once and future scientific discipline.

REFERENCES

Anderson, R. C., Hiebert, E. H., Scott, J. A., & Wilkinson, I. A. G. (1985). *Becoming a nation of readers*. Washington, DC: National Institute of Education.

Barker, R. (1978). *Ecological psychology*. Stanford, CA: Stanford University Press.

Bartlett, F. C. (1932). *Remembering*. Cambridge: Cambridge University Press.

Bereiter, C. (1985). Toward a solution of the learning paradox. *Review of Educational Research, 55* (2), 201–226.

Berry, J. W. (1976). *Human ecology and cognitive style*. New York: Sage-Halsted.

Berry, J. W. (1981). Cultural systems and cognitive styles. In M. P. Friedman et al. (Eds.), *Intelligence and learning*. New York: Plenum.

Berry, J. W. (1985). Cultural psychology and ethnic psychology: A comparative analysis. In I. Reyes & Y. Poortinga (Eds.), *From a different perspective: Studies of behavior across cultures*. Lisse: Swets and Zeitlinger.

Bronfenbrenner, U. (1979). *Experimental human ecology*. Cambridge: Harvard University Press.

Chall, J. S. (1983). *Stages of reading development*. New York: McGraw-Hill.

Cole, M. (1978). Ethnographic psychology—so far. In G. S. Spindler (Ed.), *The making of psychological anthropology*. Berkeley: University of California Press.

Cole, M. (1988). Cross-cultural research in the sociohistorical tradition. *Human Development, 31*, 137–157.

Cole, M. (in press). Cognitive development and formal schooling: The evidence from cross-cultural research. In L. C. Moll (Ed.), *Vygotsky and education*. New York: Cambridge University Press.

Cole, M., Dore, J., Hall, W. S., & Dowley, G. (1978). Situational variability in the speech of preschool children. *Annals of the New York Academy of Sciences, 318*, 65–105.

Cole, M., Gay, J., Glick, J. A., & Sharp, D. W. (1971). *The cultural context of learning and thinking*. New York: Basic Books.

Cole, M., & Scribner, S. (1977). Developmental theories applied to cross-cultural cognitive research. *Annals of the New York Academy of Sciences, 285*, 366–373.

D'Andrade, R. G. (1982). *Reason vs. logic*. Paper presented at symposium on the ecology of cognition, Greensboro, NC.

Dasen, P. R. (1977). Cross-cultural cognitive development: The cultural aspects of Piaget's theory. *Annals of the New York Academy of Sciences, 285*, 332–337.

Dasen, P. R. (1980). Psychological differentiation and operational development: A cross-cultural link. *Quarterly Newsletter of the Laboratory of Comparative Human Cognition, 2* (4), 81–86.

Dasen, P. R., Berry, J. W., & Witkin, H. A. (1979). The use of developmental theories cross-culturally. In L. Eckensberger, W. Lonner, & Y. H. Poortinga (Eds.), *Cross-cultural contributions to psychology*. Amsterdam: Swets and Zeitlinger.

Dasen, P. R., Ngini, L., & Lavallee, M. (1979). Cross-cultural training studies of concrete operations. In L. H. Eckensberger, W. J. Lonner, &

Y. H. Poortinga (Eds.), *Cross-cultural contributions to psychology*. Amsterdam: Swets and Zeitlinger.

Donaldson, M. (1978). *Children's minds*. New York: Norton.

Eckensberger, L. H. (1988, September). *From cross-cultural psychology to cultural psychology*. Paper presented at the Twenty-fourth International Congress of Psychology Meeting, Sydney, Australia.

Eckensberger, L. H., Krewer, B., & Kasper, E. (1984). Simulation of cultural change by cross-cultural research: Some metamethodological considerations. In K. McCluskey & H. W. Reese, *Life-span developmental psychology: Historical and generational effects*. New York: Academic Press.

Engestrom, Y. (1987). *Learning by expanding*. Helsinki: Orienta-Konsulttit Oy.

Erikson, E. H. (1969). *Gandhi's truth*. New York: Norton.

Fodor, J. (1983). *The modularity of mind*. Cambridge: MIT Press.

Foorman, B. R., & Siegel, A. W. (Eds.). (1986). *Acquisition of reading skills: Cultural constraints and cognitive universals*. Hillsdale, NJ: Erlbaum.

Gay, J., & Cole, M. (1967). *The new mathematics and an old culture*. New York: Holt, Rinehart and Winston.

Geertz, C. (1973). *The interpretation of cultures*. New York: Basic Books.

Goodall, J. (1986). *The chimpanzees of Gombe: Patterns of behavior*. Cambridge: Harvard University Press.

Goodman, K. S., & Goodman, Y. M. (1979). Learning to read is natural. In L. B. Resnick & P. A. Weaver (Eds.), *Theory and practice of early reading* (Vol. 1). Hillsdale, NJ: Erlbaum.

Goody, J. (1977). *The domestication of the savage mind*. Cambridge: Cambridge University Press.

Goody, J. (1987). *The interface between the written and the oral*. Cambridge: Cambridge University Press.

Goody, J., & Watt, I. P. (1963). The consequences of literacy. In J. Goody (Ed.), *Literacy in traditional societies*. Cambridge: Cambridge University Press.

Gould, S. J. (1980). *The panda's thumb*. New York: Norton.

Greenfield, P. M., & Bruner, J. S. (1966). Culture and cognitive growth. *International Journal of Psychology, 1*, 89–107.

Greenfield, P. M., & Lave, J. (1982). Cognitive aspects of informal education. In D. A. Wagner & H. W. Stevenson (Eds.), *Cultural perspectives on child development*. San Francisco: Freeman.

Griffin, P., & Cole, M. (1984). Current activity for the future. In B. Rogoff & J. Wertsch (Eds.), *Children's learning in the "zone of proximal development."* New directions for child development No. 23. San Francisco: Jossey-Bass.

Hallpike, C. R. (1979). *The foundations of primitive thought*. New York: Oxford University Press.

Harris, R. (1986). *The origin of writing*. La Salle, IL: Open Court.

Havelock, E. A. (1978). *The Greek concept of justice: From its shadow in Homer to its substance in Plato*. Cambridge: Harvard University Press.

Inhelder, B., & Piaget, J. (1958). *The growth of logical thinking from childhood to adolescence*. New York: Basic Books.

Inkeles, A., & Smith, D. H. (1974). *Becoming modern*. Cambridge: Harvard University Press.

Irvine, J. (1978). Wolof "Magical thinking": Culture and conservation revisited. *Journal of Cross Cultural Psychology, 9*, 300–310.

Jahoda, G. (1980). Theoretical and systematic approaches in cross-cultural psychology. In H. C. Triandis & W. W. Lambert (Eds.), *Handbook of cross-cultural psychology* (Vol. 1). Boston: Allyn and Bacon.

Jahoda, G. (1983). European "lag" in the development of an economic concept: A study in Zimbabwe. *British Journal of Developmental Psychology, 1*, 113–120.

Kamara, A. I., & Easley, J. A., Jr. (1977). Is the rate of cognitive development uniform across cultures? A methodological critique with new evidence from Themne children. In P. R. Dasen (Ed.), *Piagetian psychology: Cross-cultural contributions*. New York: Gardner.

Kantor, J. R. (1982). *Cultural psychology*. Chicago: Principia Press.

King, C. (1988). *The social facilitation of reading comprehension*. Unpublished doctoral dissertation, University of California at San Diego.

King, C., Griffin, P., Diaz, E., & Cole, M. (in press). A model systems approach to reading instruction and the diagnosis of reading disabilities. In R. Glaser (Ed.), *Advances in instructional psychology*.

Kozulin, A. (1984). *Psychology in utopia: Toward a social history of Soviet psychology*. Cambridge: MIT Press.

Laboratory of Comparative Human Cognition. (1982a). Culture and intelligence. In R. J. Sternberg (Ed.), *Handbook of human intelligence* (pp. 642–719). New York: Cambridge University Press.

Laboratory of Comparative Human Cognition (1982b). A model system for the study of learning disabilities. *Quarterly Newsletter of the Laboratory of Comparative Human Cognition, 4* (3), 39–66.

Laboratory of Comparative Human Cognition. (1983). Culture and cognitive development. In W. Kessen (Ed.), *Mussen's handbook of child psychology: Vol. 1. History, theory, and method* (4th ed.) (pp. 295–356). New York: Wiley.

Larsen, M. T. (1986). Writing on clay: From pictograph to alphabet. *Quarterly Newsletter of the Laboratory of Comparative Human Cognition, 8* (1), 3–9.

Latour, B., & Woolgar, S. (1986). *Laboratory life: The construction of scientific facts*. Princeton: Princeton University Press.

Lave, J. (1987). *Cognition in practice*. New York: Cambridge University Press.

Leontiev, A. A. (1970). Social and natural in semiotics. In J. Morton (Ed.), *Biological and social factors in psycholinguistics*. Urbana: University of Illinois Press.

Leontiev, A. N. (1932). Studies of the cultural development of the child: 3. The development of voluntary attention in the child. *Journal of Genetic Psychology, 37*, 52–81.

Leontiev, A. N. (1981). *Problems of the development of mind*. Moscow: Progress.

Lerner, D. (1957). *The passing of traditional society.* New York: Free Press.

Luria, A. R. (1928). The problem of the cultural development of the child. *Journal of Genetic Psychology, 35,* 493–506.

Luria, A. R. (1932). *The nature of human conflicts; or, Emotion, conflict and will.* New York: Liveright.

Luria, A. R. (1934). The second psychological expedition to Central Asia. *Journal of Genetic Psychology, 44.*

Luria, A. R. (1976). *Cognitive development.* Cambridge: Harvard University Press.

Luria, A. R. (1979). *The making of mind: A personal account of Soviet psychology* (M. Cole & S. Cole, Eds.). Cambridge: Harvard University Press.

Mandler, G., & Dean, P. J. (1969). Seriation: The development of serial order in free recall. *Journal of Experimental Psychology, 81,* 207–215.

Mandler, J. M., Scribner, S., Cole, M., & DeForest, M. (1980). Cross-cultural invariance in story recall. *Child Development, 51,* 19–26.

Marshack, A. (1972). *The roots of civilization: The cognitive beginnings of man's first art, symbol, and notation.* New York: McGraw-Hill.

McClelland, J. L., & Rumelhart, D. E. (1981). An interactive activation model of context effects in letter perception: Part 1. An account of basic findings. *Psychological Review, 88* (5), 375–407.

Miller, G. A. (1988). The challenge of universal literacy. *Science, 241,* 1293–1299.

Neimark, E. D. (1975). Intellectual development during adolescence. In F. D. Horowitz (Ed.), *Review of child development research* (Vol. 4). Chicago: University of Chicago Press.

Newman, D., Griffin, P., & Cole, M. (1989). *The construction zone.* New York: Cambridge University Press.

Nyiti, R. (1976). The development of conservation in the Meru children of Tanzania. *Child Development, 47,* 1122–1129.

Nyiti, R. (1982). The validity of "cultural differences explanations" for cross-cultural variation in the rate of Piagetian cognitive development. In D. Wagner & H. Stevenson (Eds.), *Cultural perspectives on child development.* New York: Freeman.

Palincsar, A. S. & Brown, A. L. (1984). Reciprocal teaching of comprehension-fostering and monitoring activities. *Cognition and Instruction, 1* (2), 117–175.

Pfeiffer, J. (1972). *The emergence of man.* New York: Harper and Row.

Piaget, J. (1966). Nécessité et signification des recherches comparatives en psychologie génétique. *Journal International de Psychologie, 1,* 3–13.

Piaget, J. (1972). Intellectual evolution from adolescence to adulthood. *Human Development, 15,* 1–12.

Price-Williams, D. (1979). Modes of thought in cross-cultural psychology: An historical review. In A. J. Marsella, R. G. Tharp, & T. J. Ciborowski (Eds.), *Perspectives in cross-cultural psychology.* New York: Academic Press.

Price-Williams, D. (1980). Toward the idea of a cultural psychology: A superordinate theme for study. *Journal of Cross Cultural Psychology, 11,* 75–88.

Price-Williams, D., Gordon, W., & Ramirez, M. (1969). Skill and conservation: A study of pottery-making children. *Developmental Psychology, 1,* 769.

Riessman, F. (1962). *The culturally deprived child.* New York: Harper and Row.

Rogoff, B. (1981). Schooling and the development of cognitive skills. In H. C. Triandis & A. Heron (Eds.), *Handbook of cross-cultural psychology,* (Vol. 4). Boston: Allyn and Bacon.

Sahlins, M. (1976). *Culture and practical reason.* Chicago: University of Chicago Press.

Scardamalia, M., & Bereiter, C. (1985). Fostering the development of self-regulation in children's knowledge processing. In S. F. Shipman, J. W. Segal, & R. Glaser (Eds.), *Thinking and learning skills: Research and open questions.* Hillsdale, NJ: Erlbaum.

Schmandt-Besserat, D. (1978). The earliest precursor of writing. *Scientific American, 238* (6), 50–59.

Scribner, S. (1975). Recall of classical syllogisms: A cross-cultural investigation of error on logical problems. In R. Falmagne (Ed.), *Reasoning: Representation and process.* Hillsdale, NJ: Erlbaum.

Scribner, S. (1985). Vygotsky's uses of history. In J. Wertsch (Ed.), *Culture, communication, and cognition: Vygotskian perspectives.* New York: Cambridge University Press.

Scribner, S., & Cole, M. (1973). The cognitive consequences of formal and informal education. *Science, 182,* 553–559.

Scribner, S., & Cole, M. (1981). *The psychology of literacy.* Cambridge: Harvard University Press.

Serpell, R. (1976). *Culture's influence on behaviour.* London: Methuen.

Serpell, R. (1979). How specific are perceptual skills? A cross-cultural study of pattern reproduction. *British Journal of Psychology, 70,* 365–380.

Sharp, D. W., Cole, M., & Lave, C. (1979). Education and cognitive development: The evidence from experimental research. *Monographs of the Society for Research in Child Development, 44* (1–2, Serial No. 178).

Shweder, R. A. (1990). Cultural psychology—what is it? In J. W. Stigler, R. A. Schweder, & G. Herdt (Eds.), *Cultural psychology: The Chicago Symposium on Culture and Human Development.* Cambridge: Cambridge University Press.

Stevenson, H.W. (1982). Influences of schooling on cognitive development. In D.A. Wagner & H.W. Stevenson (Eds.), *Cultural perspectives on child development.* San Francisco: Freeman.

Tomasello, M. (1989). Chimpanzee culture. *SRCD Newsletter,* Winter, pp. 1–3.

Toulmin, S. (1980). Toward reintegration: An agenda for psychology's second century. In R. A. Kasschau & F. S. Kessel, *Psychology and society: In search of symbiosis.* New York: Holt, Rinehart and Winston.

Tulviste, P. (1979). On the origins of theoretic syllogistic reasoning in culture and the child. *Quarterly Newsletter of the Laboratory of Comparative Human Cognition, 1* (4), 73–80.

UNESCO. (1970). *Literacy 1967–69: Progress throughout the world.* Paris: UNESCO

Valsiner, J. (1988). *Developmental psychology in the Soviet Union*. Bloomington: Indiana University Press.

Vygotsky, L. S. (1929). The problem of the cultural development of the child, II. *Journal of Genetic Psychology, 36*, 414–434.

Vygotsky, L. S. (1934). The genesis of higher mental functions. In J. Wertsch (Ed.), *The concept of activity in Soviet psychology*. White Plains, NY: Sharpe.

Vygotsky, L. S. (1966). *Development of the higher mental functions. Psychological research in the U.S.S.R.* (Vol. 1). Moscow: Progress. (Abridged translation of L. S. Vygotsky's extensive work published under the same title in 1930–31)

Vygotsky, L. S. (1978). *Mind in society: The development of higher psychological processes* (M. Cole, V. John-Steiner, S. Scribner, & E. Souberman, Eds.). Cambridge: Harvard University Press.

Wagner, D. A. (1974). The development of short-term and incidental memory: A cross-cultural study. *Child Development, 45*, 389–396.

Wagner, D. A. (1978). Memories of Morocco: The influence of age, schooling, and environment on memory. *Cognitive Psychology, 10*, 1–28.

Wagner, D. A. (1982). Ontogeny in the study of culture and cognition. In D. A. Wagner & H.W. Stevenson (Eds.), *Cultural perspectives on child development*. San Francisco: Freeman.

Wagner, D. A., & Spratt, J. E. (1987). Cognitive consequences of contrasting pedagogies: Effects of Quranic preschooling in Morocco. *Child Development, 58*, 1207–1219.

Wason, P. C. (1960). Regression in reasoning. *British Journal of Psychology, 4*, 471–480.

Wertsch, J. (Ed.). (1985). *Vygotsky and the social formation of mind*. Cambridge: Harvard University Press.

White, L. (1959). The concept of culture. *American Anthropologist, 61*, 227–251.

White, S. (1965). Evidence for a hierarchical arrangement of learning processes. In L. P. Lipsitt and C. C. Spiker (Eds.), *Advances in child development and behavior* (Vol. 2). New York: Academic Press.

Whiting, J. W. M. (1969). Methods and problems in cross-cultural research. In G. Lindzey & E. Aronson (Eds.), *The handbook of social psychology* (Vol. 2). Reading, MA: Addison-Wesley.

Whiting, B. (1976). The problem of the packaged variable. In K. F. Riegel & J. A. Meacham (Eds.), *The developing individual in a changing world: Historical and cultural issues* (Vol. I). The Hague: Mouton.

Whiting, B. B. (1980). Culture and social behavior: A model for the development of social behavior. *Ethos, 8*, 95–116.

Wundt, W. (1916). *Elements of folk psychology*. London: Allen and Unwin.

Subject Index

abnormal behavior, 235
  cultural influences and, 236–237,
    240
  invariant, 237–240, 267
abstraction, 7, 9, 99, 149, 309
acceptance, 68, 145
accommodation, 303
acculturation, 201–203, 213, 216, 228
  age and, 211, 229
  attitudes toward, 211, 215, 216,
    218, 219 (table), 224, 230–231
  definition of, 202, 204
  donor/receptor, 206–209, 214–
    215, 225
  education and, 204, 206, 212, 222,
    230, 231
  employment and, 212, 230
  language and, 212, 214, 217, 218,
    230
  media and, 212, 213, 218
  motivations in, 207–208
  policies, 208, 231
  psychological, 203–204, 205, 207,
    209–210, 214, 221(fig.)
  stress of, 211, 220, 222, 224–229,
    231

  types of, 216–218, 230
  variables in, 142, 203(fig.), 205,
    207–208, 212–214, 224, 230
achievement, 49, 56, 64, 68, 69, 73,
    74, 95, 106, 149, 155
  emphasis on, 105, 119(n12)
action theory, 281, 283
activity/passivity, 248, 262
adaptation, 141, 201, 224
aesthetics, 59, 113(n10)
affect, homogeneity of, 96
affiliation, 106, 112(n9)
affluence, 44, 45, 70, 72, 94, 102,
    120(n12), 180
  individualism and, 44, 45, 49, 55,
    94–95, 107, 117–119(n12), 160
Africans, 9, 23–25, 57, 75, 82, 89,
    149, 153, 213
  mental health studies of, 243,
    245, 246, 247, 262
age, 53, 153, 115(n11), 211, 229
aggression, 74, 106, 151, 220, 250,
    258, 264
  Japanese, 248–249
agoraphobia, 265
agricultural societies, 47, 71,

self-confidence, 92
self-control, 249, 263
self-development, 54, 179
self-direction, 68
self-discipline, 68
self-disclosure, 87
self-esteem, 151, 152
self-experience, 249, 255
self-fulfillment, 94
self-improvement, 266
self-interest, 48, 49, 51, 121(n12), 172
Self in the Life of Peoples (Fluegel), 11–12
selfishness, 48, 74, 113(n10)
selflessness, 250
self/other differentiation, 71
self-presentation, 80
self-reliance, 43, 45, 46, 48, 49, 50, 64, 71, 72, 74, 108(n5), 112(n9), 113–114(n10), 119(n12), 172
domination and, 102
personality and, 155
as valued, 147, 171
Self-Reliance(factor), 79, 108–109(n7)
Self-Reliance with Competition (factor), 49, 55
self-report measures, 67
self-restraint, 119(n12)
self-sacrifice, 51, 56, 83, 110(n8), 250
self-sufficiency, 155, 162, 184
semantic differential scales, 92
sensitivity, 82, 110(n8), 227
sensuality, 23
sentence completions, 67, 111(n8)
separateness, 164, 182
separation, 154, 155, 157, 184
acculturation and, 216–222, 228
Separation from Ingroups(factor), 50, 108–109(n7)
SES beliefs, 148
settlement pattern, 229
sexuality, 45, 159, 264
shaman, 240
shame, 45, 59, 60, 112(n9), 254
sharing, 60, 87

signification, 284, 296
signs (artifacts as), 284
Singapore, 156, 165–168, 172, 250, 253
Sketch of a Historical Picture of the Progress of the Human Mind (de Condorcet), 4
smallest space analysis, 68
smoking, 111(n8)
sociability, 55, 65, 114(n10), 115–116(n11), 151
social behavior, 47–48, 59, 66, 72, 73, 84, 85
social constructionism, 144, 148
social control, 56, 59, 60
socialization, 9, 47, 57, 77, 96, 137–139, 174, 178, 179, 201
children and, 74, 120(n12), 136, 137, 148
class and, 71, 152
social mold theory, 138
Social Science Research Council, 202
social support, 94–96, 110(n8), 112(n10), 162, 183
acculturation and, 215, 228, 229
sociocentric orientation, 156, 265
sociocultural context, 49, 139
sociohistorical approach, 2, 5, 10, 14, 35, 282, 320. *See also* Soviet sociohistorical school
sojourners, 214, 215
solidarity, 113(n10), 141
somatic functioning, 227
somatization, 247, 257, 259, 261, 262
son preference, 169, 170, 178, 180
South Africa, 103
Soviet sociohistorical school, *xii*, 36, 283, 284, 288, 297, 307
Soviet Union, 57, 74, 76, 104, 241
Spain, 84, 251
Spangler values, 59
spatial-perceptual abilities, 29
specialization, 44, 117(n11)
spousal relations, 75, 76, 169, 180, 220

Author Index

356

360

74753